CW01064648

ENGLISH CRIMINAL JUSTICE
IN THE
NINETEENTH CENTURY

English Criminal Justice
in the Nineteenth Century

David Bentley

THE HAMBLEDON PRESS

LONDON AND RIO GRANDE

Published by The Hambledon Press 1998
102 Gloucester Avenue, London NW1 8HX (UK)
PO Box 162, Rio Grande, Ohio 45674 (USA)

ISBN 1 85285 135 X

A description of this book is available from
the British Library and from the Library of Congress

Typeset by Carnegie Publishing Ltd, Chatsworth Road, Lancaster
Printed on acid-free paper and bound in Great Britain by
Cambridge University Press

Contents

Preface

This is a book for lawyers and historians interested in the evolution of our criminal trial system. Written from a lawyer's perspective, it is the fruit of research which I embarked upon soon after my appointment to the circuit bench in 1988. I have always been fascinated by legal history and, with my trial lawyer's background, investigating how men were tried in the last century seemed both an appropriate and an exciting project. In the space of one hundred and fifty years we have moved from a system of trial without lawyers to one in which few accused stand trial unrepresented; from a system which prohibited the accused from testifying to one which permits an adverse inference to be drawn if he fails to do so. I wanted to discover how the old system operated in practice and how and by what steps it had evolved into the present-day model.

When I began to investigate the practicability of the project, I quickly discovered that there was an invaluable but hitherto largely neglected resource readily to hand: *The Times* reports of criminal trials. Professor Langbein in his researches into the eighteenth-century criminal trial made extensive use of the *Central Criminal Court Sessions Papers*. *Sessions Papers* also exist for the nineteenth century, but a brief perusal of *The Times* reports satisfied me that they would be a far more valuable source: they contain material which the *Sessions Reports* omit (applications for postponements, the assignment of counsel, sitting hours, counsel's speeches, the judge's summing up) and include not only reports of Old Bailey trials but also of trials in the King's Bench, at Assizes, at Middlesex and other Sessions and in the London police courts. Almost as useful as these newspaper reports were journals such as the *Law Times*, the *Justice of the Peace*, the *Law Magazine*, the *Law Journal*, the *Solicitors' Journal* and the *Irish Law Journal*, written for practitioners and reflecting in their articles and correspondence columns the issues of the day and the concerns and views of the rank and file of the profession. Clearly not only was there a story to be told, but an abundance of source material. The temptation to try and tell it was overwhelming.

That it is a tale worth telling I have no doubt. The trial system is as important to an understanding of nineteenth-century criminal justice as the penal system (upon which so much has been written) and, as the centenary of the passing of the Criminal Evidence Act of 1898 approaches, there has surely never been a more appropriate time for a book such as this.

Abbreviations

Archbold	J. F. Archbold, *Pleading and Evidence in Criminal Cases* (London, 1822)
Beattie	J. M. Beattie, *Crime and the Courts in England 1660–1800* (Oxford, 1986)
Bla Comm	Blackstone, *Commentaries on the Laws of England* (Oxford, 1765)
East PC	Sir Edward Hyde East, *Treatise on the Pleas of the Crown* (London, 1803)
Co Litt	Sir Edward Coke, *Commentary upon Littleton* (1628)
Co Inst	Sir Edward Coke, *Institutes of the Laws of England* (1642–44)
Criminal Law Commissioners	
2nd Report	*Second Report* 1836 PP (343) XXXVI 183
8th Report	*Eighth Report* 1845 PP (656) XIV 161
DNB	*Dictionary of National Biography*
Foster	Sir Michael Foster, *Crown Law* (Oxford, 1762)
Hale PC	Sir Matthew Hale, *The History of the Pleas of the Crown* (London, 1736)
Halsbury's Laws	*Halsbury's Laws of England* (London, 1907–17)
Hawk PC	W. Hawkins, *Pleas of the Crown* (London, 1716–21)
Holdsworth HEL	Sir William Holdsworth, *The History of English Law* (London, 1922–52)
JN	The Twelve Judges' Notebooks, printed in part in D. R. Bentley, *Select Cases from the Twelve Judges' Notebooks* (London, 1997)
PD	*Parliamentary Debates*
PP	*Parliamentary Papers*
PRO	Public Record Office
Phillipps	S. M. Phillipps, *A Treatise on Evidence* (London, 1838)
Phipson	Phipson on *Evidence* (London, 1892)
Russell	W. O. Russell, *A Treatise on Crimes and Misdemeanours* (London, 1819)
Radzinowicz	Sir Leon Radzinowicz, *A History of English Criminal Law* (London, 1948–86)

Stephen HCL	J. F. Stephen, *A History of the Criminal Law of England* (London, 1883)
Stephen's Digest	J. F. Stephen, *A Digest of the Law of Evidence* (London, 1876)
Taylor	J. P. Taylor, *A Treatise on the Law of Evidence* (London, 1848)

Introduction

'How men were tried? There is no better touchstone for a social system than this question.' Marc Bloch, *Feudal Society.*

The nineteenth century saw great changes in the way England was policed and in the way criminals were punished. Upon both subjects there is an extensive and expanding literature. The nineteenth-century trial system has however been little studied. Work by Cockburn, Langbein and Beattie has added considerably to our understanding of the seventeenth- and eighteenth-century criminal trial but no one has performed the same service for the nineteenth century.[1] Why is this? The esteem in which any criminal justice system is held depends in no small part upon how successful it is in achieving the dual objective of punishing the guilty and acquitting the innocent. Wrongful convictions undermine confidence in the courts and those charged with the task of law enforcement, while a high acquittal rate means either that large numbers of innocent people are being caught in the law enforcer's net or that too many guilty men are slipping through it. In Victoria's day it was an article of faith with many Englishmen that their country's trial system was the best in the world. Was this merely jingoism or were there solid grounds for their claim? That the question has never been tackled may have been due to a belief that the nineteenth-century system resembled the twentieth-century model too closely to merit detailed study. Such a view, however plausible fifty years ago, rings hollow today. Over last thirty years it has been urged with increasing stridency that the trial system inherited from the Victorians is too favourable to the criminal, offers him too many chances of escape. This argument has not only been listened to but has carried the day. Wholesale changes have been made to criminal procedure and to the law of criminal evidence, all designed to raise the conviction rate. As a result, trials today are conducted very differently than they were a hundred year's ago. This purpose of this book is to attempt

---

[1] J. S. Cockburn, *A History of the English Assizes, 1558–1714* (Cambridge, 1972); J. H. Langbein, 'The Criminal Trial before the Lawyers' (1978) 45 U Chicago LR 263 and 'Shaping the Eighteenth-Century Criminal Trial' (1983 – (i)) 50 U Chicago L R 1; J. M. Beattie, *Crime and the Courts in England, 1660–1800* (Oxford, 1986).

to fill a gap in the literature and to tell how those accused of crime in nineteenth century England were tried.

It is a task which involves the consideration of not one but two modes of trial. In 1800, as today, all serious crime was tried on indictment. But there were may petty offences which by statute were triable summarily by magistrates, ranging from poaching to neglect of duty by post boys.

Trial on indictment was the trial by a jury of twelve of a sworn written accusation of crime (indictment) found by a grand jury or jury of presentment. The roots of the system lay in the twelfth and thirteenth centuries.[2] Juries of presentment date back to at least the Assizes of Clarendon (1166) and Northampton (1176), which required representatives of each hundred and township to attend before the king's justices and to present on oath the names of those suspected of homicide, robbery or theft. The trial (or petty) jury, on the other hand, was an expedient devised in the thirteenth century to fill the gap caused by a papal ban upon what until then had been the normal mode of trying suspects: the ordeal, a mode of trial involving an appeal to God to give a sign of guilt or innocence. At first, trial juries were drawn from the ranks of the presenting jurors attending before the king's justices and, like presenting juries, they were expected to act of their own knowledge. In 1352, however, the accused was given the right to object to the presence of an indicting juror on the trial jury. Also (and this development is difficult both to date and to trace) the practice grew up of calling witnesses to inform the jury. The size of the trial jury had early been set at twelve. By the mid fourteenth century it was also a requirement that its verdict be unanimous. At some unknown date, between the thirteenth and mid fifteenth centuries, the rule arose that the accused could challenge up to thirty-five jurors peremptorily and an unlimited number for cause.

By 1600, although a trial jury might still act of its own knowledge (a rule affirmed in *Bushel's Case* in 1670 and not rooted out of the law until the early nineteenth century),[3] the evidence of witnesses was the material upon which jury verdicts were based. To ensure that prosecutions did not fail for lack of witnesses, statutes of Phillip and Mary required magistrates in felony cases to examine the prisoner and his accusers, to write down what they had to say and to bind the prosecutor and his witnesses over to attend and give evidence at the accused's trial. With the use of witnesses to prove the charge against the accused, jury trial had by the sixteenth century begun to assume its modern shape. The first detailed account we have of trial procedure comes from this period. The indictment is found by a grand jury of twenty-three after hearing the Crown witnesses. The accused is arraigned upon it. If he pleads not guilty and puts himself on his country (that is agrees to jury trial), a jury is empanelled to try him. If he refuses to plead,

---

[2] See generally T. F. T. Plucknett, *A Concise History of the Common Law* (5th edn, London, 1956) 118–24 and 433–36.

[3] *Bushel's Case* (1670) Vaughan 135; *R v Sutton* (1816) 4 M & S 532.

or having pleaded not guilty refuses jury trial, he is put to the *peine forte et dure*: pressed by weights until he either agrees or expires. The jury having been empanelled, the evidence for the Crown, upon whom the proof lies, is then gone through. First, the magistrates' examinations of the accused and the witnesses against him are read. Next, the Crown witnesses are called. They testify on oath. Of their evidence the accused has had no forewarning. He is allowed no counsel to defend him. Lest he detect a flaw in the indictment, he is refused a copy of it. There are no rules of evidence. The accused is not always confronted by the witnesses who speak against him. Confessions obtained from him or his accomplices by torture are not only admitted in evidence but regarded as particularly cogent proof. He cannot himself give sworn evidence nor can he call witnesses. For his defence he is obliged to confine himself to disputing with witnesses and the prosecutor. During this altercation he may be questioned both by the judge and prosecuting counsel. After he has heard enough the judge charges the jury and proceeds to hear the next case. After two or three cases have been gone through the jury will consider their verdicts on them.

The seventeenth century saw important changes. The use of torture was abandoned. The ban on the calling of witnesses by the accused was relaxed: by mid century he was allowed to call witnesses but not to have them sworn. After the Glorious Revolution of 1688 the practice in treason trials was drastically modified by statute, the accused being granted the rights to counsel, to a copy of the indictment and to have his witnesses sworn. Also the judges, in order to ensure that there should be no return to the judicial bullying of prisoners which had been so prevalent under Scroggs and Jeffreys, now prohibited all interrogation of the accused – a protection which also had the consequence of preventing him giving evidence in his own defence. From around the same period we have the outlines of a hearsay rule.

During the eighteenth century there was further reform. In 1702 prisoners in felony were given the right to have their witnesses sworn. By about 1730 judges were also starting to allow them the help of counsel in questioning witnesses. Evidential protection for the accused increased. By 1750 it was becoming a settled rule that a confession obtained by an improper inducement was not to be left to the jury. It also became common practice for judges to warn juries against convicting on unconfirmed accomplice evidence. In 1772 *peine forte et dure* was abolished. Henceforth refusal to plead or consent to jury trial was in all cases to be treated as equivalent to a plea of guilty. By 1800 the procedure in prosecutions for indictable offences was in some ways close to the present-day model.

At the beginning of the nineteenth century there was much complacency about the trial system, particularly trial on indictment. English criminal procedure was spoken of by native and foreigner alike as liberal or tender to the prisoner. One doubts, however, whether present-day accused would have viewed it in such a light. Its shortcomings were too numerous for that. As Glanville Williams put it: 'Until one dips into legal history it is hard to realise how recent is our present notion of justice to the accused person and a fair trial.'[4]

A jurist looking at present-day English law as to trial on indictment might, given the adversarial nature of our system, identify the following as basic to the concept of a fair trial:

1. The accused's right to be tried by a tribunal consisting of an impartial and legally trained judge and an impartial jury.[5]

2. The accused's right to be legally represented at his trial (including unrestricted access to legal advice and assistance whilst in custody awaiting trial);[6] and to have the state pay for such representation if he is too poor to be able to do so himself.[7]

3. The accused to be given in advance of trial notice of the case he has to meet.[8]

4. The prosecution to make disclosure to the accused pre-trial of any material in their possession which may assist his defence.[9]

5. The accused to be protected against prejudicial pre-trial publicity.[10]

6. The accused to be given full opportunity to test and challenge the prosecution evidence by cross-examination.

7. The accused to have the right to give evidence and call witnesses in his defence.

8. The accused to have the right to the last word with the jury.[11]

9. The judge to give full and adequate direction to the jury on the law relevant to the trial.

10. A safeguard against wrongful conviction in the form of a requirement that the Crown prove its case beyond reasonable doubt.

11. The accused to have the right, if convicted, to appeal against conviction and sentence[12]

The rules of evidence may also be seen as part and parcel of a fair trial (albeit that in the last fifteen years they have been drastically revised largely to the disadvantage of the accused).

[4] *The Proof of Guilt* (3rd edn, London, 1963), 4.

[5] Supreme Court Act, 1981, s 8; as to impartiality see e.g. *R v Mulvihill* (1990) 9 Cr App R 372.

[6] *R v Kingston* (1948) 32 Cr App R 183.

[7] Legal Aid Act, 1988, Part V.

[8] Magistrates' Courts Act, 1980, s 102; *R v Wright* (1936) 25 Cr App R 35.

[9] Criminal Procedure and Investigations Act, 1996, ss 1–21.

[10] Contempt of Court Act, 1981, ss 1 and 2.

[11] Criminal Procedure (Right of Reply) Act, 1964.

[12] Criminal Appeal Act, 1968.

In 1800 only three of the above rights and protections (the rule placing on the Crown the burden of proving guilt beyond reasonable doubt and the rights to cross-examine and call witnesses) were fully conceded, the remainder being either denied completely or enjoyed to only a partial or limited extent. By 1850, as a result of legislative reform, the position of the accused had improved somewhat but was, to modern eyes at least, far from enviable.

This book will attempt to assess how far the nineteenth-century criminal trial system conformed to the present-day concept of a fair trial. The protections which nineteenth-century law conferred upon the accused, the handicaps to which he was subject, and the extent to which these were during the century variously added to, expanded, reduced and abolished will be examined. Topics such as policing and punishment will be dealt with, but only by way of background. After a short overview of the criminal justice system as a whole, summary trial is considered. The main body of the book deals with trial on indictment, the analysis of the latter broadly following the chronology of the prosecution process. As well as making use of material to be found in nineteenth-century law texts, law reports and parliamentary debates and papers, I have drawn heavily upon correspondence and articles in contemporary legal journals and upon newspaper reports of trials (in particular *The Times* police and trial reports). Irish (and to a lesser extent American and colonial) decisions and practice are cited where relevant to the way in which the law on a particular point evolved. Where (as in the case of criminal appeal and legal aid) a reform campaigned for in the nineteenth century was carried in the early years of the twentieth, the text ignores the artificial cut-off point of 1900 and strays beyond it.

1

The System

1. Common Law and Statute

Trial procedure at the start of the nineteenth century was regulated principally by the rules of common law (that part of English law which originated
in common custom and was unified and developed by the rulings of judges).
The law of criminal evidence was similarly regulated. Most crimes, however,
were statutory. During the second half of the eighteenth century there had
been 'an ever-increasing volume of statute law specifying particular offences,
some in effect reiterating common law, some embracing new territory,
much designed primarily to impose death as the penalty for crimes against
property'.[1]

The nineteenth century saw no slowing down in the output of legislation.
Growth was greatest in the field of summary offences but Parliament was
also increasingly intervening to reform and refashion the law of criminal
procedure. Periodically attempts were made to simplify both law and procedure. Obsolete statutes were repealed and, during the 1820s and again
in 1861, consolidating Acts were passed (Acts which swept up, collected and
reenacted in a single statute existing enactments on a particular subject),
bringing much needed order to several areas of criminal law. Twice during
the century (between 1834 and 1849 and between 1878 and 1883) attempts
were made to codify English criminal law and procedure. Judicial criticism
of the draft codes coupled with the determination of 'the aristocratic ruling
class ... that the criminal law should not be over-clarified'[2] ensured that
they came to nothing. It was left to textbook writers, such as Archbold,
Greaves, Phillipps, Roscoe, Stone, Stephen and Taylor, to systematise and
reduce to intelligible order the burgeoning mass of case and statute law, a
task of which they acquitted themselves well.

2. The Classification of Offences

Of the various classifications of crime employed by text writers the most

---

[1] W. R. Cornish & G. de N. Clark, *Law and Society in England, 1750–1850* (London, 1989),
545.

[2] J. Hostettler, *The Politics of Criminal Law* (Chichester, 1992), viii.

important was the procedural one.[3] Offences were classified according to the method by which they were tried into indictable and summary offences, with indictable offences in turn subdivided into treasons, felonies and misdemeanours. This last division was of great practical importance. The rights of an accused charged with an indictable offence, as to bail, representation by counsel, jury challenge, the number of offences which could be included in the indictment against him and appeal, all depended upon the category into which the offence fell.

At common law, felonies were crimes conviction for which resulted in an automatic forefeiture of all the felon's property to the Crown. They were 'venomous' offences which 'cost a man his property'. They also cost him his life. With the exception of petty larceny (theft of property worth less than twelve pence) all felony was capital. In strict law felony included treason but, because trial for treason was subject to special procedural rules, text writers commonly treated it as a separate species of offence. Indictable offences less than felony were known at first as transgressions or trespasses, later as misdemeanours. Commonly punished by imprisonment, fine, whipping or other corporal punishment (such as the pillory or ducking stool), misdemeanours were not capital, nor did they involve forfeiture.

Treason could take one of two forms: high treason (levying war against the king, adhering to his enemies or other breach of allegiance); and petit or petty treason (a wife slaying her husband, or a servant his master). It was capital, involved forfeiture, and an aggravated form of death penalty – hanging, drawing and quartering for men, burning for women (a statute of 1790 substituted hanging for burning).[4] Petty treason was abolished in 1828; such offences being converted into murder.

In the thirteenth century the list of felonies was short: homicide, larceny, robbery, burglary, arson and rape. Over the next four centuries Parliament created nearly fifty new statutory felonies. By 1800 the number of felonies stood at well over two hundred. In 1800 it still remained possible to prosecute felons by appeal of felony, an ancient mode of accusation in which trial was by battle. Well nigh obsolete by the end of the medieval period, the appeal had survived as a means by which the relatives of a deceased could still harass one who had been acquitted on indictment of his murder. In 1819 an attempt to use it for just this purpose led to its speedy abolition by Parliament. Although felony was capital, by the late eighteenth century only a small proportion of those capitally convicted actually suffered death. The Crown had the power, liberally exercised in practice, to commute hanging to some lesser penalty such as transportation, whilst for some felonies a first offender could escape the rope by pleading 'benefit of clergy'.

The privilege of benefit of clergy dated from the twelfth century. Following

[3] On this, see Plucknett, *A Concise History of the Common Law* (5th edn), 424–58 and Radzinowicz, i.

[4] 30 Geo III, c. 48.

Becket's murder, Henry II had been forced to concede the church's claim that criminous clerks be tried by the church. Thereafter, if a clerk on indictment pleaded his clergy the plea had to be allowed. It was not necessary for him to make his claim on arraignment. He could take his chance with a jury, pleading his clergy only if their verdict went against him. In course of time the latter became the usual and then the invariable course. It was for an accused claiming clergy to prove that he was a clerk; by the fourteenth century ability to read was commonly accepted as sufficient proof of entitlement. His claim admitted, the clerk would be handed over to the church for trial. Before the church court he could clear himself by swearing an oath.

By the fifteenth century the privilege was being regularly claimed by laymen. The literacy test had become largely a formality: if a lay convict could read or recite a prescribed passage from the Bible (Psalm 51, verse 1: 'the neck verse': 'Have mercy upon me, O God, according to thy loving kindness: according unto the multitude of thy tender mercies blot out my transgressions'), he would be allowed his clergy. It had also become the rule that the benefit could only be used once. In 1490 branding was introduced to prevent second claims. In 1576 the practice of handing 'clerks' over to the church was abandoned. They were instead to be imprisoned at the discretion of the court for up to a year and then discharged. In 1707 the reading test was abolished, thus admitting all the world to the privilege.

As the class of convicts by whom the clergy was claimable grew ever wider, the scope of the privilege itself grew narrower. After the Reformation a long list of statutes made murder, piracy and a host of other felonies non clergyable. In the eighteenth century the number of such felonies increased prodigiously. As Edmund Burke cynically put it: 'If a country gentleman can obtain no other benefit from the Government, he is sure to be accommodated with a new felony without benefit of clergy ...'[5] At the same time the punishment for clergyable larceny was increased to seven years' transportation. By 1800 whether a felony was clergyable often depended upon the value of the property involved. Shoplifting, for example, was clergyable where the goods stolen were worth less than forty shillings. To save the necks of petty thieves, eighteenth-century juries often returned verdicts deliberately undervaluing the goods stolen. Such 'pious perjury' continued to be a feature of trial on indictment until benefit of clergy was abolished in 1827.

After 1808 the number of felonies capitally punishable was progressively reduced until by 1861 it stood at just three (murder, piracy with violence and arson of the Queen's ships or dockyards). In 1870 forfeiture, the other hallmark of felony, was abolished along with hanging, drawing and quartering. Both had long been in disuse. No traitor had been drawn and quartered since the Cato Street conspirators in 1820, whilst forfeiture had

[5] In conversation with Sir James Mackintosh, PD 1819 XXXIX, 787.

long since ceased to be a source of profit for the Crown. Most felons had
no assets and those who did commonly evaded the penalty by transferring
them to others before trial.[6]

3. Police

England in 1800 had no professional police.[7] In country areas policing was
the responsibility of the parish constable and the local magistracy. The
parish constable was elected annually. His duties were to keep the peace,
arrest suspected wrongdoers and take them before a magistrate, and to
convey to prison those committed there by the local magistrates. The office
was unpaid. If he wished, he could instead of discharging the duties of the
office himself pay a deputy to do so. Such detective work as there was was
usually carried out under the personal supervision of the local magistrates,
who in cases of serious crime would order the arrest of suspects and examine
them when brought in. To deal with actual or anticipated disorder the
magistrates had the power to swear in special constables and, in the last
resort, to call out the military. They could also read the Riot Act, the effect
of which was to render all who failed to disperse within an hour guilty of
felony. Constables had the right to call upon members of the public to assist
them, failure to do so being a punishable offence.

This system, although capable of working tolerably well in country areas,
was quite inadequate to deal with urban crime. During the eighteenth century
many towns, copying the example of London, had obtained Improvement
Acts empowering them to supplement the parish constabulary with paid
watchmen, the cost to be met out of a local rate.

In London responsibility for policing was hopelessly fragmented. In
addition to the parish constabularies there were local watches. The City had
had a night watch since the seventeenth century and a day watch since 1737.
Many parishes outside the City also had watches. These varied enormously
in size and efficiency. Some, such as that of St George's, Hanover Square,
were large and highly efficient, whilst others employed only a few infirm
old men ('Charleys' as they were contemptuously called). There were also
nine police offices with jurisdiction over the whole of London except the
City. Attached to each were three full-time paid magistrates and a small
staff of officers. The earliest and best known was that at Bow Street. This
had had a full-time magistrate since its establishment in 1729. In 1753 the
government had been prevailed upon by Sir John Fielding, the then magistrate, to provide funds to enable him to employ a small body of full-time
officers. Known to history as 'Bow Street Runners', they quickly proved their

---

[6] See *R v Bolam* (1839) 2 M & Rob 192; and E. Bowen Rowlands, *Seventy-Two Years at the Bar*
(London, 1924), 345–46.

[7] On the history of the police, see generally Radzinowicz, ii, iii and iv.

worth. 'Their services were sought as far away as Bristol or Portsmouth; indeed ... they quickly became something of a national institution.'[8]

By 1800 Bow Street (and in this respect it was unique) also had attached to it a sixty-strong foot patrol. It was a plain clothes unit and patrolled all central London, except the City, from dusk until 1 a.m. In 1815 it was augmented by a horse patrol established to provide protection for travellers on the main roads into London. Operating during the hours of darkness, the horse patrol was a uniformed force (the uniform included a scarlet waistcoat which earned its members the nickname 'Robin Redbreasts').

By the end of the eighteenth century there were loud calls for the establishment of a paid professional police for London. The proposal encountered fierce resistance. In 1822 a Select Committee declared it irreconcilable 'with that perfect freedom of action and exemption from interference which are the great blessing of society in this country'.[9] In 1829, however, Peel carried the reform and created the Metropolitan Police Force. Directed and controlled from a new police office at Scotland Yard by two commissioners answerable to the Home Secretary, it was to be responsible for policing all London except the City. A thousand officers were recruited initially, a figure which by the end of its first year had swollen to three thousand. At first it was highly unpopular and its turnover in manpower high. But despite these and other teething troubles (not least of which was the severe criticism which it attracted in 1833 for its handling of the Spa Fields Riot), the force soon won a reputation for efficient policing. Even the City was convinced. In 1839 it procured the passing of an Act giving it a force of 500 men commanded by a commissioner answerable to the City authorities. In the meanwhile, during the great municipal reforms of 1835, the question of borough policing had been tackled. The Municipal Corporations Act required borough councils to set up watch committees charged with duty of appointing a sufficient number of fit men as constables.

In 1839 the government turned its attention to the counties. A permissive Act empowered county magistrates in Quarter Sessions to establish, with the consent of the Home Secretary, a county constabulary. It met with a mixed response. Many counties simply ignored it. In 1842 the government tried another tack. An Act was passed designed to breathe fresh life into the parish constabulary. This in turn had little impact. In 1856 the government, by now fast running out of patience, resorted to compulsion. By the County and Borough Police Act all counties which had not set up a county force were required to do so by the following winter. The Act also provided for the appointment of Inspectors of Constabulary who were to visit county and borough forces and report to the Home Secretary on their efficiency. A force receiving a certificate of efficiency would receive a central government

[8] Radzinowicz, iii, 57.
[9] PP 1822 (440) IV, 107.

grant equal to a quarter (by 1900 a half) of the cost of paying and clothing its constables. Forces for boroughs with a population of five thousand or less were, however, excluded from grant aid. The exclusion led to the disappearance of many of the smallest and least efficient borough forces. By 1870 fifty-eight had merged with adjoining county forces. Gradually policing standards rose, even in those counties and boroughs which had shown the greatest reluctance to implement the pre-1856 legislation.

In 1888, as part of the local government reform of that year, control of county forces was transferred from Quarter Sessions to a standing joint committee consisting of magistrates and county councillors. Forces of boroughs with less than ten thousand inhabitants were also required to merge with their county force.

From the first the 'new police' were organised on a military model. There were grades of rank, a distinctive uniform (including after 1852 a military style helmet), drill, the use of military style salutes and strict discipline. Many forces were commanded by ex-army officers. Pay for constables was poor and conditions of service harsh, leading to strikes in the Metropolitan Police in 1872 and 1890. Officers worked a seven day week (rest days were not introduced until 1910) and were entitled to just one week's unpaid holiday per year. Those injured in service or retiring after long service had until 1890 no right to a pension. Officers were also disqualified from voting in parliamentary and local government elections.

The first force to employ detective officers was the Metropolitan Police. The disbandment of the Bow Street Runners in 1839 left England without a detective force. In 1842 the gap was made good with the establishment of a small detective branch at Scotland Yard. For a long time the public opposed plain clothes police, regarding them as spies and 'entirely foreign to the habits and feelings of the nation'. Gradually they won acceptance, although their cause was not helped when in 1877 three detective officers were found guilty of corruption after a highly-publicised Old Bailey trial. Reorganisation followed the scandal. In 1878 detective work was concentrated in the hands of a newly formed Criminal Investigation Department. The failure of the CID to catch the perpetrator of the Whitechapel murders led to widespread criticism. However, in the 1890s it had success in a number of high profile murder cases. By now it was no longer the only police detective force. By 1900 the majority of provincial forces had their own detective departments. There was also the Special Irish Branch created in 1884 to counter the Fenian terrorist menace.

The only scientific aids available to the nineteenth-century detective were photography and plaster of Paris for taking casts of footprints. Forensic science laboratories, blood grouping and forensic ballistics lay in the future. In cases of suspicious death the opinion of a medical man and, if poison was suspected, a chemist would commonly be taken. But both pathology and toxicology were new sciences. In 1800 medical men were still resorting to the quackery of 'floating lungs' to determine whether dead infants had been born alive,[10] whilst the Smethurst (1859) and Maybrick (1889) cases demonstrated that poisoning was a field in which doctors and chemists were capable of spectacular error.[11] In 1871 a Criminal Records Office was established at Scotland Yard. In 1901 both crime records and detective work were revolutionised with the creation of a Central Fingerprint Bureau set up to exploit the technique of fingerprint identification developed by E. R. Henry.

4. Prosecution

The prosecution of criminals was in the eighteenth and early nineteenth century regarded as a private rather than a public responsibility, a matter for the victim.[12] To encourage men to prosecute the law offered both rewards and immunities. A number of statutes offered those who prosecuted felons to conviction a pardon and a reward varying according to the crime from £10 to as much as £40. In addition boroughs, parishes and local magistrates regularly offered rewards (often raised by public subscription) for the conviction of the perpetrators of particular crimes. So too did banks, insurance offices and local associations for the prosecution of felons. In cases of serious crime the Home Office would usually consent to the inclusion in the reward handbills of an offer of a pardon to any informant who was not himself a principal in the crime. The reward system inevitably gave rise of a class of professional thieftakers (the Bow Street Runners, in particular, were notorious for bounty hunting). It also served as a means of bringing pressure to bear on criminals to inform on their fellows. A criminal caught red-handed would commonly be wooed with promises of immunity and a share of the reward money to name and testify against his accomplices. There was an obvious potential for abuse. It was not unknown for men to be entrapped into or falsely accused of crime for the sake of a £40 reward. This had happened in 1756, in the notorious *MacDaniel* case,[13] and was still happening as late as the 1820s.[14] The system also led to heavy dependence upon the use of the evidence of accomplices to secure convictions.

By 1850 the picture was much changed. Although England still lacked a system of public prosecutors, prosecutions were now increasingly overseen by either the police, clerks to magistrates or borough solicitors, and were financed out of public funds. In 1879 a Director of Public Prosecutions was appointed charged with the duty of overseeing prosecutions. Rewards were now of far less importance than at the start of the century. In 1818 the

[10] E.g. *R v Green*, *The Times*, 2 July 1825.
[11] *The Trial of Dr Smethurst* and *The Trial of Mrs Maybrick* (in the Notable British Trials Series).
[12] On prosecution, see generally Radzinowicz, ii.
[13] *R v MacDaniel* (1756) 19 St Tr 745.
[14] E.g. *R v Cooper and Bennet*, *The Times*, 17 January 1806; also *The Times*, 24 February 1818 ('Blood Money').

fixed statutory rewards in felony had been replaced by rewards at the court's discretion. As for Home Office offers of rewards and pardons, these had by the 1850s only a limited life span ahead of them. In the 1880s their use was discontinued altogether because of the meagre results they were yielding in terms of the detection and conviction of criminals.[15] With the rise of the 'new police', associations for the prosecution of felons gradually fell into decay. Many were dissolved but a few lived on as clubs offering a convivial annual dinner.

5. Criminal Courts

The first court before which a person accused of crime would normally be brought was a magistrates' court.[16] Where the crime alleged was indictable the magistrates would conduct a preliminary examination, committing the accused for trial where the evidence established a prima facie case of guilt. If the offence was summary they would try the case themselves.

Another official with power to commit accused for trial (albeit only for homicide) was the coroner. It was his duty to hold an inquest into all suspicious deaths occurring in his district. When inquiring into a death the coroner sat with a jury of between twelve and twenty-three. All witnesses whom it was thought could throw light on the circumstances of the death would be summoned to give evidence, and their evidence was taken down in the form of written depositions. At the conclusion of the evidence the coroner would sum up the case to the jury. Their verdict was recorded in a written inquisition signed by the coroner and the jurors. Where it charged murder or manslaughter against a named person it was equivalent to an indictment. In such a case it was the duty of the coroner forthwith to commit the person accused for trial in custody, binding over the witnesses to attend the trial. In 1800 the carrying out of an autopsy by a medical practitioner was already a common preliminary to an inquest.

The principal courts for the trial of indictments in England were the Assizes and the Old Bailey, and in Wales the courts of Great Sessions. Between them these courts tried all capital cases, as well as a share of the non-capital felonies and misdemeanours. Below them came the courts of Quarter Sessions, held at least quarterly in every county and in such boroughs as had their own Sessions. In theory, Quarter Sessions had jurisdiction to try all crimes except treason. In practice, all they tried were cases of petty larceny and misdemeanour. Other courts having jurisdiction to try indictable offences were the court of King's Bench and the House of Lords. In the

---

15 PRO, HO 45/9961 X 6851.
16 On criminal courts, see *Crime in England, 1550–1800*, ed. J. S. Cockburn (London, 1977), 15–48 and 299–309 (J. H. Baker).

event of a major outbreak of disorder in a particular part of the country, judges could be sent out under a special commission to try offenders.

In 1830 the courts of Great Sessions were abolished, and Wales and Chester brought within the Assize system. The reform of the courts system effected by the Judicature Acts (1873–75) had relatively little effect upon the higher criminal courts. The court of Queen's Bench was abolished and its jurisdiction vested in the Queen's Bench Division of the newly created High Court of Justice. The common law judges who had been and continued to be responsible for trying all serious crime were now restyled High Court judges.

6. Criminal Procedure

In prosecutions for indictable offences, the first step following arrest would normally be the preliminary examination of the accused by a magistrate.[17] If the evidence called disclosed a prima facie case of guilt the accused would be committed for trial, usually in custody. It was, however, possible for a prosecutor to by-pass the preliminary inquiry stage. If he chose, he could apply directly to the grand jury at the court of trial for a bill of indictment against the accused. In cases of misdemeanour it was possible to initiate proceedings by laying an information in the King's Bench, such information being equivalent to an indictment. Again, an accused committed for trial on a coroner's inquisition could be tried upon it without either preliminary examination or indictment. Pending trial the accused had no right to a copy of the evidence against him, nor in felony to a copy of the indictment upon which it was proposed to try him. Protection against adverse press publicity before trial was more theoretical than real.

At the court of trial the prosecutor and his witnesses would go before the grand jury. If the grand jury found a bill of indictment against the accused he would be arraigned upon it. Arraignment consisted of calling the prisoner to the bar of the court, putting the indictment to him and calling upon him to plead to it. Most prisoners pleaded either guilty or not guilty, although occasionally an accused would raise some legal objection or bar to the indictment (such as a pardon, a previous conviction or acquittal, or a defect in the indictment). If he made no answer when called on to plead a jury would be empanelled to try whether he was mute of malice. If they found him mute of malice, or he openly refused to plead, or, having pleaded, he refused to be tried by jury, he was deemed to have pleaded guilty. Where the jury found him mute by visitation of God they might also be called upon to try his fitness to plead, on which issue the prison surgeon would normally be heard.

If the prisoner pleaded not guilty, a jury would be empanelled to try him.

---

17 On criminal procedure, see J. Chitty, *Criminal Law* (1st edn, London, 1816).

Most trial juries in criminal cases were common juries (drawn from the ranks of men between twenty-one and sixty possessing the requisite property qualification), although special juries (consisting of jurors who were bankers, merchants or of the rank of esquire or above) were normally used to try cases of misdemeanour in the King's Bench. The accused had the right to challenge jurors for cause; and in treason and felony there was also a right of peremptory challenge.

A jury having been empanelled they would be put in charge of the accused and the trial would commence. In 1800 it was unusual, except in treason, for either side to be represented by counsel. Even where the accused did have counsel, if the charge was felony, the counsel was not permitted to make a speech to the jury on his behalf. Where there was no prosecuting counsel, the judge would prosecute, calling the witnesses and examining them from the depositions sent up by the committing magistrate. After a short opening speech from prosecuting counsel (where there was one), the Crown witnesses would be called in turn and examined on behalf of the Crown. The accused had the right to cross-examine. At the close of the prosecution case the judge would call upon the accused 'to make his defence'. He could not give evidence on his own behalf (a disability commonly defended on the ground that it protected him from the 'moral torture of cross-examination' and prevented him from being forced to incriminate himself). He was, however, permitted (except in misdemeanour when represented by counsel) to make an unsworn statement. He could also call witnesses, either as to fact or character. The right to call character witnesses was one of several advantages and protections he enjoyed under the nascent law of evidence. (Others included the rule that the Crown bore the burden of proof, the rules excluding hearsay and involuntary confessions, and the practice of warning juries against convicting on uncorroborated accomplice evidence.) If he called evidence the prosecution had the last word with the jury. After the close of evidence, if the case was one of any difficulty, the judge would normally although not invariably sum up, following which the jury would consider their verdict. Often they would reach a verdict in the jury box without leaving court.

If the verdict was not guilty the accused would be discharged. If convicted it was open to him to move in arrest of judgement. One of the most common grounds for such a motion was that the indictment was bad in law. If made out, this would result in the prisoner being discharged but left him at risk of being indicted afresh. Failing a successful motion in arrest, the accused would be sentenced, along with the rest of those convicted, at the end of the session.

Against his conviction and sentence the accused normally had no appeal. The only court having jurisdiction to review a conviction on indictment was the King's Bench. This had power to grant a new trial to a person convicted before it of misdemeanour, and to quash the conviction of accused tried before any court who could prove error on the face of the record (in error there was a further appeal from the King's Bench to the House of Lords). The number of accused who benefited from these procedures was never more than a handful per year.

A less formal appeal procedure lay in the practice of judges reserving cases. In the case of a trial held at Assizes, the Old Bailey or the Great Sessions (but not Quarter Sessions), it was open to the judge, in the event of a conviction, to reserve for consideration by all the common law judges any point of law which had arisen during the trial as to which he entertained doubt. If the judges considered his ruling wrong and the conviction bad they would recommend a pardon or arrest the judgement. Whether a point was reserved was entirely at the discretion of the trial judge. In 1848 the practice of reserving cases was placed upon a statutory footing with the establishment of a Court for Crown Cases Reserved. Throughout the century the number of cases reserved never exceeded thirty-six per year and in most years was below twenty. The only other means of overturning a conviction or sentence was extra-judicial: a petition to the Home Office for a pardon.

Until 1848 trial procedure upon prosecutions for summary offences was wholly at the magistrates' discretion. In that year a procedural code was enacted which magistrates were obliged to follow when trying accused.

7. Punishment

In the eighteenth and early nineteenth century England sought to deal with crime by executing and transporting her worst criminals.[18] Between 1810 and 1835 about a third of all those convicted on indictment were either executed or transported. In 1800 over two hundred offences were capital. Public hanging was the normal method of execution. Treason and murder, however, attracted an aggravated form of death penalty. Male traitors were hanged, drawn and quartered (a ghastly procedure last employed in 1820 but not formally abolished until 1870), whilst the bodies of murderers were, after execution, delivered to surgeons for public dissection or, if the trial judge had so ordered, gibbeted (hanged in chains). Of those capitally convicted only a small number were actually put to death. Some escaped the noose by pleading benefit of clergy and many more were pardoned on condition that they undergo transportation.

Introduced in the seventeenth century as a means of ridding the country of the idle and incorrigible, transportation to the American colonies had since 1717 been the normal punishment for felons who escaped the death penalty. On the outbreak of the American War of Independence in 1776 it came to a halt. Shipment out being impractical, transportees were instead confined to warship hulks in the Thames and set to work cleansing and dredging the river or labouring in the royal dockyards. With the discovery

---

[18] On punishments, see Radzinowicz, i & v ; H. Potter, *Hanging in Judgment* (London, 1993).

of Australia transportation resumed. The first convict fleet sailed for Botany Bay in 1787 and over the next eighty years 160,000 men, women and children were transported. On arrival in Australia convicts were either employed on public works or assigned as labourers to free settlers. Good behaviour was rewarded by a ticket of leave (release on licence) towards the end of the transportee's sentence.

For most non-capital indictable offences the penalties in 1800 were imprisonment, a fine, public or private whipping, or a combination of these. Public whipping was carried out at the cart's tail (the offender was tied to the back of a cart and whipped as the cart moved along the street) or at a whipping-post. It was not the only shaming punishment the law employed. The pillory was still in use for crimes such as fraud, cheating and some sexual offences. Women convicted of the nuisance of being a common scold were still occasionally ducked. Long-term imprisonment however was virtually unknown, sentences of imprisonment rarely exceeding twelve months. For summary offences a fine, a short prison sentence or in some cases the stocks were the usual penalty.

In the first two decades of the century Sir Samuel Romilly conducted a vigorous campaign against the death penalty which, although it achieved little in the way of reform, was influential in changing public opinion. The first major inroads upon capital punishment were made in the 1820s during Peel's Home Secretaryship. In the space of five years over a hundred felonies were declared non capital, including in 1827 all clergyable felonies. In the 1830s the pace of reform was equally brisk. By 1840 the the number of capital offences stood at just seven, being further reduced to four in 1861. After 1838 for the rest of the century no person was hanged except for murder.

The penalties most commonly substituted for hanging by repealing statutes were transportation and imprisonment (with whipping sometimes an added penalty). By mid century not only was capital punishment in decline but many of the old shaming punishments, such as whipping for women, the ducking stool, the pillory and the dissection and gibbeting of murderers, had either been abolished or were in disuse. In 1861 public whipping was abolished. Henceforth floggings were to be carried out inside prison (with the press in attendance). At the same time whipping was abolished as a punishment for adult males except for vagrancy and a handful of other offences (it was, however, retained for juvenile males). But no sooner had the legislation passed than an outbreak of garrotte robberies in London led to an Act being rushed through Parliament making robbery with violence or by garrotte punishable by flogging.

The claimed success of the Garrotters Act led to recurrent demands during the rest of the century that rapists and those who attacked women and children be whipped, but the only victory the flogging constituency actually achieved was in 1898 when living on prostitution was made whippable.

The 1860s also saw the end of transportation. Its abolition had been recommended as early as 1837 and it had been clear since the 1840s that it had no long-term future. What finally sealed its fate was the reluctance and then the refusal of the Australian colonies to accept further shipments of transportees. When in 1867 the last convict ship set sail for Van Diemen's Land there was already in place a substitute form of sentence: penal servitude. First introduced in 1853, this sought to reproduce the main features of transportation. A convict would serve the first nine months of his sentence in solitary confinement. (After the construction of Parkhurst (1837) and Pentonville (1842) transportees, instead of being confined on the hulks, underwent a term of penitentiary confinement before shipping out.) He or she would then be transferred to a convict prison to be employed on hard labour, becoming eligible after serving five-sixths of his sentence for a ticket of leave. Portland, the first great convict prison opened in 1848, was followed by Portsmouth and Dartmoor (1850) and Chatham (1856).[19] Centrally administered by a Directorate of Convict Prisons, they were quite separate from the local prisons where those sentenced to imprisonment served their sentences.

In 1868 public hanging was abolished. Henceforth executions were to take place behind prison walls. Although hidden from public gaze, they would not be secret affairs. The press was to be admitted. The prison bell was to toll as the condemned man or woman began the walk to the scaffold and a black flag was to be hoisted as soon as sentence had been carried out. This was to be followed by the posting of a notice and certificate at the prison gates and a coroner's inquest inside the prison. In the 1890s, in the wake of a series of bungled executions, sheriffs began to refuse the press admission to hangings. By 1900 the ban on reporters had become universal. It was last breached in the early 1920s.

By 1870 imprisonment had become the normal punishment for all but the most petty criminal offences. Moving flogging and hanging inside prison served to emphasise the pre-eminent role prisons now had within the penal system.

8. Prisons

Early nineteenth-century criminal prisons were of two kinds: houses of correction and gaols.[20] Popularly known as bridewells, houses of correction were a Tudor creation. Their original purpose had been to discipline and put to work vagrants and workshy paupers. Gaols, on the other hand, were essentially places whose main function was the custody of prisoners awaiting trial. Each county had a gaol. There was also a number of municipal prisons: gaols and lock-ups provided by boroughs and small towns to serve their

---

[19] Erected in 1806 to house French prisoners of war, Dartmoor was converted into, not built as, a convict prison.

[20] On prisons, see S. McConville, *History of English Prison Administration, 1750–1877* (London, 1981); Radzinowcz, i & v.

courts. The largest and best known of these municipal prisons was Newgate, the county gaol for London and Middlesex. In Durham, the county gaol was actually a franchise prison owned by the bishop. Until 1815 the main sources of remuneration of most gaol staff consisted of fees exacted from inmates and the profits made from trading with them. Bennet's Act (1815), however, forbade fee-taking, magistrates being empowered to compensate gaol staff with salaries charged on the rates.

During the eighteenth century the distinction between gaols and houses of correction had become increasingly blurred. The use of houses of correction to provide work for paupers had been abandoned. Instead they had come to be prisons where vagrants and minor offenders (those convicted of offences less than felony) could be confined. Their changed role was highlighted when in 1776 an emergency Act had made hard labour in a house of correction a substitute for transportation for convicts unfit for work on the hulks. They finally disappeared from the legal map in 1865.

Gaols and houses of correction were in every sense local prisons serving their immediate localities, paid for out of local rates and supervised by the local magistrates or borough council. After 1816 they existed side by side with a handful of central government prisons: first, the short-lived National Penitentiary at Millbank (1816), Parkhurst Juvenile Penitentiary (1838) and Pentonville Model Prison (1842); then after 1853 the convict prisons for those sentenced to penal servitude.

Subject since 1823 to increasing central government control, local prisons were 'nationalised' in 1877 and placed under a Prison Commission responsible to the Home Secretary. Finally, in 1898 the Convict Prison Directorate was merged with the Prison Commission, creating a single body responsible for the management of all prisons.

By 1900, as a result of a programme of prison closure and prison building and extension begun in the 1840s, the number of prisons had fallen dramatically: fifty-eight local prisons (compared with around 300 in 1833) and six convict prisons. Although most women prisoners still served their sentences in separate wings in male prisons, there were and had been since the 1850s a scattering of women's prisons: Brixton (1853–69), Fulham (1855–88) and Woking (1869–1902).

For much of the nineteenth century there was intense debate as to the form prison discipline should take. In the last quarter of the eighteenth century there had been enthusiasm for the idea of using solitary confinement as a means of bringing prisoners to repentance. After the loss of the American Colonies, an Act was passed in 1779 providing for the establishment of two national penitentiaries, one for men and one for women, in which felons spared execution would serve their sentences. The scheme was, however, abandoned when transportation was resumed in 1787. In 1792 the Gloucester magistrates built a new prison and five houses of correction to be run on the penitentiary model. Two years later Bentham persuaded the government to revive the plan for a National Penitentiary. Eventually, after years of inactivity, Millbank was built (although not to Bentham's Panopticon design). The role it was assigned, like Parkhurst and Pentonville after it, was that of housing convicts awaiting transportation.

By the time Parkhurst and Pentonville opened, two competing system of prison discipline (both American in origin) were in widespread use: the silent (or associated) system and the separate system. Under the former prisoners ate, slept and spent their free time in their cells but worked together in silence in the prison workshop. Under the separate system prisoners spent all their times in their cells, apart from time spent on exercise or attending chapel services. When out of their cells they were forbidden to talk and wore masks to prevent recognition.

Following a House of Lords Select Committee Report, the Prison Act (1865) was passed with the avowed aim of making prisons more punitive. The object of imprisonment was to be deterrence. Henceforth the emphasis within local prisons would be upon cellular confinement and work which was penal and fatiguing ('hard labour, hard fare and a hard bed'). Prisoners were to be taught 'to hate prison but to hate crime more'. With the nationalisation of local prisons in 1877 the Prison Commission under its first chairman, Sir Edmund Du Cane, succeeded in creating a regime which was as uniformly applied as it was severe. In the 1890s the harshness of the system began to attract growing criticism. In 1894 a Home Office Departmental Committee was appointed to report on the system. It recommended that prisons concern themselves with reformation as well as deterrence. A Prison Act followed which created three divisions of imprisonment, introduced a system of remission for good conduct and reduced the number of prison disciplinary offences for which flogging could be ordered as a punishment.

9. Juvenile Offenders

At common law the age of criminal responsibility was seven years.[21] Once a child attained this age he became subject to the same punishments as an adult. In the late eighteenth and early nineteenth century children capitally convicted were regularly sentenced to death. Most but not all were pardoned on condition of transportation. As late as 1831 a thirteen-year-old (John Bell) was hanged at Norwich for murder.[22] For non-capital petty larceny juveniles were usually whipped or given a short prison sentence. If the number of juveniles hanged was small, the number transported was not. In 1825 the hulk of the warship *Bellerophon*, which ten years before had carried Napoleon to exile on St Helena, was pressed into service as a depot for juveniles awaiting transportation. Over the next twenty years it served as a

---

[21] On juvenile offenders, see Radzinowicz, v.
[22] *The Times*, 2 August 1831.

temporary home to some 2500 boys. In 1838 transportation for juveniles was remodelled. Before shipping out, they were to undergo a term of penitentiary imprisonment in the recently opened juvenile prison at Parkhurst.

With transportation in its death throes, new methods of dealing with juvenile offenders were devised. In 1854 courts were empowered to sentence offenders under sixteen to a term of at least fourteen days' imprisonment, followed by two to five years in a reformatory school. These schools were to be privately run but financed by central government grants. Three years later industrial schools were established to receive juveniles sentenced for vagrancy.

By the 1880s there were demands for England to adopt the Massachusetts system of putting juveniles on probation. Some enlightened benches of magistrates took up the call. Taking advantage of a recently conferred power to discharge offenders conditionally, and with the help of the Police Court Mission, they succeeded in establishing an English version of the Massachusetts scheme. By 1900 there were a hundred men and nineteen women police court missionaries working principally with juveniles. This initiative led in 1907 to probation being placed on a statutory basis.

Despite these advances, in 1900 it still remained possible to send juveniles to prison. Whilst whipping had been curtailed as a punishment for adults it was still widely used as a punishment for those under sixteen. Although no child had been hanged since 1833, it was not until 1908 that the death penalty was abolished as a punishment for those under sixteen.[23]

10. Crime

Crime in England and Wales began to increase sharply in the last decades of the eighteenth century.[24] It continued to mushroom until around 1850, with the rise particularly steep in the depression years of 1815–17 and 1842. Between 1805 and 1842 commitments for trial increased 700 per cent but the population by less than 70 per cent. By the 1850s, however, the tide was on the turn. Crime now began to diminish and would continue to do so for the rest of the century. Between 1868 and 1898 the population increased by 45 per cent but the number of indictable offences reported to the police fell by a quarter; prosecutions fell from 890 to 506 per 100,000 of the population. Early nineteenth-century pessimism and fear of crime now gave way to unfaltering optimism. 'Property', declared *The Times* in 1881, 'is safer than it has ever been against depredations of every sort',[25] and with this conclusion the government's crime statistician agreed. In 1899

---

[23] Children Act, 1908, s 103.

[24] On crime, see H. O. Pike, *History of Crime in England* (London, 1876); Radzinowicz, v; D. Jones, *Crime, Protest, Community and Police in Nineteenth-Century Britain* (London, 1982), 3–23.

[25] *The Times*, 8 August 1881 (leader).

a *Times* editorial, commenting on the latest criminal statistics, was rash enough to describe the thief as a disappearing species.[26]

Most crime was against property. The high incidence of property offences was the dominant characteristic of urban crime throughout the century. The typical urban offence was theft. Nowhere was crime more prevalent than in London. The world's wealthiest and most populous city, it had a teeming criminal underworld. It was the receiving centre of England; its 'swell mob' (high-class pickpockets) were to be seen at race meetings and other gatherings up and down the country; its river and docks were a magnet for thieves; shoplifting thrived; amongst its huge servant population stealing was endemic; pickpockets prowled its streets by day, with handkerchiefs a favourite target for boys learning the trade; child strippers preyed on well-dressed children, luring them away and then stealing their clothes and shoes. At night footpads prowled the streets and burglars plied their trade. In the early years of the century the main routes leading into the city were infested with highwaymen. Fraudsters and forgers flourished; counterfeit-bank notes (mostly of Birmingham manufacture) and forged bills of exchange were daily passed across the counters of its shops and business houses. Much of the bad coin in circulation was London made. The century's major thefts and frauds were London-based: the 1814 Stock Exchange fraud, the £4,000,000 fraud on the Bank of England for which Henry Fauntleroy was hanged in 1824, the theft of £12,000 in gold and bullion from Folkestone express in 1855 (the so called 'First Great Train Robbery'). In 1862–63 it was the use of the garrotte by London footpads which triggered the so-called Garrotting Panic.

By the 1890s the volume of property crime was much diminished. Pickpocketing, in particular, was not the scourge it once had been. The highwayman, already a vanishing breed by 1812, had, like the stage coaches he once robbed, passed into history. Currency offences had declined into insignificance. Large-scale bank-note forgery had ended with the conviction in 1863 of a Birmingham gang of forgers: after 1890 the number of forged notes presented to the Bank of England never exceeded fifty a year; in 1816–20 it had been over 5000 a year. One offence of which there was no falling off was burglary. Nor was there any shortage of spectacular high-value City frauds. In 1894 the collapse of Jabez Balfour's fraudulent financial empire involved the public in such massive losses that *The Times* dubbed it 'a national calamity'.

Whilst recorded property offences declined by over a third relative to population between 1868 and 1907, offences against the person fell by only a fifth. Assault, often drink related, was common. Murder, however, was not. Between 1857 and 1900 there were rarely more than 400 homicides reported to the police each year (in the 1890s the average was below 350), while the

---

[26] *The Times*, 6 February 1899 (leader).

number tried for murder was under seventy. Of those prosecuted roughly half were convicted and a quarter executed (during the first half of the century executions for murder averaged twelve a year). Most murders were of women by men, with as many as half of the victims wives, mistresses or sweethearts. Of those convicted 60 per cent were in the age group twenty-one to forty and most came from the poorer classes. Child murder was distressingly frequent (between 1878 and 1892 20 per cent of all known killings were infanticides). Most such murders were by single women made pregnant and then abandoned by their seducers; or by baby-farmers (women who took in unwanted babies for a small cash sum).[27] Serial sexual killers although rare were not unknown. The highest killing tally was almost certainly run up by a woman: Mary Ann Cotton, the West Auckland poisoner, believed responsible for twenty-seven deaths.[28]

Statistics for offences reported and numbers committed for trial suggest a relatively low level of sexual crime. In 1805 there were just eight prosecutions for rape. The figures were, however, misleading, as rape was a much underreported crime and, until the law was amended in 1885, the obstacles to the conviction of child abusers were so great that many escaped prosecution. Until 1885 the evil of child prostitution went almost wholly unchecked (due in no small part to the low age of consent: twelve raised in 1885 to sixteen), while incest was not made criminal until 1908.

In the opening decades of the century Despard, the Cato Street Conspirators and the leaders of the Pentrich Rising were tried and executed for treason, whilst hundreds of radicals were prosecuted for sedition. There was also much industrial unrest. Luddite outrages led to machine-breaking being made a capital offence and to a crop of hangings at York in 1813. In 1839 there was a Chartist uprising at Newport which led to convictions for treason. 1842 saw the so-called Plug Plot in which Lancashire strikers, in a campaign of industrial sabotage, withdrew the plugs from industrial boilers. By mid century, however, with Chartism a spent force, fear of revolution began to recede. Protest crime was also on the wane. After 1870 there was a marked downturn in rick-burning and animal-maiming in rural areas, while prosecutions for sedition, which had been running at the rate of nearly 250 a year in 1848, had dwindled almost to nothing. The main threat to public tranquillity came from the Fenian bombing campaigns in 1867 and in the 1880s.

Most crime was committed by men, women only making up between a fifth and a third of the prison population. The juvenile crime rate, high in the first half of the century, showed signs of dropping off by the 1890s (in 1890 60 per cent of the prison population were aged thirty or over; in the 1830s and 1840s 50 per cent had been aged twenty-five or less).

---

[27] See e.g. *R v Waters and Ellis*, *The Times*, 22–24 September 1870, and *Makin v A G for New South Wales* [1894] AC 57.

[28] For her criminal career, see R. S. Lambert, *When Justice Faltered* (London, 1935), chapter 5.

2

Summary Trial

'As a great part of the business of the magistrates in Manchester consisted in settling disputes of masters with their workmen, a magistrate who was himself engaged in manufacture might be suspected by some persons as not impartial'. Bathurst, *Parliamentary Debates* 1813.

The overwhelming majority of those accused of crime were tried summarily: by 1900 over 98 per cent of all criminal trials were summary.[1] F. W. Maitland writing in 1885 commented: 'summary jurisdiction ... is yearly becoming of greater importance ... only in the present century have we begun to think of [it] as normal'.[2] The power to try summarily derived from and depended entirely on statute. The number of summary offences was by 1800 already large: in 1765 Blackstone had warned that summary jurisdiction had 'been so extended, as, if a check be not timely given, to threaten the disuse of ... trial by jury'.[3] After 1840 growth in summary offences was particularly rapid. Not only did the list become longer each year, by 1850 magistrates had also acquired power to try summarily theft and other lesser indictable offences, if the accused consented. Limited initially to juveniles charged with larceny, in 1855 the jurisdiction was extended to adults.[4] By 1879 it applied, in the case of adults, to offences of larceny, embezzlement and receiving involving forty shillings, or without limit of value where the prisoner pleaded guilty and, in the case of children, to all offences except homicide.[5] The new procedure was much used. From the accused's point of view being tried summarily rather than on indictment offered two substantial advantages. First, he would be dealt with more speedily. Secondly, statutory restrictions upon magistrates' sentencing powers meant that he would, in the event of conviction, be likely to receive a lighter sentence than if convicted at Quarter Sessions. Larceny, for example, carried a maximum sentence of seven years upon conviction on indictment but only three months

[1] See the statistics for 1893–1912 given by G. G. Alexander, *The Administration of Criminal Justice* (Cambridge, 1915), 202–3.

[2] F. W. Maitland, *Justice and Police* (London, 1885), 89.

[3] Bla Comm, iv, 277–78.

[4] See the Juvenile Offenders Act, 1847, Larceny Act, 1850 and Criminal Justice Act, 1855.

[5] Summary Jurisdiction Act, 1879, ss 10–14.

upon summary conviction. By 1900 80 per cent of all indictable offences were dealt with summarily.[6]

1. Magistrates

Justices of the peace were appointed by the Crown for each county and for such boroughs as had their own commission of the peace.[7] London however had a different system: for the City the lord mayor and aldermen were ex officio justices, whilst for the rest of the metropolis there were nine police offices attached to which were paid magistrates. The holders of some offices (e.g. privy councillors) were justices of the peace ex officio.

Separate commissions of the peace were issued by the Crown for each county (for this purpose the three ridings of York and the three divisions of Lincolnshire were separate counties). There were also individual commissions for a handful of ancient liberties: Ripon, the Isle of Ely and Peterborough being the best known. The magistrates named in the commission were appointed by the Lord Chancellor upon the recommendation of the lord lieutenant of the county who was invariably the *custos rotulorum* (keeper of the rolls) of the county bench. By an Act of 1723 county justices, unless privy councillors, peers, the eldest sons of peers or the holders of certain public offices (e.g. after 1888 the chairmen of county, rural and urban district councils), had to own or occupy land in the county worth £100 p. a. This, and the fact the office was unpaid, made the county magistracy largely the preserve of the landed classes. An important factor in appointments to the county bench was political affiliation: 'Liberals alleged that the Lords Lieutenants were Conservatives and that this reflected overwhelmingly in ... appointments to the bench'.[8] Whilst some Lord Chancellors tried to be even-handed, others did not. Halsbury was alleged to have seldom appointed anyone who was not a Conservative. Of those named in the commission not all were acting justices ('very many perhaps one half of those who are named in the commission are titular justices; they have not taken the requisite oaths and so become acting magistrates'.)[9] A striking feature of the first quarter of the century was the large number of clerical justices on the county bench. There were three clergy amongst the twelve justices who ordered the troops to attack the crowd at Peterloo in 1819. By the 1820s, however, 'there was a growing feeling that service on the bench was incompatible with a clergyman's duty to his flock'. In spite of this many continued to serve for a time and as late as 1832 a quarter of all JPs were members of the clergy,[10] but by the latter part of the ... century

---

6 Alexander, *The Administration of Criminal Justice*, 202–3.
7 Maitland, *Justice and Police*, 81–85, 88–90, 94, 96 and 102.
8 A. H. Manchester, *Modern Legal History* (London, 1980), 75.
9 Maitland, *Justice and Police*, 83.
10 S. & B. Webb, *The Parish and the County* (reprinted London, 1963), 384 n 2.

it was generally accepted that no ... clergyman or minister of any denomination ... ought to be appointed a JP unless no other suitable person could be found locally'.[11] A county magistrate could in theory sit in any part of the county but in practice justices tended to sit only in their own locality. In 1828 Quarter Sessions were empowered to divide the county for the purpose of Petty Sessions (sittings for the trial of summary offences). This was followed in 1836 by an attempt to make these Petty Sessional divisions, as they came to be called, roughly coincident with the new poor law unions.

In every borough the serving mayor and his immediate predecessor were ex officio justices of the peace. Boroughs having their own commission of the peace had, in addition, their own bench of magistrates. Appointed by the Lord Chancellor on the recommendation of the borough council, they were not subject to a property qualification but had either to be resident or have a house or trade premises in the borough. Until the link was severed by statute in 1835, borough appointments were confined to those close to the corporation.

In the City of London the lord mayor and aldermen, as well as being ex officio justices of the peace, were also ex officio judges of the Old Bailey Sessions, which were not properly constituted unless there was at least one alderman on the bench. When sitting in Petty Sessions they had wider powers than ordinary justices, any one of them having the same powers and jurisdiction as a bench of two or more county or borough magistrates. For London outside the City there were in 1800 nine police offices. Attached to each were three stipendiary magistrates. Bow Street (established in 1723) was the oldest. Seven more had been created in 1792 and the ninth (the Thames Police Office) in 1800. At these offices the magistrates sat daily from 10 a.m. to 8 p.m. They were paid a salary of £400 p.a. and, when sitting, possessed all the powers and jurisdiction of a bench of two or more county or borough magistrates. When Peel was Home Secretary he adopted the practice of appointing lawyers as police magistrates. Hitherto most had been laymen. When the Metropolitan Police was created in 1829 the police office model was adopted. The new force was attached to an office at Scotland Yard under two commissioners who were also the magistrates therefor. The commissioners were, however, magistrates in name only; they exercised no judicial functions and the new office was from the start a purely policing establishment. In 1839 the metropolitan magistracy was reformed by statute.[12] Only barristers of at least seven years' standing were to be eligible for appointment, the office of Chief Metropolitan Magistrate was created and the name police court substituted for police office. By 1900 the number

---

[11] Sir T. Skyrme, *The History of the Justices of the Peace* (Chichester, 1991), ii, 36. Even today, clergymen (although exempt from jury service) are not disqualified from being justices of the peace but, in practice, are simply not appointed, R. Cross & P. A. Jones, *An Introduction to Criminal Law* (5th edn, London, 1964), 328.

[12] Metropolitan Police Act, 1839.

of metropolitan police courts had increased to fourteen and the number of magistrates to twenty-seven. In the meanwhile, the magistrates' salary had increased to £1400 p.a. and their sitting hours had decreased (they now sat from 10 a.m. to 5 p.m.).[13]

The first town to be granted a stipendiary magistrate was Salford in 1805, followed by Manchester in 1813. In 1835 the Municipal Corporations Act provided that any municipal borough might have a stipendiary if it chose to ask the Crown to appoint one and undertook to pay his salary. Only barristers were eligible for appointment. In 1863 provision was made for the appointment of stipendiaries for populous places (towns with a population of 25,000 or more). Relatively few towns availed themselves of these provisions; by 1900 only twenty towns had stipendiaries.

2. Trial Procedure

Statutes conferring summary jurisdiction on magistrates commonly left the subject of procedure unprovided for. An accused could, unless the Act creating the offence excluded the remedy, test the legality of the procedure adopted by the bench who tried him by suing out a writ of certiorari in the King's Bench. This was normally his only avenue of appeal and the cost was prohibitive. The lack of an effective appeal remedy left magistrates free to try accused as they saw fit.[14]

A reasonably reliable picture of how summary offences were tried in London pre-1848 can be gained from newspaper reports. There such trials were held in open court, in well-appointed court rooms and regularly reported in the press. Although accused were permitted legal representation, it was unusual for either side to have a lawyer. In 1800 it was rare for lawyers to be employed in criminal cases even in the higher courts. Most summary cases did not warrant the expense of a lawyer even where a party could afford one. Amongst the first to be dealt with each day would be the 'night charges' (those arrested overnight). Others appeared in answer to summonses issued by the magistrate on the information of complainants. Where the accused denied guilt the evidence of the complainant and any witnesses would be taken first, with the magistrate interposing with questions so as to ensure the story came out clearly. The accused would then be called upon for his answer. This would be given unsworn with the magistrate intervening with questions to clear up ambiguities. If he had witnesses they would be heard on oath. The magistrate would then give his decision and, if he found the case proved, impose sentence.

In country areas matters were ordered less satisfactorily. Many active justices had a 'justice room' in their homes where they would sit to hear

---

13 See *Whittaker's Almanack* for 1900, 180–81.
14 Skyrme, *History of the Justices of the Peace*, ii, 63; Manchester, *Modern Legal History*, 162.

applications for warrants and summonses and to try those offences which a single justice could try.[15] Offences triable by two or more justices were also sometimes heard in the private house of one of the bench. More usually, they were tried in a hired room in a public house or other public building. In some districts public and press were routinely excluded from hearings and, even when they were not, the lack of regular sitting days and times made comprehensive newspaper coverage difficult.[16] Some benches, as well as sitting behind closed doors, barred lawyers. Being laymen country justices had to rely upon their clerk and upon handbooks such as Burn's *Justice of the Peace* for their law.[17] But the clerk himself might know little law. Clerks varied enormously in their industry and competence and some had no legal qualifications at all. Knowing little or no law and bound by no rules of procedure, magistrates tried cases as they saw fit. In country areas summary justice had in the eighteenth century often meant 'a travesty of a trial conducted in secret in a justice's parlour',[18] with the accused refused all legal representation and his answer barely listened to. Stories of the highhandedness of eighteenth-century justices in petty sessions and out abound. Their early nineteenth-century counterparts often behaved little better. In 1822 a farmer, summonsed by one of the Duke of Buckingham's gamekeepers for an offence under the Game Acts, was tried and convicted by the duke in the duke's home upon the evidence of another of his gamekeepers.[19] All this would have been serious enough had justices' powers of punishment been limited to fining but they were not. Many summary offences were punishable with short-term imprisonment and magistrates were not slow to imprison. In Sheffield the fondness of the local bench for gaoling petty offenders earned the Cutlers' Hall where they sat the nickname 'Bang Beggars Hall'.[20]

In 1836 the practice of excluding lawyers from summary proceedings was outlawed, the Prisoners' Counsel Act giving accused the right to be defended by counsel or attorney and to have witnesses examined and cross-examined by them. Comprehensive reform of summary trial came in 1848. Jervis's Summary Proceedings Act obliged magistrates to sit in open court when

[15] Skyrme, *History of the Justices of the Peace*, ii, 63; in the late eighteenth century the Rev. Wilkinson, the resident magistrate for Sheffield, had such a room built on to his house at Broom Hall, see J. P. Bean, *Crime in Sheffield* (Sheffield, 1993), 22.

[16] B. Osborne, *Justices of the Peace, 1361–1848* (Sedgehill, 1960), 205.

[17] 'The practical accuracy, great learning and convenient arrangement [of Burn] made it from its first appearance in 1755 the standard reference for magistrates and overseers and led to the issue of no fewer than thirty editions extending over more than a century', Webb, *The Parish and the County*, 354. It was after 1850 displaced by Stone's *Justices' Manual* (1st edn, London, 1842), which is still the standard work. It was not, of course, obligatory for a justice or a justice's clerk to use or familarise himself with Burn and such law as many knew they had picked up from colleagues rather than from books.

[18] Osborne, *Justices of the Peace*, 203.

[19] PD 1828 XVIII, 166.

[20] J. E. Vickers, *A Popular History of Sheffield* (3rd edn, Sheffield, 1992), 192.

exercising summary jurisdiction. It also laid down a mandatory code of procedure: after the charge had been read out, the accused was to be asked whether or not he admitted it; if he denied it, the magistrates were to hear evidence, first from the prosecutor and his witnesses and then from any witnesses whom the accused chose to call. In 1849 Parliament turned its attention to the problem of courthouses. County Quarter Sessions and borough councils were empowered to provide suitable buildings for the holding of Petty Sessions.[21] The reform was timely. A parliamentary return of 1845 had shown just how unsatisfactory magistrates' court accommodation was.[22] A few country benches had the use of the local town hall, but most sat in inns or worse; at Chesterfield petty sessions were held in a converted carpet warehouse. At Newmarket the magistrates met in the subscription room there by permission, except during race weeks when they sat where they could. The rent for the hire of accommodation was almost invariably paid by the magistrates or the clerk out of their own pockets; in a few places the premises used were either owned or had been erected by the clerk or one of the bench at his own expense. The 1849 Act did not solve the problem overnight. Justice rooms and inns were still in use in some places in the 1880s, a practice the Summary Jurisdiction Act (1879) sought to discourage by limiting the powers of punishment available to magistrates sitting in such premises. Not until 1902 was the use by magistrates of licensed premises finally outlawed.[23]

The growth in summary jurisdiction after 1850 was accompanied by the introduction of increased safeguards for the accused. First, those charged with offences punishable on summary conviction with three months' imprisonment or more were in 1879 given the right to elect jury trial.[24] At the same time the maximum punishment which magistrates could impose by way of consecutive sentences was limited to six months' imprisonment,[25] and the powers of punishment available to a single magistrate, or to a bench sitting elsewhere than in a petty sessional courthouse, restricted to imprisonment for two weeks and a fine of twenty shillings. Secondly, appeal rights were steadily enlarged. Even after Jervis's Act those summarily tried had no general right of appeal against conviction or sentence. A few statutes such as the Combination Act (1800) and the Vagrancy Act (1824) gave those summarily convicted thereunder a right of appeal to Quarter Sessions, but this was unusual. In 1857 a right of appeal on law was granted and in 1879 a general right of appeal against conviction was given to those sentenced to imprisonment without the option of a fine.[26] Yet the change was more

---

21 Petty Sessions Act, 1849.
22 PP 1845 (606) XXXVI, 295 summarised (1845) 9 JP, 673–74; see also (1845) 9 JP 703.
23 Licensing Act, 1902, s 21, which came into force on the 31 March 1907.
24 Summary Jurisdiction Act, 1879, s 17.
25 Ibid., s 18.
26 Summary Jurisdiction Act, 1857; Summary Jurisdiction Act, 1879, s 19.

apparent than real. The right of appeal under both the 1857 and 1879 Acts was hedged with restrictive procedural rules, including a requirement that the appellant give security for costs. As a result, appeals were few. The low incidence of appeals was seized upon by some as 'evidence of the satisfactory working of our courts of summary jurisdiction'. All it in fact showed was that appeal was a remedy beyond the means of most accused.[27] Despite the reforms of 1848–79, an important right still denied to accused in summary cases was advance disclosure of the prosecution evidence.

After 1850 police prosecutions in magistrates' courts came increasingly to be conducted by solicitors employed by the police. The practice was not universal. Some forces preferred to entrust the work to senior officers. Bitterly resented by solicitors, the lawfulness of officers acting as advocates was questioned by legal journals and in the Queen's Bench.[28] In 1862 Lord Chief Justice Cockburn refused to condemn the practice, observing that it was for the magistrates to decide whether they would allow it.[29] In *Webb v Catchlove* (1886) Denman and Hawkins JJ came out strongly against police advocacy describing it as an 'unfortunate' and 'very bad practice'.[30] The following year Lord Chief Justice Coleridge expressed his disapproval.[31] It persisted none the less. It was most prevalent in country areas but also survived in a number of large towns (Hull, Plymouth and Oldham were still using police officers to conduct magistrates' court prosecutions as late as 1931).[32] Although after 1836 those accused of summary offences had a right to be legally represented, few in fact were. Lawyers were a luxury beyond the means of most prisoners. There was no system of legal aid in magistrates' courts nor was any introduced until 1930.[33]

3. The Justices' Clerk

The century also saw important changes in the office of magistrates' clerk. At common law every justice of the peace had the right to appoint a clerk, but the usual practice was for the justices for a town or petty sessional division to appoint one clerk to serve them all. In 1800 all clerks were paid by fees, but in 1851 power was given to pay a salary in lieu of fees.[34] After this date payment by fees fell gradually into disuse. Until 1877 magistrates' clerks were not required to be legally qualified. The Justices' Clerks Act of that year, however, required all new appointees to be either legally qualified or

---

[27] Alexander, *The Administration of Criminal Justice*, 66–67.
[28] E.g. (1907) 71 JP 604, and (1908) 72 JP 16 & 75.
[29] *Ex p Leamington Local Board* (1862) 5 LT 637.
[30] *Webb v Catchlove* (1886) 3 TLR 159.
[31] *Duncan v Toms* (1887) 56 LJMC 81
[32] P. Howard, *Criminal Justice in England* (New York, 1931), 183.
[33] Poor Prisoners' Defence Act, 1930, s 2.
[34] Criminal Justice Administration Act, 1851, s 9.

to be qualified by experience.[35] Clerks to county magistrates who were attorneys were free to undertake the prosecution of prisoners committed for trial by their bench. A Bill was introduced in 1866 to disqualify them from doing so but it failed to pass.[36] Their position was in sharp contrast to that of clerks to borough magistrates, who were prohibited by statute from undertaking prosecutions. Prevented from having the justices' clerk get up cases committed for trial, borough authorities desirous of ensuring that such cases were properly prepared and conducted were obliged either to appoint a prosecuting solicitor or to have the police bound over to prosecute. Clerks to metropolitan stipendiaries were subject to a special regime. Paid by salary from the outset, they were brought under direct Home Office control by an Act of 1839. This gave the Home Secretary the power to appoint them, required that the chief clerk at each office be an attorney of seven years' standing (or to have previously served as a subordinate clerk), and prohibited all clerks from holding any other office or employment. The salary for a chief clerk it set at £500 p.a., that for a second clerk at £300 p.a.

4. Justices' Justice

Magistrates' justice had a poor reputation throughout the century. A charge often levied against the lay magistracy is that it enforced the criminal law in its own class interest. There is undoubtedly truth in the claim. Drawn predominantly from the upper class, magistrates, like most other people at their social level, tended to be prejudiced against the lower classes. In 1833, rather than serve with a magistrate who had previously kept a retail grocer's shop and who 'still belonged to the Methodists', the Merioneth bench went on strike.[37] The landed gentry who sat on county benches were notorious for their harsh enforcement of the Game Laws. Brougham in 1828 declared that no worse tribunal existed than a brace of sporting magistrates.[38] The verdict of the Webbs was equally severe: 'in the hands of the country gentlemen of the eighteenth and still more of the beginning of the nineteenth century Game Laws became an instrument of terrible severity leading not infrequently to cruel oppression of individuals of the lower orders suspected of poaching'.[39] Before the advent of the 'new police' the duty of suppressing public disorder rested with the magistracy. It was they who had the responsibility of ensuring popular protest and demonstration did not

[35] Justices' Clerks Act, 1877, s 7.
[36] PP 1866 (53), II, 1.
[37] Webb, *The Parish and the County*, 385.
[38] Brougham; see also 'Justices' Justice', *The Times*, 25 November 1842 (Woodstock Bartlett a married man of good character fined 15s. with fourteen days in default (which he served) for throwing stones in the road at one of the Duke of Marlborough's rabbits).
[39] Webb, *The Parish and the County*, 598.

degenerate into riot and disorder. This inevitably strengthened the perception of magistrates as being both bastions of the established order and being anti-working class. It also fell to them to punish those who breached the laws against trade combinations. Under the Combination Act of 1800 a workman who combined with others for an increase in wages or a decrease in hours, or attended a meeting for such purpose, committed a summary offence. The offences of intimidation of workmen and breach of contract created by the Combination Act (1825), the Master and Servant Act (1867), the Criminal Law Amendment Act (1871) and the Conspiracy and Protection of Property Act (1875) were also summary. In the new manufacturing districts the magistrates were often drawn from the ranks of the local employers. As such they carried onto the bench 'the hostilities over discipline and conditions that infected many work places'.[40] In 1828 the only magistrates in the hundred of Caerphilly and Merthyr were 'two ironmasters employing four or five thousand workmen apiece who were continuously trying their workmen for offences against themselves'.[41] Even where the magistrate trying workmen's case was not himself an employer his sympathies and instinct would often lead him to take the employer's side. 'Colonel Fletcher of Bolton was a coalowner, and he took care that his brother magistrates put his workmen in prison when they struck for an advance of wages.'[42] In Sheffield in the 1840s a doctor called Overend earned such notoriety for his biased adjudication that there were calls in Parliament for him to be replaced.[43] Before such benches 'Masters easily secured convictions against men who left their employment without due notice, who left work unfinished or [who committed other offences under the Master and Servant laws]. Conviction could be secured [before] a single justice of the peace ... and the penalty was always imprisonment.'[44] At Derby in 1834 a woman was sentenced to three months' imprisonment for shouting 'Bah!' at a blackleg.[45] Such prosecutions and sentences were far from rare. In the 1830s in areas where employers had a monopoly on the bench the Factory Acts often went unenforced. 'In 1828 factory inspectors reported that the Factory Acts were a dead letter at Wigan because all the magistrates there were manufacturers and therefore disqualified from trying breaches of the Act. Consequently they all broke it at their pleasure'.[46] Likewise with the Truck Acts which

---

[40] W. L. Cornish & G. de N. Clark, *Law & Society in England, 1750–1950*, 20.

[41] J. L. and B. Hammond, *The Town Labourer* (1995 edn, Abingdon), 65. After 1840 Parliament began to intervene to prevent justices who were manufacturers trying offences connected with their own trade, see e.g. Hosiery Act, 1843, s. 25; Trade Union Act, 1871, s. 22; Coal Mines Regulation Act, 1887, s. 69, and Truck Act, 1887, s. 13.

[42] Hammond, *The Town Labourer*, 64–65.

[43] PD 1847 XCII, 1056–62.

[44] P. Gregg, *A Social and Economic History of Great Britain, 1750–1955* (2nd edn, London, 1956), 337–38.

[45] *Pioneer*, 15 March 1834.

[46] Hammond, *The Town Labourer*, 65.

prohibited paying workmen in kind. Bias against the labouring classes was not, of course, confined to the magistracy. The savage sentence upon the Tolpuddle Martyrs in 1833 was imposed by a judge not a magistrate.[47] Juries, drawn in the main from the ranks of shopkeepers and small landowners, also tended to display a similar bias.

Before 1848 the secrecy and unfairness of proceedings of many provincial benches resulted in their being held in low public esteem. The problem was at its most acute in the towns. In 1833 a royal commission reported that there was widespread distrust of the muncipal magistracy, often accompanied by a contempt for the magistrates themselves.[48] Jervis's Act did much to improve the reputation of justices' justice but a general perception of lay magistrates as pro-police and over harsh in sentencing (particularly at county Quarter Sessions) was one which has followed them into the present century. The survival of the lay magistracy, despite its unpopularity, was due principally to the problem of devising a substitute for it. Not even radicals were 'prepared for elections to the magistracy nor for the appointment of a vastly increased number of stipendiaries'.[49] Quite apart from the expense, the use of stipendiaries had proved far from an unqualified success. There had been a number of thoroughly bad appointments. During his time as chief Bow Street magistrate Frederick Roe proved an implacable opponent of the new Metropolitan Police and did all he could to discredit and undermine them.[50] There was also much press complaint in the 1830s and 1840s about the rudeness of magistrates towards the poor and defenceless. The worst offender Laing, the Hatton Garden magistrate whom Dickens had used as the model for Fang in *Oliver Twist*, was eventually dismissed. Another, Samuel Twyford, a Bow Street magistrate, resigned after press criticism of the way he had handled a child prostitution case.[51]

[47] *R v Lovelass* (1834) 6 C & P 596; the judge was Williams B.
[48] Manchester, *Modern Legal History*, 76.
[49] Ibid.
[50] J. Lock, *Marlborough Street* (London, 1980), 39–40.
[51] J. Lock, *Bow Street* (London, 1982), 95–98.

3

Committal for Trial

'[Though] the ... statutes authorise an examination, they are not compulsory on the prisoner to accuse himself. There is no mode of extorting [a] confession or other statement from the prisoner. And indeed ... he is generally cautioned that he is not bound to accuse himself and that any admission may be produced against him at his trial'. Chitty, *Criminal Law* (1st edn, 1816), i, pp. 84–85.

1. The Examination

A suspect arrested for an indictable offence would as soon as practicable be taken before a magistrate for examination. Statutes of 1554–55 obliged magistrates to examine suspected felons and from felony the practice had spread to treason and misdemeanour.[1] In the sixteenth and seventeenth centuries preliminary examinations were regarded as a means of obtaining evidence sufficient to secure the accused's conviction.[2] Depositions were taken from prosecution witnesses in his absence. The magistrate would then question him, taking care to write down any incriminating answers he made. Unless it was clear that no felony had been committed, he would be committed for trial. In the eighteenth century the procedure became more favourable to accused. In London it had been customary since at least the 1740s to hold examinations in public, which had led to 'Newgate solicitors slipping in ... to extricate notorious offenders from their difficulties'.[3] By 1800 the practice of keeping the accused in ignorance of the evidence of Crown witnesses had been abandoned. By this date depositions were taken from (or at least read over to and confirmed by) the witnesses in the accused's presence, he having the right to cross-examine. This change had been forced upon the magistracy by the ruling of Gould J in *R v Dingler* (1791) that the deposition of a witness who had died or was ill could not be read at a prisoner's trial, unless the latter had been present when it was taken and had had the opportunity to cross-examine.[4]

Magisterial interrogation of accused, finally outlawed in 1848, had been

---

[1] 1 & 2 Ph & M, c. 13 and 2 & 3 Ph & M, c. 10.
[2] Holdsworth, HEL, i, 296; Beattie, 271–72.
[3] Beattie, 278.
[4] *R v Dingler* (1791) 2 Leach 561.

in decline throughout the previous half century. In *Wilson* (1817), Richards LCB had refused to allow the answer of a prisoner upon his examination to be given in evidence at his trial, declaring: 'it was irregular for magistrates to examine prisoners, for an examination itself imposed an obligation to tell the truth and so amounted to a form of compulsion'.[5] Questioning of prisoners under oath had long been prohibited on this very ground, and for a time the new doctrine enjoyed a certain currency. Indeed Richards' ruling was still being cited in Burn's *Justice of the Peace* as late as 1830.[6] It had, however, been questioned by Littledale J in 1826.[7] A succession of cases in the 1830s, upholding the right of magistrates to interrogate, robbed it of all authority.[8] The reenactment of the provisions of the Marian statutes in 1826 with their wording on this point essentially unaltered had in fact made its demise inevitable.[9]

Lambard (1581)[10] and Dalton (1618)[11] had spoken of the Marian statutes as permitting confessions to be wrung out of prisoners. This was not how preliminary examinations were viewed two centuries later. 'An examination', wrote Chitty in 1816 was to be considered 'not as an additional peril to the prisoner, but as a privilege to him, an opportunity for him to clear himself of the charge at the preliminary stage.'[12] As a precaution against his being compelled to incriminate himself, there was the safeguard of the caution. Before putting any question to the prisoner, the magistrate was expected first to warn him that he was not obliged to answer and that any answer he gave might be used against him. The practice of magisterial cautioning, which has been traced back to 1730 (and is almost certainly older), was not merely a protection to the prisoner.[13] It also had, from the Crown's point of view, the advantage of rendering it less likely that any confession which he went on to make would be held inadmissible at his trial by reason of prior out of court inducements.

There was also by 1800 a general feeling that a prisoner under examination ought not to be pressed unduly. In 1824 a metropolitan magistrate, stung by newspaper criticism that he had not attempted to get a confession out of an accused, protested that he was not there to drag confessions out of prisoners.[14] Nor was he alone in adopting this stance. It is clear from

---

[5] *R v Wilson* (1817) Holt 597.

[6] (25th edn, 1830), i, 982.

[7] *R v Ellis* (1826) Ry & Moo 432.

[8] *R v Court* (1836) 7 C & P 486; *R v Rees* (1836) 7 C & P 568; *R v Bartlett* (1837) 7 C & P 832.

[9] 7 Geo IV, c. 64, ss 2 and 3.

[10] W. Lambard, *Eireenarcha* (1581), c. 21, 208.

[11] M. Dalton, *Country Justice* (London, 1619), 273.

[12] Chitty, *Criminal Law* (1st edn, 1816), i, 84.

[13] Report of the Royal Commission on Police Powers and Procedures: PP 1928/29 (Cmnd 3297) ix, 127, app 4.

[14] *R v Foster, The Times*, 1 and 2 October 1824.

press reports of committal hearings that in the 1820s and 1830s magistrates, when they asked questions at all, in the main confined themselves to seeking to clarify statements made by the prisoner; often the only question put was whether he had anything to say in answer to the charge.[15] Indeed, in the 1820s one can find examples of the practice (much criticised in 1843 in evidence to the Criminal Law Commissioners) of magistrates shutting the mouth of a prisoner when he began to volunteer a confession by advising him not to commit himself.[16] Since the mid eighteenth century magistrates had become far readier to discharge a prisoner against whom the evidence was weak than had once been the case. The advice of seventeenth-century text writers, that the best and safest course was to commit 'even though it shall appear ... that the Prisoner is not guilty for it is not fit that a man once arrested and charged with felony (or suspicion thereof) should be delivered upon any man's discretion without further trial', now often went unheeded.[17] Finally, in 1836, prisoners were given the right, long denied at common law, to a copy of the depositions taken against them.[18]

In 1848 the law as to preliminary examinations was placed on its modern footing. Jervis's Indictable Offences Act required that the depositions of prosecution witnesses be taken in the presence of the accused and gave him the right to cross-examine. He was to be allowed to make any statement or call any witness he chose but was not obliged to do either and the magistrate was to inform him of this. The only question the magistrate was to be permitted to ask him was whether he wished to make a statement or to call any witness.[19] If he went beyond this and put any questions, any answers he got would be excluded at trial.[20]

On the eve of Jervis's Act the features of the preliminary examination which pointed most strongly to its Marian origins were denial of legal representation to the accused, the practice of omitting from depositions those parts of the witnesses' evidence favourable to him, and the refusal to hear witnesses tendered on his behalf. All three practices, although not universally adopted, were sanctioned either by statute or decisions of the judges.[21] Surprisingly, despite recommendations to the Criminal Law Commissioners that representation be allowed,[22] the 1848 Act instead of

---

[15] See *The Times* police reports for the period.

[16] See e.g. *Reynolds*, Marylebone Police Office, *The Times*, 3 and 5 January 1824; and Criminal Law Commissioners, 8th Report, app A at 242 and 256; W. W. Pue, 'The Criminal Twilight Zone' (1983) 21 Alberta L R 335 at 346–47; also W. Eagle,*The Magistrate's Pocket Companion* (2nd edn, London, 1844), 112.

[17] Dalton, *Country Justice*, 270.

[18] Prisoners' Counsel Act, 1836.

[19] S 18.

[20] *R v Pettit* (1850) 4 Cox 164; *R v Berriman* (1854) 6 Cox 388.

[21] See *R v Staffs JJ* (1819) 1 Chit KB 217; *R v Borron* (1820) 3 B & Ald 432; *Cox v Coleridge* (1822) 1 B & C 37; 2 & 3 Ph & M, c. 10 and 7 Geo 4, c. 64, ss 1 and 2.

[22] Criminal Law Commissioners, 8th Report, app A.

stripping magistrates of their discretion to bar lawyers appeared by section 19 to affirm it.

Denial of legal assistance even in 1800 had never been universal. In London representation by attorney had been permitted since the 1750s. In country areas, however, there were as late as the 1840s benches which routinely refused to admit lawyers, regarding their presence as an obstruction to justice. Attorneys, complained a group of Lancashire justices in a letter to the Solicitor-General, 'interrupt the magistrates and direct the prisoners "to hold their tongues, not to answer any questions and to say nothing" which prevents the prisoners from the discoveries which they might otherwise be inclined to do and thereby discover their accomplices'.[23] During the second half of the nineteenth century the practice of refusing to allow accused to be represented was abandoned. By 1915 a text writer could confidently assert 'the assistance of an advocate (at a preliminary hearing) would never now be denied to an accused if he were able to pay for it'.[24]

Jervis's Act also marked the end of the role of the Privy Council in preliminary examinations. After 1848 the Council never again exercised the right which it had long possessed, and in the early nineteenth century had occasionally exercised (as in 1819 at the time of the Cato Street conspiracy), to examine and commit for trial those accused of treason or other great political crimes. In 1840 the madman, Oxford, who was accused of shooting at the Queen, was examined by the Council before being sent in front of an examining magistrate, which seems to have been the last time the jurisdiction (never formally abolished) was exercised.[25]

2. Bail

In 1900 just under a quarter of those committed for trial were bailed. In 1800 the percentage had been far lower. Those committed for capital offences were seldom, if ever, given bail. By statute treason was expressly declared non bailable, as were certain felonies and certain classes of offender.[26] Even where they had a discretion, magistrates would rarely exercise it in favour of the accused. The presumption against bail in felony extended even to non-capital petty larceny; in 1800 no more 10 per cent of those so accused were bailed.[27] Only where a prisoner was of good character and the evidence doubtful had he a hope of bail. Further, as a safeguard against corruption, the Marian statutes required the grant of bail in felony to be in open court and by at least two justices. In misdemeanour a more liberal

---

23 Beattie, 276.
24 G. G. Alexander, *The Administration of Criminal Justice*, 26.
25 Stephen, HCL, i, 183.
26 Statute of Westminster I, 1275 and 1 & 2 Ph & M, c. 13; and see generally Bla Comm, iv, 295.
27 Beattie, 281–82.

regime applied. Here the accused's prospects of bail depended upon his character and antecedents, and upon the gravity of the offence charged. In petty misdemeanour and in cases of assault (in which there was no risk of the victim dying of his injuries) bail was readily granted to those who could offer sureties. If a man could not produce suitable sureties, however (and poor prisoners, strangers and foreigners often could not), he would, even for a small offence, languish in gaol until trial. Those refused bail by an examining magistrate could (if they had the means) apply to a judge of the King's Bench for bail (the usual method of bringing the issue before a judge was by writ of habeas corpus).[28] The success rate upon such applications appears to have been low.

In 1826 the law as to bail was recast. It was enacted that justices should have a discretion whether to commit in custody or on bail both in felony and in misdemeanour, although they were enjoined to commit in custody in felony where the evidence raised a strong presumption of guilt. The prohibition upon the grant of bail in felony by a single justice was retained.[29] In 1848 the law was further reformed. Jervis's Act declared that in felony and certain specified cases of misdemeanour (e.g. obtaining by false pretences), the examining magistrates should have a discretion to commit either in custody or on bail, but in all other cases of misdemeanour the grant of bail should be mandatory.[30] The prohibition upon the grant of bail by a single magistrate in felony was abolished. But the power to refuse bail to those who could not find sureties was left unaffected. In treason bail was to be grantable only by the Home Secretary or a judge of the Queen's Bench.

In a succession of cases in the 1840s and 1850s, the judges stressed that, when considering bail, the question magistrates had to decide was the likelihood of the prisoner appearing to take his trial if bailed; that in assessing the risk of absconding they might have regard to the strength of the case against him and the severity of the punishment likely to be imposed on conviction.[31] The result of this approach was that bail was almost never granted in murder and seldom allowed in any serious case. In 1898 Parliament attempted to end the evil of prisoners, otherwise deserving of bail, being remanded in custody for want of sureties. The Bail Act of that year authorised magistrates to dispense with sureties where to do so 'would not tend to defeat the ends of justice'. The Act was in practice widely ignored and within a decade had become largely a dead letter.[32]

---

[28] *Ex p Allen* (1834) 3 Nev & MKB 35; J.J. Tobias, *Prince of Fences* (London, 1974), 76.

[29] 7 Geo IV, c. 64.

[30] Indictable Offences Act, 1848.

[31] *R v Scaife* (1841) 9 Dowl 553; *Ex p Baronnett* (1852) 22 LJMC 25 at 28; *R v Robinson* (1853) 23 LJQB 286.

[32] Alexander, *The Administration of Criminal Justice*, 33–34.

3. The Court of Trial

At the same time as committing the accused for trial the magistrate would bind over the prosecutor and witnesses to attend the trial to prosecute and to give evidence. He would also send to the court of trial the depositions and the accused's examination. From these the clerk of the court or one of his staff (usually the clerk of indictments) would draw the indictment. The court to which the accused would be committed for trial would be the next Assize, or Quarter Sessions, for the place where the offence had been committed. The common law rule as to venue had long been that an accused was to be tried by a jury from the county where the crime occurred. But there were exceptions.[33] For example special rules as to venue applied in the case of offences committed abroad or on the high seas. Until 1830 Welsh offences could be tried in the next adjoining English county. Coining and counterfeiting offences could be tried in the county where the accused was apprehended, and theft in any county into which the accused had brought the stolen goods. After 1826 offences committed on a journey on a stage coach or other conveyance could be tried in any county through which the conveyance had passed. Palmer's Act created a further significant exception, as did the system of grouping Assize counties brought in by the Winter and Spring Assizes Acts of 1876–79.

---

[33] Archbold (20th edn, 1886), 28–42

4

Preparing for Trial

'The sessions are on', said Kaggs, 'if they get the inquest over and Bolter turns King's evidence; as of course he will ... they can prove Fagin an accessory before the fact, and get the trial on on Friday ... and he'll swing in six days from this.' Dickens, *Oliver Twist* (1838), chapter 50.

1. Knowing the Case to be Met

A prisoner committed for trial by an examining magistrate would, by the time he was arraigned, know both the charge he faced and the evidence on which it was based.[1] He would learn what offence was alleged at the time of arrest,[2] and he would be told again at the preliminary examination. In most cases the information given would be perfectly adequate for his purposes but not in all. To tell a man that he was charged with conspiracy to defraud or with embezzling £5 might leave him no wiser as to the particular transaction impugned. In such a case it was open to the accused to ask the prosecutor for particulars of the charge and, if these were refused, to apply to a judge.[3] In barratry and nuisance cases the practice of ordering particulars dates back to the eighteenth century,[4] but it was only in the 1820s and 1830s that it began to be extended to embezzlement and conspiracy.[5] Unrepresented prisoners, of course, would seldom know of their right to apply for particulars and, even where they did, lack of means might prevent their exercising it before arraignment.[6]

The accused would learn what evidence the charge was based on at the preliminary examination. To secure his committal for trial the prosecutor

---

[1] Although the Marian statutes applied only to felony in 1800 preliminary examinations were commonly held in treason and misdemeanour, see *R v Hunt, Jones and Moorhouse*, *The Times*, 30 August 1819 and *The Times* police reports for 1800–26; statutory authority to hold preliminary examinations in misdemeanour was given in 1826 (7 Geo. IV c. 64) and in treason in 1848 (Indictable Offences Act, 1848).

[2] See *MacKalley's Case* (1611) 9 Co Rep 61b; R. Burn, *The Justice of the Peace and Parish Officer* (1st edn, London, 1755), i, 302 and Hale, 2 P C, 82.

[3] See *R v Curwood* (1835) 3 Ad & E 815; and *R v Hamilton* (1836) 7 C & P 448.

[4] Barratry: *R v Ward* (1701) 12 Mod Rep 516; nuisance: *R v Marquis of Downshire* (1836) 4 Ad & E 698.

[5] *R v Hodgson* (1828) 3 C & P 422; *R v Bootyman* (1832) 5 C & P 300.

[6] A pre-arraignment application had to be supported by an affidavit, *R v Esdale* (1857) 8 Cox 69.

had to adduce evidence sufficient to establish a prima facie case and, by 1800, the depositions usually were[7] (and after 1848 had to be)[8] taken in the presence of the accused. In treason he was, by statute, also entitled to have delivered to him, ten days before trial, a list of the Crown witnesses (with their addresses and occupations).[9] But this marked the limit of the law's indulgence. From fear of concocted defences, inspection of or a copy of the depositions was denied him. In all but a few courts this denial was firmly maintained down to the coming into force of the Prisoners' Counsel Act (1836).[10]

What a prisoner could not obtain from the court, he could sometimes obtain indirectly. The practice of reporting committals meant that, if his case was of interest (and even if it was not), some newspaper (local or national) might well carry details of the evidence given. Even if there was nothing in the press, if he was represented at the committal by an attorney the latter would invariably take a full note of the evidence.[11] If unrepresented, but literate, he could take his own note. None of these expedients was foolproof. Examining magistrates had the power to exclude both press and attorneys from preliminary hearings and some benches were not slow to do so.[12] Secondly, the taking of a full and accurate note by anyone but a shorthand writer was made extremely difficult where the depositions, instead of being taken in the accused's presence, were taken out of court by a clerk and then merely read over and confirmed by the witnesses in open court.[13]

It is impossible to guess how many prisoners ended up with some note of the committal evidence but the number must have been small. The vast majority were unrepresented and, even if they appreciated the advantage of a note (the first offender might not do so), were often prevented by illiteracy from taking one.[14] Without a note, a prisoner trying to prepare his defence would have to try and remember the evidence given. Here the old hand, familiar with the procedure and able to appreciate the points against him, would be likely to fare better than the tyro.

Reform came in 1836 with the Prisoners' Counsel Act, which gave accused

---

[7] In the first quarter of the century the accused was not always present at 'the initial hearing and sifting of evidence from which depositions eventually grew', W. W. Pue, 'The Criminal Twilight Zone' (1983) 21 Alberta LR 335; see e.g. *Kepple and Others*, The Times, police reports, 11 June 1823.

[8] Indictable Offences Act, 1848, s 17.

[9] 1 Anne, st 2, c. 9 re-enacting and extending 7 & 8 Will III, c. 3.

[10] See e.g. *R v Holland* (1792) 4 T R 691; *R v Sheridan* (1811) 31 St Tr 543 and PD 1836 XXXV, 185.

[11] See PD 1836 XXXV, 184–85, 228–29.

[12] *R v Staffs JJ* (1819) 1 Chit KB 217; *Cox v Coleridge* (1822) 1 B & C 37 and *R v Borron* (1820) 3 B & Ald 432.

[13] This practice persisted even after being outlawed by the Indictable Offences Act, 1848, see e.g. *R v Calvert* (1848) 2 Cox 491 and *R v Christopher* (1854) 4 Cox 76.

[14] See the statistics as to prisoners' literacy given in the *Judicial Statistics* for 1857 onwards.

the right to inspect the depositions and to a copy of them.[15] Welcome though the Act was, it had a number of shortcomings. First, it gave the prisoner no right to inspect or take copies of any statement he himself had made at the committal hearing,[16] nor to take copies of other documentary exhibits.[17] (Anatomical exhibits seem not to have been subject to the prohibition on inspection.)[18] A potentially more dangerous loophole appeared in 1845 when Patteson J held that the Act gave no right to copies of witness statements taken post-committal.[19] This ruling left it open to prosecutors to adopt the Irish practice of deliberately keeping witnesses back at committal.[20] In Ireland the defence was in such cases refused even the names of the new witnesses.[21] English judges, after initially adopting the same stance, proved more accommodating, allowing defence counsel to inspect the back of the indictment to get the witnesses' names.[22] Another defect was that copies of the depositions had to be paid for.[23]

When in 1848 this provision of the 1836 Act was reenacted, with its wording altered, nothing was done about the problem of keeping back witnesses. However, later in the same year, in *R v Ward*,[24] Cresswell J said that he thought that the fair course was for the prosecution to apprise the defence of the character of the additional evidence. Within a few years this became settled practice.[25] It was strongly affirmed by Willes J in 1867 and Brett J in 1870.[26] But what redress did the defence have if notice was not given? To this question the Australian courts gave a bold answer: the evidence could not be given.[27] The most English judges were, however, willing to offer was an adjournment to give the defence the opportunity to consider and meet the new evidence, but it was not until 1884 that even this right

[15] For the parliamentary debate on the reform, see PD 1834 XXIV, 1098, and 1836 XXXV, 184 and 228; the fear that the courts would be swamped with applications for copy depositions proved ill founded, see *The Times*, Central Criminal Court report, 21 September 1836.

[16] *R v Aylett* (1838) 8 C & P 669 followed in Ireland in *R v Glennon and Others* (1840) 1 Craw & D 359; see also (1884) 9 Law Mag (4th series) 61 referring to the problem of documentary exhibits in fraud cases.

[17] *R v Sargent* (1851) 5 Cox 499.

[18] *R v Spry and Dore*, *The Times*, 23 August 1848 (application for leave for a chemist instructed by the defence to examine the deceased's stomach contents granted but described by the court as 'unusual').

[19] *R v Connor* (1845) 1 Cox 233.

[20] For the Irish practice, see PD 1834 XXIX, 1099, and 1836 XXXI, 1159–60.

[21] *R v Lacey Cuffey and Fay* (1848) 3 Cox 517.

[22] *R v Duffy* (1843) 1 Cox 283 (in *R v Gordon* (1842) 6 Jur 996 Patteson J had followed the Irish practice).

[23] A sum not exceeding 1 1/2d per folio. The Bill in its original form had proposed a charge of 4d per folio.

[24] *R v Ward* (1848) 2 C & K 759.

[25] Note in 11 Cox 413.

[26] *R v Stiginani* (1867) 10 Cox 552; *R v Greenslade* (1870) 11 Cox 412.

[27] *R v Brown* (1869) 6 WW & A'B 239; for an attempt to establish the same rule in Ireland, see *R v Petcherini* (1855) 7 Cox 79.

was clearly established.[28] In 1867 the furthest Willes J had been prepared to go was to say that failure to give notice was a matter about which the defence would be entitled to make strong comment.

There was also the question whether the 1836 Act applied to coroners' depositions. This was a point of some importance. The accused was not necessarily present at the coroner's inquest; and although the majority of those committed for trial for murder or manslaughter by coroner's inquisition also underwent a preliminary examination, not all did.[29] Decisions on the point were conflicting.[30] The accused's right to a copy of such depositions was not finally placed beyond doubt until 1887.[31]

Committal upon a coroner's inquisition was not the only procedure whereby an accused could be brought to trial without the safeguard of a preliminary examination. At common law it was possible for a prosecutor to by-pass the magistrates' court completely, and simply go before the grand jury with his witnesses and ask for a bill of indictment. If the grand jury found a true bill, the first the accused would know of the proceedings was when he was arrested pursuant to the court's warrant. He would then stand his trial without knowing what the evidence against him was.[32]

In 1859 the freedom of prosecutors to apply to the grand jury in this way was curtailed by the Vexatious Indictments Act.[33] This declared that thenceforth no indictment for perjury, conspiracy, indecent assault or certain other specified misdemeanours should be presented to or found by a grand jury, unless the accused had been committed for trial; or the prosecutor bound over to prosecute; or the indictment was preferred by the direction of or with the consent of a judge of one of the superior courts. The Act applied only to this limited class of offences and, as the Criminal Code Commissioners pointed out in 1879,[34] in all other cases the potential for abuse still remained. Within months of their report just such a case occurred, with its victim an alderman of the City of London.[35] The Criminal Code Bills sought

---

[28] *R v Flannagan and Higgins* (1884) 15 Cox 403.

[29] The practice of putting a man on trial on a coroner's inquisition without any preliminary examination was viewed with disfavour because the verdict of a coroner's jury could be brought in behind the accused's back and inevitably created prejudice against him; after 1850 attempts were made to deprive coroners of the power to commit for trial (not least by the Criminal Code Bills); as to procedural snares see *R v Quaill, The Times*, 5 March 1862.

[30] *R v Greenslade* and *R v White* (1852) 5 Cox 562; the Manslaughter Act, 1859, gave those committed by a coroner on a charge of manslaughter the right to a copy of the depositions but was silent as to murder.

[31] Coroners' Act, 1887, s 18(5).

[32] See Tindal CJ in *R v Simpson and Others* (1842) Car & M 669.

[33] For the debates on the Bill see PD 1859 CLII, 1045–50, CLIV 296–97 and CLV 443–45. A defect in the Act was exposed in *R v Lord Mayor of London ex p Gosling* (1886) 16 Cox 77.

[34] Report of the Criminal Code Commissioners, PP 1878/79 (Cmnd 2345) XX, 169 at pp. 32–33.

[35] He was Sir Francis Truscott; for the facts see *The Times*, 23 September 1879 (leader); the Criminal Code Bills all contained clauses to close the loophole.

to close the loophole but, after the dropping of the 1883 Bill, nothing further was done.[36]

Nor was there any preliminary examination in prosecutions for misdemeanour begun by criminal information. Indeed where the information was ex officio there was no disclosure whatever of the prosecution evidence before trial (a state of affairs which remained unaltered until informations were abolished in 1967).[37]

2. The Right to a Copy of the Indictment

Just as it was the policy of the common law to deny the accused a copy of the Crown's evidence, so also it denied him a copy of the indictment.[38] The rule had been abolished as regards high treason in 1695,[39] and was abolished in misdemeanour in 1819,[40] but as regards felony it remained unreformed throughout the nineteenth century.[41]

The hardship denial of the indictment caused to an accused was not that it left him uncertain as to the offence for which he was to be tried (in the vast majority of cases this could not be in doubt) but that it made it more difficult for him to make indictment objections. Indeed, there is some ground for believing that judges may have regarded this as a powerful reason for maintaining the rule.[42] Hawkins claimed that the court would grant the accused copy of the indictment to enable him to take an exception to it or draw a special plea,[43] but it is doubtful whether this represented early nineteenth-century practice.[44] However, a counsel determined to obtain a copy of the indictment would often be able to get one. He had a right to have the indictment read over once slowly. If this were done, he would of course be able to copy down what was read.[45] Such was the prolixity of nineteenth-century indictments that the mere threat to call for the indictment to be read (in practice all that was usually put on

---

[36] But see the Assizes & Sessions Act, 1908, s 1(5), which required five days notice of the intention to present a Bill.

[37] See J. ll. J. Edwards, *The Law Officers of the Crown* (London, 1964), 267.

[38] The rule is stated in Hale 2 P C 236 and Foster, 228–29. Kelyng (Rep 3) mentions a resolution passed by five of the Old Bailey judges in 1670 as the reason for the rule.

[39] 7 Anne c. 21, s 11.

[40] 60 Geo III and 1 Geo IV, c. 4, s 8, held in *R v Brown and O'Regan* (1844) 1 Cox 114 to apply to all cases of misdemeanour; according to Pennefather B the accused had a common law right to a copy on payment.

[41] The right to a copy in felony was finally conceded by the Indictments Act, 1915, schedule r 13(1).

[42] Polexfen CJ in *R v Grahme* (1691) 12 St Tr 646 at 660–61.

[43] Hawk 2 P C, c. 39, s 13.

[44] *R v Vandercomb* (1796) 2 Leach 708.

[45] *R v Parry* (1837) 7 C & P 836; *R v Mitchel* (1848) 3 Cox 1; *R v Dowling* (1848) 3 Cox 509.

arraignment was a summary) would often induce the Crown to furnish a copy.[46]

During the second half of the century repeated calls were made for reform of the rule, and clauses conferring upon those accused of felony the right to a copy of the indictment were included in all of the Criminal Code Bills and many of the Criminal Appeal Bills.[47] In reality, the matter had by the 1850s become less urgent, due to the fact that the scope for successful indictment objections had been greatly reduced by Lord Campbell's Act (1851). A final irony was that, for all the calls for reform, the scope of the rule was in 1848 actually extended when the Treason Felony Act gave the Crown the option to prosecute certain treasons as felony, a course which, if adopted, deprived the accused of his right to a copy of the indictment.[48]

3. Disclosure of Information by the Crown

In a murder case in 1838 Patteson J insisted that the prosecution call all eye-witnesses to the killing, irrespective of their supposed sympathies and whether or not their names were on the back of the indictment.[49] In *R v Pook* in 1871 Cockburn LCJ went even further,[50] declaring it the duty of the police to ensure that the defence were given all information available about the crime. Neither doctrine took root and by 1900 the law still imposed no duty on the prosecution or police to disclose information in their possession helpful to the defence case.

4. Access to Legal Advice and Representation

Most of those committed for trial were committed in custody. Save in treason, where the prisoner's counsel had a statutory right of access to him,[51] the right of a remand prisoner to see a lawyer depended upon the rules of the prison in which he was detained. Most prisons seem to have allowed fairly generous access to lawyers.[52] Indeed, in Newgate in the mid 1840s the regime was, if anything, too liberal, with sham attorneys and clerks of low

---

[46] *R v Grace* (1846) 2 Cox 101 was such a case; normally only a summary would be read to the jury; cf. Tindall CJ in *R v Newton* (1844) 1 C & K 469. The trend towards long indictments did not abate in the second half of the century, see (1876–77) 21 Sol J 475 and the *Albion Insurance Case* (*The Times*, 13 June 1878, leader).

[47] See e.g. the call for reform by Taylor (7th edn 1878), 1253.

[48] *R v Mitchel, R v Dowling* supra; *R v Casey Mullaney and Burke, The Times*, 29 February 1868.

[49] *R v Holden* (1838) 8 C & P 606 (one can find a scattering of other cases to the same effect: *R v Orchard* (1838) 8 C & P 559 n, *R v Stroner* (1845) 1 C & K 650 and *R v Holland* (1896) 30 Ir LT 395).

[50] *R v Pook* (murder), *The Times*, 8 June 1871.

[51] Treason Act, 1695, s 1: 'such counsel shall have free access at all seasonable times.'

[52] See e.g. The Rules for Newgate, Report of the Select Committee on London Gaols, PP 1813–4 (157), IV, 249 app. 8.

attorneys allowed to prowl amongst the remand prisoners touting for business. In the end, in order to protect prisoners from exploitation (which ranged from gross overcharging to out and out fraud),[53] the City authorities were obliged to deny access to all save duly qualified attorneys and their properly accredited clerks.[54]

A recurrent problem for much of the century was the practice of some prison governors and police of insisting that interviews between attorneys and prisoners take place in rhe presence of a prison or police officer (defence medical examinations and the interviewing of possible prisoner witnesses were sometimes made subject to a similar requirement).[55] The problem was finally tackled in the 1870s, both the Metropolitan Police General Orders (1873) and the Prison Rules (1878) providing for interviews to take place in the sight (but not the hearing) of police or prison staff.[56]

During the first half of the century a serious obstacle to remand prisoners hiring lawyers lay in the practice of the police, in some areas, of taking from a prisoner all money found on him on arrest. In the 1830s judges repeatedly intervened to stress the impropriety of the practice (except in cases where it was clear that the money seized was stolen),[57] but for all that it continued well into the 1840s.[58] In the 1890s a small but important improvement in police practice was made by a Home Office circular directing that an arrested person be allowed to make immediate communication with a friend or lawyer.[59]

5. Time to Prepare for Trial

The time available for a prisoner to prepare for his trial varied according to the nature of the charge he faced. An accused charged with high treason could not be put on trial until at least ten days after he had been served with a copy of the indictment, a list of the witnesses and a copy of the jury panel.[60] In misdemeanour the accused, if not in custody, had the right to

[53] For a useful summary of these abuses, see *The Times*, 28 October 1844 (letter signed 'Veritas').

[54] The matter was referred to by Alderman Wood in *R v Pond*, *The Times*, 23 September 1844.

[55] Warders: *R v Potts Tucker and Others*, *The Times*, 22 July, 1839; *R v Conroy and Others*, *The Times*, 3 March 1856; *R v Cunningham and Burton*, *The Times*, 13 May 1885; police: (1866) 30 JP 46 and (1882) 46 JP 268; medical examination: *R v Hinson*, *The Times*, 28 October 1869; other prisoners, *R v Watts and Hall*, *The Times*, 5 June 1896.

[56] Prisons: Prison Act, 1877, s 39 and Prison Rules, 1878; police: Metropolitan Police General Orders, 1870 (PR0, MEP 8/3) and Metropolitan Police General Orders & Regulations, 1893 (PRO, MEP 8/4).

[57] *R v Barnett* (1829) 3 C & P 600; *R v Jones* (1834) 6 C & P 343; *R v O'Donnell* (1835) 7 C & P 138; *R v Kinsey* (1836) 7 C & P 447; *Ex p Griffiths* (1845) 1 New Prac Cas 119; but contra *R v McKean*, *The Times*, 12 August (1826) and *R v Pierce* (1852) 6 Cox 117.

[58] See (1845) 9 JP 97–98; *R v Carter and Others*, *The Times*, 16 March 1849, and *R v Bass* (1849) 2 C & K 822.

[59] The circular is referred to in reg 309 of the 1893 General Regulations & Orders above.

[60] Treason Act, 1708, s 14.

traverse, that is to put off his trial until the session of the court next after that at which he was arraigned.[61] In felony no such indulgence was given. There the prisoner would be put on trial at the session immediately following his committal (usually on the same day as the indictment was found against him by the grand jury). Where he had been committed just before the session began, this could mean his being tried within days of arrest.[62] In 1812 Bellingham was tried for the murder of Spencer Perceval three days after the deed, being hanged four days later. Nor was his an isolated case. At the Old Bailey, where even in 1800 there were eight sessions a year, prisoners frequently took their trial within days and sometimes hours of their committal. At Assizes and Quarter Sessions, with their less frequent sittings, the problem was not so acute. In 1844 the *Law Magazine* called for all prisoners to be allowed fifteen clear days between committal and trial.[63] However, the only reform made was in the opposite direction, namely the abolition in 1851 of the right to traverse in misdemeanour.[64]

Where his case was called on before he was ready, it was always open to the accused to apply for a postponement. In the early years of the century the attitude of judges to such applications was markedly unsympathetic. In *Bellingham's case* an application by counsel for a postponement to allow evidence to be called as to the accused's sanity was brushed contemptuously aside.[65] In 1835 a protest staged by the Old Bailey bar against prisoners having their cases called on when they were unprepared with either counsel or witnesses merely drew from the Common Serjeant the retort: 'Every prisoner is bound to be ready to take his trial on the first day of the session'.[66] The courts gradually became less hostile to applications for postponement.[67] But even in 1900 it still remained the law that a prisoner indicted for felony could not demand of right a single day to prepare for his trial. It was regarded as neither unusual nor unfair to expect counsel, briefed from the dock or assigned by the court, to conduct the defence after a hurried conference with the prisoner over the dock rail.

[61] Chitty, *Criminal Law* (1st edn, 1816), 483–84.

[62] See *R v Anon.*, The Times, 7 February 1835 (prisoner not in gaol a quarter hour); *R v Cooper*, The Times, 13 May 1842; *R v Conner*, The Times, 14 April 1845; *R v Thomas and Thomas*, 2 January 1844.

[63] The article is reprinted as Appendix C of the 8th Report of the Criminal Law Commissioners.

[64] S 27 (the right had been curtailed in the eighteenth century by 30 Geo II, c 24 and 39 & 40 Geo III, c. 87) and again in 1819 by 60 Geo III & 1 Geo IV, c 4, ss 3 & 5.

[65] *R v Bellingham*, The Times, 13,15 and 16 May 1812.

[66] *R v Lyon*, The Times, 29 October 1835.

[67] See e.g. *R v Cooper*, *R v Conner*, and *R v Thomas and Thomas* supra; *R v Mellish*, The Times, 28 November 1851 and *R v Taylor* (1869) 11 Cox 340 (postponement granted in murder case despite looseness of supporting affidavit).

5

Pre-Trial Publicity

'It was much to be lamented that ... no case now occurred ... which was not forestalled by [accounts in the newspapers] which created a prejudice against accused persons from which it was very difficult, if not impossible, to divest themselves.' Gaselee J, Old Bailey, 11 September 1828.

In 1800, as now, stirring up prejudice against an accused awaiting trial was prohibited on pain of committal for contempt.[1] But it was a prohibition to which the press paid little heed. Newspapers had since the 1780s habitually reported evidence given at inquests and preliminary examinations of accused;[2] and such reports did not confine themselves simply to the evidence given. If an accused committed for trial was known to be of bad character the public would be told.[3] In notorious cases every scrap of information and rumour which could be gleaned about the accused and the crime would be laid before the reading public.[4] Any confession which he had made since being taken into custody would be reported, and where possible reproduced verbatim,[5] as would any letters by him upon which the press had been able to get their hands.[6] Not infrequently what was published was wholly false. In 1823 Thurtell had to stand trial for murder falsely accused by *The Times* of

---

[1] *St. James Evening Post Case* (1742) 2 Atk 469.

[2] 1 St Tr NS 672 n.

[3] *The Times* police reports regularly included such descriptions of persons committed for trial as 'both have been in custody before for swindling' (*Hawkins and Underwood, The Times*, 17 March 1800); 'an old hand who has been transported and is otherwise well known to the police' (*Oates, The Times*, 1 and 8 November 1826); and 'the associate and occasional leader of a gang of burglars' (*Bedsar, The Times*, 27 September 1836).

[4] Before the trial of Carter Tuck in November 1811 for fraud, a number of damaging articles about him appeared in *The Times*, one (of 7 August) accused him of performing illegal marriages; another (of 8 August) contained the observation 'when the irons were put on his legs he handled them and appeared to know how to tie them to prevent them rattling as well as one of the oldest thieves in town'.

[5] See e.g. *Leary* (*The Times*, 5 August 1813), *Thurtell and Hunt* (*The Times*, 1 November 1823) and *Greensmith* (*TheTimes*, 10 April 1837).

[6] See e.g. *The Times*, 13 January 1817, where an extract from a letter written by Watson after his committal for treason was published.

having murdered before.[7] Worse still, false reports were often coupled with blatant attempts to prejudge guilt. In 1824 the banker Fauntleroy was tried for forgery at the Old Bailey, having already been tried and convicted in the press. In the press campaign against him no newspaper had behaved worse than *The Times*, which published a long but untrue biography depicting him as a voluptuary who had spent his ill-gotten gains on women and gaming.[8]

The press's bad example was copied by others. A notorious case would before the trial spawn handbills, pamphlets and ballads about the crime, often containing the most scurrilous untruths about the accused;[9] and, on the day of the trial, placards advertising such wares would be on display outside the court building.[10] Whilst Thurtell was awaiting trial he had to take proceedings in the King's Bench to prevent the Surrey Theatre putting on a play, based upon the murder of which he was accused, depicting him as the murderer.[11]

Largely unsuccessful attempts to prevent the reporting of preliminary examinations and inquests (ex parte proceedings as they were called) had been made since the 1780s. In 1782 when newspaper reports of Bow Street examinations first began to be published, the Attorney-General threatened to take action unless they ceased. The threat was heeded for a short time but soon things were as bad as ever. In 1796 the press appeared to have won a victory when, in *Curry v Walter*, it was held that no action would lie for publishing a true report of an unsuccessful ex parte application to the King's Bench for a criminal information.[12] They were further encouraged three years later when, in *Wright*, Lawrence J expressed his agreement with this ruling.[13] In 1804, however, the trend was reversed when Heath J gaoled for contempt the printers of the *Sussex Journal* for publishing an account of the evidence given at the preliminary examination of an accused for murder;[14]

---

[7] The allegation appeared in the issue for 6 November; for a full account of the way Thurtell's case was prejudged and prejudiced by *The Times* and other newspapers, see A. Borowitz, *The Thurtell-Hunt Murder Case* (London, 1987), chapter 7.

[8] Thurtell and Fauntleroy were not the only accused to suffer in this way. In 1839 it was suggested in the Newcastle papers that an accused called Bolam had conveyed away his freehold property in anticipation of his forthcoming trial for murder (see 2 M & Rob 192). How damaging pre-trial press comment could be to an accused is shown by a murder case tried at the Old Bailey before Grose J where the jury, after a direction to acquit, surprised everyone by remaining out for several hours; on their return they told the judge that the cause of their difficulty was that they were unable to keep clear in their minds what they had heard in evidence and read elsewhere (referred to by Serjeant Best, 1806, PD VI, 796).

[9] See e.g. *R v Jane Scott* (*The Times*, 10 September 1827) and *R v Edens Wolfe and Wolfe* (*The Times*, 17 August 1819).

[10] *R v Mead*, referred to in *R v Geach* (1840) 9 C & P 500, and *R v De Vidil*, *The Times*, 23 and 24 August 1861.

[11] *R v Williams* 2 LJ (OS) 30; cf. *R v Gilham* (1827) Moo & M 165.

[12] *Curry v Walter* (1796) 1 Bos & Pul 526.

[13] *R v Wright* (1799) 8 TR 293 at 298.

[14] *R v Lee* (1804) 5 Esp 123.

the mere publication of ex parte evidence before trial being, he declared, highly criminal. In 1806 Serjeant Best, in an attempt not to clarify the law (which was he claimed clear) but to make it better known and to give it teeth, sought leave to introduce a Bill making the publication of all ex parte proceedings in criminal cases an offence punishable with fine and imprisonment, and giving a penalty of £100 to anyone who would prosecute in such a case.[15] In the end he bowed to arguments that the Bill infringed the liberty of the press and dropped it. In *Fisher* in 1811 the King's Bench condemned such publications in trenchant terms.[16] 'Their only tendency', declared Lord Ellenborough CJ, 'is to prejudge those whom the law still presumes to be innocent and to poison the well of justice.' Seven years later in *Fleet* the court, in making clear that the embargo applied equally to reports of coroners' inquests, was equally forthright.[17] The press, however, continued to ignore the prohibition, although some provincial magistrates and coroners were by now seeking to prevent ex parte hearings being reported by holding them in private.[18]

In 1823 Park J took up the topic. During the trial of Thurtell and Hunt he condemned the ex parte reports which had circulated pre-trial, not only on the grounds that they created prejudice, but also because they led to the accused being furnished with what they had no right to, namely a written account of the evidence against them.[19] Months later, during the trial of Pallett, he warned that, if the press continued to publish reports of inquests, it would be the duty of coroners to exclude them.[20] These comments stung *The Times* into a fierce reply. Giving publicity to inquests, was, it claimed, in the public interest. It helped to ensure that those responsible for atrocious crimes were detected, and also served as a check on coroners (it cited a recent case in which press reports of an inquest had helped to expose an attempt by a coroner to stifle a murder prosecution).[21] Park was not deterred. The next year, at Fauntleroy's trial,[22] he repeated his strictures, and later

---

[15] 1806 PD VI, 795–96 and 902–3.

[16] *R v Fisher* (1811) 2 Camp 563.

[17] *R v Fleet* (1818) 1 B & Ald 379.

[18] In 1819 the Birmingham magistrates banned reporters from their courts, J. Lock, *Marlborough Street*, 120. In the same year the Oldham coroner purported to ban reporting of an inquest into the death of a man mortally injured at Peterloo, R. Walmsley, *Peterloo: The Case Re-Opened* (Manchester, 1969), 319.

[19] *The Trial of Thurtell and Hunt* (Notable British Trials Series), 193–94.

[20] *R v Pallett, The Times*, 13 and 15 December 1823 (report); 15 December 1823 (leader).

[21] *The Times*, 22 and 25 December 1823 (leader and reprint of an article from the *Leeds Intelligencer* respectively). The coroner was Whitcombe, one of the four county coroners for Shropshire; he was indicted in the King's Bench and tried and convicted at Assizes in July 1823; he suffered no punishment; the magistrates who had brought the prosecution announced that they would not move for judgement provided the defendant resigned his office (which he did); it was the deceased's relatives and not the press who were instrumental in exposing him; see generally the *Salopian Journal*, 12 February, 21 March, 7 May, 30 July and 6 August 1823; *The Times*, 29 July and 14 November 1823, and *R v Whitcombe* (1823) 1 C & P 124.

[22] *The Times*, 1 November 1824.

that year Abbott CJ stressed that the fact that such reports were so numerous and frequent did not render them in any way lawful.[23]

How little the press was inclined to obey judicial bans on publication is illustrated by the way it behaved during the trial of the Cato Street conspirators in 1820. There, upon the accused severing their challenges, the court directed that no part of the proceedings in any of the trials should be published until the conclusion of all. Its reasons for making the order were twofold: preventing prejudice to the accused and also preventing Crown witnesses from reading what others had said in evidence. Such orders were by no means new. They had been made three years previously in *Watson* and *Brandreth*,[24] but, as in those two cases, the order was no sooner made than it was breached. This time the editor of the culprit newspaper, the *Observer*, was brought to book.[25] Denman, his counsel, argued that he had done no wrong. There was no risk of prejudice to waiting jurors since they were obliged to sit in court during all the trials in order to be ready when called, while there was real advantage in such publication from the accused's point of view: if false evidence was given, members of the public reading the same might thereby be induced to come forward on behalf of the defence. Abbott CJ would have none of it and imposed a heavy fine.

By mid century the attitude of the press to such bans was still obdurate. In 1848 *The Times* ignored a ban imposed by Perryn J in relation to a case of treason-felony which he was trying in Dublin, boasting in its leader: 'We care as little for the solemn warning of Mr Justice Perryn as for a veto of the Grand Llama of Thibet.'[26] Had the Law Officers, instead of merely bemoaning in opening speeches to juries the conduct of the press, sought vigorously to enforce the law, there might have been some prospect of putting an end to the evil, but no Law Officer was ever prepared to go that far.

That the freedom of newspapers to comment upon pending cases was bitterly resented by prisoners is demonstrated by the frequency with which the topic was broached before juries by them and by their counsel.[27] What could a prisoner do about such damaging publicity? If he had the means, he could bring proceedings to restrain further publication; but to do so would often merely make matters worse.[28] While an alternative course was

---

[23] *Duncan v Thwaites* (1824) 3 B & C 556 at 583; for other examples from this period of judicial condemnation of reports of ex parte proceedings, see *Scott and Wife v Clement*, *The Times*, 13 –16 July 1827 (case report) and 14 and 16 July (leaders); and *R v Fenn*, *The Times*, 11 September 1828.

[24] *R v Watson* (1817) 32 St Tr 1; *R v Brandreth* (1817) 32 St Tr 755 at 766.

[25] *R v Clement* (1821) 4 B & A 218.

[26] *R v Duffy* (1848) 7 St Tr NS 795.

[27] See e.g. *R v Despard*, *The Times*, 8 February 1803; *R v Henry Hunt*, *The Times*, 21 March 1820 and *R v Corder*, *The Times*, 8 August 1828.

[28] A point made by Serjeant Best when introducing his 1806 Bill and by Russell LCJ in *Re Fowler and Milsom*, *The Times*, 18 May 1896.

to apply for a postponement of the trial, it was rare for such applications to be granted.[29] In cases of extreme prejudice it was open to the King's Bench to order a change of venue; but there were doubts as to the scope of such jurisdiction (particularly in capital felony) and applications were sparingly granted;[30] the remedy was in any event beyond the means of a poor prisoner. In the vast majority of cases the only antidote to prejudicial publicity which the law could offer was a direction to the jury in the summing up (often reinforced by observations from Crown counsel in his speech) to put all that they had heard and read about the case out of their minds.

In 1856 local prejudice against Palmer, the Rugeley poisoner, stirred up in no small measure by the newspapers,[31] led the Attorney-General to decide to move the trial to London. Certiorari was granted by the Lord Chief Justice removing the case into the Queen's Bench.[32] The object of the removal was to transfer the case to the Old Bailey. Then doubts arose as to the power of the court to order such a transfer (if it did not have such power the only alternative would be the inconvenience of a trial at bar). To get round the problem, a special Act was passed giving the Queen's Bench power to order the trial at the Central Criminal Court of indictments found elsewhere.[33] Thereafter most applications for change of venue were made under this Act. The Act did not however change the court's attitude to such applications. To have any prospect of success an applicant had to make out a very strong case.[34]

By the time Palmer's Act was passed the attitude of the courts to reports of ex parte proceedings was changing. In 1843 Denman, who by now was Lord Chief Justice, in his evidence before the House of Lords Select Committee on the Libel Law, argued that the publication of reports of preliminary examinations before magistrates was in the public interest. Such reports, he claimed, often led to the detection and punishment of crime and the vindication of character; the accused was not prejudiced thereby as the public, realising that they were ex parte, postponed judgement on the case until after trial.[35] In 1858 in *Lewis v. Levy*, Lord Campbell, citing Denman's arguments, refused to lay down that the publication of reports of preliminary examinations was unlawful;[36] it was important, he said, that the proceedings

---

[29] A postponement was granted to Thurtell and to Bolam in 1839 but refused in *Geach* (1840) 9 C & P 499, *R v Graham*, *The Times*, 7 August 1845, and in *R v Oscar Wilde*, *The Times*, 25 April 1895.

[30] *R v Holden* (1833) 5 B & Ad 347; (1856) PD CXL 2199: 'changes of venue were rare indeed.'

[31] (1856) 20 JP 65–66.

[32] Ibid., 70.

[33] 19 Vict, c. 16 (commonly known as Palmer's Act); the parliamentary debates are reported in (1856) PD CXL 218–19, 512–13, 1768–70 and 2194–2200.

[34] See e.g. *R v Ruxton* (1862) 26 JP 773 and *R v Rudge Baker and Martin*, *The Times*, 19–21 January 1886.

[35] 1843 PP (513) V 259 (Minutes of Evidence, Q. 419).

[36] *Lewis v Levy* (1858) EI B&L 537.

of courts of justice should be universally known. In *Gray* (1865) the Irish judge, Le Froy (a sometime fiance of Jane Austen), offered another argument in favour of such reporting: it was important that the public should know that magistrates did their duty impartially.[37] Three years later in *Wason v Walter* Cockburn LCJ declared that the publication of a fair account of what took place in public courts was of great advantage to the public, and that this was as true of ex parte proceedings as any other.[38] The coup de grace was administered in *Usill v Hales*, in 1878, where it was held that the publication of a fair and accurate report of proceedings in open court upon an ex parte application to a magistrate for a summons for perjury was not only lawful but privileged.[39]

The courts' new stance upon ex parte reports left the press free to publish with impunity all the evidence given at an accused's committal, including evidence which would or might be held inadmissible at trial.[40] They were thus able to publish and did publish (often verbatim) alleged confessions of guilt;[41] and evidence about previous convictions given at bail applications.[42] It left unaltered the old rule that it was contempt to publish prejudicial comment.

The behaviour of the press in this regard gradually became more responsible. By 1865 the only details of an accused's past which were given in police reports in *The Times* were those spoken to in evidence. Comments prejudging guilt were only occasionally to be found in its columns.[43] However, the latter vice was one which it had only recently given up. In 1850 whilst the Mannings were awaiting trial for murder, both *The Times* and the *Observer* left their readers in no doubt as to their belief in the guilt of the accused.[44] The behaviour of other newspapers was slower to change. As late as 1886 the *Barnsley Chronicle* was to be found regaling its readers with an unflattering biography (including the whole criminal record) of a local man awaiting trial for murder.[45] In 1894 the *People* published an article alleging,

37 *R v Gray* (1865) 10 Cox 184.
38 *Wason v Walter* [1868] LR 4 QB 73.
39 *Usill v Hales* (1878) 14 Cox 61.
40 This was still giving rise to problems in the 1930s: see *The Times*, 24 February 1931 (*R v Rouse*, letter).
41 See e.g. *R v Carr*, *The Times*, 2 July, 1866; *R v Fish*, *The Times*, 21 April 1876, and *R v Greany*, *The Times*, 27 November 1890.
42 See e.g. *Brown*, *The Times*, 4 June 1860 ('who has recently undergone penal servitude'); *Fearman*, *The Times*, 25 May 1870 ('a ticket of leave man'); *Harris and Proughton*, *The Times*, 9 March 1899 ('previous convictions were proved against both prisoners').
43 For instances of prejudging in *The Times* during this period, see e.g. *Ellis, Ellis and Ellis*, 17 February 1855, 'evidence was given (at committal) which rendered the case perfectly conclusive against all the prisoners'; *Butler*, 11 May 1865; *McCann* 27 May, 1870; and *Jones*, 1 June 1870.
44 *The Times*, 18 August 1850; and generally A. Borowitz, *The Bermondsey Horror* (London, 1989), chapter 7.
45 *Barnsley Chronicle* (supplement), 2 October 1886.

quite falsely, that a woman called Hermann awaiting trial for murder had been convicted of a similar offence some years previously.[46] In 1895 the *Review of Reviews* published an article containing a scurrilous attack on Jabez Balfour then awaiting trial for fraud.[47] In 1901 Bennett, the Yarmouth murderer, was the target of a vicious press campaign both before and during his trial.[48]

Much of the blame for this state of affairs must be laid at the door of the Law Officers for failing to act to stamp out such abuses. Proceedings for contempt in such cases were rare and, when they were brought, it was usually the victim of the attack who brought them.[49] Indeed, during the latter half of the century, the only notable intervention by the Law Officers to prevent comment upon a pending criminal trial appears to have been the contempt proceedings brought against the Tichborne Claimant, then awaiting trial for perjury, and against two MPs for asserting at a public meeting that he was innocent and the victim of a conspiracy: proceedings which scarcely had an even-handed look about them when one reflected that the Attorney had not lifted a finger to stop the constant press attacks on the Claimant.[50]

[46] *R v Armstrong, The Times,* 9 May 1894.

[47] See *Re Stead* (1895) 11 TLR 492.

[48] See (1901) 110 LT 417 and E. Marjoribanks, *The Life of Sir Edward Marshall Hall KC* (London, 1929), 145–46 and 151.

[49] Proceedings for contempt in *Parnell* 1880 14 Cox 474, *Barnado, The Times,* 29 November 1892, *Re Fowler and Milsom, The Times,* 18 and 20 May 1896, and *Ex p Smith* (1869) 21 LT 294, were instituted by the accused or his representatives.

[50] *R v Onslow & Whalley* (1873) 12 Cox 358.

6

The Court of Trial

'upon the bench, there are the aldermen, reading the daily papers or writing letters, attired in their purple silk gowns trimmed with fur; … and the under-sheriffs in their court suits … and all on the same seat with the full wigged judges'. H. Mayhew and J. Binny, *Criminal Prisons of London*, p. 74.

1. Assizes

Twice a year, Lent and Summer, commissions were issued to the twelve judges of the three common law courts (King's Bench, Common Pleas and Exchequer) directing them to travel the kingdom to take the Assizes (the name derives from the principal civil commission under which they sat).

For Assize purposes England was divided into six circuits (Home, Midland, Norfolk, Northern, Oxford and Western). The counties within a circuit were visited in a set order with a given number of days allotted to each Assize town. Usually the county town was the Assize town but not always. Kent Assizes, for example, were held at Maidstone not Canterbury. Where a city or town was itself a county (and twelve were),[1] its Assize would usually be combined with that for the adjacent county. A yet further variant was for the Assize to be held in two or even three towns in a county in rotation.[2] Worst served by the system were the four northern counties (Cumberland, Durham, Northumberland and Westmoreland), which had a Summer but no Lent Assize.

The entry of the Assize judges into a county was, and was intended to be, an impressive affair. Having been met at the county boundary by the under-sheriff, as they neared the county town the high sheriff and the county gentry would ride out to meet them. They would enter the town with an escort of javelin men to the sounding of trumpets and the ringing of church bells. There, still attended by the high sheriff, they would proceed to the lodgings provided for them by the county. By the evening the town, swollen by an influx of barristers, attorneys, constables, jurors and witnesses, as well as county society, would be near to bursting.

On the first day of the Assize the judges in their scarlet robes would attend

---

[1] For a list see Stephen, HCL, i , 116.

[2] E.g. Surrey assizes were held at Guildford alternately with Croydon in Summer and Kingston in Spring.

divine service at the cathedral or parish church. They would then process
to the courthouse. There proceedings would open with the reading by the
clerk of assize of the commission and the king's proclamation against vice.
This was followed in the criminal court by the calling of the grand jury and
the judge's charge to them. After being sworn, the grand jury would retire
to their room. As bills of indictment began to emerge from the grand jury
room, the work of trying prisoners would begin. Meanwhile in the adjoining
Nisi Prius court the civil judge would be beginning his list. On the last day
the convicted prisoners would be brought up for sentence. Before the judges
departed they would hand to the sheriff a list of those left for execution
(i.e. not to be recommended for pardon).[3]

With roots going back to the eleventh century, the Assize system and its
attendant ceremonial had changed little since medieval times. In the Isle of
Ely a chief justice, appointed by the archbishop of York and regularly named
in the Assize commission, still presided over its Assize as had been the
practice for four centuries.[4] The large manufacturing towns of Manchester,
Liverpool, Birmingham and Leeds, because they were not county towns, had
no Assize, but backwaters like Appleby and Oakham did.

The practice of holding Assizes at towns where there were rarely more
than a handful of cases to try was extremely wasteful. The more towns the
judges had to visit, the less time they could spend at each, while at busy
centres there was often more work than they could hope to cope with in the
time available. This led to the twin evils of rushed cases and late sittings.

Slowly and grudgingly the claims of the great industrial towns to their
own Assize were conceded. In 1833 Liverpool was made an Assize town,
followed in 1864 by Manchester and Leeds. Birmingham, however, had to
wait until 1884. As for Sheffield, refused an Assize in 1865, it would remain
outside the system until 1955. The creation of new Assize towns in the north
led to a redrawing of the circuits. In 1864 Yorkshire was transferred to the
Midland circuit. Twelve years later it was (as had been recommended in
1844) combined with Durham and Northumberland to form a new circuit:
the North Eastern.

One of the worst evils of the Assize system was the length of time prisoners
spent in custody awaiting trial. In 1800 a prisoner committed for trial soon
after the Summer Assize faced a wait of almost twelve months in the northern
counties and seven months elsewhere. Eventually the problem was tackled.
In 1820, following two years vigorous campaigning by the MP for Durham,
the northern counties were given a Lent Assize.[5] In 1822 the experiment
was tried of holding a third (Winter) criminal Assize on the populous Home

---

[3] Beattie, 316–18; J. R. Lewis, *The Victorian Bar* (London, 1982), chapter 1.

[4] J. S. Cockburn, *A History of the English Assizes, 1558–1714* (Cambridge, 1972), 34; the office
was abolished by Liberties Act, 1836 s 4.

[5] PD 1819 XXXIX, 293–96.

circuit.[6] In 1834, however, Brougham ordered it discontinued.[7] In 1843 the idea was taken up again. The experiment was tried of holding a third criminal Assize in all counties where there was the work to justify it.[8] It proved successful and by 1870 it had become the practice to hold a Winter Assize in all counties which, at the end of October, had six or more prisoners awaiting trial. This reduced but did not eliminate the problem. In small counties waits of up to seven months were still commonplace. In the late 1870s growing complaints about waiting times led the government to act.[9] By the Winter Assizes Acts (1876–77) the Home Secretary was empowered to direct the holding of a fourth Autumn Assize and to order that both this and the Winter Assize be held only at selected towns, these to take all cases pending in a specified group of counties. Under this new regime no prisoner would have to wait more than three months for trial. To the reform there was, however, a serious drawback. The practice of grouping counties caused considerable hardship to jurors, witnesses and to prisoners. Men tried at a town remote from their home county had difficulty finding lawyers to represent them, had even greater difficulty getting their witnesses to court and, if acquitted, found themselves turned loose often penniless and many miles from their homes.

There was a storm of protest. Grand juries made presentments against the new system.[10] The legal journals complained that London was being denuded of common law judges in the middle of busy civil sittings to provide manpower for the extra Assize.[11] From the judges there was loud grumbling about the increased travelling. The office of judge was already becoming undesirable. This made it more so. If the best men declined judgeships, 'the country would suffer grievously, far more grievously than it suffers because in a small minority of cases prisoners are kept too long in gaol'.[12] If the government continued to insist upon a fourth Assize, the number of Assize towns ought to be drastically reduced. To this the government would not agree. It knew full well that stripping counties of their Assizes would be highly unpopular. In the early 1890s the judges changed their tack. Grouping should be abandoned. There should be a criminal Assize in every county three times a year, with a four month gap between.[13] In 1893 the government gave way. An Order in Council was made reducing the number of criminal Assizes to three a year, except at Manchester, Leeds and Liverpool.[14] The result was a lengthening of 'the period during which an innocent member

---

6 PD 1819 XL, 1067–77; PD 1822 VI, 1317–21.

7 *The Times*, 15 November 1834.

8 Report of the Royal Commission on Circuits of Judges, PP 1845 (638) XIV, 535.

9 See PD 1876 CCXXVIII, 488, 625, 919–20.

10 See (1879) 14 LJ 163

11 (1878–79) 68 LT 346.

12 Report of the Committee of Judges respecting Circuits, PP (311) 1878 LXIII, 1.

13 (1892–93) 94 LT 135.

14 (1893) 95 LT 341–43.

of the public may languish in prison' and a renewal of complaints about prisoners having to wait four, five and even six months for trial.[15] For the rest of the century complaints about the Assize system rumbled on. In 1894 the *Law Times* protested at the absurdity of holding Assizes at Appleby: 'It has a population of eight hundred. There is no gaol in the county to deliver. Yet a judge still goes thither as he does to Manchester and Liverpool'.[16] The following year it scouted a proposal that Assizes should not be held at towns which had no gaol.[17] In 1899 the Bar Council published a report highlighting the injustice to prisoners of holding Assizes at unequal intervals, and proposing that henceforth they be held at regular intervals.[18] There was however to be no further reform.

The reform of the court system effected by the Judicature Acts (1873–75) had little effect on the Assizes. The common law judges (now styled High Court judges) continued to go out on circuit. For a few years Chancery, Divorce and Appeal judges were sent out with them. The experiment was not a success, however, and was soon abandoned.[19]

By the 1860s the old pageantry and pomp was fast disappearing. Judges now arrived at Assize towns by train. Often there were neither trumpeters nor javelin men to greet them. The opening of the Assize was no longer invariably preceded by a church service. After 1884 the proclamation against vice was no longer read.[20] Only in towns such as Appleby, anxious to hang onto their Assize, were judges sure of being welcomed in the old lavish style. For this state of affairs they were in part to blame. Since the coming of the railways they had too often shown a lack of respect for the old traditions and local sensibilities. In 1849 Denman LCJ and Williams J, having arrived at Salisbury station in plain clothes, instead of making their presence known decided to walk to their lodgings, leaving the sheriff and his javelin men to search everywhere for them.[21] In 1854 Jervis LCJ told a crowded Coventry courtroom that the judges' lodgings there were: 'a cesspool ... a place fit only for pigs or for people brought up in Coventry'.[22] In 1858 Hill J had given great offence to the corporation of Ludlow when he wrote declining the traditional hospitality of 'cakes presented on a silver salver and wine in a loving cup'; the courtesy was never offered again.[23] Once the rot had set in it was difficult to stop.

---

[15] (1896) 31 LJ 659; (1899) 34 LJ 61.

[16] (1894) 97 LT 238.

[17] (1895) 99 LT 384.

[18] (1899) 107 LT 203.

[19] (1885) 20 LJ 133; R. M. Jackson, *The Machinery of Justice in England and Wales* (4th edn, Cambridge, 1964), 47; B. Abel-Smith and S. Stevens, *Lawyers and the Courts* (London, 1967), 85.

[20] PD 1884 CCXCII, 252–55.

[21] Lewis, *The Victorian Bar*, 12.

[22] Ibid., 13.

[23] B. Nield, *Farewell to the Assizes* (London, 1972), 159.

2. The Old Bailey

In London and Middlesex there were no Assizes. Prisoners instead were tried at the Old Bailey Sessions held eight times a year in the Sessions House adjoining Newgate Prison.[24] The commissions under which the court sat issued to the lord mayor and aldermen of the City of London, the recorder and common serjeant of London, all the common law judges and certain others. In fact only two common law judges attended. They would try the most serious cases, with the City judges trying the remainder. At least one alderman was present at all sittings, occasionally proffering, if asked, an opinion on sentence but for the most part paying scant attention to the proceedings.

In 1800 each Old Bailey Sessions lasted four or five days. The Sessions House had only one court room and so sitting hours were long – from 9 a.m to 9 p.m. and later. On the first day the recorder would charge the grand jury; as soon as the first indictment was returned he would embark on the trial of prisoners. In the late afternoon the common serjeant would replace him on the bench, sitting on into the evening with a fresh jury. On the Wednesday of the session two of the common law judges would attend to try the heavy cases. They would take their seats on the bench at 10 a.m. and sit until late afternoon. One would preside while the other read the depositions in the next case. After they had risen at around 5 p.m. there would be an evening sitting before one of the City judges. Sittings would follow this pattern until the work for the judges was exhausted. After their departure the recorder and common serjeant would try what cases remained.[25] When the trials were finished all those convicted would be brought up before the recorder to be sentenced. The Old Bailey was also the venue for Admiralty Sessions held before specially appointed commissioners for the trial of offences committed within the Admiralty jurisdiction, i.e. on the high seas or in navigable rivers.

The story of the court during the century was one of ever longer and more frequent sittings. Between 1800 and 1820 the court's workload doubled, ten days being by now the usual length of the sessions. In 1824, to help with the increase, the clerk of arraigns' record office was converted into a second court room ('the New Court') at a cost of £4500.[26] An additional judge – the judge of the Sheriff's Court – was also drafted in. In 1834 the Central Criminal Court Act, as well as placing the court on a statutory footing and extending its territorial jurisdiction so as to take in metropolitan Essex,

[24] They were usually held in December (the first session of the mayoral year), January, February, March, May, July, September and October.

[25] HL Select Committee on the Prisoners' Counsel Bill, PP 1835 (HL 130) XLVI, 317 (evidence of Phillipps); see also the Final Report of the Royal Commission on County Rates PD 1836 (58) XXVII, I at p. 23.

[26] *The Times*, 4 June 1824.

Kent and Surrey, vested in it the jurisdiction of the Admiralty Sessions and directed that it hold at least twelve sittings a year.

In 1844 evening sittings were discontinued.[27] This increased the daytime workload and led to the cramped grand jury room being used as an overflow court. Nicknamed by the bar 'The Cellar Down There' it was really quite unsuitable.[28] In 1848 a third court room was built. This time the indictments office was sacrificed to provide the space.[29] Work continued to increase. Soon the grand jury room was back in use, this time as a fourth court, and would so remain for the rest of the century.[30]

With its poor lighting and worse ventilation (the death of Coltman J in 1847 was blamed on a three-day stint in the Old Court),[31] its lack of proper accommodation for the judges and the bar (the judges had two retiring rooms between them; the bar a tiny robing room and squalid mess facilities),[32] and its lack of waiting room for witnesses, the court house was by mid century far too small for the volume of people daily passing through its doors. In 1878, after part of the building had been destroyed in a fire, the City Lands Committee recommended it be demolished and rebuilt.[33] Work finally began in 1902. Newgate was pulled down and on its site the present Central Criminal Court building was erected. It opened in 1907.

By 1900 the reputation of the City judges and the Old Bailey bar stood fairly high. It had not always done so. Well into the 1840s judges conducting the evening trials often came onto the bench the worse for drink, whilst the bar, notorious for its touting, bullying of witnesses and rudeness to the bench, was an open disgrace.[34] By the 1860s such former prevalent abuses as doorkeepers demanding payment for admission to the public gallery, and sham attorneys prowling the court corridors touting for work amongst prosecutors and prisoners' friends and families, had been rooted out.

3. The Courts of Great Sessions

In Wales and Chester the principal criminal courts were the courts of Great Sessions. Created in 1536, they possessed both civil and criminal jurisdiction. A circuit system operated with the Welsh counties grouped into four

[27] *The Times*, 25 November and 17 December 1844; (1844) vol. 7 *Punch* 246.
[28] *The Times*, 21 August 1857.
[29] R. Sharpe, *Memorials from Newgate Gaol and the Sessions House, Old Bailey* (London, 1907), 23.
[30] H. Mayhew and J. Binny, *Criminal Prisons of London* (reprint, London 1971), 607.
[31] Lewis, *The Victorian Bar*, 19.
[32] F. W. Ashley, *My Sixty Years in the Law* (London, 1936), 79–80.
[33] Sharpe, *Memorials from Newgate Gaol*, 29–30.
[34] See *The Times*, 4 November 1834 (leader) and 1 November 1836 (letter); see also Lewis, *The Victorian Bar*, 24.

circuits,[35] each circuit being visited twice a year by two judges. The judgeships, which were part time and carried no pension, were filled from the ranks of the practising bar. Once appointed, a judge would travel the same circuit year in year out. In the late eighteenth and early nineteenth centuries there were repeated parliamentary complaints about the Great Sessions.[36] The judges, it was said, were for the most part of indifferent ability. There were also allegations of unseemly familiarity with local attorneys. A rife abuse was that of attorneys obtaining in advance the opinion of a judge upon a case which he was due to try by putting the facts to him under fictitious names. In 1828 the Common Law Commissioners were told how one of the late judges on the Carmarthen circuit had actually had an attorney stand up in court and wave one of his opinions in his face demanding to know how 'he dared take his money for declaring one opinion, and the King's money for pronouncing another'.[37] The end came in 1830. The Great Sessions were abolished by the Law Terms Act and Wales and Chester brought within the Assize system. To help it cope with the increased volume of Assize work, the size of the common law bench was increased from twelve to fifteen.

4. Quarter Sessions

County Quarter Sessions were held before the justices of the peace for each county four times a year or more frequently if necessary. Two justices were enough to constitute a court but in practice a large number of justices from all parts of the shire would attend. When the court was trying criminal cases the chairman would act as judge.

In 1800 there were nearly 250 boroughs in England and Wales, the majority of which had by charter the right to hold their own Quarter Sessions. The jurisdiction and constitution of these borough sessions varied enormously. Some had no jurisdiction to try felony while others could try all crimes and impose any punishment including death. In some the mayor and aldermen were the judges of the court, in others a salaried recorder (appointed by the borough and usually but not always a practising barrister) acted as judge of the court. In yet others the Quarter Sessions were held before the justices of the peace for the borough.[38]

In 1835 borough Quarter Sessions were reformed. By the Municipal

---

[35] They were Chester (Chester, Flint, Denbigh and Montgomery), Anglesea (Anglesea, Carmarthen, and Merioneth), Brecknock (Brecknock, Glamorgan and Radnor) and Carmarthen (Carmarthen, Cardigan and Pembroke); the senior judge of a Circuit was known as the Chief Justice, the junior as the puisne or second judge.

[36] For a description of the Great Sessions and their shortcomings see First Report of the Common Law Commissioners, PP 1829 (46) IX, 1.

[37] Ibid., app E, 388 (letter from J. H. Allen).

[38] Report of Royal Commission on Municipal Corporations, Analytical Index, PP 1839 (402) XVIII, 1 (pp. 535–38, 550–59).

Corporations Act 178 boroughs listed in the schedules to the Act were given the right to apply to the Crown for a separate court of Quarter Sessions. This court, if granted, was to be presided over by a recorder to be paid by the borough. He was to the appointed by the Crown from the ranks of barristers of five years' standing or more, and was to be the sole judge of the court. Most took up the Act. In the years which followed many of the new industrial towns which were not incorporated at the time of its passing were granted borough status and their own Quarter Sessions. These included Birmingham (1839), Manchester (1842), Bradford (1847) and Sheffield (1880).

In the first half of the century, as the number of capital felonies dropped, so the felony jurisdiction of Quarter Sessions, limited in 1800 to petty larceny, steadily grew. In 1842 it was enacted that they should have no jurisdiction to try capital offences or offences punishable on first conviction by transportation for life,[39] but this merely brought the law into line with existing practice. Subtractions and additions to and from Quarter Sessions jurisdiction were made by a number of later statutes, not least by an Act of 1896 empowering them to try cases of burglary which were not of a grave or difficult character.[40]

Although the City of London and Middlesex lay outside the Assize system, both had Quarter Sessions. The City of London Sessions, held before the recorder, was of little importance, concerning itself principally with appeals.[41] The Middlesex Sessions (held at Clerkenwell Sessions House) was, however, a busy court. Even in 1800 it sat as frequently as the Old Bailey. In 1844 it was enacted that it should sit twice a month and be presided over by a paid and legally qualified assistant judge.[42] It was supplanted in 1888, however, and its paid judge transferred to the newly-created County of London Sessions.[43] After this it lingered on as a small sessions court with little work.

5. The Court of King's Bench

The King's Bench was the only one of the three courts of common law to possess a criminal jurisdiction.[44] While its primary role as a criminal tribunal was as a court of review, it also had a trial jurisdiction. It was in the King's Bench that prosecutions for sedition and other high misdemeanours were customarily commenced, usually by information (a document filed with the court by the Attorney-General or by the Master of the Crown Office on the

---

39 Quarter Sessions Act, 1842.
40 Burglary Act, 1896.
41 Second Report of Commission on Muncipal Corporations, PP 1837 (239) XXV, 1 at 135.
42 7 & 8 Vict, c. 71, s 8; the first Quarter Sessions to have a paid chairman was Salford.
43 Local Government Act, 1888, s 42.
44 See generally Holdsworth, HEL, i, 212–17.

relation of a private individual alleging misdemeanour against a named person). Also each year a number of indictments for misdemeanour were transferred there for trial. Very occasionally high profile treason and felony cases were tried there 'at bar' i.e. before three judges. When the Queen's Bench was abolished in 1875, its criminal jurisdiction passed to the Queen's Bench Division of the newly created High Court.

6. The House of Lords

The House of Lords had jurisdiction to try those impeached before it by the House of Commons.[45] Also any peer or peeress indicted for treason, felony or misprision of either was, when Parliament was in session, triable only by the House of Lords. Out of session such trials took place before the court of the Lord High Steward. The indictment in such cases was found by a grand jury in the ordinary way and then transferred to the Lords or the court of the Lord High Steward.

In trials before the House of Lords the Lord High Steward presided (the Lord Chancellor was invariably appointed) but the peers of Parliament, both lay and ecclesiastical, were the judges of both law and fact. The verdict was by majority, each peer giving his verdict separately and publicly.

In trials before the Lord High Steward the court consisted of the Steward and such peers of Parliament as were summoned for the trial, the Lord High Steward being the sole judge of law and the lords triers (as the peers were called) the judges of fact. In treason all the peers of Parliament had to be summoned, in felony at least twelve, the verdict being by a majority.

Trial by peers as a mode of trial was open to serious objection. The excessive size of the tribunal meant that the sense of personal responsibility of the triers was weakened. The accused peer had no right of challenge. The privilege was not claimable in cases of misdemeanour (peers accused of misdemeanour or of summary offences were tried in the ordinary courts) and yet by mid century there were many misdemeanours which were more severely punishable than felonies.

In practice, both impeachment and trial by peers were by 1800 almost obsolete. The last ever impeachment was that of Lord Melville in 1805. The Court of the High Steward had not sat to try a peer since 1689 and during the whole of the nineteenth century only one peer stood trial in the House of Lords (Lord Cardigan in 1840).

---

[45] For the criminal jurisdiction of the Lords see Holdsworth, HEL, i, 379–90.

7

Conditions at Trial

'[The] Fourth [Court at the Old Bailey was] a room rather than a court where the dock and the jurybox completely filled two sides, counsel and the clerk of the court having to squeeze themselves into a narrow row of seats. The public had the choise of standing in the gangway or passage or not patronising the court at all'. F. W. Ashley, *My Sixty Years in the Law*, p. 79.

1. Courthouses

In most counties the Assizes and county Quarter Sessions were held in the shire hall in the county town. Borough Quarter Sessions were usually held in the town hall or another public building. Court house accommodation was least impressive in the small Welsh counties. At Welshpool, for example, Assizes were until 1873 held in a church.[1] Some English courthouses were little better. In the eighteenth century in every assize town on the Oxford circuit the Nisi Prius court and the Crown court were held in the same room without any partition or division, a state of affairs which continued at Gloucester until 1816.[2] At Guildford in the 1880s the assizes were held in an old theatre; the judge sat on the stage, counsel solicitors and the public on red plush seats in the stalls; there were no cells and prisoners had to be brought into court through the waiting crowd outside.[3]

2. Conditions for Prisoners

Where the court sat in a town with no gaol, the prisoners for trial had to be brought from the gaols where they were being held. Usually, but not always, they were taken in an open cart. In the West Riding, as late as the 1820s, they were marched to and from court chained together. Not until the 1830s did conveyance by closed wagon become the norm.[4] The conditions in which prisoners were held whilst waiting for their cases to be called on were often equally deplorable. At Reigate in 1800 a twelve by nine foot cage

---

[1] B. Nield, *Farewell to the Assizes*, 220.

[2] (1856) 26 LT 126.

[3] T. Humphreys, *Criminal Days* (London, 1946), 59; for a description of the court-house in the 1860s, see *The Times*, 7 August 1862.

[4] S. and B. Webb, *English Prisons under Local Government* (London, reprint 1963), 79.

was used as a holding cell for Quarter Sessions prisoners.[5] At Croydon Assizes prisoners were kept chained together in stables at an inn and taken thence directly into court. Eighty years later things were little better. In 1887 a Home Office Committee reported that at eight courthouses prisoners waiting to be brought up were held in cupboard-like boxes, with bases measuring about two feet square, whilst at other places the practice was to keep them unsegregated in a single dark room, with no seats, no heating and inadequate sanitary facilities.[6]

When a prisoner was brought up into court he was brought up unshackled (the use of fetters had been abandoned in 1770). But in some courts he was still required to hold up his hand (as an acknowledgement of identity) on arraignment and verdict taken. Also, unless he was infirm, he was expected to stand however long his trial lasted.[7] As today, he would have to communicate with his lawyers by notes or whispered instructions from the dock. Only in misdemeanour was the prisoner allowed to sit with his counsel and even there the privilege was unusual.[8]

Since it was the practice for courts to sit until late at night, a prisoner might find his case called on or continuing at an hour at which both he and his counsel (if he had one) were physically exhausted. At the Old Bailey late sittings were traditional (fostered in part by the sheriffs' practice of holding a dinner at 5 p.m. for the judges).[9] At Assizes the cause was more usually a heavy list and too few days allotted to get through it. Protests about the practice were made in Parliament from time to time, but usually to little effect. When in 1834 an MP complained that at the last Armagh Assizes Baron Smith had tried fourteen cases (some of them capital) between 6 p.m. and 6 a.m., several MPs sprang to the judge's defence, claiming that he had

[5] Beattie, 312.

[6] Report of Home Office Committee on the Accommodation in Court Houses and Other Places for Prisoners awaiting Trial at Assizes and Quarter Sessions, PP 1887 (Cmnd 4791) XLI, 905. The the most commodious boxes were those at Clerkenwell Sessions which had a base of four feet by two feet nine inches, the smallest those at Bodmin the base of which measured only two feet four inches by two feet six inches. At seven courts the committee found that there were no sanitary facilities whatsoever for prisoners.

[7] The practice was severely criticised in an article in *The Times* (3 January 1844), which complained of the inhumanity of calling on a prisoner to make his defence after he had been on his legs for ten to fourteen hours.

[8] In trials for felony the judges always insisted that the prisoner take his trial in the dock, see *R v Egan* (1839) 9 C & P 485 n; even if he was a foreigner who had no English, see *R v Zulueta* (1843) 1 C & K 215. At the start of the century a laxer rule prevailed in misdemeanour, with defendants often allowed to sit at the table of the court, especially in trials in the King's Bench, see e.g. *R v Carlile* (1834) 6 C & P 636 n. By the end of the century misdemeanants were invariably required to take their trial in the dock. For a case which went against the trend see *R v Edmunds*, *The Times*, 9 May 1872, where Bramwell B with considerable reluctance allowed a solicitor charged with manslaughter to sit with counsel.

[9] See e.g. R. Harris, *The Reminiscences of Sir Henry Hawkins* (London, 1904), 39–40; the dinners were discontinued after a fire at the Old Bailey in 1877, W. E. Hooper, *History of Newgate and the Old Bailey* (London, 1935), 17 and 134.

been merely trying to spare the prisoners the hardship of having their cases put over to the next Assize. The Commons voted to hold an inquiry into this and other charges against him but nothing came of it.[10]

Courts gradually moderated their sitting hours but late sittings continued to occur from time to time both at the Old Bailey and at Assizes right through until the end of the century.[11] By the 1860s it was also becoming usual to allow the prisoner a chair, whether he was infirm or not.[12]

3. Conditions for the Jury

If conditions for prisoners were bad, the treatment meted out to jurors was only marginally better. If a trial did not finish within the day, the judge had power to adjourn it.[13] If he did so, and the case was one of treason or felony, the jury were not permitted to separate over the adjournment. Instead they would be taken either to a room in the court building,[14] or more usually to a hotel, and kept there overnight in the charge of a bailiff sworn to allow no one to speak to them. Old Bailey juries were normally taken to a hotel. The London Tavern, the London Coffee House, the City Terminus Hotel and the Cannon Street Hotel were all used at different times during the century.[15] Provincial juries did not always fare so well. In 1848 a York jury complained that all they had been provided with had been six shake-downs on the floor; the under-sheriff, when taxed by the judge, claimed that this was the accommodation normally provided.[16] The purpose of the rule against

---

[10] PD 1834 XX1, 272–350; during the debate there was reference to an occasion when Chambre J (JCP 1800–15) had despatched twenty cases in one night; see also PD 1816 XXXII, 1146 and the complaint there made that, at Lord Cochrane's trial, Ellenborough LCJ had insisted on sitting until 3 a.m. despite protests from his counsel that they were exhausted.

[11] Old Bailey: see the Report of the Royal Commission on the state of the Corporation of the City of London, PP 1854 (1772) XXV1, 701, p.290 (reference to the practice of the City Judges sitting until 9 p.m. to try London cases); also R v Dyer (murder) 1896 where Hawkins J (who was notorious for late sitting) began the trial at 7 p.m. and concluded it at 9.30 p.m., F.W. Ashley, *My Sixty Years in the Law*, 177–78; *The Times*, 22 and 23 May 1896. Assizes: see *The Times*, 10 December 1888 (Stephen J sitting till 11 p.m. on the Western Circuit); and *The Times*, 12 December 1898 (Hawkins J sitting at Maidstone until well past 9 p.m. on four nights and till 11 p.m. on another).

[12] See e.g. *R v Desmond*, *The Times*, 21–28 April, 1868, and *R v Staunton and Others*,*The Times*, 19–28 September 1877 (Old Bailey)

[13] *R v Hardy* (1794) 24 St Tr 199; *R v Stone* (1796) 6 TR 527 at 530 ('necessity justified what it compelled').

[14] At the end of the eighteeenth century there was a hostel in Westminster Hall where county juries were lodged during adjournments, see *R v Hardy* above; in the 1860s jurors at Dublin Assizes were lodged overnight in the grand jury room; Cork juries were also lodged at the court house: PD 1865 CLXXVII, 1717 and PD 1866 CLXXXI, 869 et seq.

[15] See *The Times* reports of Old Bailey trials.

[16] *R v Metcalfe and Robinson*, *The Times*, 15 December 1848.

separation was to prevent the jury being tampered with.[17] It never applied in misdemeanour (there the jury were allowed to return home overnight).[18] To jurors it caused huge inconvenience, particularly at weekends when they were locked up not merely overnight but on two consecutive nights and for the whole of Sunday, with a communal outing to church, or an airing in a quiet spot such as the Temple Gardens the only relief from the tedium.[19]

It also had an unfortunate impact on the way trials were conducted. It was one of the causes of late sittings. To avoid having to lock the jury up judges would sit late to finish a case,[20] with the result that the defence case was taken at a time when the powers of concentration and comprehension of jurors as well as accused were at their lowest ebb. Later on in the century, it bred an unwillingness to start felony trials after lunch. In the *Tichborne Case* it was the principal reason why the Claimant was charged with the misdemeanour of perjury rather than the felony of forgery.[21]

4. Accommodation for the Public and Press

Most courts had a public gallery or public seats and benches set aside for the press. Friends of the judge and distinguished guests would sit with him on the bench.[22] In smaller court rooms the accommodation for the public was often limited (in the fourth court at the Old Bailey there were no seats at all and spectators had to stand in the gangway). Even here access was never denied. Rowdiness would lead to threats to clear the public gallery, and judges would discourage women and children from remaining in court whilst indecent cases were being tried,[23] but the trial of cases in camera was, in the higher courts, wholly unknown.

[17] If there was an improper separation the jury would be discharged: *R v Ward* (1867) 10 Cox 573.

[18] *R v Kinnear* (1819) 2 B & Ald 462.

[19] See e.g. *R v Coates*, *The Times*, 6,8 and 9 March 1875; *R v Foster*, *The Times*, 14 May 1859; see also *R v Dove*, *The Times*, 18 and 19 July 1856 (York jury allowed to walk in Clifford's Tower).

[20] PD 1866 CLXXXI, 870–71.

[21] *Ex p Castro* (1873) 37 JP 260 (Cockburn LCJ) and Russell LCJ at PD 1897 XLIX, 86–89.

[22] See the correspondence between McVane and Coleridge LCJ published in *The Times*, 8 June 1891.

[23] See e.g. *R v Woodward*, *The Times*, 24 March 1817.

8

Judges

'It is a disgrace to the county to impose on the judge the necessity to act as counsel against the prisoners'. Patteson J, in *R v Anon.*, *Bedford Mercury*, 23 March 1844.

1. The Judicial Hierarchy

In 1800 of the judges who tried criminal cases only twelve – the judges of the three common law courts – King's Bench, Common Pleas and Exchequer – held full-time appointments. Even they, for all that they tried the heaviest English cases, were principally civil judges. Welsh crime and lesser indictable offences were tried by part-time judges. The City judges, the eight Welsh judges and the recorders of borough Quarter Sessions all held part-time appointments. Nearly all were practising barristers and several were MPs. The chairmen of County Sessions also sat only part-time.

By the end of the century the position had changed little. In 1830 Wales and Chester had been incorporated into the Assize system and three additional common law judges had been created, but this was the only increase. In 1900 the number of common law judges (now restyled judges of the Queen's Bench Division of the High Court) still stood at fifteen, while the figure for part-time judges, although lower than in 1800 was just under 180.[1]

2. The Common Law Judges

The common law judges, known collectively (until 1830) as 'the Twelve Judges' or more simply 'the Judges', were recruited exclusively from the practising bar. The power of appointment was split between the Prime Minister and the Lord Chancellor. The former appointed the Lord Chief Justice and the Chief Justice of the Common Pleas, the latter the Lord Chief Baron and the puisne judges.[2] Under the Act of Settlement of 1701 a judge once appointed was removable only on a joint address by both Houses of Parliament. In 1830 an Irish judge was so removed but no English judge ever has been.[3]

---

[1] G. G. Alexander, *The Administration of Criminal Justice in England*, 125.
[2] D. Duman, *The Judicial Bench in England, 1727–1875* (London, 1982), 78.
[3] The judge was Sir Jonah Barrington.

Throughout the century the common law judges enjoyed enormous prestige. The cases they tried were extensively reported by all sections of the press, and their names were well known to the public. Dickens thinly veiled allusion to Gaselee J (Stareleigh in *The Pickwick Papers*) was one most readers would have picked up. Appointed from the leading advocates of the day, they were in the main men of high ability. More than a third of those appointed during the century had taken first-class university degrees.[4] Several were the authors of leading legal textbooks, one a distinguished scientist and inventor who ultimately abandoned the bench for physics, another a moderately successful playwright.[5] In 1863 a high reputation for legal scholarship was enough to win a judgeship for Blackburn, who had never enjoyed a substantial practice at the bar. His case was, however, unique.

A common route to the bench was via politics. The bench was throughout the century used as a means of rewarding past political services. Of 139 judges of the higher courts, appointed between 1832 and 1906, eighty were MPs at the time of their appointment; of whom sixty-three were appointed whilst their party was in office.[6] In 1897 Lord Salisbury openly acknowledged the fact. 'Party claims', he declared, 'should always weigh very heavily in the disposal of the highest legal appointments.'[7] Indeed in the case of the Attorney-General there was a convention that he was entitled to first refusal of the chief justiceship of the Common Pleas, should it become vacant during his tenure of office. The Attorney's claims, repudiated by Gladstone, would resurface in the 1920s when Hewart successfully asserted his right as Attorney to first refusal of the then vacant Lord Chief Justiceship.[8]

Influence and connection also played their part.[9] Hotham B, who sat until 1805 and when appointed was wholly unknown to the London bar, owed his preferment to the influence of the Duke of Portland. Vaughan 'the Judge by Prescription' had his brother-in-law, the queen's physician, to thank for his elevation in 1827. Connection rather than merit won Heath and Graham their judgeships, whilst the appointment of Martin B in 1850 was widely regarded as out and out nepotism – his father-in-law was Pollock LCB.

Although some, on appointment to the bench, suffered a large drop of income (Scarlett's acceptance of the office of Lord Chief Baron cost him £13,000 p.a.), the remuneration was none the less generous.[10] In 1800 the Lord Chief Justice received an annual salary of £4000, the Chief Justice of the Common Pleas and the Chief Baron of the Exchequer £3500, and the

4 Duman, *The Judicial Bench in England*, 45.
5 Ibid., 149–53.
6 H. J. Laski, *Studies in Law and Politics* (London, 1932), 168.
7 Quoted by A. H. Manchester, *Modern Legal History*, 80.
8 J. Ll. J. Edwards, *The Law Officers of the Crown*, chapter 15.
9 Duman, *The Judicial Bench in England*, 81–82.
10 Ibid., 111–13, 119–20 and 122.

puisne judges £3000. In addition, all received a substantial income from fees, while the two Chief Justices also had at their disposal a lucrative judicial patronage. In Ellenborough's day the office of Lord Chief Justice is thought to have been worth at least £16,000 p.a. to the holder.

In 1825 the system of paying judges was reformed. Henceforth they were to receive increased but inclusive salaries. The Lord Chief Justice was given a salary of £10,000 p.a., the Chief Justice of the Common Pleas £8000, the Lord Chief Baron £7000 and the puisne judges £5500. In 1832 Denman, on his appointment as Lord Chief Justice, volunteered to accept a salary reduction of £2000. The same year also saw the salary for puisne judges cut to £5000. The cuts proved permanent. Indeed, salaries were to remain at their 1832 level for the next 120 years.

The judges were not subject to a retiring age. In 1799, in the hope of discouraging them from hanging on to office into extreme old age, judicial pensions had been introduced. In 1825, as part of the restructuring of judges' remuneration, the pensions were enhanced.[11] The introduction of pensions served to bring down the number of judges dying in harness from 65 per cent in the years 1727 to 1790 to 39 per cent in the period 1790 to 1875.[12] Part of the reason why so many still died in office was the late age at which they were appointed. Between 1850 and 1875 the average age of appointment was fifty-seven, with appointments of men in their late sixties by no means unknown. Fitzroy Kelly was actually seventy when he was appointed Lord Chief Baron in 1866. Another reason why judges stayed on was that it took fifteen years to earn a full pension. Of those who did retire many did so with a bad grace. In 1891 it took a series of parliamentary questions and a *Times* leader about his mental capacity to induce Stephen J to retire.[13] None showed greater reluctance to let go of the reins than the holders of the office of Lord Chief Justice. Of the nineteenth-century Lords Chief Justice no less than five died in harness, while Ellenborough and Denman, the two who did retire, both went on far longer than they should have done. So adhesive was Ellenborough's grip that he continued to sit even when he could scarcely totter to his seat, while Denman, being so badly disabled by a stroke that he could scarcely sign his name, sat on for two years in a vain attempt to prevent Campbell succeeding him.[14] Cases of judges actually dying on the bench were not unknown, particularly on circuit. Between 1844 and 1863 four judges – Abinger, Talfourd, Watson and Wightman – suffered fatal strokes whilst on Assize. Watson and Wightman both succumbed whilst in the act of charging the grand jury. There was one judicial suicide (that of Willes J who shot himself in October 1872 in a fit

11 Ibid., 124–25.
12 Ibid., 72–73.
13 *The Times*, 10 March and 8 August 1891; J. R. Lewis, *The Victorian Bar*, 147–48.
14 A. Mockler, *Lions under the Throne* (London, 1983), 185 and 195–96.

of depression after a long Assize).[15] Watkin Williams J, so local legend has it, died in a brothel whilst on circuit in Nottingham in 1884.[16]

A majority of those appointed to the bench in the nineteenth century had a public school and Oxbridge background,[17] with Eton, and Trinity College and Trinity Hall, Cambridge particularly well represented. This trend became more pronounced in the second half of the century, but the bench was still far less public school and Oxbridge oriented than its twentieth-century counterpart. A handful of those appointed after 1850 (Charles, Day, Quain and Wills) were London University men. Although some came from landed families, most were men from the professional and business classes (a trend which became more pronounced as the century wore on). A very few, including a Lord Chief Justice (Abbott, the son of a barber), came from the artisan classes, whilst a couple (Garrow and Graham) were sons of schoolmasters.

Similarity of background and education was no guarantee of judicial amity. Lord Campbell was almost universally unpopular with his brethren, whilst Lord Chief Justice Cockburn's dislike of Willes J and the mutual antipathy between Blackburn and Bramwell BB were equally notorious.[18] During a Commons debate in 1879 it was claimed that 'recently ... attacks of one judge upon another ... had almost become epidemic'.[19] Secure in their position, some indulged in behaviour on the bench which would today be considered unseemly. Emotional judges, like Willes, would weep when passing sentence of death.[20] Hawkins took immense delight in inconveniencing the bar. A widespread and unattractive habit was that of castigating juries for 'wrong verdicts'.[21] Rudeness to the bar was commonplace. In civil suits, though happily not in criminal cases, it was not unknown for judges to read newspapers or write letters whilst counsel was addressing them.[22] In trade union cases the judges' class bias was often plain. Nor were all above making party political speeches when charging a grand jury – conduct which invariably attracted parliamentary censure.[23]

From legal memoirs we gain a vivid picture of the foibles and mannerisms of individual judges: Heath's refusal to accept a knighthood on appointment (he wanted to remain plain John Heath); Cockburn's philandering (Lady

15 Holdsworth, HEL, xv, 505.

16 E. Bryson, *A Portrait of Nottingham* (London, 1983), 196; a report of the inquest appears in *The Times*, 26 July 1884.

17 Duman, *The Judicial Bench in England*, 38–45.

18 Lewis, *The Victorian Bar*, 52.

19 PD 1879 CCXLIV, 1455.

20 Lewis, *The Victorian Bar*, 52.

21 See e.g. PD 1859 CLIII, 1557, Bramwell B, and 1875 CCXXIII, 462, Lawson J (Irish) and Cockburn LCJ.

22 E. S. Turner, *May it Please your Lordship* (London, 1971), 173.

23 See e.g. PD 1843 LXVI, 1037–68 (where Abinger LCB was fiercely attacked on this ground).

Cockburn always accompanied him on circuit – but it was a different Lady Cockburn each time); Maule's hastiness (on a hot summer's day at Lincoln in 1852 he ordered the court room windows smashed rather than wait for court staff to climb on the roof to open them), his keen wit and his demonstrations in court of his skill at picking locks; Martin's love of the turf; Jervis's delight and skill at card sharping; Erle's loathing for boxing; Day's slovenly standards of dress; Channell's dropped aitches; Willes' indecisiveness; and the pleasure Campbell is said to have taken in passing sentence of death.[24]

One of the prime, although not necessarily the most reliable, sources of information about his contemporaries was Campbell, whose *Lives of the Chief Justices* was described as having 'added a new pang to death'. A criticism voiced by Serjeant Ballantine, and still true today, was that some of those appointed came to the common law bench with little or no previous experience of criminal cases, having spent the whole of their professional lives in the civil courts.[25] For such novices, help was readily at hand from fellow judges, it being the practice at this time in criminal cases for judges to rise in mid case to consult with their brothers should a point of difficulty arise. It has also long been fashionable to depict the nineteenth-century bench as reactionary and opposed to reform of the criminal law. Instances commonly quoted include Ellenborough's unremitting hostility to the relaxation of the capital laws;[26] and Park J's threat (never carried out) to resign his judgeship if the Prisoners' Counsel Bill became law.[27] Such criticism ignores the fact that during the century the judges substantially remodelled the rules of evidence to the advantage of prisoners, and that several of the most important reform Bills were actually promoted and supported by judges.

3. The Part-Time Judges

The Welsh judgeships were Crown appointments. Not so the borough recorderships, 171 out of 183 being in the gift of the corporation or its governing body. The City judgeships were also elective. The Court of Aldermen appointed the recorder, and the Court of Common Council the common serjeant and the judge of the Sheriff's Court.

In 1835 borough recorderships were made Crown appointments. But, despite the unseemly aspect of City elections (Ellenborough's eldest son, for example, owed his appointment as recorder in 1833 to lobbying and influence,[28] and his was not an isolated case), and the notoriously bad

---

[24] See *DNB* ; Lewis, *The Victorian Bar*; and E. S. Turner, *May it Please your Lordship.*

[25] W. Ballantine, *A Barrister's Experiences* (8th edn, London, 1883), 373–76.

[26] Mockler, *Lions under the Throne*, 182–83.

[27] W. B. Odgers, *A Century of Law Reform* (London, 1901), 50.

[28] Ballantine, *A Barrister's Experiences*, 8; as to City elections see G. Pitt Lewis, *Mr Commissioner Kerr* (London, 1903), chapter 4.

appointments which they had produced over the previous thirty years, the government failed to take up the recommendation in the report of the Royal Commission on Municipal Corporations that the City judgeships be made Crown appointments. This was all the more surprising given that by mid century the work load of the City judges had become such as to make theirs practically full-time posts. In the 1880s there were City judges in the House of Commons but by then private practice at the bar had long been out of the question. Eventually, in 1888 the right to appoint the common serjeant and the judge of the Sheriff's Court was transferred to the Crown (the Act which effected the change also abolished elective county coronerships).[29] The recordership, however, remained elective until well into the present century.

For the twelve weeks sitting they did each year, the Welsh judges received salaries ranging from £1150 to £1630 p.a. The chief justice of Chester was the highest paid and in addition had a fee income.[30] Borough recorders were often unpaid or paid only a token salary (such as the £4 p.a. paid to the recorder of Coventry). Only a handful received more than £100 a year. By far the best rewarded was the recorder of Liverpool, who, in addition to an annual salary of £525, was also briefed in all prosecutions brought by the borough at the Assizes.[31] Chairmen of county Sessions were (except for Salford, Middlesex after 1844 and the County of London Sessions after 1888) unpaid.[32] The recorder and common serjeant, on the other hand, were handsomely remunerated. In 1800 the recorder was paid £1000 p.a. and the common serjeant £550. In 1837 these salaries were increased to £3000 and £1500 respectively.[33] By 1900, with salaries of £4000 and £3000, of all judges below High Court rank they were the best paid (the salaries of county court judges at this date were in the bracket £1500 to £1800 whilst the chairman of County of London Sessions was paid £2000).[34] Borough recorders even after 1835 continued to be poorly paid, the salary in the case of some of the smaller boroughs being barely enough to cover the expenses of the office (in 1859 the recordership of Newark paid £59 p.a.).[35] However, a recordership being seen (as today) as a stepping-stone to a full-time judicial appointment, there was usually no shortage of applicants.

[29] Local Government Act, 1888.

[30] W. R. Williams, *The History of the Great Sessions in Wales, 1542–1830* (Brecknock, 1899), 18.

[31] Royal Commission on Municipal Corporations, Analytical Table, PP 1839 (402) XVIII, 1 (pp. 550–59).

[32] 45 Geo III, c. 59 (Salford); 7 & 8 Vict, c. 71 (Middlesex) and Local Government Act, 1888 (County of London).

[33] Reports on officers holding appointments, vol. 1 (Corporation of London Records).

[34] *Whittaker's Almanack* for 1900, 178, 181 and 334.

[35] Lewis, *The Victorian Bar*, 58; in 1901 the recordership of Bury St Edmunds carried a salary of £40 p.a., E. Hume Williams, *The World, the House and the Bar* (London 1930), 41.

4. *Nineteenth- and Twentieth-Century Criminal Judges Compared*

Between the nineteenth-century criminal judge and his present-day counterpart there are three striking differences. First, he would conduct the prosecution where no counsel was briefed to do so. Secondly, except where he agreed to reserve a point of law or in a King's Bench trial for misdemeanour, his rulings, jury directions and conduct were not subject to review by a higher court. Thirdly, he was not always legally qualified.

5. *Judges Prosecuting*

At the start of the century judges prosecuted the majority of indictments.[36] Only in government prosecutions (for treason or sedition) and in Mint and Bank cases were prosecuting counsel regularly to be seen.[37] These cases apart, it was unusual to find counsel retained on either side. At the Old Bailey at the July session of 1800 counsel prosecuted in only one case in eight. In the rest the judge prosecuted.

None the less, prosecuting counsel were now seen in greater numbers than they had been a hundred years before. In 1700 it was almost unheard of for counsel to prosecute in felony. It was only when, in the 1730s, the courts relaxed the prohibition on counsel appearing for prisoners that a trickle of barristers instructed to prosecute began to appear.[38] Some incentive had been given for the employment of counsel in felony by statutes of 1752 and 1788,[39] which gave the courts power to award prosecutors their legal costs in such cases, but, despite this reform, the numbers of prosecutors employing counsel had remained small. Many were simply too poor to do so. Even where a prosecutor had means, his inclination would be not to do so. Why incur the expense (by no means certain to be reimbursed) of employing counsel to prosecute a prisoner who, almost certainly, would not have counsel himself? What was the need? Why not do what most people did and leave it to the judge? After all, he would perform the task for nothing.

By the end of the nineteenth century, the position had been completely reversed. Most cases on indictment were now prosecuted by counsel, the only place where the practice of the judge prosecuting still lingered on being at Quarter Sessions and, to a very limited extent, before the City judges. It had recently been dealt a terminal blow by the Criminal Evidence Act (1898). Once this was in force, the judge who prosecuted would, as part of that task, have to cross-examine the prisoner, and this might look most unfair. None

---

[36] I.e. examine the prosecution witnesses.

[37] C. Emsley, *Crime and Society in England, 1759–1900* (London, 1987), 138; see also *The Times* trial reports for the period.

[38] J. H. Langbein, 'The Criminal Trial before the Lawyers', 50 U Chicago L R, 1 at 311–12.

[39] 25 Geo II, c. 36 and 18 Geo III, c. 19.

the less, it was to be a few years dying, receiving a mention in the 1904 edition of Pritchard's *Quarter Sessions Practice*.[40] The coup de grace came in 1908 with the Costs in Criminal Cases Act of that year.

The first calls for change had come in the 1830s. An early landmark was the Report of the Royal Commission on County Rates in 1836.[41] This had condemned the practice of judges prosecuting in complicated cases as inefficient and a false economy. It had recommended that a prosecuting counsel's fee be allowed both at Assizes and Quarter Sessions in all cases involving an arguable point of law, or in which there were three or more witnesses. A decade later the common law judges (from whom there had been rumblings on the subject since the early 1830s),[42] increasingly irked at having themselves to prosecute serious cases, decided to make a stand on the issue. Complaining that it was unseemly for a judge to act as prosecutor,[43] they refused to have any further truck with the practice. When cases came before them, with no counsel briefed to prosecute, they now simply handed the depositions to one of the counsel in court, with a request that he prosecute.[44] Their stand, which was applauded in *The Times*, the Commons and in legal journals,[45] proved a turning-point: in the second half of the century the practice of judges prosecuting died out entirely at Assizes and became much diminished at Quarter Sessions.[46]

How was this change effected, given that even by the end of the century a system of public prosecutors still had not been established? There appear to have been two main factors. First, money to finance prosecutions was made increasingly available. The courts' power to make awards of costs to prosecutors was extended.[47] At the same time the burden which such awards made on the rates was reduced when the government in 1835 agreed to

[40] T. S. Pritchard, *Quarter Sessions Practice* (2nd edn, London, 1904), 248.
[41] 1836 PP (58) XXVII, 1 at pp. 22–23; cf. the evidence of Lord Wharncliffe to the HL Select Committee on County Rates, 1835 PP (206) XIV, 1 at p. 72.
[42] See the evidence of Tindal CJ and Park J to the 1835 Select Committee.
[43] See e.g. *R v Anon.* (1843) 1 Cox 48; *R v Anon.*, *Bedford Mercury*, 23 March 1844; *R v Hezell* (1844) 1 Cox 348; *R v Page* (1847) 2 Cox 221.
[44] See e.g. *R v Lawrence* (1844) 1 Cox 61; *R v Robins* (1847) 1 Cox 114; *R v Farrell and Moore* (1848) 3 Cox 169; Criminal Law Commissioners, 8th Report, app. B (Q 201).
[45] See *The Times*, 18 June 1847; PD 1847 XCIII, 761; and (1847) 9 LT 256 and 283.
[46] 5th Report of the Judicature Commission, 1874 PP (C 1090, 2345) XXIV, 307, app 1 (p 14); even as late as the 1870s it was possible to come across cases at Assizes in which no prosecuting counsel had been briefed, see letter from Bramwell B (ibid. app 1, p 3).
[47] The power to award costs in certain cases of misdemeanour had been given by 7 Geo IV, c. 64 (1826) and extended by later statutes. But even in 1900 there still remained a considerable number of misdemeanours in respect of which there was no such power, see Report of the Departmental Committee on Allowances to Prosecutors and Witnesses in Public Prosecutions, 1903 PP (Cmnd 1650) LVI, 357. As to the unwillingness of some courts to exercise the power to award costs, see Report of Royal Commission on County Rates, 1836 above (p 33), the evidence of Tindal CJ to the 1835 Select Committee (Q 803); the Report of the Select Committee on County Rates, 1834 PP (206) XIV, 1 and the Return of Rates and Allowances 1845 PP (in 390) XLI, 411.

meet half the cost.[48] Secondly, it was no longer being left simply to the prosecutor to decide whether counsel should be employed. At the Old Bailey and at some Quarter Sessions there was by the 1830s a 'soup' system in operation, under which briefs in cases in which no counsel had been retained to prosecute were handed out by the clerk of the court to members of the bar mess in rotation.[49] In Liverpool, Manchester and Leeds responsibility for briefing counsel in prosecutions rested with an attorney, appointed and paid by the council to prosecute all cases within the borough. Liverpool had been the first with such a scheme in the 1830s, followed in less than a decade by Manchester and Leeds.[50] In many petty sessional divisions of counties, the clerk to the magistrates would act as prosecuting attorney in all cases where the examining magistrates had certified that counsel ought to be retained to prosecute.[51] In the metropolis and in boroughs (where by statute the clerk to the magistrates was prohibited from undertaking prosecutions) the police were pressed into service.[52] One of the police officers in the case would be bound over to prosecute, thereby investing him with the authority to instruct an attorney and through him counsel.[53] Private enterprise also made a contribution. Poor prosecutors were now openly touted by attorneys with offers to conduct their cases for such costs as the court allowed.[54]

That recorders and chairmen were still to be found prosecuting at Quarter Sessions in the last years of the century was due in part to a gap in the law (the statutory power to award prosecutors their costs, although it had been extended during the century to certain classes of misdemeanour, still did not apply to all), but more to a belief, on the part of county benches in particular, that it was wrong to spend public money employing counsel to prosecute simple and straightforward cases.[55] Nowhere was this view held more tenaciously than in Surrey, which in the last quarter of the century

---

[48] See 5th Report of the Judicature Commission above, app. 1, p 14.

[49] See Select Committee on Prosecution Expenses, 1862 PP (402) XI, 1 (Evidence Qs 2257 and 2399); A. Crew, *The Old Bailey*, 50; 5th Report of the Judicature Commission above, app 1, p 25.

[50] See Report of Select Committee on Public Prosecutors 1854/55 PP (481) XII, 1 (Qs 76, 106, 975, 1379, 2767) and PD 1870 CCI, 242 and 1871 CCV, 1766.

[51] Report on County Rates, 1836 above, p 23; 5th Report of Judicature Commission above, p 13; and PD 1854/55 CXXXVI, 1656–57 where the objections to the practice are set out.

[52] Municipal Corporations Act, 1835, s 102 and Municipal Corporations Amendment Act, 1861, s 5.

[53] Report on Public Prosecutors 1854/55 above (Qs 882–85 and 2140–42); 5th Report of Judicature Commission above, p 13; PD 1854 CXXX, 666 (claim that system led to corruption); in some areas the risk of corruption was avoided by appointing a reputable solicitor as attorney to the police with instructions to act in all cases in which prosecutors were bound over to prosecute, see *R v Yates* (1853) 7 Cox 361.

[54] 5th Report of Judicature Commission above, app 1, p 13 and PD 1871 CCV, 1746.

[55] The argument was one which had been accepted by the 1835 Select Committee and the 1836 Royal Commission on County Rates as well as by the 1859 Commission on the costs of prosecutions 1859 PP (2575 Sess. 2) XIII, Part 1, 13.

was still applying costs rules made fifty years before, refusing prosecutors a counsel's fee in any case where the prisoner had no counsel, a practice which resulted in almost all undefended prisoners being prosecuted by the chairman.[56]

From the accused's point of view, the obvious objection to judges prosecuting was the look of the thing and the potential for unfairness. If there was no prosecuting counsel, and Crown witnesses went back on what they had said in their depositions, it was the judge who had the task of cross-examining them about the inconsistency. If the accused called witnesses or gave evidence himself (as he could do after 1885 in most cases of sexual assault), it was the judge who had to cross-examine. This descent of the judge into the arena looked unfair. When done in a partisan spirit (an ever-present danger where counsel appeared for the prisoner), it could actually work injustice. Occasionally, however, having the judge prosecute would work to a prisoner's advantage. Depositions often came to a judge too late for him to have any hope of mastering them and, if a case was complicated, for it to be prosecuted by a judge who was not master of his brief inevitably increased the prisoner's chances of escape.[57]

6. Unappealability

The fact that the conduct and behaviour of judges were not subject to review had two unfortunate consequences. First, it had an adverse effect upon the standards of summing up. The fact that appeal on questions of law was in the judge's discretion led to the absence of a body of law (such as that developed by the Court of Appeal in the present century) as to the legal directions which a summming up must contain and the form such directions should take. (This was a gap which the pitiful precedents of summings up in books such as Chitty and the occasional ruling from the Court for Crown Cases Reserved did little to close.)[58] There being no authoritative guidance on the question, judges summed up as they thought fit. The lack of an appeal remedy also meant the absence of a vital check on judicial misconduct.

Amongst the common law judges standards of conduct appear, on the whole, to have been reasonably high. At Assize trials in the 1820s prisoners can be seen asking the judge to act as their counsel, and receiving an assurance from him that he would watch their interests (which was, of course, all that the maxim meant).[59] The promise was usually kept. If there was a pleading or other legal point available to an unrepresented prisoner the

---

[56] The practice of Surrey Sessions is described in many reports including the 5th Report of the Judicature Commission above, app 1, p 14.

[57] Royal Commission on County Rates, 1836 above, p 22 and PD 1851 CXIV, 828.

[58] Chitty, *Criminal Law* (1st edn, 1816), iv, 331–32.

[59] See e.g. *R v Nuttall*, *The Times*, 8 September 1817; *R v Redding*, *The Times*, 11 August 1823; as to the meaning of the maxim, see Bla Comm, IV, 349.

judge would take it on his behalf.[60] A prisoner who pleaded guilty to a capital charge would be strongly urged to retract his plea and take his trial so that the case against him could be scrutinised to see whether there was in fact a defence available to him.[61] Where judicial pressure proved unavailing, it was not unknown for the judge to direct that the evidence be gone through[62] or even that a plea of not guilty be entered.[63] To jurors, called on to try on overwhelming evidence the guilt of a man whom they had themselves heard plead guilty, such a proceeding must have seemed bizarre but, occasionally, it was the means of saving a prisoner's life.[64] If prosecuting counsel opened a case unfairly he would be stopped.[65] Witnesses called to prove a confession would be subject to a rigorous judicial interrogation as to the events leading up to its being made, so as to leave no doubt as to its voluntariness.[66] A medical man, who in an infanticide case sought to rely upon the discredited test of floating the lungs as proof that the child was born alive, would leave court with a judicial flea in his ear.[67] On occasions, in joint trials, one even finds a defence counsel seeking to cast blame on an undefended prisoner being warned from the bench not to try and hang the judge's client to save his own.[68]

For all the generally high reputation of the red judges, some inevitably fell short of the standard expected. Ellenborough, for instance, was notorious for his petulance and for his browbeating of juries. Abinger LCB throughout his judicial career had a reputation for arrogance and lack of impartiality. In 1843 his conduct towards Chartist prisoners, when presiding over a special commission in Lancashire and Cheshire, was the subject of protest both in the press and the Commons.[69] Gurney B was noted for his severity and the unseemly haste with which he despatched cases: 'rushing through the calendar like a wild elephant through a sugar plantation'.[70] Later in the century, Stephen J earned criticism for his habit of late sitting (a penchant which he

---

[60] See e.g. *R v Rawlings* (1835) 7 C & P 150; *R v Donnelly and Murray* (1835) 1 Moo 438; and *R v Wilson* (1837) 8 C & P 111.

[61] See Chitty, *Criminal Law*, i, 429 and PD 1826 XV 289. By the later years of the century, judges were contenting themselves with merely ascertaining whether the prisoner understood the consequences of his plea, see *R v Constance Kent, The Times*, 22 July 1865, and *R v Bradford, The Times*, 25 July, 1872.

[62] See e.g. *R v Cashon and O'Brien, The Times*, 13 December 1828; *R v Wakely, The Times*, 15 August 1839; *R v Bury, The Times*, 6 March 1873.

[63] *R v Rodanbosh, The Times*, 18 December 1856 (foreigner accused of attempted murder).

[64] See e.g. *R v Barber, The Times*, 8 April 1842, and *R v Moore, The Times*, 26 March 1860.

[65] *R v Knowles* (1820) 1 St Tr NS 497; see also PD 1826 XV, 607 (*R v Evans*).

[66] See e.g. *R v Day* (1847) 2 Cox 209.

[67] See e.g. *R v Green, The Times*, 2 July 1825.

[68] *R v Hicks, The Times*, 30 December 1830; and *R v Salter and Kettle* (1877) 41 JP 187.

[69] PD 1843 LXVI, 1037.

[70] 1st Report of the Judicature Commission PP 1868–69 (4130) XXV 1 at 17; Gurney also had a reputation for harshness towards prisoners: see Serjeant Robinson, *Bench and Bar* (London, 1889), 158.

shared with Hawkins),[71] and for subjecting to an *interrogatoire* prisoners who gave evidence under the Criminal Law Amendment Act.[72]

It was, however, on the lower rungs of the judicial ladder that the effects of the lack of a remedy against judicial misconduct were most pronounced. In the 1830s and 1840s trials before the City judges were a by-word for unfairness. They were rushed through so fast that prisoners sometimes did not even take in what was happening;[73] often a trial would take no more than three or four minutes from start to finish.[74] In one year in the 1830s the average length of the trials held at successive Old Bailey sessions was calculated to be no more than eight and a half minutes. Worst conducted of all were the evening trials. During the sessions it was the custom for the sheriffs to give two lavish dinners a day, one at three o'clock and a second at five o'clock. The City judges, who dined at five o'clock, were notorious for returning to the bench afterwards the worse for drink.[75] In 1837 a City alderman made an attempt to put a stop to these dinners;[76] but they continued, albeit somewhat better conducted in later years, until a fire in 1877 destroyed the Sessions House dining-room.[77]

The way Old Bailey trials were conducted was a regular subject of press comment at this time.[78] The only occasion, however, when such comment seems to have had any effect was when *The Times*, in December 1838, made a particularly strong attack on Mirehouse, the common serjeant, for the way he had tried a sixteen-year-old called Saunders for theft: 'five or six witnesses ... examined; as many clever jokes perpetrated; a prisoner bantered; a jury charged; the verdict returned; the criminal sentenced to transportation; all in six minutes'.[79] After the article Mirehouse, for a time at least, mended his ways.[80] The second half of the century, happily, saw a considerable improvement in judicial behaviour so far as the Old Bailey was concerned (due in large measure to the efforts of Russell Gurney, recorder from 1857 to 1878).

---

[71] *The Times*, 10 December 1888; as to Hawkins' liking for late sitting see F. W. Ashley, *My Sixty Years in the Law*, 176–78.

[72] (1886) 21 LJ 323.

[73] 1833, 'Old Bailey Experiences' (1833) 10 Law Mag (1st series) 259 at 276.

[74] Ibid., 276–277; see also (1847) 9 LT 319.

[75] See A. Hayward, 'The Origins of Dinners Clubs etc' (1836) 55 *Quarterly Review*, 455 at 474–75; *'Justice after Dinner'* (1844) vol. 7 *Punch*, 218–19; Ballantine, *A Barrister's Experiences*, 54–55; Montagu J. Williams, *Leaves of a Life* (2nd edn, London, 1890), 162.

[76] Motion by Alderman Lott, 21 April 1837 (Misc. Papers, Administration of Justice Committee, Corporation of London Records Office).

[77] The fire occurred on 26 February 1877 (*The Times*, 27 February 1877). When the dining room had been repaired the question of reinstating the dinners was referred to the judges who were against it, Bowen Rowlands, *Seventy-Two Years at the Bar*, 19.

[78] See e.g. (1847) 9 LT 319 and PD (1831) V, 648.

[79] *The Times*, 25 December 1838 and 'Indecent Haste' (1839) 3 JP 2.

[80] *The Times*, 2 January 1839 ('a marvellous change for the better' in the Common Serjeant's behaviour).

Not so at county Quarter Sessions, however. The reputation of such courts remained consistently bad throughout the century. Amongst the more serious criticisms regularly levelled against them were failure by chairmen to take a proper note of the evidence,[81] the display of open bias against prisoners and pressing them unfairly.[82] It was also a commonplace that county Sessions were generally more severe than Assize judges in the matter of sentence (notwithstanding that they tried far less serious offences than did the latter).[83]

7. Lay Judges

Chairmen of county Sessions also represented after 1835 the only class of judge not required to be legally qualified. Later in the century a few chairmen were judges or retired judges,[84] but at the start of the century the nearest most benches came to having a legally qualified chairman was a man who had read for the bar but never practised.[85] The majority could not boast even that slender link with the law. Prior to the Municipal Corporations Act of 1835 a similar state of affairs had prevailed at many borough Quarter Sessions. In 1835 the Royal Commission on Municipal Corporations had found that in only seventy-eight of the 183 boroughs where the Quarter Sessions was presided over by a recorder was there any requirement that he be legally qualified;[86] and that in a number of Quarter Sessions the court was constituted in much the same manner as at county Quarter Sessions.[87] The 1835 Act changed all this by providing that henceforth the sole judge at all borough Quarter Sessions should be a recorder appointed by the Crown from the ranks of barristers of at least five years standing.[88] In 1844 it was made obligatory for the chairman of Middlesex Sessions to be legally qualified.[89] When the County of London Sessions was established in 1888 the county council were empowered to apply to the Crown to appoint a legally-qualified chairman, which they did.[90] Calls for it to be made compulsory for all chairmen to be legally qualified were repeatedly heard during

---

[81] (1875–76) 20 Sol J 74.

[82] (1873–74) 18 Sol J 196; (1875–76) 20 Sol J 74.

[83] (1848) 11 LT 445; (1849) 13 LT 293.

[84] In the last quarter of the century Amphlett and Kay LJJ were both Chairmen of County Sessions, see (1894) 97 LT 372–73); a few county court judges also sat, see *The Times*, 22 September 1899 (letter).

[85] A. Foote, *Pie Powder* (London, 1911), 69.

[86] Report of Commission on Municipal Corporations, Analytical Table, PP 1839 (402) XVIII, 1 at 551–58.

[87] Ibid.; there was no office of recorder in 46 out of 237 boroughs.

[88] Municipal Corporations Act, 1835 ss 103 and 105.

[89] 7 & 8 Vict, c. 71, s 8 (to be a serjeant or barrister of at least ten years' standing).

[90] Local Government Act, 1888, s 42.

the century but went unheeded.[91] It was not until 1962 that this modest reform in fact went through.[92]

The consequences of having laymen acting as judges were inevitably unsatisfactory. They were wholly unequipped to act as counsel for unrepresented prisoners. What law they knew, and the technique of summing up, they picked up in the main from watching other chairmen. If a difficult legal point cropped up the chairman would often be left floundering. It was seldom much use for him to look to the clerk of the peace for help, for clerks of the peace (or their deputies), although solicitors, were rarely practitioners in or knowledgeable about criminal law.[93] At some courts it was the practice for the chairman to canvass the view of a member of the bar not engaged in the case.[94] At others he would muddle through as best he could without giving reasons for his rulings.[95] Nor was it uncommon to find the law misstated in a chairman's summing up. In 1844, the *Law Times* declared that county Quarter Sessions could not, as presently constituted, hope to survive the establishment of an appeal system, so bizarre were the propositions daily laid down as law by county chairmen.[96] With no appeal remedy (apart, after 1848, for the reservation of a case at the court's discretion), there was no higher court to expose their errors and mistakes, and the matter could be brushed under the carpet.

The unsatisfactory way in which points of law were dealt with at county sessions stood in sharp contrast to the careful way in which they were dealt with at Assizes. If a point of difficulty cropped up during an Assize trial, the judge would usually immediately rise and take the view of his brother judge sitting in the adjoining Nisi Prius court (a useful practice but one which has now died out).[97]

8. Other Questionable Practices

As surprising as the use of lay judges was the survival of vestiges of practices which had flourished in the days of Scroggs and Jeffreys but had been outlawed following the Glorious Revolution of 1688. One was judicial questioning. Judges who in mid century condemned police questioning, as the impertinent assumption of a power which even the bench did not possess, had short memories. In the first quarter of the century, it had been by no

---

[91] See e.g. PD 1838 XLI, 335; Criminal Law Commissioners, 8th Report, app A; (1844) 2 LT 364; (1846) 7 LT 478; (1875–76) 20 Sol J 74; *The Times*, 6 June 1882 and 22 September 1899.

[92] Criminal Justice Act, 1962, s 5.

[93] (1894) 97 LT 372–73.

[94] Criminal Law Commissioners, 2nd Report, app 1 (pp 92 and 95).

[95] (1875–76) 20 Sol J 74.

[96] (1844) 2 LT 364; F. W. Ashley, *My Sixty Years in the Law*, 219.

[97] For examples of the practice see *R v Gibbons* (1823) 1 C & P 97; *R v Evans* (1839) 8 C & P 765; *R v Coley* (1868) 10 Cox 536; *R v Goddard* (1882) 15 Cox 7; *R v Hirst* (1896) 18 Cox 374.

means unknown for a prisoner who made an unsworn statement to the jury to be questioned on it by the judge (and often in anything but a friendly spirit).[98] Also occasionally still to be found were traces of the obnoxious seventeenth-century practice of discharging a jury where the prosecution case broke down, in order to give the Crown the chance to plug the gap in its case. In 1825 Bayley J discharged a jury where the adult complainant in a rape case proved wholly ignorant of the nature and obligation of an oath, in order that she might receive instruction;[99] while in 1861 Hill J discharged a jury where the principal prosecution witness, after refusing to give evidence, was committed for contempt (a course which the Queen's Bench refused to condemn).[100]

[98] See e.g. *R v Webb* (1799–1800) CCC Sess Pap, 469; *R v Hanson* (1805) CCC Sess Pap, 380; *R v Voss* ibid., 381; *R v Taylor* ibid., 425 (all tried by the recorder); and *R v Buckingham, The Times*, 17 July 1824 (Burrough J).

[99] *R v Wade* (1825) 1 Moo 86. The problem of inability to understand the oath most commonly arose in the case of young children and often gave rise to applications that the trial be postponed so that the child could receive instruction, see *R v White* (1786) 1 Leach 430; *R v Williams* (1836) 7 C & P 320; *R v Nicholas* (1846) 2 Cox 136 and *R v Baylis* (1849) 4 Cox 23; also *R v Whitehead* (1866) 30 JP 391.

[100] *R v Charlesworth* (1861) 9 Cox 44.

9

Officials

'The Clerk of Assizes Act was passed after the appointment of Mr Bovill, who had been a cavalry officer. He did not really know much about it at first.' 'Was he the son of a judge?' 'He was the son of a Lord Chief Justice and that meant rather a scandal: his military methods did not quite accord with the practice.'

Sixth Report of the Royal Commission
on the Civil Service, Minutes of Evidence

1. The High Sheriff

Every county had a high sheriff who held office for a year. In shire counties the sheriff was a Crown appointee. The sheriffs of cities and boroughs which were counties in their own right were, however, elected; Middlesex and the City of London had two sheriffs elected by the Court of Aldermen for the City.[1]

The principal duty of the sheriff was to receive and protect the king's judges whilst they were in his county. It was his responsibility to ensure that there were lodgings for their accommodation and javelin men to guard them. His other duties included the execution of sentences of death and whipping, the enforcement of fines, and in shire counties but not elsewhere, the summoning of jurors. He had the right to call out the posse (all the able-bodied males of the county) to suppress insurrection or civil disorder; in 1830 the posse was used to suppress an enclosure riot in Oxford.[2]

Sheriffs invariably discharged the duties of their office through an under-sheriff who was usually a practising solicitor. It was the under-sheriff who would summon jurors and make the arrangements for and supervise executions. The sheriff's role was essentially ceremonial. He would attend the judges, conveying them to their lodgings in his coach, escorting them to the courthouse and to the Assize service, and would sit with them on the bench for part, if not the whole, of the Assize. It was also traditional for him to provide hospitality not merely for the judges but for the bar and local dignitaries. Usually he was a man of wealth and position. Indeed it

---

[1] G. G. Alexander, *The Administration of Criminal Justice*, 89–90; S. and B. Webb, *The Parish and the County*, 484–88.

[2] S. and B. Webb, *The Parish and the County*, 488 n 4.

was an office to which only the well to do aspired. Of all the shrievalties none involved the holder in greater expense than those of London and Middlesex. According to a witness before an 1854 Royal Commission, the expense of being a City sheriff was never less than £3000.[3]

2. The Clerk of Assize

Each circuit had a clerk of assize whose duty it was to oversee the running of the Assizes.[4] At Assize time he and his staff would follow the judges from town to town. Between them they would clerk the Crown and the Nisi Prius courts, drawing up all necessary indictments and orders, and taxing the costs of prosecutors and their witnesses. Originally these offices had been saleable. In the eighteenth century, however, the judges had taken the power of appointment into their own hands and used it as a means of providing for their sons and relatives.

Before 1853 clerks of assize were paid entirely by fees. In 1852, however, a salary was assigned to them for their duties on the civil side and in 1856 the fees for their duties on the criminal side were also commuted. At the same time they were relieved of the responsibility for paying their subordinate staff. The level of salaries, fixed by the Treasury with the concurrence of the three chief judges, was generous. By the 1880s the three best paid clerkships (those of the Northern, Oxford and Western Circuits) carried the salary of £1000 p.a. Their deputies (who also held the appointment of clerk of arraigns) were paid half this.[5]

Until 1852 the clerk was not obliged to perform his duties in person. Until 1869 he was not required to be legally qualified. The havoc caused by the attempt of a cavalry officer son of Bovill CJ to run a circuit on military lines led to the passing of the Clerks of Assizes Act. This made it obligatory for appointees to be either lawyers or to have served as a subordinate to a clerk of assize. It did little to stop judicial nepotism. As late as 1915 no less than five of the seven clerks of assize were judges' sons.[6]

At the Old Bailey the clerk of the peace for the City of London acted as clerk of the court. He had under him a clerk of arraigns and a clerk of indictments. In 1854 his office was worth some £350 p.a. in fees.[7]

---

[3] Report of the Commissioners appointed to inquire into the existing state of the Corporation of London, 1854 PP (1772) XXVI, 701, evidence of Wire (Q 7933); Wallis (Q 1356) put the cost at £2000 to £2500; the expense in other counties was far less, *The Times*, 2 October 1879 (letter) and 11 October 1879 (leader).

[4] See 5th Report of the Judicature Commission, 1874 PP (C 1090, 2345) XXIV, 307, app 1, pp. 7 and 9.

[5] See generally, *Whittaker's Almanack* for 1882 (pp 152–53) and for 1900 (p 183).

[6] R. M. Jackson, *The Machinery of Justice in England* (4th edn), 287.

[7] Report of 1854 above.

3. The Clerk of the Peace

Every Quarter Sessions had a clerk known as the clerk of the peace.[8] The clerk of the peace for county Quarter Sessions was appointed by the *custos rotulorum* of the county (the justice of the peace for the county charged with the custody of its rolls and records). Carrying with it a large fee income, the office was in the eighteenth and early nineteenth century usually filled by a friend or dependent of the *custos rotulorum*. He would rarely discharge the duties of the office himself. Instead he would appoint a solicitor from a firm in the county town to act as his deputy in return for a share of the fees. In Middlesex in 1829 the fee income of the sinecurist clerk of the peace amounted to £2088, of which he gave £855 to his working deputy to cover all expenses. After 1852 payment by salary was gradually substituted for payment by fees. By 1861 four fifths of the county clerks of the peace were receiving fixed salaries. In Surrey, however, payment by fees survived until 1904. In 1888 the office was combined with that of clerk of the county council with the power of appointment vested for the future in the county council.

Prior to 1835 the office of clerk of the peace of borough Sessions was in all but ten boroughs combined with that of town clerk. The Municipal Corporations Act of 1835 vested the power of appointment in the borough council. The appointee had to be a fit person and the council was required to determine what fees he should be entitled to. In most boroughs the practice of combining the office with that of town clerk continued. Where it did not, a local solicitor would usually be appointed. As in the case of county Quarter Sessions after 1852, payment of the clerk by salary instead of fees gradually became the norm.

All courts employed ushers and often doorkeepers. The practice of door-keepers charging for admission to the public gallery was one practised at Assizes as well as the Old Bailey.[9] At the Old Bailey it proved remarkably long lived, only finally being stopped in 1860. There was a rumour that the sheriffs received a share of the fees. If true this would explain why it survived so long in the teeth of constant complaints in the press and to the City authorities.[10]

4. Public Prosecutors

In 1800 England had no system of public prosecutors. Prosecution was regarded as a private rather than a public responsibility: 'a matter for the

---

[8] 5th Report of Judicature Commission above, app 1, pp. 8–10, and Webb, *The Parish and the County*, 502–7.

[9] *The Times*, 12 May 1842 (letter).

[10] *The Times*, 11 May 1842, 30 September 1844 (letters); Report of 1854 above, evidence of J. Acland Qs 492–501; A. Crew, *The Old Bailey* (London 1933), 43.

victims themselves or other private individuals who could be persuaded to take a sufficient interest in the matter'.[11] As has been seen, clerks to county justices, the police and others would gradually come to exercise a de facto responsibility for prosecutions on indictment, but even in 1900 England still lacked a national system of public prosecutors.

Until 1879 the only person who could be described as a public prosecutor was the Attorney-General. Appointed from the practising bar, he and the Solicitor-General (the junior Law Officer and the Attorney's deputy) were members of and legal advisers to the government of the day and changed with the government. Although the greater part of his work lay in the civil field, the Attorney had always been responsible for advising the government on important criminal matters. He traditionally led for the Crown in State Trials. He had the power to intervene to halt a private prosecution by entering a nolle prosequi and, during the century, it became increasingly common for statutes to provide that prosecutions for certain offences should not be brought without his consent. When appearing for the Crown in a prosecution the Attorney possessed a number of prerogative rights which no other prosecutor enjoyed. In misdemeanour he could commence proceedings by ex officio information laid in the Queen's Bench (which had the effect of by-passing both committal proceedings and the grand jury). He could demand that any indictable offence be tried 'at bar', that is before three judges. He had the right to demand that the case be tried in any county of his choice (at common law the normal rule as to venue was that a prisoner was to be tried in the county where his crime was committed by a jury from that county). He also had the right in all cases to the 'last word' with the jury.[12]

Another government officer with a measure of responsibility for prosecutions was the Treasury Solicitor. Recruited (after 1806) from the practising bar,[13] his duty was to represent the Crown in its legal business. In the criminal field he was responsible for preparing and for briefing counsel in state prosecutions for treason and sedition. In 1834 Brougham had suggested that Treasury counsel be appointed to prepare and superintend all Old Bailey prosecutions.[14] Later in the century this suggestion was taken up: it became the practice for the Treasury Solicitor to nominate counsel to represent him in the more serious cases tried at the Old Bailey.[15] In 1849, upon the abolition of the office of Solicitor to the Mint, he took over counterfeiting and coinage prosecutions.[16]

---

11 W. R. Cornish & G. de N. Clark, *Law and Society in England, 1750–1950*, 552.
12 Alexander, *The Administration of Criminal Justice*, 135–7; J. Ll. J. Edwards, *The Law Officers of the Crown*, chapter 13.
13 T. Heath, *The Treasury* (London, 1927), 186.
14 Edwards, *The Law Officers of the Crown*, 346.
15 Ibid., 372.
16 Ibid.

What, however, was wholly lacking was a network of local public prosecutors (such as existed in Ireland and Scotland) responsible for the preparation and conduct of prosecutions in their respective areas. Reformers argued that the establishment of such a network would bring a host of benefits. Criminals would no longer escape justice because victims were unable or unwilling to prosecute. Prosecutions would no longer break down at trial for want of proper preparation; and there would be an end to blackmailing suits, the bribing of prosecutors and collusive compromises. Also judges would be spared the necessity of acting as prosecutors in cases where no prosecuting counsel had been retained.

As early as 1824 Denman, a future Lord Chief Justice, had argued in an article in the *Edinburgh Review* that the absence of a public prosecutor was a strange anomaly.[17] The matter was considered in 1833 by a House of Commons Committee;[18] and in 1845 by the Criminal Law Commissioners. The record of the proceedings of the 1833 committee has not survived. The Report of the Criminal Law Commissioners was, however, strongly for reform. In 1854 Lord Chief Justice Campbell (who during his own term as Lord Chancellor had not been able to accomplish anything in this direction) upbraided the Attorney-General in open court about the government's inaction in the matter, saying that it was absolutely incumbent upon them to do something.[19]

Shortly after this a Private Member's Bill was introduced but dropped after an assurance from the Attorney that the government was working on a Bill of its own.[20] No government Bill having been forthcoming, this Bill was reintroduced the following year.[21] Its scheme was that each circuit should be divided into districts, with a salaried prosecuting attorney (to be known as a district agent) and one or more salaried prosecuting barristers (to be known as public prosecutors) appointed by the Lord Chancellor for each district. The district agent was to prosecute indictable offences up to committal; after committal the public prosecutor would advise whether the prosecution should continue. If it was to continue he would prosecute, unless it was a Quarter Sessions case in which event it would be prosecuted by an assistant public prosecutor. Private prosecutors were to have the right to apply to the grand jury for a bill of indictment but were otherwise to be excluded. The Bill was referred to a Select Committee which reported in favour, but recommended that the district agent should intervene in prosecutions only after committal and that each circuit should have a salaried barrister to advise on prosecutions and to prosecute in difficult cases. Briefs

---

[17] (1824) XL *Edinburgh Review*, 191.
[18] Referred to by Brougham in his Evidence to the Select Committee on Public Prosecutors, 1854–55 PP (481) XII, 1.
[19] Recounted by Attorney-General Cockburn in his evidence to the Select Committee.
[20] PP 1854 (15) V, 571.
[21] PP 1854/55 (26) V, 615.

in other cases should be open to the whole bar. After the committee's report the matter was allowed to sleep until 1870 when Eykyn brought in a Bill.[22]

The scheme which Eykyn proposed was broadly that which the Select Committee had recommended in 1856. The main differences were that district agents (or public prosecutors as the Bill called them) were to be appointed by the Home Secretary rather than by the Lord Chancellor, and were to have power to prosecute *ab initio* all indictable offences for which costs were allowable in law. The Bill was referred to a Select Committee which recommended a number of alterations. The following year it was reintroduced by the recorder of London but made no progress.[23] In 1872 it was introduced again.[24] During its passage through the Commons the government proposed an amendment, the effect of which would have been to make the appointment of a public prosecutor obligatory so far as the Central Criminal Court district was concerned but permissive in all other areas. Lack of parliamentary time prevented further progress. Over the recess the government circulated copies of the amended Bill to the judges and to chairmen of Quarter Sessions. Only four of the judges thought fit to reply. Quarter Sessions chairmen were generally critical. They thought the Bill unnecessary and that the existing system worked well. They also objected to the expense it would entail and to the patronage and power which it would confer on the Home Secretary.[25] In 1873 the government introduced a fresh Bill (which was to be compulsory in all areas) but it had to be withdrawn due to lack of parliamentary time.[26] In 1875 the Fifth Report of the Judicature Commission came out strongly in favour of a national system of public prosecutors, with Lord Chief Justice Cockburn particularly forceful in his calls for reform.

The next legislative initiative came from the government. In 1879 it introduced its Prosecution of Offences Bill. This provided for the appointment of a Director of Public Prosecutions, whose duty it would be to undertake and carry on prosecutions in such cases as the Attorney-General should by regulation specify, included amongst which would be all cases of importance or difficulty, or where his intervention was required to secure the due prosecution of an offence. He would also have the duty of giving advice and assistance to chief officers of police and others concerned with prosecutions. This very limited reform was, the government insisted, all that was necessary. The existing system worked well but there was a need for overall supervision of prosecutions. This the Bill would provide. The Bill became law and in the same year Sir John Maule was appointed as the first DPP. Maule adopted a timid and conservative approach to his duties, being

---

22 PP 1870 (45) IV, 69.
23 PP 1871 (35) V, 249.
24 PP 1872 (28) IV, 583.
25 Edwards, *The Law Officers of the Crown*, 352.
26 PP 1873 Bill (173) IV 279.

slow to intervene to take up cases. In his first three years in office, out of 2324 cases referred to him, only 809 were taken up. Given also that in cases where his office did intervene the conduct of the prosecution was turned over to the Treasury Solicitor, the Director and his staff quickly came to be regarded 'as a sort of fifth wheel of the coach'.[27] The upshot was a Select Committee Report followed in 1884 by an amending Act which merged the offices of DPP and Treasury Solicitor.[28] Henceforth all prosecutions taken up by the Director would actually be conducted by his office. The Act also made it obligatory for chief officers of police to make periodic returns to the Director, giving details of abandoned prosecutions and other cases in which his intervention was considered necessary.

The passing of the Act was followed by the appointment of Sir Augustus Stephenson as the new DPP. In 1886 revised regulations were issued requiring the Director to prosecute where the offence charged was capital or of a class formerly prosecuted by the Treasury Solicitor, when instructed to do so by the Attorney-General or Home Secretary, and in all other cases where his intervention was required in the public interest. Stephenson was a high-profile Director who managed to get on the wrong side of a number of judges. Indeed an unseemly feud with the Lord Chief Justice ended only with Stephenson's compulsory retirement in 1894. After his departure his office passed out of the public spotlight. By 1900 it was still only handling four to five hundred cases per annum.[29]

---

[27] Edwards, *The Law Officers of the Crown*, 370–71.
[28] Prosecution of Offences Act, 1884.
[29] Edwards, *The Law Officers of the Crown*, 380–87.

10

Trial Juries

'The composition of the jury list seems to be conducted on the principle of selecting the most uneducated and incompetent persons in the county with the requisite property qualification.' (1847–48) 10 *Law Times* 319.

The hallmark of trial juries in the nineteenth century was their wholly unrepresentative character. The only persons eligible to serve were men aged between twenty-one and sixty, and possessed of the requisite property qualification.[1] In 1800 the qualification for Assize and county Sessions jurors was the ownership of freehold land worth £10 a year or leasehold land worth £20 a year; the occupation of a house with fifteen or more windows; or occupation of a dwelling with an annual value for rating of at least £20 (£30 in London and Middlesex). In Wales the qualification was (until 1870) three-fifths of that for English counties. In the City of London and in boroughs it depended upon local custom.[2]

Most of those tried on indictment were tried by common juries (juries selected from the general pool of those eligible for service), but a handful were tried by a special jury or by a jury *de medietate linguae*. A special jury consisted of jurors who were either of the rank of esquire or above or bankers or merchants (after 1870 those who satisfied a special rating qualification were also eligible to serve).[3] Trial by such a jury was available upon the application of either prosecutor or accused but only in cases of misdemeanour pending in the King's Bench or on the Revenue Side of the Exchequer.[4] To have a country case tried by a special jury it was necessary first to remove the indictment into the King's Bench. An order for a special jury having been made, the case would then normally be tried at Assizes.[5] Special jurors, unlike common jurors whose service in criminal cases was unpaid,[6] received a fee of one guinea for each case they tried. Nor was it the practice to fine them for non-attendance.[7]

---

[1] Juries Act, 1825, ss 1, 8, and 50; Juries Act, 1870, s 7.
[2] Juries Act, 1825, s 31.
[3] Juries Act, 1870, s 6.
[4] Chitty, *Criminal Law* (1st edn, 1816), i, 522.
[5] Halsbury's *Laws* (1st edn), xviii, 260.
[6] (1852) 17 LT 202; *The Times*, 21 December 1858.
[7] J. Bentham, *Elements of the Art of Packing as Applied to Special Juries* (London, 1821).

Down to 1852 one of the most distinctive features of the special jury was the way in which it was selected. It was not, as was a common jury, selected by ballot from a panel returned by the sheriff. Instead it was 'struck'. The sheriff would attend upon the proper officer of the court with the freeholders' book, and the latter in the presence of the Crown solicitor and the defendant's attorney would nominate forty-eight jurors out of the book. Of the forty-eight the Crown solicitor would strike out twelve and the defendant's attorney a further twelve. The twenty-four remaining would then be returned for the trial, and of those of the twenty-four who attended in answer to summons the twelve whose names appeared first on the list would serve.[8] The backgrounds of special jurors meant that they could usually be relied upon to find for the Crown in political cases. In the first third of the century out of the small number of cases tried each year by special jury, a significant number were political prosecutions (some 183 between 1816 and 1834).[9]

The jury *de medietate linguae* had its origin in a statute passed in Edward III's reign with the object of attracting wool merchants to England.[10] By this statute any alien might upon arraignment claim the right of being tried by such a jury. If he did, a jury would be empanelled consisting as to one half of aliens (if so many could be found) and as to the rest of native-born citizens.[11] The alien jurors did not have to be of the same nationality as each other or as the accused. Nor did they have to possess the property qualification required of English jurors. The privilege was abolished in 1870,[12] on the ground that to continue it was to suggest that foreigners could not receive a fair trial from an English jury.[13] Up to its abolition it was anything but a dead letter. Each year a number of accused would claim the right of being so tried,[14] although counsel would often try to dissuade clients from doing so for tactical reasons.[15]

Special issues (e.g. fitness to plead) would normally be tried by a common jury empanelled in the usual way. To this rule there was an important exception. The issue of whether a woman capitally convicted was pregnant (pregnancy entitled her to a respite of execution until the child was born) was tried by a jury of matrons,[16] selected from amongst the women present

---

8 Chitty, *Criminal Law*, i, 523–24.

9 L. Woodward, *The Age of Reform* (2nd edn, Oxford, 1962), 31.

10 28 Ed III, c 13 confirming 27 Ed II, st. 2, c. 8.

11 Chitty, *Criminal Law*, i, 525.

12 Naturalisation Act, 1870, s 5 (the Special & Common Juries Bill, 1868 had contained a similar clause).

13 PD 1870 CXCIX, 1129.

14 The most celebrated example of an attempt to invoke the privilege was in the trial of the *Mannings* (1849) 2 Car & K 887; *The Times* trial reports up to 1870 contain a number of examples of aliens being tried by such juries. For an attempt to invoke the privilege as late as 1882, see *R v Howard, The Times*, 3 April 1882.

15 E. Bowen Rowlands, *Seventy-Two Years at the Bar*, 32.

16 Bla Comm, iv, 388. Prior to the Sex Disqualification (Removal) Act, 1919 it was the only jury on which a woman could serve.

in court, who would, with the assistance of a surgeon if they required it, examine the accused and deliver a verdict.[17] By the 1840s the procedure was widely discredited.[18] As a safeguard against a mistaken verdict, the Home Office would usually order a medical examination of any woman found not pregnant.[19] 1848 saw the abandonment of the policy of granting only a temporary respite to convicts found pregnant. Henceforth the reprieve in such cases was permanent.[20] Despite a number of attempts to abolish it, the jury of matrons survived until 1931.[21]

3. Jury Packing

In Ireland jury packing (achieved by ruthless use by the Crown of its stand-by powers to get Catholics off juries) was a source of grievance throughout the century.[22] In the first quarter of the century there were also loud complaints about packed English juries. These centred around the special juries used to try Crown cases in the King's Bench and the Exchequer. The same men, it was said, sat upon such juries term after term. They were chosen because they could be relied upon to find for the Crown, and if they ever failed to do so they were never called to serve again. This state of affairs arose, it was claimed, because of the way the forty-eight jurors to be struck were chosen. The Crown, so the allegation went, had an unofficial list of jurors regarded as 'sure men', and if a name was drawn by the officer of the court which was not on that list, the Crown solicitor would ensure that he was passed over by urging objections such as that he would not attend if summoned, or that he was dead. If this failed, the jurors objected to would be got rid of by the Crown solicitor naming him amongst the twelve he desired to have struck. In this way a body of jurors amenable to the Crown could be and was obtained.[23]

Allegations of packing had been made by Horne Tooke at his trial in 1794,[24] and thereafter the subject would not go away. In 1808 it was raised

---

[17] As to the procedure when a plea of pregnancy was raised see *R v Wycherley* (1838) 8 C & P 262n.

[18] See *The Times*, 5 October 1847 (leader and letter) which referred to numerous recorded instances of erroneous verdicts by juries of matrons.

[19] See Taylor, *Principles of Medical Jurisprudence* (8th edn, London, 1928), 31, citing *R v Hunt* (1847) 2 Cox 261.

[20] F. Bresler, *Reprieve* (London, 1965), 54; public clamour in the case of Charlotte Harris (*The Times*, 3 and 8 August 1849, report and leader) led to the change in practice.

[21] The Criminal Code Bills had proposed to abolish the jury of matrons. It was actually abolished by the Sentence of Death (Expectant Mothers) Act, 1931 (as to which see PD 1931 CCLXVII, 1817).

[22] See J. McEldowney and P. O'Higgins, *The Common Law Tradition* (Dublin, 1990), 136–53.

[23] T. J. Wooler, *An Appeal to the Citizens of London against the Alledged Lawful Mode of Packing Special Juries* (London, 1817); J. Bentham, *Elements of the Art of Packing*, 5 and 32–35; PD 1809 XIV, 183–84 and *R v Henry Hunt, The Times*, 23 March 1820.

[24] *R v Horne Took* 1794 25 St Tr 127.

by one of the sheriffs with the Chief Baron.[25] In the following year it was the subject of a petition and debate in the Commons.[26] In 1818 a report from a special committee set up by the City appeared to lend weight to the complaint.[27] In 1821 Bentham joined in with a devastating attack, published under the title *Elements of the Art of Packing*. Faced with mounting public unease, Peel decided to act: by the Juries Act of 1825 it was provided that in London and Middlesex the forty-eight jurors from whom a special jury was to be struck should henceforth be selected by ballot.[28] This put an end to complaints of packing. In 1852 the system was further reformed, with the Common Law Procedure Act providing that special juries at Assizes should no longer be struck but that instead the sheriff should be directed to return a specified number of special jurors, not exceeding forty-eight, from which the jury should then be selected by ballot.[29] In 1870 this procedure was applied to London and Middlesex as well.[30] Henceforth a struck jury could only be had by special order of the trial judge.[31]

Packing of common juries does not appear to have been a problem in England at any stage during the century. The potential for abuse was, however, certainly there, for the law left it entirely to the discretion of the sheriff how the panel was selected (with the only safeguard for the accused being his right to challenge the array, upon which he bore the burden of proof).[32] In 1881 a Select Committee had commended the Irish system of mechanical selection of panels but the idea was never taken up.[33]

4. The Poor Quality of Common Juries

The main shortcoming of common juries was their poor quality.[34] Educated men, it was claimed, were rarely to be found on them. Instead, they consisted in the main of small farmers and shopkeepers, often wholly unfitted either by education or intelligence to try complicated issues. That the educated and well to do rarely served on common juries was due to several factors. First,

---

[25] Bentham, *Elements of the Art of Packing*, 126–33.

[26] The petition of Henry White, PD 1809 XIV, 175–90.

[27] *The Times*, 24 January 1818. The report appeared to confirm the existence of an unofficial list of jurors and that the claim that the same men sat as special jurors term after term.

[28] Juries Act, 1825 s 32. Peel had first proposed the reform in his Juries Empanelling Bill of 1824.

[29] Common Law Procedure Act, 1852, s 108.

[30] Juries Act, 1870, s 16.

[31] Common Law Procedure Act, 1852, s 109; Juries Act, 1870, s 17.

[32] Report of Departmental Committee on the Jury Laws, PP 1913 (Cmnd 6817) XXX, 403, para 104.

[33] Report of Select Committee on Irish Jury Laws, PP 1881 (430) XI, 1, para 51.

[34] See the 2nd Report of the Common Law Commissioners, PP 1852–53 (1626), XL, 6; Select Committee on Special and Common Juries, PP 1867/68 (401) XII 677 (Q 1335 and app 2); Select Committee on the Irish Jury Laws, para 10; (1847–48) 10 LT 425 and PD 1873 CCXIV, 547.

the vast majority of those exempt from jury service came from those classes.[35] Secondly, it was comparatively easy for a man who was not exempt to buy his way out of jury service. Until the 1825 Act transferred the duty to parish overseers, the task of compiling jury lists fell to the parish constable, who 'in consideration of some trifling gratuity often omitted the names of persons best qualified to serve'.[36] After the Act, the same result could be achieved by an approach to one of the poorly paid sheriff's officers by whom the work of compiling jury panels was in practice done.[37] Yet another factor was the law's insistence on making land the basis of the qualification for jury service, thereby placing outside the net those whose wealth consisted of personal property.[38] Even more important was a practice, going back it would seem at least to the 1820s,[39] of not including special jurors on common jury panels. This practice, for which there was no warrant in the 1825 Act, was repeatedly condemned by both judges and royal commissions but continued largely unabated.[40] An 1870 Act went so far as to declare that special jurors were not to be exempt from serving on common juries, but even this made little difference.[41] In 1878 Serjeant Cox, the second judge at Middlesex Sessions, wrote to *The Times* saying that he doubted whether any judge or counsel had ever seen a special juror at those sessions.[42] By 1913 the practice still had not been wholly eliminated,[43] despite repeated judicial fulminations.[44]

At the Committee Stage of the Juries Bill of 1873 the Attorney-General, arguing that the quality of juries would thereby be improved, introduced an amendment proposing that all common juries should henceforth consist of four special and eight common jurors.[45] The amendment was strongly attacked as an attempt to introduce caste justice and was in the end withdrawn. Nor did a clause in the 1873 and 1874 Bills, proposing that a trial judge should have power to direct trial by special jury in felony, fare any better.[46]

---

[35] (1864–65) 40 LT, 112 and 197 and PD 1874 CCXIX 289.

[36] PD 1825 XII, 968 (Peel).

[37] Report of the Select Committee of 1867–68, app 2; the practice had been declared illegal and made punishable by a fine by s 43 of the Juries Act, 1825.

[38] The Jurors Qualification Bills of 1823 and 1824 had sought to make the possession of government or company stock above a certain value a qualification.

[39] *The Times*, 8 January 1879 (letter from 'B'), 10 January 1879 (letter from 'An Officer of the Court').

[40] Common Law Commissioners, 2nd Report, PP 1830 (123) XI, 547 at p 6; 1st Report of the Judicature Commission PP 1868/69 (4130) XXV, 19; Report of Select Committee of 1867–68, app 2.

[41] Juries Act, 1870, s 15.

[42] *The Times*, 5 October 1878.

[43] Report of Departmental Committee above, para 111.

[44] Fry J (Gloucester Assizes) *The Times*, 9 August 1880; (1877–78) 22 Sol J 472; *Linscott v Jupp* (1891) 8 TLR 130.

[45] PD 1873 CCXVI, 1510.

[46] The provision appeared as cl 80 in the 1873 Bill and cl 77 in the 1874 Bill; for parliamentary reaction, see PD 1874 CCXIX, 804–7.

5. Working-Class Jurors

The last quarter of the century saw increasingly vociferous demands, particularly from the Trades Union Congress (the matter was the subject of resolutions at every annual congress between 1873 and 1883), that working men be allowed to serve on juries.[47] By the 1870s a trickle of artisan jurors had already begun to appear at London and borough sessions.[48] In his letter to *The Times*,[49] Serjeant Cox described his experiences of this new breed of juror: most asked to be excused on the ground of financial hardship. The Trades Union Congress itself accepted that its reform proposals would never work unless working men received compensation for the financial loss which jury service involved, and demanded that they be so compensated. This led to jibes in *The Times* that working men wished to share in the privileges but not the burdens of jury service.[50]

Although the calls to widen the base of jury service fell largely on deaf ears, the demand that jurors be paid did not. As early as 1821 Bentham had pointed to the anomaly of paying those jurors who were best able to afford to serve, namely special jurors, a guinea per case, whilst the humble common juror received only eight pence a day in civil cases and nothing at all when sitting on a criminal jury.[51] Bills providing for the payment of common jurors were introduced in 1863 and 1868.[52] In 1870 the battle appeared won when the Juries Act passed with a section included which provided for common jurors to be paid ten shillings a day out of fees paid by civil litigants.[53] Unhappily, the provision proved unworkable. In many courts there was simply no money with which to pay the common jurors. Early in 1871 the government had to repeal the section.[54] Between 1874 and 1898 no less than thirteen Bills on the subject were introduced in Parliament,[55] but none reached the statute book. Only in 1949 would this blot on the law be removed.[56]

[47] TUC, *Annual Congress Reports*, 1873–83, 1892 and 1894.

[48] The phenomenon was a consequence in the increase in the burgess rolls cause the the Representation of the People Act, 1867 (Report of the Select Committee on the Juries Bill, PP 1870 (306) VI, 61).

[49] *The Times*, 5 October 1878.

[50] *The Times*, 17 September 1878 (leader).

[51] Bentham, *Elements of the Art of Packing*, 140.

[52] Jurors' Remuneration Bill, 1863 and Special and Common Jurors Bill, 1868.

[53] S 22.

[54] Juries Act Amendment Act, 1871; for the background to the repeal, see PD 1871 CCIV 372.

[55] Beginning with the Juries Bill, 1874 and ending with the Jurors Expenses Bills of 1897 and 1898.

[56] Juries Act, 1949.

6. *Jury Challenge as a Protection against Jury Bias*

Given the make up of common juries, it was inevitable that there should be complaints of class bias, and there were. In 1913 the Departmental Committee on the Jury Laws reported that there was a belief that jurors discriminated against trade unionists and those holding different political views from their own,[57] the same complaint that had been made from time to time by the Trades Union Congress.[58]

The only means the accused had of countering jury bias was through exercise of his right of jury challenge. His most valuable right in this respect was that of peremptory challenge, but the extent of this varied according to the nature of the offence being tried. In treason he had up to thirty-five such challenges;[59] in felony up to twenty (in Ireland the right was confined to capital felony).[60] In misdemeanour he had, in strict law, no right of peremptory challenge but, in practice, he was often allowed to challenge without assigning cause until he had exhausted the jury panel.[61] In addition to the right of peremptory challenge, an accused had, whatever the charge, the right to challenge individual jurors for bias or other sufficient cause.

For the effective exercise of his right of challenge the accused needed to know the background of prospective jurors. But this information the law was loath to grant. In treason he had by statute the right to have a copy of the jury panel delivered to him ten days before trial, a document which, after 1825 at least, would state the full name, address, occupation and qualification of every juror on the panel.[62] In felony and misdemeanour, however, there was no right to see the panel. In 1844 the *Law Magazine* argued that felony should be placed on the same footing in this respect as treason, but the judges were wholly against such a reform, refusing to allow the prisoner copy of the panel even in treason felony.[63] In *R v Dowling* and *R v Lacey* in 1848 counsel tried a new tack.[64] They claimed the right to examine jurors before they were sworn, with a view to discovering whether grounds for challenge existed. In making such application they were doubtless seeking to copy American practice, where the right to conduct such an examination had been upheld by the courts as a necessary corollary of the

---

[57] Para 180.

[58] TUC, *8th Annual Report*, 1875.

[59] Chitty, *Criminal Law*, i, 540–51.

[60] H. H. Joy, *Challenges to Jurors in Criminal Cases* (Dublin, 1842), 150–53.

[61] *R v Blakeman* (1850) 3 C & K 97; *Creed v Fisher* (1854) 9 Ex 472; at some courts it was the practice simply not to call jurors in respect of whom either side had raised objection before trial, see Chitty, *Criminal Law*, i, 534–35 and (1872–73) 17 Sol J 232.

[62] Treason Act, 1695, s 7; Juries Act, 1825, s 21.

[63] Printed as Appendix C to the 8th Report of the Criminal Law Commissioners.

[64] *R v Dowling* and *R v Lacey* (1848) 3 Cox 509 and 517 respectively; for an earlier but equally unsuccessful attempt see *R v Edmonds* (1821) 4 B & Ad 471. In the 1840s some of the Irish judges had shown a disposition to adopt the US Practice, see *R v Francis* (1841) Ir Circ Rep 274.

right to trial by an impartial jury guaranteed by the constitution.[65] The judges, however, would have no truck with such a procedure. English law permitted jurors to be examined only after the ground of challenge had been stated, and even then only to a limited extent.[66] For the rest of the century judicial practice on the question never shifted. The largest concession counsel was ever able to wring from a court was to be allowed to put a question to the jury panel as to whether any of them had, for example, any conection with the body which was financing the prosecution.[67]

---

[65] As to which see C. La Rue Munson, 'Selecting the Jury' (1894–95) 4 Yale LJ, 173 at 179.

[66] Chitty, *Criminal Law*, i, 550.

[67] Questions allowed as to whether jurors came from a particular locality (*R v Edwards, The Times*, 16 August 1822), whether they had any connection with the Bank of England (*R v Rigand, The Times*, 17 February 1826); whether any of them belonged to the society which had brought the prosecution, *R v Carlile* (1819) 1 St Tr NS 1387; and *R v Nicholson* (1840) 4 Jur 558. Questions were disallowed in *R v Swann, The Times*, 15 January 1820, as to who a juror's landlord was, and in *R v Davidson, The Times*, 24 October 1820, as to whether any juror was a member of the society bringing the prosecution.

11

Lawyers

'I shall not allow attorneys to practice at this court when four barristers are present. That is my order'. Sir Gregory Lewin, Recorder of Doncaster (1845) 4 *Law Times* 300.

1. Barristers

Barristers had the right of audience in all criminal courts and an exclusive right of audience before the House of Lords, the King's Bench, the Assizes, the Old Bailey and the more important Quarter Sessions. In 1800 the bar did not, however, normally attend the Welsh Quarter Sessions which, for the most part, were difficult to reach, had little work and that badly paid. Nor was there a bar at Cornwall or Rutland Sessions; nor at some of the smaller English borough sessions, such as Derby, Doncaster and Pontefract. At these courts attorneys had a right of audience, as they did at the Welsh Great Sessions.[1]

In the 1840s the bar (who had of late seen a sharp drop in their work) began to attend Quarter Sessions which they had formerly neglected. They then tried to exclude attorneys from them. They achieved an important victory in 1844 when the Queen's Bench held lawful a ruling by Denbigh County Sessions that the bar (which had only recently begun to attend) should enjoy an exclusive right of audience whenever at least five barristers attended.[2] The practice adopted at Denbigh was soon followed elsewhere.

---

[1] Barristers were persons who had been called to the bar by one of the four Inns of Court. Their principal work was advocacy and the giving of legal advice. They were entitled to appear as advocates before all courts. It was a rule of bar etiquette that a barrister might only accept instructions from an attorney and not from the client direct, but the rule did not at this period apply to all species of work. Attorneys were persons who had been admitted by the judges of the superior common law courts to conduct proceedings therein on behalf of clients. As well as conducting litigation, attorneys gave legal advice to and drew up legal documents for clients. They also had the right to act as advocates before magistrates and other inferior courts. For the extent to which they enjoyed rights of audience before Quarter Sessions, see Report of the Royal Commission on Municipal Corporations, Analytical Table PP 1839 (402) XVIII, 1 (at 28–29 and 152–53). After the Judicature Acts, 1873–75 attorneys adopted the style 'solicitors of the Supreme Court'. After 1877 admission to the profession was superintended by the Law Society on behalf of the judges. In 1888 the power of disciplining solicitors was delegated to a committee appointed by the Master of the Rolls from the Council of the Law Society.

[2] *Ex p Evans* (1846) 9 QB 279; sub nom *R v Denbigh JJ* (1846) 10 JP 371.

At some places, however (Doncaster in particular) attorneys fought hard to hang on to their right of audience. In 1900 they still retained rights of audience in four county and three borough sessions.

Criminal work was for the most part badly paid so far as the bar was concerned. Worthwhile fees could be earned by those fortunate to be retained to prosecute by the Bank, the Mint or the Treasury Solicitor. Most prosecution work, however, rarely attracted a fee of more than two guineas even at Assizes or the Old Bailey.[3] As with prosecution work, so with defence briefs. Counsel retained to defend a client of means (such as the banker Fauntleroy tried in 1824 for forgery) could expect a handsome fee. So too could those briefed for a prisoner for whom a defence fund had been raised by public subscription (such as the Tichborne Claimant), or whose defence was funded by a newspaper (a practice which was steadily creeping in in the 1890s). Most prisoners, however, when they, their family or friends could afford a lawyer at all, could rarely run to a brief fee of more than a guinea or two. Where in a capital case counsel was assigned by the judge to represent a poor prisoner he was obliged to give his services free.

Much of the heavy criminal work was concentrated in the hands of the London bar. Twice a year the common law bar would leave London to go on circuit for six weeks. While for most the attraction was civil briefs marked with high fees, they would also expect to pick up briefs in important criminal cases. They gradually began to face competition from local bars. At Leeds, Manchester and Liverpool, where it had since the 1830s been the practice to brief barristers to prosecute in all cases at Assizes and Quarter Sessions, local bars (small at first) soon grew up. By the end of the century there were local bars in many of the large towns;[4] in 1876 Sheffield, although it did not even have a borough Quarter Sessions, none the less had a small bar.[5]

The size of the criminal bar in the nineteenth century is difficult to estimate. According to the *Law List*, there were 257 barristers in 1780, 810 in 1828, 3268 in 1850 and 9454 in 1900. These figures cannot be accepted at face value, since the lists make no distinction between practising and non-practising barristers. In 1850 the Attorney-General told a Parliamentary Committee that the number earning a living at the bar was between 100 and 1000.[6] An author, writing on the professions in 1857, put the figure at 500.[7] Of his figure of 500 he estimated that 250 were common lawyers. It was from the common law bar that the criminal practitioners came, but there were many who did little or no criminal work.

---

[3] *The Times*, 16 August 1837 and 17 December 1850; see also Return of Rates and Allowances for Attornies and Counsel as settled in each County, PP 1845 (in 390) XLI, 411.

[4] R. L. Abel, *The Legal Profession in England and Wales* (Oxford, 1988), 102.

[5] W. White, *General and Commercial Directory of Sheffield and Rotherham 1876* (Sheffield, 1876), ii , 467.

[6] Report of Select Committee on Official Salaries, PP 1850 (611), XV, 180.

[7] H. Byerly Thomson, *The Choice of a Profession* (London, 1857), 96–97.

There were three ranks or gradations at the bar: King's Counsel, Serjeant at Law and barrister. King's Counsel were appointed by the Lord Chancellor from the senior bar. They were the leaders of the profession, wore silk gowns as a mark of rank and commanded the highest fees. The order of Serjeants at Law, which in medieval times had enjoyed huge prestige, had been in decline since at least the eighteenth century. Until 1846 it enjoyed an exclusive right of audience in the Court of Common Pleas. The appointment of serjeants was in the hands of the Lord Chancellor. After 1868 no further serjeants were created and gradually the order dwindled away.[8] To become a barrister a man had to secure admission to one of the four Inns of Court (for this he required a certificate of respectability signed by two barristers) and to keep twelve law terms there. He did this by dining at the Inn on a set number of occasions per term. Not until 1872 were candidates required to submit themselves to examination (thirty-six years after the Law Society had introduced examinations for attorneys). Prior to the introduction of examinations, the usual training for a would-be barrister was pupillage with a special pleader or practising barrister, or work in an attorney's office (Kenyon LCJ and Kelly LCB both started their legal careers in attorneys' offices, as did several puisne judges).

Most of the high flyers at the criminal bar came from landed or professional families.[9] William Ballantine and Montagu Williams (the most famous Old Bailey barristers of their day) were both lawyers' sons. Marshall Hall's father was a doctor. But there were exceptions. Sir Edward Clarke, who defended Oscar Wilde, was the son of a watchmaker. Because of the difficulty in getting started, with or without connections, many during their early years sought to supplement their income by other activities. The more able practised journalism or wrote legal text books. A few had more questionable sidelines, such as running a public house. The practice at some courts of allocating prosecution briefs on a 'soup' basis provided the briefless with an opportunity to show their ability. But it remained notoriously hard even for able men to get a start. To try and attract work some resorted to questionable practices. Nowhere was this more true than at the criminal bar. Throughout the century the rule of etiquette which forbade barristers from accepting instructions from the client direct was widely breached in criminal defence work, especially in London.[10] There was a good deal of touting for criminal briefs both by barristers and their clerks.[11] Etiquette forbade a barrister to appear in court for a fee of less than a guinea, but there were more than a few who were prepared to work for less in return for a steady supply of small cases. In 1824 during a row between counsel at Middlesex Sessions, Alley, an Old Bailey hack, openly accused his opponent of

---

[8] J. H. Baker, *The Order of Serjeants at Law* (London, 1984), chapter 8.
[9] For these and other biographical details in this chapter see *DNB*.
[10] See e.g. (1845) vol 13 *Punch*, 177; *The Times*, 21 August 1845.
[11] See e.g. (1861–62) 6 Sol J 151.

accepting half-guinea briefs.[12] In mid century there were recurrent rumours that bar clerks were paying policemen commission to put briefs the way of their principals. As late as 1907 the Bar Council found it necessary to include in its annual statement a condemnation of the practice of barristers' clerks paying prison officers a fee for briefs received.[13] Also it was through the complicity of the bar that sham attorneys were able to prosper at the Old Bailey and elsewhere in the first half of the century and beyond.[14]

Malpractices, which had long given barristers a bad name with civil litigants, were also prevalent at the criminal bar. None was more so than that of accepting a fee to appear for a client and then, if a more lucrative case turned up, either not appearing at all or handing the brief at the last minute to a substitute who knew little or nothing about the case.[15] To add insult to injury the bar (until the 1880s) resolutely maintained the stance that the fee paid by the abandoned client was not refundable.[16] This unworthy attitude ensured that the barristers received little public sympathy when they complained of attorneys cheating them of their fees. Then there were the bar's restrictive practices (applied in criminal and civil suits alike), such as the rule that a KC must appear with a junior barrister and that a client who wished to brief a barrister to appear on a circuit, or at a closed Quarter Sessions of which he was not a member, must pay a special fee.

The largest criminal bar was at the Old Bailey. It had a foul reputation. When William Ballantine was blackballed at the Reform Club it caused no surprise: 'An Old Bailey barrister would be blackballed if he were Jesus Christ'.[17] In 1834 a *Times* leader expressed the hope that the coming into force of the Central Criminal Court Act would be accompanied by an improvement in manners on the part of the bar.[18] It was not. Bullying cross-examination of witnesses and rudeness to the bench continued to be the stock in trade of its practitioners. So bad was the behaviour of counsel that on occasions jurors actually stood up to protest. Particular targets for the bar's discourtesy were the judges at Middlesex Sessions. Serjeant Adams, who was assistant judge there in the 1840s and 1850s, seemed to one journalist 'only to occupy the bench as a mark for the impertinence of the bar'.[19] And if members of the bar were rude to the bench they were ruder still to each other. In 1816 a particularly vituperative exchange between

---

12 *The Times*, 13 April 1824 (Middlesex Sessions reports); see also (1871) 51 LT 327.

13 Bar Council, *Annual Statement 1906/7* and *Annual Practice* 1906, ii, 686.

14 *The Times*, 21 August 1845.

15 *The Times*, 1 January 1836, 7 December 1841, 2 June 1842 and 25 January 1845 (letters); *Barrington v Liddell*, *The Times*, 23 and 25 November 1852; *The Times*, 8 June 1842 (article) and 19 August 1859 (leader); (1846) vol 14 *Punch*, 257.

16 *The Times*, 28 May 1833, 10 February 1836 and 8 August 1885 (letters); (1845) vol 13 *Punch* 210.

17 J. R. Lewis, *The Victorian Bar*, 24.

18 *The Times*, 4 November 1834.

19 J. R. Lewis, *The Victorian Bar*, 22–24.

Alley and Adolphus, the law reporter, led to the two fighting a duel on Calais beach.[20] Bad behaviour was not the exclusive preserve of the Old Bailey bar or even the criminal bar. In 1848 at Hull Sessions the recorder was reduced to tears by the insolence of a barrister called Dearsley. The previous year the profession had been scandalised when two Chancery QCs exchanged blows in open court.[21] In the second half of the century the behaviour of the bar both at the Old Bailey and elsewhere gradually improved. But the process was a slow one. In 1874 Dr Kenealey QC was disbarred for his behaviour towards Cockburn LCJ during the trial of the Tichborne Claimant. Even in the 1880s the judges at the London Sessions were often treated with great rudeness by the bar.[22]

2. Attorneys

The task of an attorney instructed to prosecute or defend a prisoner committed for trial was to prepare the case and to brief counsel. Only at the Great Sessions, and at Quarter Sessions where attorneys had the right of audience, could the attorney himself conduct the case in court. In 1859 an attorney was allowed to conduct a prosecution at Wells Assizes when the counsel he had briefed did not appear, but this seems to have been a wholly exceptional course.[23] In London in the nineteenth century three firms (Humphreys & Morgan, Wontner & Son and Lewis & Lewis) did the bulk of the criminal work.[24] In provincial towns there would usually be at least one attorney prepared to take on criminal work, although many chose not to soil their hands with it (not least because it was in the main poorly paid).

Throughout the first half of the century the higher criminal courts and the prisons which served them were plagued with sham attorneys. Such men, themselves unqualified, sometimes worked under the cover of the name of a qualified attorney (George Cannon in Arnold Bennett's novel *Hilda Lessways* was of this breed) but more often they simply passed themselves off as attorneys. Nowhere were they thicker on the ground than in the London courts. Before the start of the Old Bailey Sessions they would tour Newgate touting for business amongst the prisoners. They were also to be seen regularly at the police offices, the Old Bailey, the Clerkenwell Sessions House and the public houses around offering to conduct defences for prisoners. Nor was it only prisoners and their families on whom they preyed. They habitually approached prosecutors with offers to conduct their prosecutions for such fee as the court allowed. Once he had managed to persuade a

[20] W. Ballantine, *A Barrister's Experiences* (8th edn), 56–57.
[21] *The Times*, 27 July 1847; for a similar incident in 1907, see D. Pannick, *Advocates* (Oxford, 1993), 54.
[22] T. Humphreys, *Criminal Days*, 39–41.
[23] *R v Paul and Others*, *The Times*, 15 August 1859.
[24] T. Humphreys, *Criminal Days*, 25.

prisoner or his family to employ him, the sham attorney would commonly extract every penny from his victim that he could get (sometimes as much as £10 and more). He would then brief a barrister for a fee of a guinea (less if possible) and pocket the rest of the money. Sometimes no barrister was instructed at all, the sham attorney simply keeping the fee and making himself scarce when the prisoner's case was called on.[25] In 1844 the Court of Aldermen sought to stop this abuse by issuing regulations prohibiting access to prisoners by any except duly-qualified attorneys or their clerks duly authorised in writing.[26] This did not end the problem and cases of prisoners standing trial unrepresented, after paying a sham attorney to retain counsel for them, remained unhappily all too common. Occasionally a miscreant was prosecuted or barred from a court house. Although the evil was particularly pronounced in the capital it was by no means confined to it. At most Assizes and Quarter Sessions outside London sham attorneys could be found plying their trade.[27] Had the bar refused to have any truck with such men the abuse could have been stamped out, but competition at the bar was too fierce and etiquette on the point too doubtful for there to be any hope of that.[28]

Nor was touting for criminal work and the fleecing of criminal clients an activity confined to sham attorneys. Criminal work tended to attract a low class of attorney to whom overcharging was second nature.[29] At the bar it was a standing joke that the brief delivered by a solicitor consisted of no more than a copy of the depositions wrapped in a back sheet. In the 1850s the idea was canvassed but unhappily never adopted of making it compulsory for attorneys retained on behalf of prisoners to submit their bills of costs for taxation (scrutiny and possible disallowance) by court officials.[30] Although it had, in fact, been possible to demand taxation of an attorney's bill in a criminal case since the eighteenth century, few clients knew of the right and correspondingly few exercised it.[31] Nor were prisoners and their families the only victims of attorneys' dishonesty. A barrister could not by law sue for his fees and, if he neglected to insist on fee with brief (something a young man would be reluctant to do for fear of giving offence), he ran a great risk of having the attorney pocket his fee. Some attorneys were quite shameless about it. In 1842 a barrister's clerk, who had called at an attorney's home in a vain attempt to persuade him to pay a nine guinea fee which

25 *The Times*, 28 October 1844 (letter from 'Veritas'); *R v Miller Dawer and Edge*, *The Times*, 29 November 1844; *R v Denny*, *The Times*, 29 October 1847; (1847) 9 LT 466.
26 (1844) 3 LT 134; *R v Joblyn and Pettigrew*, *The Times*, 11 and 13 May 1844.
27 (1844–45) 4 LT 31.
28 *The Times*, 28 April 1847 (leader) and 2 November 1852 (letter).
29 See e.g. *The Times*, 25 October 1847 (leader); 23 August 1850 (Old Bailey reports); 2 November 1852 (letter); (1850) 15 LT 533; and (1852) 18 LT 161.
30 (1850) 15 LT 533–34.
31 For the right to claim taxation, see *Ex p Williams* (1791) 4 T R 496; *Curling v Sedger* (1838) 6 Dowl 759.

had been owing to his principal for six years, was given in charge to the police for repeatedly ringing the door-bell.[32] The problem was not confined to the criminal bar. In the 1840s the parliamentary bar adopted a blacklisting system to compel railway companies to pay arrears of fees, only to have the profession declare the scheme illegal.[33] After 1870 it became possible to take disciplinary proceedings against an attorney who declined to pay counsel after being put in funds to do so by the lay client, but many barristers hesitated to take this step for fear of thereby getting a bad name with attorneys generally.[34] In 1876 a shipowner MP introduced a Bill to enable barristers to sue for their fees and to render them liable for negligence.[35] It was blocked by the bar.

The second half of the century saw the demise of the sham attorney; and with the abolition of the courts of common law in 1875 the word attorney passed out of use in favour of the title solicitor. Since the introduction of the preliminary examination for attorneys in 1860 there had been a general improvement in educational standards in the profession generally. This in turn had led to an improvement in the social standing of solicitors, confirmed in 1893, so far as criminal practitioners were concerned, by the knighting of George Lewis, the senior partner in Lewis and Lewis, the firm which had long had the lion's share of London criminal work.[36] Complaints about the villainies practised by solicitors on their criminal clients were still heard but by 1900 they were less frequent.[37]

[32] *The Times* police reports, 30 May 1842.
[33] *The Times*, 17 May 1848 (leader).
[34] See e.g. *Re F* (1883) 18 LJ 352; *Re A Solicitor* (1894) 63 LJQB 397; *Re W D, The Times*, 17 June 1899.
[35] See Barristers and Advocates Fee Bill, PP 1876 (18) I, 125; debate, PD 1876 CCXXIX, 307–49.
[36] J. Juxon, *Lewis and Lewis* (New York, 1984), 263.
[37] J. Hay, *A Gross Miscarriage of Justice* (London, 1894), 3.

12

Representation by Counsel

'Trials would take too long if men of law were allowed.'

Staunford, *Pleas of the Crown*.

1. The Right to Counsel

In 1800 a prisoner's right to counsel varied according to the nature of the charge he faced. In treason he had by statute the right to 'full defence by counsel'.[1] In misdemeanour he had a right to counsel by common law.[2] In felony, however, the position was more complicated. In strict law the accused had no right to counsel but the prohibition had in practice been much eroded.[3] It had since as early as the fifteenth century been customary in capital cases to allow prisoners to have counsel to argue law.[4] In the course of the eighteenth century a further exception had been added: judges began to permit prisoners in felony cases to have counsel to examine and cross-examine witnesses.[5] This left the felony prisoner subject to only one (albeit important) handicap: he could not have counsel to address the jury on his behalf.[6]

2. The Prisoners' Counsel Act (1836)

Between 1821 and 1836 repeated attempts were made to remove this handicap and to give those charged with felony the right to make full defence by counsel. At first there was little enthusiasm for reform. Of five Bills

[1] 7 & 8 Will III, c. 3 (indictments for treason) and 20 Geo II, c. 30 (impeachment).

[2] Bla Comm, iv, 349.

[3] Holdsworth, HEL, v, 192, and the authorities there cited. For explanations for the rule see Coke 3 Inst. 137, J. Staunford, *Pleas of the Crown* (1557), f. 151, Hawk 2 P C, c. 39, s 2, and Sir John Hawles in *Colledge's Case* (1681) 8 St Tr 723.

[4] The prisoner had to propose the point and only if the court thought it arguable would counsel be allowed, see *The Trial of Lord Preston* (1691) 12 St Tr 646 at 655–60. For other exceptions, see Hawk 2 P C, c. 39, ss 5.

[5] J. H. Langbein, 'The Criminal Trial before the Lawyers' (1978) 45 U Chicago LR, 263 at 311–12.

[6] Two devices commonly employed by counsel to outflank the prohibition were to make a speech 'under the mask of cross-examination', and making jury points under guise of a legal submission to the judge, see PD 1824 XI, 215, and *R v Casey*, *The Times*, 21 August 1821. Of the two the first appears to have been both generally employed and also tolerated by the judges (Criminal Law Commissioners, 2nd Report, pp. 3–4 and app).

introduced between 1821 and 1828 only one got beyond the second reading stage. Twice (in 1824 and 1826) leave to bring in a Bill was refused outright, by a large majority.

In the 1830s, however, the tide began to turn. The year 1834 saw a Prisoners' Counsel Bill for the first time pass all its stages in the Commons.[7] The Bill of the following year did even better, passing all its stages in the Commons and being referred by the Lords to a Select Committee. In February 1836 the legislative round began again for what was to be the last time. The 1836 Bill, which was identical to that of the previous year, was referred by the Commons to a Select Committee. The committee reported in favour and it was passed by a substantial majority. In the meanwhile, the Home Secretary had asked the Criminal Law Commissioners to report on the question. Their report came out strongly in favour of the principle of the Bill.[8] It duly passed the Lords but with amendments (the most important being that striking out clause 2, which gave the prisoner's counsel the right to the last word). The Commons with reluctance accepted the amendments and in August the Bill received the royal assent.

The promoter of the first Bills was Richard Martin, a Galway landowner whose liberalism had earned him the nickname 'Humanity Martin'. The driving force behind the reform campaign in the 1830s was, however, William Ewart, a Liverpool merchant who, for the next thirty years, took an active part in the movement for the reform of the criminal law. Bentham took no interest in the question. Lawyers who did and whose support was important in changing opinion within parliament and the profession included Brougham, Lord Lyndhurst, Thomas Denman (the future Lord Chief Justice) and Sir Frederick Pollock (the future chief baron).[9]

Throughout the parliamentary debate the stance taken by the supporters of the Bill was that the case for reform was unanswerable.[10] The state of the law was, they argued, anomalous: a man was allowed counsel to defend him for a twopenny trespass but denied the like privilege where his life was at stake. That was illogical. It was also unjust, for it denied the prisoner on trial for his life counsel to speak for him, however unequal he might be to the task of addressing the jury himself. It was no answer to say (as Hawkins had in his *Pleas of the Crown*) that an innocent man needed no counsel to

---

[7] The first Bill to complete all its stage in the Commons was that of 1833. The 1834 Bill got as far as a first reading in the Lords.

[8] 2nd Report, PP 1836 (343) XXXVI 18, which recommended limiting the reform initially to capital felonies and cases in which prosecuting counsel addressed the jury.

[9] Brougham and Lyndhurst were at first against the Bill, PD 1826 XV 626 and Holdsworth, HEL, XVI, 6.

[10] For the parliamentary debates, see PD 1821 IV, 945–46, 1512–14; 1824 XI, 180–220; 1826 XVI, 590–633; 1833 XVI, 1199–1203; XVIII 607–13; 1834 XXIV, 158–70, 822–27, 1097–99; 1835 XXVIII, 628–33, 865–73; XXIX 356–63, 434; 1836 XXXI, 225–26, 497–501, 1142–54, 1156–61; XXXIV, 760–78, 1061–63; XXXV, 171–86, 228–32, 599–603, 612–14, 1210–11, 1247–49, 1323–25.

make a simple honest defence. The vast majority of prisoners were uneducated and incapable of making a speech explaining the facts of the case intelligibly, be they innocent or guilty. Even an educated man might find the task daunting. And so unbending was the law that the rule was enforced against children and the infirm: 'Your counsel cannot speak for you, you must speak for yourself ... this is the reply given to a poor girl of fifteen, to a foreigner, to the feeble, to the blind, to the old.' The result was that men, who with counsel to speak for them would be acquitted, were for want of counsel convicted. England and Ireland were alone among the countries of Europe in denying this right to prisoners. They were also out of step with the practice in the United States and in the colonies.

Their arguments left many in Parliament and the profession unmoved. They could see no need for the Bill. It was not true that innocent prisoners had difficulty in explaining themselves to juries and in any case the judge acted as counsel for unrepresented prisoners. The Bill was simply not wanted. The judges and the bar were hostile to it, nor was there any popular demand for change. If it became law, serious disadvantages would follow: the length and therefore the cost of criminal trials would be vastly increased;[11] and counsel would appeal to the passions and emotions of juries and lead them astray by ingenious and unmeritorious arguments. The Bill would also lead to judges and prosecuting counsel adopting a less temperate attitude towards prisoners. In his summing up the judge would have to deal with the arguments raised by counsel, and expose the fallacies therein, whilst prosecuting counsel would tend to conduct cases with more heat if the defence counsel had a speech.

The reform lobby answered these objections point by point. To say that the judge was the prisoner's counsel was misleading. The judge was incapable of defending a prisoner satisfactorily, for he had no access to him and so could not possibly know the details of his defence. Also it was his duty to hold the balance between the parties, not to act as advocate for one side. All the saying meant was that it was the duty of the judge to watch the interests of the prisoner and to see that no point of law which told in his favour was overlooked. That the legal profession and the judges were against the Bill proved little. Both were notorious for their conservatism. As for the lack of public demand for the Bill, this was no yardstick of merit. There had been no public demand for the Act of 1695 which granted prisoners the right to counsel in treason, yet all now acknowledged the value of that reform. The argument about expense and delay was unworthy. As Romilly had put it: 'too much time could not be consumed when the object was to discover the truth and administer justice'. In any event, it was false. Most prisoners went undefended through

---

[11] It was widely believed that the Act had caused a considerable increase in the length and expense of Old Bailey sittings, see *The Times*, 27 January 1837. In 1837 the salaries of the recorder and common serjeant were increased by £500 p.a. each in consequence of increased burdens imposed on them, particularly since the passing of the Prisoners' Counsel Bill (City of London, Administration of Justice Committee Records).

want of means, and that situation the Bill would not alter one iota. Rather than leading to wrongful acquittals, the Bill would be likely to result in more convictions, for juries would no longer acquit out of sympathy excited by the prisoner's inability to defend himself. As for the claim that judicial impartiality and prosecutorial fairness would be compromised, experience in trials for treason and misdemeanour did not bear out the claim, nor did the experience of the courts of the United States and the colonies.

3. Poor Prisoners

To the majority of prisoners the Act was cruelly irrelevant. Whatever their legal right, in practice they were denied counsel by their poverty. In 1800 less than one prisoner in four tried at the Old Bailey was defended and, by the end of the century, although things had improved, defended prisoners were still in the minority.[12] Nor was the position any better in the country.[13] Indeed at county Quarter Sessions it was markedly worse.

Public opinion was prepared to tolerate prisoners being tried for their lives undefended. Criminal procedure was viewed as essentially liberal. Cottu and other foreign observers had commented upon how favourable English law was to the accused. The judge would see that the prisoner had the benefit of any legal point in his favour; and he could be convicted only if a jury of twelve were unanimously of the view that his guilt had been proved beyond a reasonable doubt. Given these safeguards, the risk of an undefended prisoner being wrongfully convicted was surely minimal. Also the employment of counsel in criminal trials was still a comparatively recent phenomenon. It was still the exception rather than the rule to find counsel instructed for the prosecution even in serious cases, and if the prosecution had no counsel, how could it be said that the accused was at a disadvantage?

During the campaign for the Prisoners' Counsel Bill, the question of legal representation of poor prisoners was in fact raised. A clause entitling poor prisoners to have counsel assigned to them was included in each of the 1833–36 Bills (counsel so assigned to act without fee). Before the Lords' Select Committee on the 1835 Bill members of the bar spoke out against the clause, claiming that it would cause inconvenience and loss to the profession.[14] Although it appeared in the 1836 Bill, it was dropped before the Bill reached the Lords.

The subject once raised would not go away. In 1843 Serjeant Cox treated

---

[12] Of the 104 prisoners tried at the Old Bailey at the July 1800 Session twenty-five (24 per cent) had counsel (CCC Sess Papers), a figure which ties in with what Beattie found.

[13] See D. Phillips, *Crime and Authority in Victorian England* (London, 1977), 104 n 16. At the 1841 Summer Assizes the calendar for Nottingham county contained twelve cases; in only one did the prisoner have counsel, *The Times*, 26 July 1841.

[14] PP 1835 (HL 130) XLVI, 317; see also PD 1834 XXIV, 1097–98 and *The Times*, 10 February 1836.

the launching of the *Law Times* as an opportunity to revive the topic.[15] Counsel should, he argued, be assigned to poor prisoners from the pool of unemployed barristers who attended criminal courts. They ought to be paid out of the same fund as counsel briefed by the prosecutor, but if need be they would almost certainly work without fee. The correspondence to which the article gave rise revealed that in 1835 one of the sheriffs had, out of his own pocket, funded a free representation scheme for Newgate prisoners, only to see it break down after one session (despite encouraging results), due to opposition from the lawyers.

In 1856 the call for the state to provide legal aid was repeated by Charles Greaves in a Report to the Lord Chancellor on Criminal Procedure.[16] An attorney and counsel paid for out of public funds should, he argued, be assigned to any poor prisoner found by the visiting magistrate of a gaol to have reasonable grounds of defence.

Calls for state-funded criminal legal aid were doomed to go unanswered.[17] A scheme utilising the free services of the unemployed bar was, however, less easily dismissed. Not only would it answer (however imperfectly) the needs of poor prisoners, it would also provide young men seeking to break into the profession with much-needed experience and an opportunity to show their worth. Moreover, it was all perfectly practicable. In Scotland a free representation scheme for poor prisoners had been operated successfully by the profession since the sixteenth century.[18]

During the second half of the nineteenth century variants on Cox's scheme were proposed. In 1860 one of the City judges announced that he would be glad to see members of the bar defend all unrepresented poor prisoners, and said that he would provide all facilities in his power for the purpose.[19] In 1882 it was suggested, in a letter to the *Law Times*, that barristers willing to defend prisoners for a nominal fee (say 2s. 6d. to be paid out of the rates), should write their names on a special list to be lodged with the gaoler or an officer of the court.[20]

In 1899 it was suggested in the *Irish Law Times* that defence briefs should be allotted to counsel willing to undertake such work without fee on a soup basis.[21] Nothing came of any of these proposals. All foundered on the rule of professional etiquette which prohibited a barrister from appearing in court without a brief marked with the minimum fee of one guinea.[22]

---

[15] (1843) 1 LT 635. He also suggested a Society for the Defence of Prisoners to be funded by popular subscription.

[16] PP 1856 (456) L 79.

[17] See e.g. PD 1882 CCLXVII, 431 (Lord Harcourt).

[18] A. Alison, *Principles of the Criminal Law of Scotland* (Edinburgh, 1832–33), ii, 379; see also (1899) 33 Ir LT 322.

[19] G. Pitt Lewis, *Mr Commissioner Kerr*, 259.

[20] (1882) 74 LT 32, itself prompted by a letter in *The Times*, 25 October 1882.

[21] 3 Ir LT 452.

[22] (1843) 1 LT 635 (Cox).

By the 1890s the subject was one which was coming to be raised with increasing frequency in debates upon the Criminal Evidence Bills which the government was seeking to get through Parliament, but the breakthrough did not come until the Dorset Sessions scheme of 1902, which in turn led to the Poor Prisoners' Defence Act of 1903.

Prior to 1903, assignment of counsel and defence *in forma pauperis* were the only provision which the law made for the needs of poor prisoners, and they benefited but a handful.

4. Assigning Counsel

Assignment was a practice developed by the judges as a means of ensuring that prisoners facing grave charges did not go undefended for want of means. The judge would ask one of the counsel present in court to undertake the prisoner's defence without fee, a request never in practice refused. It was suggested in a letter published in *The Times* in 1903 that the practice dated from the time of the 1836 Act.[23] The suggestion has the attraction of neatness but is certainly wrong. During the debates on the Prisoners' Counsel Bill of 1834, one of the arguments used against the assignment of counsel clause which it contained was that the judges already had power to assign counsel, and that counsel never refused to act.[24] Also one can find in *The Times* reports of criminal trials instances of counsel being assigned to poor prisoners in felony as early as the 1820s.

Assignment of counsel to argue a point of law on behalf of a poor prisoner can in fact be traced back to at least the seventeenth century. The practice of assigning counsel to conduct a defence appeared first in treason. The Treason Act (1695) required the court to assign to the accused, immediately on his request, such counsel (not exceeding two) as he should desire, but was silent as to what was to happen if he was too poor to fee them. By the late eighteenth century, if not earlier, the gap had been supplied by a rule of bar etiquette, requiring counsel assigned to a poor prisoner to act without fee. Erskine spoke of the rule in 1800 when accepting assignment as counsel for the penniless lunatic Hadfield charged with shooting at King George III.[25]

By around 1820 the practice in treason had begun to spread to felony. *The Times* for 1818 reports a judge at Lancaster Assizes asking counsel to undertake the defence of two brothers called Fitzpatrick, charged with robbery and too poor to afford counsel.[26] No further such cases appear in *The Times* reports of trials until 1825 when two are reported (the first a trial of two brothers called Daw at Horsham Assizes for murder;[27] the second a

23 *The Times*, 14 April 1903.
24 PD 1834 XXIV, 1098.
25 *R v Hadfield*, *The Times*, 19 June, 1800.
26 *R v Fitzpatrick and Fitzpatrick*, *The Times*, 22 August 1818.
27 *R v Daw and Daw*, *The Times*, 28 March 1825.

trial for murder at Monmouth where the accused was a pauper who had no English).[28] There is reason, however, to think that the practice was at this date still new for, at the Old Bailey in April of that year, a horse thief called Probert,[29] who applied to the court to assign him counsel, was told by the Lord Chief Justice that the court had no power to assign counsel to undertake his defence; it could only assign counsel to argue law. In the event the day was saved by one of the counsel in court volunteering his services. Nor does Probert's Case stand alone. In 1823 at Monmouth a prisoner called Redding,[30] charged with capital felony, who requested assistance on the ground that he was too poor to employ counsel, was merely told by Park J that he would see justice was done to him. A further, and in some ways even stronger, indication of the novelty of such practice is to be found in cases such as *Nuttall* (1817),[31] where poor prisoners are found asking not for counsel to be assigned but for the judge to act as their counsel. Certainly, assignment in felony appears to have been unknown when Chitty published his treatise on *Criminal Law* in 1816, for he made no mention of it, despite discussing in detail both assignment of counsel in treason (for which he actually gives a precedent of an assignment) and defence *in forma pauperis*.[32]

So far as one can judge from trial reports, assignment of counsel to poor prisoners in felony cases was, and remained, a rare occurrence during the late 1820s and 1830s, but became increasingly common during the 1840s and 1850s.[33] From the start, the power to assign seems rarely to have been exercised save in murder cases, and there was certainly not at any time during the first half of the century anything approaching a policy of assigning in all capital cases.[34] Given the number of capital offences on the statute book, and given also that the majority of capital convictions for offences other than murder did not result in executions, this is not surprising. But even in murder cases (where execution would normally follow conviction) practice was far from uniform. During the period 1820 to 1850, year in year out, prisoners were tried for murder (convicted and, in some cases, executed) without counsel to defend them.

Occasionally, the prisoner's lack of representation in such cases was out

---

[28] *R v Thomas, The Times,* 11 August 1825.

[29] *R v Probert, The Times,* 6 and 8 April 1825.

[30] *R v Redding, The Times,* 11 August 1823.

[31] *R v Nuttall, The Times,* 8 September 1817; see also *R v Sullivan* (Limerick Assizes), *The Times,* 4 August 1820.

[32] Chitty, *Criminal Law* (London 1816), i, 407–14.

[33] See D. R. Bentley, 'Trial on Indictment in Nineteenth-Century England' (Sheffield University PhD thesis), 383 n 59.

[34] Occasionally one finds assignments in cases other than murder: e.g. *R v Smith, The Times,* 10 August 1848 (manslaughter); *R v Clarke, The Times,* 19 June 1849 (arson); *R v Chesham, The Times,* 7 March 1851 (poisoning); *R v Jones, The Times,* July 28 1855 (theft); and *R v Hetherington* and *R v Chipchase* n 42 below.

of choice,[35] but more usually it was because he was poor and the court had not seen fit to assign him counsel. In some cases, the reason why no counsel was assigned was almost certainly that the judge, having read the depositions, considered the case weak and thought counsel unnecessary. Where the accused was obviously insane, judges, rather than assign counsel, would simply call the surgeon of the gaol to prove the fact.[36] In infanticide cases (where due to the primitive state of medical science it was notoriously difficult to prove a live birth), the judge would often, without troubling to appoint counsel, himself demolish the prosecution case by his cross-examination of the medical witnesses.[37] This judicial technique was indeed responsible in no small measure for the very high acquittal rate in this class of case. On the other hand, if the case was complex this might incline the judge to assign. In *Johnson*,[38] a case of murder tried in 1859, the judge assigned counsel to the prisoner well into the prosecution case, the reason for the belated assignment apparently being that the case had turned out to involve more difficulty than had initially been thought. With some judges, failure by a prisoner to ask that counsel be assigned would result in his going undefended. During an Old Bailey trial in 1844 Abinger LCB excused his failure to assign on the ground that the accused had not requested counsel.[39] In *Geering* in 1849, counsel was not assigned until application was made by the prisoner's daughter, by which time one of the prosecution witnesses was already in the middle of his evidence.[40] This despite the fact that the case (being one of murder by poisoning in which the Crown were seeking to put in evidence of other deaths from poison) was one which cried out for an assignment. In an Irish case from the same period, it was actually laid down that the court would not assign counsel of its own motion.[41] In other cases the decisive factor appears to have been that the judge did not intend to leave the prisoner for execution if convicted.[42] Then again some judges seem to have been more reluctant than others to assign. One such was Martin B. In each of the years 1857, 1858, 1859, 1861 and 1862 he is to be found presiding over a murder trial with the prisoner undefended.[43] In two of the cases it is possible to justify the failure to assign, for in one a

---

[35] E.g. *R v Jackson, The Times*, 14 December 1861; *R v Dethridge, The Times*, 26 July 1869.

[36] See e.g. *R v Hodkinson, The Times*, 19 August 1853; *R v Andrew, The Times*, 3 August 1874.

[37] E.g. *R v Anncliffe, The Times*, 15 March 1842 (a clear case); *R v Crawford, The Times*, 20 July 1840.

[38] *R v Johnson, The Times*, 16 December 1859; also *R v Orrell, The Times*, 27 March 1835.

[39] *R v McGregor and Lambert* (1844) 1 Cox 346.

[40] *R v Geering, The Times*, 2 August 1849.

[41] *R v Frith* (1859) 9 Ir Jur 367.

[42] Compare *R v Hetherington, The Times*, 27 February 1837 with *R v Chipchase, The Times*, 28 February 1837 (cases of attempted murder tried by the same judge at the 1837 Spring Assizes).

[43] The cases were *R v Plant, The Times*, 17 December 1857; *R v Murray, The Times*, 2 August 1858; *R v Jones, The Times*, 30 March 1859; *R v Jones, The Times*, 21 December 1861 and *R v Hunnisett, The Times*, 4 August 1862.

pro-defence summing up secured an acquittal, and in the other it looks as though it was his intention from the beginning to spare the prisoner in the event of conviction. But it is difficult to offer any reason, other than dislike of the practice, for his not securing representation for Jones, a young woman indicted at Kingston Assizes in 1859 for the murder of her child, and convicted after a trial in which she had been in a fainting state throughout; or for his refusal at Stafford Assizes in 1861 of an application by another Jones (the only one of five prisoners jointly indicted for murder who was undefended) to have counsel assigned to him. The fifth case appears to have been one in which he overestimated his power to get the jury to do as he wished, a pro-defence summing up failing to procure the acquittal of the prisoner for the murder of her child.

By 1860 assignment in murder cases had become an almost routine practice, with judges often taking the initiative in the matter. But the occasional case in which an accused stood trial undefended could still be found. Nine such cases appear in *The Times* trial reports for 1860–69 and six for the period 1870–79.[44] The last case in those reports of an undefended prisoner convicted of murder is *Eastwell* in May 1864,[45] while the the last case of a prisoner tried for murder undefended is *Sherwood* in May 1879 (where the jury convicted of manslaughter only).[46] After 1880 one hears no more of such cases, it by then being the invariable practice to assign in murder. However, it was still extremely rare to find counsel assigned in any other class of case. Factors such as youth and mental disability, or the severity of the punishment which would follow conviction, rarely influenced judges to assign counsel where the charge was not capital.[47] Indeed as late as 1910 the Court of Criminal Appeal found it necessary to say that in rape cases 'the judge should endeavour to secure the representation of the prisoner by counsel'.[48] In 1903 Grantham J sought to justify, to the Select Committee on the Poor Prisoners' Defence Bill, the illiberality of the judges in the assignment of counsel:

> I do not very often do it except in murder cases. I always do it then. I do not do it in any other cases because I defend the prisoners myself if they are not defended. I could in murder cases but I think it better not. My difficulty is to get a man that I think can do it properly and that I think I ought to ask, because at the present time he gets no fee for it ... if you go to a good man and ask him to do that you may be depriving him of an opportunity of earning a fee in another case or in another court.[49]

[44] They are listed in Bentley, 'Trial on Indictment', 384–85 n 75.
[45] *R v Eastwell*, *The Times*, 5 March 1864.
[46] *R v Sherwood*, *The Times*, 5 May 1879.
[47] See Bentley, 'Trial on Indictment', 385 nn 76–77.
[48] *R v Gillingham* (1910) 5 C A R 187.
[49] PP 1903 VII 590; also (1904) 68 JP 40.

As a means of providing representation for the poor in capital cases, assignment was far from ideal. The counsel assigned would have no brief to work from. Having in most cases been brought in only when the case was about to start and, sometimes at an even later stage (instances are by no means uncommon of a prisoner requesting, or the judge making, an assignment only after the prosecution opening or even during the course of the evidence),[50] he had generally to try and pick the case up as he went along. He would normally be allowed access to the depositions, and the court might also grant him a few moments to confer with his client, but usually he got little more indulgence than that. If during the course of the case enquiries needed to be made, he had no attorney to assist him.

Nor was there any guarantee that the counsel assigned would be proficient. The selection was made from amongst those in court not already engaged in the case. Sometimes the judge would call on the most senior counsel in court.[51] Sometimes one of the barristers present in court would volunteer his services.[52] Occasionally the accused would be invited to choose from the barristers in court.[53] However the choice was made, the risk was that the prisoner would end up with a counsel lacking the experience and ability necessary for an effective defence.[54]

In England one occasionally finds assigned counsel bemoaning in jury speeches the lack of an attorney to assist them.[55] In Ireland matters went further than mere grumbling. In a number of cases around the mid century, the court's power to assign counsel without also assigning an attorney was openly questioned. In January 1848, on the trial of the Codys for murder, counsel assigned by the court expressed doubt as to the propriety of taking an assignment without an attorney but, under pressure from the Lord Chief Justice of Ireland, with reluctance agreed to do so.[56] In *Fogarty*, tried at Down Assizes in 1850, counsel, requested by Pigott LCB to undertake the defence of a prisoner charged with murder, declined to do so unless an attorney was assigned.[57] He was supported by one of the leaders present who told the judge that there was a feeling among the bar that no counsel could with propriety undertake the defence of a prisoner without receiving

---

[50] *The Times* report of *R v Luie and Brown*, 9 April 1874, suggests that the usual course by then was for the judge, upon the conclusion of the prosecution opening, to inquire whether any counsel represented the prisoner.

[51] E.g. *R v Daly and MacFarlane, The Times*, 5 April 1851.

[52] E.g. *R v Beveridge, The Times*, 8 March 1847.

[53] See *R v Thompson and Mullaly, The Times*, 17 March 1868 (Fenian case).

[54] See (1868) 3 LJ 270; one finds from time to time traces of a doctrine that counsel asked to watch the case on a prisoner's behalf (which was one of the form of words used to assign) was not obliged to address the jury on his behalf but merely see that he was tried according to law, see e.g. *R v Atter, The Times*, 20 July 1848 (the counsel involved was called Missing); and *R v Mahaig, The Times*, 25 December 1863.

[55] *R v Doidge, The Times*, 8 August 1862.

[56] *R v Cody and Cody, The Times*, 31 January 1848.

[57] *R v Fogarty* (1850) 5 Cox 161.

instructions from an attorney. He further asserted that where counsel was assigned the Crown should pay him a fee, as up to a very recent period had been the rule. Pigott retorted that it was his opinion that a judge might properly call on a barrister 'to give his honorary services to a prisoner who was unable to employ one', citing a case recently tried at Clonmel, where counsel had at the request of the judge defended a prisoner without the assistance of an attorney. He conceded, however, that he could not compel counsel to act. The impasse was eventually broken when a solicitor present agreed to act. The case was deemed worthy of reporting in an English series of law reports. There is reason to think that in Ireland the reluctance to accept an assignment without an attorney continued after 1850. Certainly, as late as 1873, the *Irish Law Times* was receiving letters from correspondents denying the power of the court to assign counsel without an attorney, and criticising members of the bar who accepted such assignments.[58] In England, however, the practice seems always to have been and continued to be to assign without an attorney.[59]

5. *Defence in Forma Pauperis*

The other method whereby poor prisoners could in theory secure legal representation was by applying to defend *in forma pauperis*. Under the statute 11 Henry VII, c. 12, paupers (by the nineteenth century the definition of a pauper was a person who was not worth £5 in the world) were granted the right to sue and defend causes with the assistance of counsel and attorneys assigned by the court (who were to act without fee) and were exempted from all court fees.[60]

In the course of the eighteenth century defendants had occasionally been allowed to defend *in forma pauperis* in criminal proceedings in the King's Bench, on the analogy of the 11 Henry VII, c. 12.[61] It is not clear, however, from the reports of such cases whether the judges regarded the procedure as available in criminal cases generally, or only in cases pending in the King's Bench.

In 1818 a prisoner called Stokes, convicted of murder at York Assizes, made application in the King's Bench to sue out a writ of error *in forma pauperis*. Parke B, before whom the application came, said that he was not aware of any precedent for such a proceeding, but was not prepared to say that it could not be done.[62] He suggested that a simpler course would be

---

[58] (1873) 7 Ir LT 3, and see evidence of O'Shaugnessy before Select Committee on the Poor Prisoners Defence Bill above.

[59] *Doe d Bennett v Hale* (1850) 19 LJQB 353.

[60] Chitty, *Criminal Law*, i, 413.

[61] *R v Wright* (1736) 2 Str 1041; *R v Morgan* (1745) 2 Str 1214.

[62] *R v Stokes* (1818) 3 C & K 189.

to get the trial judge to reserve the case. This was in the end done, and no final ruling on the application was ever given.

In *Page* in 1831 and *Nicholson* in 1840 defendants were granted leave to defend *in forma pauperis*.[63] Predictably, both were prosecutions in the King's Bench, the first for perjury, the second for libel. After this little is heard of *in forma pauperis* in criminal cases, but it continued to be treated by text writers as a means whereby poor prisoners could obtain free legal representation.[64]

Whatever its theoretical availability, it appears in practice to have been a dead letter. How little used it was is demonstrated by a leading article which appeared in the *Solicitors' Journal* in 1856, suggesting that the procedure be extended to criminal cases.[65] The problem, as much as anything, may have been prisoners' ignorance of the right. While old hands would know of the court's power to assign counsel, there must have been few either amongst the criminal population or amongst the hangers-on around gaols and police offices, who had heard of this King's Bench procedure with its Latin name and its requirement for a supporting affidavit.

6. The Dock Brief and the IP system

The bar, had it chosen to do so, could have solved the problem of the undefended prisoner by sanctioning a free representation scheme of the type urged on it repeatedly during the century. In fact (apart from its cooperation in the assignment system) the only concession it made to the plight of the poor prisoner was to permit counsel, in such cases, to accept briefs direct from the prisoner, his friends or family.

The rule of etiquette that a barrister might not accept instructions save through an attorney was, at the start of the nineteenth century, relatively new and was not regarded as applying to all species of work.[66] In particular, it was generally believed not to apply to non-contentious work. As late as 1888 the Attorney-General, in a letter to *The Times*, repeated an opinion, given by his predecessor in 1872, that it was not a breach of etiquette for counsel to deal with the client direct in non-contentious matters.[67]

So far as the criminal courts were concerned, it was commonplace as late as the 1840s, at least in London, for barristers to accept briefs for both

---

[63] *R v Page* (1831) 1 Dowl 507; *R v Nicholson* (1840) 8 Dowl PC 489; 4 Jur 506.

[64] Archbold (20th edn, 1886) devotes four lines to the assignment of counsel in capital cases but over a page to defence *in forma pauperis*.

[65] Sol J 702.

[66] See 'The Bar, The Attorney and the Client' (pamphlet 1852); (1844) 3 LT 500; (1845) 5 LT 359 and (1850) 15 LT 173; (1860–61) 36 LT 462 and 492; the Bar meeting reported in *The Times*, 25 February 1852; and (1887–88) 13 Law Mag (4th series) 195.

[67] *The Times*, 29 and 30 June 1888; also report of the Bar Council's Professional Conduct Committee, 29 January 1897.

prosecution and defence from the client direct. This came out into the open in 1844 when two Old Bailey barristers, who had acted for a prosecutor without an attorney, found themselves severely censured both by the court and the press.[68] The pair sought to defend themselves against the criticism by asserting that it had long been the practice, both at the Central Criminal Court and the Middlesex Sessions, for counsel to accept briefs for both prosecution and defence without the intervention of an attorney; indeed on 24 September of that year a meeting of the Central Criminal Court Bar Mess passed a resolution asserting the existence of a custom to that effect.[69] Significantly, neither the resolution nor the assertions of the two barristers at the centre of the row were contradicted by any senior member of the bar.[70]

In the debate which followed, the legal periodicals were firm in their condemnation of counsel who conducted prosecutions without an attorney,[71] but they found the matter of defence briefs less easy. The *Law Times*, in a leader on 19 October 1844, was prepared to accept that acting for a prisoner without an attorney was permissible, provided that the brief was handed to counsel by the prisoner over the bar. In the following month, in a case at the Old Bailey where it turned out that counsel had been retained for a prisoner called Ball not by an attorney but by the governor of Newgate, Rolfe B refused to condemn the proceeding, despite prosecuting counsel's assertion that the more proper course was for the prisoner to brief counsel from the dock.[72]

In 1850 the practice of counsel acting for prisoners without an attorney received apparent judicial approval in *Doe d Bennett v Hale* with Lord Chief Justice Campbell's observation that 'in criminal cases it is conceded that the practice of a barrister not to plead unless instructed by an attorney does not prevail ...'[73] It is arguable that Campbell was merely referring to the practice of judges assigning counsel to poor prisoners – indeed the passage concludes with a reference to the practice. That is not how his words were interpreted by the *Law Times*, which, in a leader discussing the decision, spoke of it being 'common practice on some circuits, as on that of North Wales for instance, for a prisoner when arraigned, to hand a fee to counsel who was bound to defend him without the requirement of a brief and an attorney'.[74] The justification which the *Law Times* offered for the practice was one which a correspondent had offered nearly six years earlier, necessity: it would be manifestly a hardship on a poor prisoner to be deprived of the

---

[68] The cases giving rise to the scandal were *R v Pond*, *The Times*, 23 September 1844 and *R v Thompson* (1844) 3 LT 500 and see generally (1844) 3 LT 500–01 and (1844–45) 4 LT 7, 8, 12, 25 and 44.

[69] (1844–45) 4 LT, 8 and 44.

[70] (1844) 3 LT, 501.

[71] (1844–45) 4 LT 45 and (1844) 32 Law Mag (1st series) 175 and 178.

[72] *R v Ball*, *The Times*, 25 October 1844 and also (1844) 8 JP 721.

[73] (1850) 19 LJQB 353.

[74] (1850) 15 LT 174.

protection of defence by counsel because he was unable to raise a double fee and, in truth, defences could usually be conducted almost as well without a brief as with one.[75] In fact, the practice of accepting briefs from prisoners direct was certainly, so far as London was concerned, one of long standing. In 1836 a report on the state of Newgate Prison disclosed that two wardsmen (both serving convicts) were permitted to draw briefs for fellow prisoners for a fee of five shillings per brief, which they were allowed to retain.[76] Such briefs when drawn would then be placed in the hands of counsel either before trial by the prisoner's family or friends or by the prisoner himself on arraignment.

One species of defence brief, which appears to have evolved from the practice of briefing counsel direct, was the dock brief or 'docker'.[77] In the twentieth century the dock brief represented a method whereby a prisoner could secure the services of counsel for a nominal fee. Its essential features were these: counsel was briefed by the prisoner in open court, the prisoner being entitled to have the services of any counsel in court who was not already engaged in the case, upon tendering a fee of one guinea plus clerk's fees (after 1951 two guineas plus clerk's fees). As in a case where the court assigned counsel, there was no attorney and no written brief, save where the prisoner had chosen to write one or have one written for him.

The Report of the Committee on Legal Aid and Advice in 1945 treated the dock brief as an institution which had existed from time immemorial. Abel-Smith and Stevens speak of its having existed for many centuries before the general right to counsel was conceded. Neither cites any evidence to support these assertions.[78] In fact, there is good reason for supposing that the dock brief is far more modern than this. It is important to begin by ridding oneself of the notion that the dock brief represented a means of obtaining representation for a purely nominal sum. True, that is what it had become by the mid twentieth century, due to the ravages of inflation, but in the nineteenth century the fee payable on a dock brief was anything but derisory. It represented in the first half of the century more than a week's wage for a working man.[79] It was the minimum brief fee which a barrister was allowed to accept, and it represented the standard brief fee

---

[75] (1844–45) 4 LT 25; see also a letter to like effect in *The Times*, 30 September 1844 (Bar etiquette).

[76] Reply of the Inspectors to the Report of the Court of Aldermen so far as relates to the Prison of Newgate, PP (1836) (486), XLII, 283, pp. 2 and 6.

[77] Halsbury's *Laws* (4th edn), iii, para. 1141; as to the fee of £1 3s 6d, see Bar Council, *Annual Statement 1906/7*; the privilege of choosing from the counsel in court appears occasionally to have been afforded to prisoners assigned counsel by the court, see *R v Thomson and Mullaly* above).

[78] PP 1944–45 (Cmnd) 6641) V, 187, p 6; Abel Smith & Stevens, *Lawyers and the Courts*, 32.

[79] The dockers' strike of 1889 was for a minimum wage of 6d per hour; see also (1901) 10 (NS) *Cornhill Magazine* 446 and (1882) 74 LT 32.

being paid for prosecutions at the Old Bailey, Middlesex Sessions, Assizes and county Quarter Sessions.[80]

The size of the fee alone indicates that it almost certainly had a nineteenth-century origin, and indeed there are other reasons for so dating it. In the first place, it is difficult to believe that the right to deliver a dock brief can have antedated the right to employ counsel in felony cases. So far as felony is concerned, it appears that it was only in the 1720s that the courts began to allow prisoners to have counsel to assist them to examine witnesses. Secondly, one finds no references to dock briefs in any of the early nineteenth-century practitioners' text books, not even in Chitty's *Criminal Law*, which discusses in minute detail the assignment of counsel in treason and defence *in forma pauperis*.[81] Thirdly, the earliest references to something resembling a dock brief come from the 1840s. Fourthly, there was the case of *Ball* (1844) referred to above. This was significant for two reasons. First, for the fact that the governor of Newgate thought it necessary to shoulder the burden of briefing counsel for prisoners who could afford to pay a brief fee but not an attorney's fee. If the dock brief was then a known and well-established right, what need was there for him to do so? Also, for the comment made on the case in the *Justice of the Peace:*

It was not foreseen [by the aldermen when they barred all but attorneys and their properly authorised clerks from Newgate] that many a prisoner might raise a guinea to pay a counsel's fee without being able to pay an attorney, and that all who were in this situation would consequently remain without a counsel.[82]

Then there is a comment made by Phillipps, the barrister and text-writer, in his evidence to the 1835 Select Committee upon the proposal that counsel should be assigned to all poor prisoners desiring representation: 'Where are [such counsel] to get their instructions? Are they to communicate with the dock? That would be rather new in the practice of the Bar.'[83]

Finally, there is the fact that, in the nineteenth century, some very elementary rules concerning dock briefs were uncertain. For example, was a prisoner charged in a magistrates' court entitled to a dock brief? Was counsel entitled to take a fee of more than one guinea for a dock brief? Was counsel entitled, where the prisoner was charged on more than one indictment, to a separate one guinea fee for each indictment?[84] This scarcely suggests an institution of much antiquity.

---

[80] *The Times*, 17 December 1850 and 26 August 1837; and the Report of Departmental Committee on Allowances to Prosecutors and Witnesses etc., PP 1903 (Cmnd 254, 264) VII, 583; as to willingness of counsel to undertake defences for one guinea, see *R v Answell and Simpson*, *The Times*, 27 March 1878.

[81] Chitty, *Criminal Law*, i, 407–14; Archbold (20th edn, 1886) is wholly silent about dock briefs.

[82] (1844) 8 JP 722.

[83] PP 1835 (HL 130) XLVI, 317 (at p 8 of his evidence).

[84] Bar Council, *Annual Statement 1900–1*.

A feature of the dock brief which requires explanation is why the briefing of counsel took place in court rather than beforehand. A partial explanation is offered by a letter, published in *The Times* during the 1844 controversy, from a correspondent signing himself Veritas.[85] The letter, after arguing strongly in favour of prisoners being allowed to instruct counsel direct, made this point: if the prisoner delivered his brief to counsel and the grand jury then threw out the bill, the prisoner would lose the brief fee, for the invariable rule of the bar was never to return brief fees come what may. Accordingly, a poor prisoner, who could not afford to lose a guinea, was well advised to hold back his brief until he knew that a bill had been found (by no means a certainty with grand juries at the Old Bailey in the first half of the century, even in clear cases). Taking this course usually meant counsel being briefed in court. Nor is it difficult to imagine other circumstances which could compel a prisoner to brief counsel in open court, for example difficulty in raising the fee.

The dock brief appears simply to have represented one of two alternatives open to a prisoner who wanted to brief counsel but either could not afford or did not wish to have the services of an attorney. The first was to have his friends or family brief counsel direct before trial. This had the advantage that counsel would have plenty of time to prepare the case, but the prisoner risked losing the fee if the grand jury threw out the bill. The second was to leave the briefing of counsel until his case was called on, which was the course he would have to take where the fee had only been raised at the last minute, and the choice which he might wish to make in order to ensure that he did not pay over a fee unnecessarily.[86]

If the dock brief offered the prisoner the opportunity of avoiding paying out a brief fee unnecessarily, its obvious disadvantage was that counsel instructed in this way had little time to take proper instructions from the client. Some prisoners would hand over with their fee a prepared statement of the case, but many did not; in which case counsel would have to work from such scrambled instructions as he might be able to get over the dock rails. Some counsel made light of these difficulties. It was Montagu Williams' boast that the only defence brief he ever required was a copy of the depositions.[87] In days when prisoners could not give evidence, such a robust approach certainly left counsel free to develop what he considered the most promising line of defence, without the embarrassment of being tramelled by instructions from the client. The other advantage of the dock brief to the very poor was that the fee, although far from derisory, was low – the lowest for which a barrister's services could be got – and remained unchanged

---

85 *The Times*, 28 October 1844.
86 The dock brief also prevented swindling. As to the common forms of swindle see (1844) 8 JP 721.
87 Per the recorder of London in *R v Nunzio Calendo* (1904) 68 JP 40.

during the nineteenth century despite inflation. Whatever its merits, at no time during the second half of the nineteenth century does the dock brief appear to have been particularly popular wth prisoners. Some evidence of how relatively uncommon it was is to be found in the periodic complaints in the last quarter of the century that prisoners were ignorant of their right to a dock brief.[88]

In London the dock brief was overshadowed by a rival system which (like the dock brief) cut out the need for a solicitor, but which (unlike the dock brief) allowed counsel time to get up the case properly. This was the IP (In Person) system. A barrister's clerk who joined the profession in the 1870s described in his autobiography how, during the 1870s, 1880s and 1890s, IP work, although confined to the less reputable of the profession, yielded those who had it a rich living. He described the way the system worked thus:

> After a prisoner had been committed for trial, his friends would procure, at the cost of a few shillings, a copy of the depositions ... hand them over to the barrister of their choice, who would accept them as a brief, decide if witnesses were to be called and fight the case in court for a small fee paid in cash. The fee ... was generally made up of shillings or florins not always too clean.[89]

He goes on to say that IP defences were eventually stopped when abuses crept in, and large IP fees were taken for work which obviously should have been done in a more conventional manner.[90] What he says about the taking of large fees for IP work receives some confirmation in the proceedings of the Select Committee on the Poor Prisoners' Defence Bill. One of the suggestions put to Grantham J, when giving evidence to the committee, was that the normal fee for an IP brief was five to ten guineas. Grantham was in fact able to offer little information about the matter. He said that he thought the IP system a lot less used than fifteen or twenty years before when he had heard a good deal of it, adding that it was a form of practice which had been very much discouraged by the bar, but he was unable to contradict his questioner's claim that there were still about half a dozen IP cases every session.[91]

The IP system appears to have represented simply a continuation of the tradition which existed in the 1830s, to which the Central Criminal Court bar vouched in 1844. Its survival was no doubt due to uncertainty as to the scope of the prohibition upon counsel receiving instructions from a client direct, which until the end of the century was far from total. How much uncertainty there was about the matter, even as late as 1900, is demonstrated by an incident in October of that year. A member of the Manchester bar

---

[88] See (1903–4) 116 LT 493, and the Report of the Special Committee of the Bar Council on Dock Defences, 1900.

[89] F. W. Ashley, *My Sixty Years in the Law*, 81.

[90] Ibid. 82.

[91] PP 1903 (254, 264) VII, 583.

telegraphed the secretary to the Bar Council, asking whether it would be in order to accept a brief from a woman to defend her husband in the police court the next day. The secretary telegraphed back 'believe counsel so entitled; have no direct decision here'.[92] Before the year was out the practice had been condemned by the Council, but what is revealing is the secretary's reaction when confronted with the problem. The Report of the Committee of the Bar Council on Dock Defences, published late in the same year, mentioned IP defences in police courts, observing that the practice, which at one time had prevailed in London to a considerable extent, was highly undesirable and had, it was believed, almost ceased.[93]

7. Charity and Other Sources of Assistance

For the prisoner who was destitute and could not afford to brief counsel, his only hope of representation (assignment apart) lay in private charity or the efforts of his friends.[94] In 1896 it was out of money raised by her friends that counsel was, at the last minute, procured for Mrs Dyer, the baby farmer.[95] Even after the passing of the Poor Prisoners' Defence Act (1903) one still finds examples of prisoners (especially those charged with murder) being defended out of a fund raised by subscription.[96] Amongst those most likely to have their defence funded by friends were members of criminal gangs (usually the money was raised by holding a 'benefit' in a public house).[97]

For those who had no friends, or no friends able to raise money on their behalf, charity was an occasional provider of representation. In 1813 the murderer Cornwell was defended at the expense of the committing magistrate, who had been moved by his complaint that he was friendless and unable to fee counsel.[98] In 1844 a prisoner at Berkshire Sessions had his counsel's fee paid by a member of the bar who took pity on him.[99] In the same year, during a piracy trial at the Old Bailey, one of the jurors trying the case offered to pay for counsel for the prisoners, an offer which Abinger LCB declined on the ground that no counsel could do justice to a case who came into it half way through.[100] In 1873 a local man came forward to offer a substantial sum for the defence of the West Auckland poisoner Mary Ann Cotton, when he heard that her furniture had had to be sold to provide her with counsel.[101]

---

92 Bar Council, *Annual Statement 1900–1*.

93 Published 21 November 1900.

94 PD 1859 CLIII, 402; see also *R v Boreham*, *The Times*, 5 February 1896; and *R v Prince*, *The Times*, 14 January 1898.

95 F. W. Ashley, *My Sixty Years in the Law*, 177.

96 See e.g. (1904) 68 JP 100, 294 (*R v Samways*) and 533 (*R v Hunt*).

97 See Montagu Williams, *Leaves of a Life*, 90, and *R v Buck*, *The Times*, 1 March 1860.

98 *R v Cornwell*, G. T. Wilkinson, *The Newgate Calendar* (1963 abridgement), iii, 45–46.

99 *R v Jackson*, *The Times*, 23 October 1844.

100 *R v McGregor and Lambert* (1844) 1 Cox 346.

101 R. Lambert, *When Justice Faltered*, 128–29.

In the first half of the century, particularly, one comes upon instances of members of the bar stepping forward to defend unrepresented prisoners for nothing. In 1801, at the Old Bailey trial of a woman called Harvey for the murder of her child, the 'prisoner appearing very much affected', counsel humanely volunteered to defend her.[102] In 1831 at Chelmsford Assizes, while the trial of a fourteen-year-old boy for murder was under way, William Clarkson, a London barrister in a substantial way of practice, intervened to offer his services to the lad, who would otherwise have gone undefended.[103] Even as later as the 1880s one finds Gerald Geoghegan, one of the best-known juniors at the criminal bar, stepping forward to offer his assistance to a fellow Irishman.[104] Such interventions, since they were subject to judicial approval, were presumably regarded as analagous to an assignment and therefore no breach of etiquette.

From time to time complaints appeared in the press of barristers doing criminal work for less than the minimum brief fee. Usually touting rather than charity was the motivation here, but not always: Marshall Hall is said to have accepted a dock brief at a fee of less than a guinea because he had taken pity on the accused.[105] Where the charge was capital, a foreigner without means would sometimes be provided with counsel by his government.

One of the few examples of systematic charity in the matter of prisoners' representation was to be found at the Central Criminal Court. There had in 1835 been the scheme of Sheriff Salomon. He had paid a Mr Yorston, out of his own pocket, to attend at Newgate to take from prisoners written statements of their defences, so that they could be handed to such counsel as they selected or to the court by which they were tried. Yorston had also to advise him of the names of the prisoners who appeared to be innocent, but who were without defence, and for such prisoners he had retained counsel at his own expense. The scheme worked well but came to an end after only one session due to opposition from the profession.[106] A less ambitious but more enduring scheme was that, dating back at least to the 1820s, whereby the sheriffs of London and Middlesex intervened in selected cases to provide counsel from prisoners who would otherwise have been unrepresented. The first case in which *The Times* trial reports mention counsel being so retained is the trial of Sheen in 1827 for murder.[107] In the main the sheriffs' intervention was confined to murder cases, but occasionally one finds them providing counsel for a poor prisoner charged

---

[102] *R v Harvey*, *The Times*, 2 November 1801.

[103] *R v Bell*, *The Times*, 30 July, 1831; see also *R v Nuttall*, *The Times*, 8 September 1817, and *R v Probert* above.

[104] *R v Nash*, *The Times*, 24 September 1884.

[105] (1852) 48 Law Mag (1st series) 229 and (1871) 51 LT 327; Marjoribanks, *Life of Marshall Hall KC*, 35–36.

[106] (1843) 1 LT 635.

[107] *R v Sheen*, *The Times*, 14 July 1827; also *R v Calken*, *The Times*, 9 January 1832 (child murder).

with a lesser crime. In 1851, for instance, they provided counsel for a foreigner charged with theft,[108] and for a 'strange sickly looking girl' called Adams charged with perjury.[109] In 1859 they briefed counsel to defend a girl called Sloman charged with concealment of birth.[110]

Where the sheriffs did intervene, no attorney was employed, the attorney's work being done by one of the under-sheriffs. This was done, for example, in *Gould* (1844), where the under-sheriff swore an affidavit in support of an application for postponement and was present in court giving instructions to counsel during the application.[111]

During the course of an Old Bailey trial in November 1892, counsel referred to a fund maintained by the sheriffs out of which the fees for counsel were paid.[112] It is not possible to identify with certainty the fund referred to but it may have been the Sheriffs' Fund, a charitable fund founded in 1807–08 to help distressed prisoners and their families. The London system may not have been unique. A scattering of cases suggests that it was in the second half of the century being copied outside London and Middlesex.[113]

Towards the end of the century another source of representation for those charged with major crime was the press. Newspapers would from time to time set up defence funds for prisoners whose plight had caught the public imagination. One of the earliest examples was that established in 1888 by the *Sussex Daily News* for Sabina Tilley, charged with child murder.[114] Another form of press involvement was less desirable: that whereby those accused of sensational crimes sold their life stories to a newspaper in return for the funds to employ fashionable counsel.[115]

108 *R v Anon.*, *The Times*, 27 October 1851.

109 *R v Adams*, *The Times*, 27 November 1851.

110 *R v Sloman*, *The Times*, 1 February 1859; also *R v Parker*, *The Times*, 23 September 1854 (attempted murder).

111 *R v Gould*, *The Times*, 11,14 and 15 April, 1840; also *R v Waller Balch and Noble*, *The Times*, 17 November 1892.

112 *R v Waller Balch and Noble*, *The Times*, 19 November 1892.

113 *R v Gould*, *The Times*, 1 March 1862 (sheriff of Berks); *R v Brown*, *The Times*, 29 March 1864 (sheriff of Suffolk); and *R v Gaydon*, *The Times*, 24 October 1879 (sheriff of Essex); all three were murder cases.

114 Majoribanks, *Life at Marshall Hall KC*, 51–52

115 The Home Office was always unhappy about this practice. In 1915, in the case of Smith ('Brides in the Bath' murderer), it refused to allow the prisoner to assign the copyright in his projected life story to a newspaper (a refusal which led to a strong letter to the Home Secretary from Marshall Hall, the counsel who was to have been retained out of the funds the newspaper had agreed to provide, see Marjoribanks, *The Life of Marshall Hall KC*, 328–33). The Home Office concern was well founded. By the 1930s some newspapers were no longer content with life stories but were demanding, as the price of legal representation for notorious murderers, a sealed letter confessing guilt not to be opened until after the prisoner's execution, see PRO, HO 45/2, 1330; and R. M. Jackson, *The Machinery of Justice in England* (4th edn), 139.

8. The Amicus Curiae and the Mackenzie Adviser

For prisoners who took their trial undefended (as so many did) the only possible sources of assistance other than the judge were the *amicus curiae* and what in the twentieth century has become known as the Mackenzie adviser. The practice of counsel present in court intervening as *amicus curiae* to suggest points of law in favour of an unrepresented prisoner was of considerable antiquity;[116] such interventions were common at busy courts well into the 1850s.[117] It is not hard to understand why. At such courts there would at any one time be sitting in court counsel who were not engaged in the case being tried, some waiting to be called on, others briefless and trying to improve their skills by watching their seniors and to get their faces known amongst the attorneys (all the while hoping against hope that a brief might come their way). An experienced counsel would be unlikely to stand by and watch a prisoner convicted for want of anyone to draw the judge's attention to a point of law in his favour, while for a briefless barrister intervention would be a means of getting noticed and gaining experience on his feet.

The right of a prisoner to have a friend sit near him 'to take notes, quietly make suggestions and offer advice' was upheld by the King's Bench in 1831.[118] The privilege appears, however, to have been little exercised in trials on indictment.

9. Reform

By the 1890s the pressure to remove the accused's incompetence to testify, coupled with the increasing number of statutes which actually did so, made the issue of legal representation even more urgent. It was obviously only a matter of time before the government got a Prisoners' Evidence Bill on the statute book. When it did so, every unrepresented prisoner would face the problems which undefended prisoners already experienced in those cases where statute made them competent. In addition to having to cross-examine and state his case to the jury unaided, he would have to make (without legal advice) the crucial decision whether to give evidence. If he went into the witness-box without counsel to take him through his evidence in chief and to re-examine, there was great danger of his defence (and, in particular his

---

[116] Dalton, *Country Justice* (1635 edn), 275, cited examples from the reigns of Henry IV and Elizabeth 1.

[117] PD 1834 XXIV, 167; (1862) 6 Sol Jo, 860; for examples of counsel intervening as *amicus*, see e.g. *R v Skinner, The Times*, 10 February 1834; *R v Greensmith, The Times*, 7 August 1837; *R v Hawtin* (1836) 7 C & P 281.

[118] *Collier v Hicks* (1831) 2 B & Ad 663 cited with approval in *Mackenzie* (1971) P 33 whence the institution derives its name; see also *R v Jones, The Times*, 27 March 1843, and PD 1843 LXIX, 189.

answer to prosecution cross-examination) not being adequately laid before the jury, even if the judge intervened to assist.

The matter had first been taken up in 1883 when Leighton had moved an amendment to the Criminal Code Bill that no Bill would be satisfactory which did not provide for the assignment of counsel to poor prisoners.[119] In 1893 the Society of Chairmen of Quarter Sessions in England and Wales passed a resolution to the effect that provision should be made in the Evidence in Criminal Cases Bill, then going through Parliament, for the assignment of counsel to poor prisoners who desired to be legally represented, such counsel to be paid out of public funds. The Lord Chancellor, believing that such a clause might remove some of the objections to the Bill, decided to refer the question to the judges. Of the judges only Cave J was wholeheartedly in favour of the proposal, the attitude of the majority being that reform was not needed and was likely to lead to a host of evils, not least of which would be waste of court time and great public expense. Faced with such an overwhelming majority against the proposal, it was quietly dropped.[120]

In 1894 the *Law Journal* took up the question again, suggesting that in the case of poor prisoners the conventional docker fee ought to be paid by the county.[121] The matter was next raised during the debate on the 1897 Criminal Evidence Bill, when the MP for Leeds proposed that the Bill should include provision for the defence of poor prisoners.[122] The proposal was lost but led the Senior Treasury Counsel, Sir Harry Poland QC, to argue, in a letter to *The Times*, that a system of assigning counsel alone would not meet the need. It was essential that a solicitor should also be assigned to get up the case. During the Committee Stage of the 1898 Bill an unsuccessful attempt was made by Gibson Bowles to move an amendment providing for the assignment of counsel to poor prisoners.[123]

While the Bill was on its way through Parliament, pressure for reform was mounting. At a meeting of the Bar Council on 17 January 1898 a motion was proposed by Lord Robert Cecil: 'That in the opinion of the Council it is desirable that every prisoner should be defended by counsel'. The next month, the Council appointed a special committee to report upon the matter. During the following months, the committee made extensive inquiries as to the practice in other parts of the English-speaking world. The replies made interesting reading. In Scotland, agents (i.e. solicitors) 'for the poor' were appointed annually by the Faculty of Advocates; the agents visited the gaols and 'counsel for the poor' were then instructed by them, appearing at trial without fee. In Victoria in Australia by Order in Council all persons without

---

[119] PD 1883 CCLXXVIII, 97–98.
[120] PRO, HO 45/9784/B2907E.
[121] (1894) 29 LJ 275.
[122] PD 1897 XLVIII, 813 (Walton).
[123] PD 1898 LX, 720–21, and LXII, 748.

means charged with capital offences, and all aboriginals charged with an indictable offence, might on application to the sheriff be provided with the services of such barrister and solicitor as they might select, the fees being paid out of monies voted by Parliament. Substantially the same practice obtained in New South Wales and New Zealand. In Queensland, however, only aboriginals and Polynesians were defended at government expense. In Canada, it was the practice of the superior courts to assign counsel to prisoners who were unable to afford to retain one, but the services of such counsel were honorary and unpaid. In Massachusetts, prisoners accused of capital crime were defended at the expense of the government by counsel assigned by the court.

In November the committee reported.[124] It came out strongly in favour of free legal representation for poor prisoners. In 1899 the annual general meeting of the bar approved the report, passing a resolution (framed in words borrowed from the report) that: 'it is in the interests of all prisoners (considering their interests alone) that they should be defended by counsel, and that the passing of the Criminal Evidence Act (1898) renders it more desirable than before that they should be so defended'. However, the resolution having been passed, the Bar Council took no steps to secure its implementation. Eventually the Dorset Sessions bar gave a lead. In 1902 they put into operation at their Sessions a free representation scheme based on the Scottish system. According to a letter published in *The Times* in April 1903, the scheme was a great success. Even in the absence of assistance of solicitors, declared the writer,

> remarkable results were achieved; it is considered that at least five persons were acquitted who would otherwise have been convicted, in cases involving either indecent assault, housebreaking or uttering false coins. The length of sittings was not increased because in clear cases prisoners pleaded guilty on the advice of counsel, and relied upon an appeal for the mitigation of sentence.[125]

Unfortunately, when news of the scheme got abroad, it was attacked by other members of the bar as improper and a breach of etiquette. The matter was referred by the Sessions bar to the Attorney-General, and he recommended them to discontinue it which they did.

The Dorset scheme had created a very favourable impression, and in 1903 a group of barrister MPs introduced a Poor Prisoners' Defence Bill, providing for a national scheme of free representation for all prisoners committed for trial.[126] Any prisoner not having the resources to instruct counsel might apply to have solicitor and counsel allotted to him. The solicitor should be allotted from a list, kept in counties by the clerk of the peace and in boroughs

[124] (1899) 63 JP 115.
[125] *The Times*, 14 April (letter) and 27 April 1903 (leader).
[126] See PD 1903 CXIX, 703.

by the town clerk, of solicitors who had given notice of their willingness to undertake poor prisoners work without fee. The Bill received an enthusiastic reception in *The Times* and its correspondence columns,[127] but it was attacked by Poland and some of the judges. Poland complained that the scheme was unworkable and would fail for want of solicitors prepared to work without fee, arguing that it was anomalous that it was limited to proceedings on indictment.[128] There was also opposition amongst the London bar: it was declared unnecessary and undesirable by the Central Criminal Court Bar Mess and unworkable by the Bar Messes of Middlesex and the County of London Sessions.[129]

Despite this opposition, the Bill was referred to a Select Committee. The committee, in its Report, accepted the principle that a prisoner without means ought to be in no worse a position to establish his innocence than the prisoner who was able to pay for legal assistance.[130] It also acknowledged that, although it was the business of the judge to see that the prisoner's defence was fully developed, the judge was not in a position to do this as efficiently as counsel, because he had no opportunity of communicating with the prisoner and ascertaining the details of the defence. It stressed that the problem was particularly acute where, as at county Quarter Sessions, the judge was not legally qualified. Although it accepted the principle of free representation, the committee recommended that the Bill be altered in two respects. First, solicitors and counsel defending a poor prisoner under the Bill were to be paid out of funds provided by Parliament. Secondly, legal assistance should only be afforded to a prisoner where this seemed desirable, having regard to the nature of the defence set up by him in evidence given or statements made at the committal hearing.

The requirement that the prisoner should disclose his defence at committal was something which had been urged upon the committee by the judges who,[131] ever since the coming into force of the 1898 Act, had been inveighing with regularity and ferocity against the practice of prisoners 'reserving their defence'.[132] It was, they argued, against the prisoner's interests and calculated to lead to sham defences.

All of this, of course, ignored the fact that, under Jervis's Act, a prisoner was at committal required to be cautioned against speaking. However, the judicial hostility to the reserved defence carried the committee with it: an honest defence ought to be disclosed at the first opportunity, and a prisoner

---

127 PP 1903 (285) III, 817.

128 *The Times*, 2 April and 3 August, 1903 (letters); see also letter from Poland dated 12 August 1883 in PRO, LCO2/148.

129 PRO, LC02/148.

130 PP 1903 (254, 264) VII, 583.

131 Ibid., evidence, Q 625.

132 See *R v Simpson*, *The Times*, 24 November 1898; *R v Larder*, *The Times*, 26 January 1899; (1903) 67 JP 557, 571 and 583; and (1904) 68 JP 557.

not disclosing his defence at committal was not deserving of legal assistance paid for by the state.

The Bill, as amended, received the royal assent on 14 August 1903 with a commencement date of 1 January 1904. Section 2 provided for the making of rules to carry the Act into effect, and work upon the rules began in late 1903. It did not go smoothly. When the draft rules were produced they contained a rule intended to ensure that prisoners were left in no doubt that disclosure of defence was a precondition to legal aid. The rule in question (draft rule 3) provided that the examining magistrates might, after delivering to the prisoner the statutory caution under section 18 of the 1848 Act, explain to him that they had the power to certify that the case was one in which legal aid should be given at the public expense – if the nature of his defence, as disclosed in his statement or evidence, satisfied them that it was desirable to do so, and it appeared that he had not himself the necessary means. Both the bar and the Law Society protested strongly against the rule, arguing that it would practically compel the prisoner to make a statement committing himself to a line of defence and would be contrary to the statutory caution.[133] There was no answer to the point and the rule was dropped.

The reception the Act got in the higher courts when it came into force was very mixed. None of the judges who saw fit to comment on its provisions welcomed it as a long overdue reform. At Middlesex Sessions the judge, Sir Ralph Littler QC, told the grand jury that the Act was useless and 'probably mischievous as well'. At Manchester Assizes Bigham J painted the Act as being positively disadvantageous to prisoners: it robbed them of a line of defence which in the past had served them well, namely 'I am a poor man and cannot get the assistance which a rich man can get. Therefore my case is not put before the jury as it ought to be'.[134]

From the Lord Chief Justice it received a favourable reception, but not because it conferred a boon on prisoners. To him its merit was that it compelled prisoners to disclose their defence: the scheme and motive of the legislature, he declared (adding that this was the opinion of his brethren too) was

> to induce innocent people, who are unjustly charged and who have a true defence to disclose their defence at the earliest possible moment, and to induce them to abstain from the practice, which has worked so much harm in the past, of prisoners under all circumstances whether innocent or guilty reserving their defence.[135]

The *Justice of the Peace*, when reporting this speech, commented: 'judges

---

[133] PRO, LCO2/148.

[134] (1904) 68 JP 29 and 76; the *Law Times* was also unenthusiastic, see (1903) 115 LT 2.

[135] (1904) 68 JP 557. He had expressed the same view earlier that year at Hertford, see (1904) 68 JP 100.

generally seem to think that the Act was passed to assist only innocent people unjustly charged'. Other judges contented themselves with indicating that they proposed to construe the Act restrictively. Clearly, attitudes had changed little since 1883.

13

The Indictment

'Mr Montagu Williams ... anticipating that a true bill might be found in the Empion case applied to the Recorder in that event to appoint Wednesday in the February session for ... the trial. Mr Williams said he made the application on the ground of the formidable dimensions of the indictment, which he said, amid some laughter, he understood had taken three learned gentlemen to draw and three other learned gentlemen to carry into court'. *The Times*, Central Criminal Court report, 12 January 1875.

1. Finding the Indictment

Proceedings at the court of trial began with the finding of the bill of indictment by the grand jury. The grand jury was a filter whose purpose was to weed out weak and baseless cases. Only a grand jury could find a bill of indictment, and a prosecutor seeking a bill had to lay his evidence before it for its scrutiny. It consisted of not less than twelve and not more than twenty-three jurors and reached its decisions by majority vote.[1] Assize grand juries were drawn in the main from the county magistracy.[2] At the Old Bailey and Quarter Sessions, however, the grand jury consisted of common jurors.[3] Care was usually taken to ensure that those selected were, by rateable value of description of a better class than the ordinary common juryman.[4] Even so it was not unusual to find Quarter Sessions grand jurors signing indictments with a cross because they could not read.[5]

At the start of the session for which they had been summoned, the grand jurors would be sworn and the judge would then deliver his charge to them, in which he would give them legal directions about any case likely to give difficulty.[6]

---

[1] At least twelve jurors had to concur in any majority verdict: Hawk 2 P C, c. 25, s 15.

[2] J. F. & H. Stephen, *Digest of Criminal Procedure* (London, 1883), 187; this was however a matter of practice.

[3] By s 1 of the Juries Act, 1825 the qualification for grand jurors at county Quarter Sessions was the same as for common jurors. The Act laid down no qualification for Assize or borough Sessions grand jurors.

[4] See Report of the Departmental Committee on the Jury Laws, PP 1913 (Cmnd 6817) XXX, 403, para 58.

[5] (1845) 9 JP 207 (letter).

[6] Until 1856 they were sworn in open court by the common crier, often whilst a trial was going on; the Grand Juries Act, 1856, substituted a more seemly procedure; henceforth they were to be sworn in the grand jury room by the grand jury foreman.

The witnesses in the various cases would then be sworn in batches in open court, and sent along to the grand jury room to wait their turn to be examined by the jury. The examination was conducted in private and in the accused's absence. If in a case the jury were satisfied that there was prima facie evidence of guilt, they would indorse the bill 'true bill' and it would be carried into court to be tried. If it did not so satisfy them, they would indorse it 'no true bill', in which event the accused would, at the end of the session, be discharged by proclamation (which would usually be an end to the prosecution).[7]

In the first half of the century a complaint frequently levelled at London grand juries was that they regularly threw out clear cases which had already passed the scrutiny of examining stipendiary magistrates. In the 1820s and the 1830s they threw out 10 per cent of the bills sent before them. Indeed, so bad was their reputation in this respect that it earned them the nickname 'The Hope of London Thieves'.[8]

For this state of affairs, there were several reasons.[9] First, London grand jurors, not being magistrates, had little legal knowledge and no experience of examining witnesses, and were thus poorly equipped for the task they had to perform. They also had to 'work in the dark': they were not furnished with the depositions; all they had to work from was the bill and the names endorsed on the back (this was in marked contrast to the practice in Ireland where grand juries worked from the depositions and never saw the witnesses).[10] They thus had no idea what the witnesses were expected to say. The inevitable result was that on occasions they would fail to get from witnesses evidence vital to the prosecution case. Another factor was interference with witnesses. Of the cases which broke down at the grand jury stage, many did so because the prosecution witnesses were either kept away by the defence, or bribed to change or water down their evidence. By changing his evidence a witness ran little risk. The fact that the grand jury hearing took place in private, with no record kept, before jurors without depositions, made perjury difficult to detect and impossible to prosecute. Eventually a partial solution was found: that of allowing a clerk to attend the grand jury, furnished with the depositions, to explain the case to them and to assist in the examination of witnesses. Already in use in the Queen's

---

[7] When a bill was thrown out this did not rank as an acquittal but a second bill could not be preferred against the accused at that session, see *R v Humphreys* (1842) C & M 601. This was, however, no bar to the preferment of a fresh bill at a later session, see Archbold (20th edn, 1886), 88.

[8] See Report of Select Committee on Metropolitan Police Offices PP 1837–38 (578) XV, 321 (Q 249); see also a draft report in the City of London records dated 3 August 1838 from its Administration of Justice Committee.

[9] As to which, see PD 1857 CXLV, 1425–37, CXLVI, 1433–56 and 1859 CLII, 1610–17, and the evidence given before the Select Committee on Metropolitan Police Offices above, especially Qs 168, and 250–51.

[10] See Bill, PP 1816 (416)(O. 14) II, 903; debate, PD 1816 XXXII, 547–48.

Bench in the 1830s, the procedure was in 1838 adopted at the Old Bailey. The result was a sharp drop in the number of bills thrown out.[11]

Reform was not, however, enough to satisfy critics of the grand jury. They wanted to see it abolished – in London at least. To them the grand jury was unnecessary; if a stipendiary magistrate had found a prima facie case, what need was there to have his decision reviewed by a jury of laymen? Nor was this all. There was the inconvenience to witnesses and the expense to the public caused by grand jury hearings. Even where it was known that the accused was going to plead guilty at trial, the prosecution witnesses still had to appear before the grand jury, whilst in contested cases the system meant their having to attend court twice; and for this dual attendance the public paid.[12] Others criticised the secrecy of grand jury proceedings: the public were not admitted and if a bill was thrown out no one knew why. Then there were the opportunities the system offered to the vexatious and to blackmailers. Anyone could go straight to the grand jury and ask for a bill without troubling with a committal hearing and without any notice to the accused; in such a case the first the accused would know of the matter was on arrest after bill found. Even worse, a prosecutor, having obtained his bill, was under no obligation to bring it on for trial, a state of affairs which was an incentive to blackmail.[13] In 1859 Parliament tried to stem the abuse with a Vexatious Indictments Act.

Some of the loudest demands for reform came from the grand jurors themselves. In the 1840s and 1850s grand juries at the Old Bailey and the Middlesex Sessions repeatedly made presentments 'as to their own inutility'. Bills for the abolition of metropolitan grand juries were introduced in 1849, 1852 and 1857; all were lost through lack of parliamentary time.[14] Following his translation to the Lords, Frederick Thesiger, the promoter of the 1852 and 1857 Bills, introduced Bills there in 1860 and 1861 but with no greater success.[15] Opposition to the reform both in the Commons and Lords centred around claims that the Bill was the thin end of the wedge (the first step to the abolition of all grand juries), and that it would mean the sweeping away of a valuable constitutional safeguard (for the future the decision as to

[11] The Queen's Bench practice is described in the 8th Report of the Criminal Law Commissioners, app B, Qs 36–41. Its adoption at the Old Bailey was approved by the judges on 2 November 1838 (*The Times*, 3 November). The result was that the number of bills thrown fell from 12 to 5 per cent (1846) 6 LT 219. The Jury Laws Amendment Bill, 1892, proposed that grand juries be furnished with copies of the depositions.

[12] The *Law Magazine* estimated that the attendance of witnesses before Old Bailey grand juries involved a cost to the county rates of £3500 p.a., 8th Report of the Criminal Law Commissioners, app C; see also PD 1857 CLXV 1433.

[13] See PD 1857 CXLV, 1425–37.

[14] The Bills were the Administration of Justice (Metropolitan District) Bill, 1849, and the Grand Juries (Metropolitan District) Bills, 1852 and 1857. The basic scheme of the Bills was that an information drawn up by the clerk of the court based upon the committal charges take the place of the indictment.

[15] Indictable Offences (Metropolitan Districts) Bills, 1860 and 1861.

whether a man should stand trial would in London rest with an official removable at the pleasure of the Crown).[16] After the loss of the Bill of 1861 calls for abolition were still heard periodically;[17] indeed in 1892 a Bill was actually introduced for the abolition of grand juries at Quarter Sessions but lost.[18] The Criminal Evidence Act (1898) led to a short-lived controversy as to whether an accused had a right to give evidence before the grand jury, but with the number of bills thrown out running at less than 1 per cent per annum, grand jury reform had ceased to be a burning issue.[19]

2. Pleading Rules

The indictment which came back from the grand jury room would, even in a simple case, be a prolix document, often well nigh unintelligible to anyone but a lawyer. And within its pages might lurk an error or flaw which would win a prisoner an unmeritorious acquittal. The law required indictments to be certain: both offender and offence had to be described with accuracy and minute particularity. Indeed so complex were the rules of criminal pleading that it took Chitty, writing in 1816, over 130 pages to expound them.[20] Since the law did not permit amendment of indictments, the effect of the accused's being able to point to a defect was that the prosecution automatically failed.

Nor was it merely indictment defects which would bring a prosecution to a halt. A variance between the indictment and the evidence called to support it had the same effect. To try and reduce the risk of variance to the minimum, it was usual for the pleader to include in an indictment a number of alternative counts all founded on the same transaction, hardly differing from each other except in small particulars but intended to cover every possible combination of facts the evidence might prove.[21] This, of course, also served to add both to the length of the document and to the risk of formal error creeping in.

Where there was an indictment defect, the accused would normally take the point after verdict by motion in arrest of judgement.[22] It was open to him to raise the objection on arraignment (by plea of abatement or demurrer), but there were grave disadvantages in so doing. First, in misdemeanour, if a plea in abatement or demurrer was determined against the accused, he

---

[16] See PD 1857 CLVI, 1434–55, 1859 CLIII 1530 and 1538; and 1860 CLVI, 901.

[17] See e.g. presentment by Middlesex grand jury (1861) 31 LT 468; presentment by Old Bailey grand jury (1864) 40 LT 86; and paper read to the Law Society's annual provincial meeting, 1888 (*The Times*, 17 October 1888).

[18] Jury Law Amendment Bill, 1892.

[19] In 1898 just 0.0025 per cent of all bills were thrown out, see Judicial Statistics, PP 1900 CIII, 1.

[20] Chitty, *Criminal Law* (1st edn, 1816), i , 168–304.

[21] 8th Report of the Criminal Law Commissioners, 1845, pp. 12–13.

[22] Chitty, *Criminal Law*, i, 442–43.

would not normally be allowed to plead over.[23] Secondly, if the plea succeeded it would not result (as would a successful motion in arrest of judgement) in his discharge, but would merely delay the proceedings for a short time: the indictment would be quashed and a fresh bill sought from the grand jury with the accused remanded in custody in the interim.[24] In theory a fresh bill could also be preferred against an accused who was discharged upon motion in arrest, but it was not usual for this to happen.[25]

For an example of how minor indictment defects and variances could win a prisoner an unmeritorious acquittal one need look no further than *Sheen's Case*.[26] In 1827 Sheen killed his child, by deliberately cutting its throat in its mother's presence, and was indicted for murder. In the indictment the name of the child was given as 'Charles William Beadle'. At the trial the only evidence adduced as to the child's name was to the effect that he was always called 'William' or 'Billy', in the light of which the judge directed an acquittal on the grounds of variance. A fresh indictment was at once preferred again charging the accused with murder of the child, but this time containing no less than thirteen counts, varying the name and description of the child in every conceivable combination. On arraignment the accused pleaded *autrefois acquit*, averring in his plea that the child mentioned in both indictments was the same, and that he was as well known by the names of Charles William Beadle as by any of the names and descriptions in the new indictment. The plea being supported by evidence, the jury were directed to bring in a verdict of *autrefois acquit*. Sheen's was not an isolated case: a perusal of the Nisi Prius reports of the time throws up many other examples: a prisoner acquitted of murder because the indictment misstated the cause of death;[27] of arson because the indictment omitted the word 'unlawfully';[28] of burglary because the ownership of the premises burgled was laid in the wrong person;[29] of forgery because the indictment misdescribed the forged document,[30] or failed to follow its wording exactly.[31]

It is important not to overstate the problem. In the main, it was only in cases where the prisoner had counsel that indictment points were taken,

[23] Abatement was the appropriate plea where the name or description of the accused was misstated; a demurrer was a plea that the indictment was defective in substance or form; for the prohibition on pleading over, see Chitty, *Criminal Law*, i, 435 and 445; cf Bla Comm, iv, 334.

[24] Chitty, *Criminal Law*, i, 443 and 450.

[25] Ibid. 443 and *The Times*, 31 December 1842 (leader) and 3 January 1843 (letter); an accused whose crime was particularly atrocious would sometimes be re-indicted, see e.g. *R v Sheen* below and *R v Clarke*, *The Times*, 30 March and August 3 1818 and August 6 1819.

[26] *R v Sheen* (1827) 2 C & P 634; *The Times*, 14 and 16 July, 1827.

[27] *Re Kelly* (1825) 1 Lew 193; cf. *R v Thompson* (1826) 1 Moo 139 and *R v McDermott* (1813) Russ & Ry 356.

[28] *Turner and Reader's Case* (1830) 1 Lew 9; cf. *R v Pearson* (1831) 1 Moo 313.

[29] *R v Wilson* (1806) Russ & Ry 115 (this was a common cause of acquittal).

[30] *R v Wilcox* (1803) Russ & Ry 50 (indictment failed to state what the forged instrument was).

[31] *R v Anon.* (1827) 1 Lew 235; *Wright Roden and Holgate's Case* (1828) 1 Lew 236; *R v Goldstein* (1822) Russ & Ry 473.

and throughout the first half of the century the percentage of prisoners who had counsel was small (although it must be conceded that where counsel did appear the indictment would invariably claim their attention, many displaying great ingenuity in the points taken).[32]

The first attempt at reform came in 1826. By his Criminal Law Act of that year, Peel made two small changes in the law.[33] First, the Act set out a list (and unfortunately from a reformer's point of view only a short list) of formal defects which were not to be a ground of arrest of judgement or proceedings in error.[34] The effect was that where an indictment contained one of the specified defects the objection had to be taken by demurrer or not at all; and, if taken by demurrer, would only delay and not defeat the prosecution. Secondly, it gave the court power to amend the indictment where, upon a plea of abatement, it was shown that the name or addition (that is the rank, occupation or residence) of the accused was misstated.[35]

In 1828 came another small reform, 9 George IV, c. 15, empowering the court in cases of misdemeanour to amend the indictment where there was a variance between the indictment and a written document or record produced in evidence – a power which was extended in 1848 to cases of felony tried at sessions of Oyer and Terminer and Gaol Delivery;[36] and, in 1849, to cases of felony tried at Quarter Sessions.[37]

Useful as these reforms were they only scratched the surface of the problem. By the 1840s there were calls for root and branch reform. The acquittal in 1841 of Lord Cardigan of attempted murder by reason of the misnomer of his victim in the indictment brought the problem into the public eye.[38] The following year saw a *Times* leader calling for legislation of the subject during the coming parliamentary session.[39] In 1844–45 the subject was considered by the Criminal Law Commissioners. Their Eighth Report made clear the need for reform but was guarded as to the form it should take.[40] Not so Charles Greaves in his answer to a questionnaire from them. The whole system of criminal pleading, he argued, needed to be remodelled: indictments should be framed in the simplest and plainest form so as to be intelligible to anyone of average intelligence, with the courts given power in cases of defect or variance to order amendment.[41]

For a time it looked as though the campaign for reform would come to

---

[32] See e.g. *R v Fry and Fry* (1822) Russ. & Ry. 482.

[33] Peel had originally planned a more thoroughgoing reform, see PD 1826 XV, 1235–36.

[34] S 20.

[35] Ibid. s 19.

[36] By the 11 & 12 Vict, c. 46, s 4.

[37] By the 12 & 13 Vict, c. 45, s 10.

[38] *The Times*, 17 February 1841 (trial) and 17 and 18 February 1841 (leaders).

[39] *The Times*, 31 December 1842.

[40] 8th Report above, pp. 8–16.

[41] Ibid., app A, p 249, also pp. 217, 231–32; Cobbett, at p 296, actually defended the existing law.

nothing but eventually, in 1851, reform did come in the shape of Lord Campbell's Criminal Procedure Act. This declared that the indictment defects listed in the 1826 Act should not invalidate an indictment,[42] that all formal objections to the indictment must be taken before the jury was sworn and not afterwards, and that the court should have power upon such objection to order the indictment to be amended.[43] It gave the court in cases of variance the same power to amend as possessed by a judge at Nisi Prius:[44] power to amend in the case of any variance not material to the merits of the case, which did not prejudice the accused in his defence.[45] It also simplified the forms of indictment in the case of certain crimes, in particular homicide and those involving criminality in relation to documents.[46] In its objective of seeking to prevent acquittals based on unmeritorious pleading points, the Act was largely (although not completely) successful.[47] Certainly there was a marked reduction in the number of indictment points reserved and taken upon writ of error. What it did not tackle was the problem of prolixity (itself a by-product of the rules as to certainty and variance). An attempt was made to address the problem along the lines suggested by Greaves in the Criminal Code Bills of 1878–83, but it was not until 1915 that this nettle was in fact grasped.[48]

3. Arraignment

The grand jury having returned a true bill, the accused was then arraigned. In 1800 there were aspects of the law as to arraignment and plea which were anything but favourable to him. Mention has already been made of the law's refusal to allow the accused to plead over in misdemeanour. Even more harsh was its treatment of those who refused to plead. If when called on to plead a prisoner made no answer, a jury would be empanelled to try whether he was mute of malice or by visitation of God.[49] If they found him mute of malice, or if on arraignment he had expressly declined to plead or answer directly (which conduct was taken as dispensing with the need for a jury's verdict on the question), or if having pleaded not guilty he refused to put himself on his country, his contumacy was treated as equivalent to a conviction and the court would proceed forthwith to sentence.[50] This had always been the law in treason, petty larceny and misdemeanour. When the

---

[42] S 24.
[43] S 25.
[44] Under 3 & 4 Will IV, c. 42, s 23.
[45] Criminal Procedure Act, 1851, s 1.
[46] Ibid. s 4 (murder, manslaughter); s 5 (theft, forgery etc. of documents).
[47] See e.g. *Sill v R* (1853) 1 El & B 553.
[48] Indictments Act, 1915.
[49] See Chitty, *Criminal Law*, i, 424–25.
[50] By 12 Geo III, c. 20; and see *R v Mercier* (1777) Leach 183.

peine forte et dure was abolished in 1772 the rule was applied to felony as well. In 1827 the law was reformed, Peel's Criminal Law Act providing that henceforth an accused who, on arraignment, pleaded not guilty was deemed thereby to have put himself on his country; and that where a prisoner, on arraignment, was mute of malice or refused to answer directly, the court should direct that a plea of not guilty be entered.[51]

Another problem and one at least as common in practice as contumacy was that of the prisoner who had (or might have) a defence in law, but who, despite the judge's (and his counsel's) entreaties insisted on pleading guilty, conceiving that to plead not guilty would be to add falsehood to crime. In 1860 Brougham, in an attempt to deal with this difficulty, introduced a Bill into the Lords which proposed that the question put on arraignment be altered from 'Are you guilty or not guilty?' to 'Do you wish to be tried or do you plead guilty?'[52] This sensible small reform, although having the support of the Lord Chancellor and of many outside the House (not least prison chaplains), failed to pass into law.

[51] Ss 1 and 2.
[52] Plea on Indictment Bill, PP 1860 (241) V, 207; debate, PD 1860 CLIX, 757–59.

14

The Prosecution Case

'The self-defending prisoner, unless he is an old hand, usually does not cross-examine at all, or attempts to put his cross-examination into controversial assertions for which he gets pulled up. What questions he does ask result in emphasising the case against him.' A. M. Sullivan, *The Last Serjeant*, p. 124.

The accused having pleaded not guilty, and having been given in charge to the jury, the prosecution would begin to call its evidence. Before calling his witnesses, prosecuting counsel could, if he thought fit, make an opening speech. If there was no prosecuting counsel, the judge would prosecute, calling the witnesses and examining them from the depositions sent up by the committing magistrate.

What witnesses the prosecution called was a matter for its discretion. During the first half of the century there was a tendency for judges to react to a refusal by the prosecution to call a witness whose name appeared on the back of the indictment either by calling the witness themselves,[1] or by insisting that the Crown tender him for cross-examination.[2] After 1860, however, this practice was abandoned, the only obligation now cast upon the Crown in respect of witnesses it chose not to call being to have them at court in case the defence wished to call them (a rule change which, in an age when the calling of evidence by the defence gave the Crown the last word with the jury, had major implications for trial tactics).[3] The defence had the right to require that those witnesses the Crown did call remained out of court until called.[4] Where the prisoner was represented this right was invariably insisted upon.

A Crown witness who proved hostile (that is to say went back on what he had said at committal) would in the early part of the century get short shrift. He would be confronted with his deposition and warned by the judge against perjury. Nor until 1865 was the Crown given the right to cross-examine him

---

[1] See *R v Simmonds* (1823) 1 C & P 84; *R v Bodle* (1833) 6 C & P 186.

[2] *R v Beezley* (1834) 4 C & P 220; *R v Bull* (1839) 9 C & P 22; *R v Barley* (1847) 2 Cox 191.

[3] *R v Woodhead* (1847) 2 C & K 520; *R v Edwards* (1848) 3 Cox 82; *R v Cassidy* (1858) 1 F & F 79; *R v Thompson* (1876) 13 Cox 181.

[4] See *R v Goodere and Others* (1741) 17 St Tr 1003; *R v Colley and Sweet* (1829) Moo & M 329; *R v Wylde* (1834) 6 C & P 380.

on his deposition. To undermine and discredit the evidence of prosecution witnesses the accused had the tool of cross-examination. At this date its effectiveness was limited by two factors: the denial of legal representation to poor prisoners; and legal rules placing curbs upon cross-examination.

1. Lack of Legal Representation

Attempts by unrepresented prisoners to cross-examine were, for the most part, pitifully ineffective.[5] Sometimes the judge would make the task even harder by insisting that all questions be put through him. In trial reports, one occasionally finds an example of effective cross-examination by an undefended prisoner, but few prisoners displayed such skill and those who did were apt to be regarded with suspicion.[6]

2. Leading Questions

As for legal curbs, the propriety of defence counsel putting leading questions in cross-examination was at the start of the century regarded by some judges as doubtful.[7] The objection was still being taken (albeit unsuccessfully) as late as 1836.[8]

3. Cross-Examination of Witnesses as to their Pasts

More important were the obstacles to the cross-examination of witnesses as to their discreditable pasts. Of these the most obvious was the rule which rendered a person who had been convicted of (and received judgement for) treason, felony or *crimen falsi* (forgery, perjury and cognate offences),[9] incompetent to testify.[10] (After 1828 competency was restored, save in *crimen falsi*, once the convict had served his sentence.)[11] Any prisoner wishing to raise such a conviction against a witness had to produce a copy of the record or judgement, whereupon unless a pardon was produced the witness would be held incompetent.[12] If he failed to produce a copy of the record, not

---

[5] See the evidence of the recorder of Leicester to the Select Committee on the Poor Prisoners' Defence Bill PP (1903) (254, 264) VII, 583; see also F. C. Gurney Campion, *Justice and the Poor in England* (London, 1926), 50–51.

[6] PD 1826 XV, 594; for examples of cases where the prisoner's skill in cross-examining attracted attention, see e.g. *R v Palmer*, *The Times*, 8 November 1810; *R v Redding*, *The Times*, 11 August 1823; and *R v Clover and Another*, *The Times*, 20 March 1824.

[7] *R v Hardy* (1794) 24 St Tr 199.

[8] *Parkin v Moon* (1836) 7 C & P 408.

[9] *Crimen falsi* included forgery, perjury, subornation of perjury, bribing a witness to absent himself and barratry but not conspiracy to defraud, see Phillipps (8th edn, 1838), 17.

[10] Ibid. 19.

[11] 9 Geo IV, c. 32; competency could also be restored by a pardon.

[12] East, 1 P C 78; Phillipps, 19–20.

only would the witness be permitted to testify, but the prisoner would be debarred from cross-examining as to the conviction.[13]

Then there was the privilege against self-incrimination which in 1800 had a wider scope than it does today, entitling a witness to decline to answer not only on the ground of incrimination of crime but also where the answer would expose him to a penalty, forfeiture or ecclesiastical censure.[14] In 1806 the judges advised the Lords that the privilege also excused a witness from answering a question which would expose him to an action for debt,[15] but this ruling was reversed by statute the following year.[16] In the latter half of the century the scope of the privilege was gradually reined in by the judges. In particular, while acknowledging that a witness might lawfully refuse to answer a question where the answer would provide a link in a chain of evidence leading to his conviction,[17] they insisted that they, not the witness, were to be the judges of whether a question was incriminating, although controversy on the point lingered on until the 1860s.[18]

In the 1850s Brougham was advocating that the law go further than this. In 1853 he included in his Law of Evidence and Procedure Amendment Bill of that year a clause abolishing the privilege, substituting for it a rule forbidding incriminating answers being used against the witness in subsequent proceedings.[19] The clause met strong opposition. It was argued that such a change in the law would be a means of circumventing the prohibition upon the interrogation of prisoners, and might also result in a witness being compelled to disclose facts which would lead to the discovery of other evidence against him which could be used to procure his conviction. These arguments carried the day and the clause was lost.[20]

The most troublesome aspect of the privilege was, however, that part of it which related to degrading questions. In a number of seventeenth- and eighteenth-century cases it had been held that a witness was not obliged to answer a question which would degrade or disgrace him (e.g. whether he had been whipped for petty larceny).[21] The rule had also been applied to attempts to question jurors upon the trial of a challenge for cause.[22] According

---

[13] Archbold (1st edn) 95.
[14] Penalty: *R v Gordon (Ld)* (1781) 21 St Tr 485; forfeiture: *R v Newell* (1707) Park 269; ecclesiastical censure: *Chetwynd v Lindon* (1752) 2 Ves Sen 450 (incest); *Finch v Finch* (1752) 2 Ves Sen 491 (concubinage).
[15] Phillipps (8th edn), 914–915 n.
[16] 46 Geo III, c. 47.
[17] *Cates v Hardacre* (1811) 3 Taunt 424; *Fisher v Ronalds* (1852) 12 C B 762.
[18] *R v Boyes* (1861) 9 Cox 32 and the cases there cited; the judges also refused to countenance a claim for privilege being made on behalf of a witness by counsel in the suit, see *R v Adey* (1831) 1 M & Rob 94.
[19] PP 1852–53 (610) III 337.
[20] PD 1853 CXXIV, 1379–80.
[21] *R v Freind* (1696) 13 St Tr 1; *Layer's Case* (1722) 16 ST 94 at 259.
[22] *R v Cook* 1696) 13 St Tr 311.

to Peake,[23] the rule fell into desuetude during the eighteenth century, only to reemerge with a vengeance at the start of the nineteenth, with Lord Ellenborough holding not merely that degrading questions need not be answered but that they should not be put.[24] He sought to justify his ruling on the ground of public policy: if such questions were allowed witnesses would not come forward. Others offered as a justification the grievance to a witness of having old disgraces dragged up after he had rehabilitated himself.[25] But, as Best CJ pointed out, there was another side to the coin: if such questions were not permitted juries would be prevented from learning facts about a witness's character which it was important for them to know, and innocent men might suffer.[26] So far as one can judge from contemporary trial reports, the new rule was far from universally enforced. One finds, for instance, numerous examples from the first quarter of the century of accomplices called by the Crown being cross-examined unmercifully as to their character.[27] Reported cases also afford instances.[28] Indeed, it appears that Lord Ellenborough himself may have had a change of heart on the subject, for, in a case in 1818, he is reputed to have threatened to commit a witness for contempt unless he answered a question as to whether he had previously been imprisoned.[29]

From the defendant's point of view, the important thing, so far as cross-examination was concerned, was not to be able to compel an answer but to be able to put the question; a refusal to answer being generally treated by the jury as tantamount to an admission. His right to do so had by 1850 been clearly established. The last case in which a judge is reported as disallowing a question as degrading was *Pitcher* in 1823.[30] A severe blow was dealt to the authority of such cases by Denman's Act of 1843, which restored to competency those convicted of *crimen falsi* or undergoing punishment for treason or felony. For it was scarcely to be believed that Parliament's intention that those who, by reason of their infamy, had formerly been incompetent as witnesses should now not merely be competent but also protected from questioning about their infamy. If such questions could be put to witnesses of this sort, why not to all witnesses? Indeed, by the 1850s, serious doubt was being expressed as to whether there was in fact any privilege to refuse to answer degrading questions.[31] In 1853 Brougham, in his Evidence Bill,

---

[23] T. Peake, *A Compendium of the Law of Evidence* (2nd edn, London, 1801), 130 et seq.

[24] *R v Lewis* (1802) 4 Esp NPC 225; see also *MacBride v MacBride* (1802) 4 Esp NPC 242.

[25] Phillipps, 918.

[26] *Cundell v Pratt* (1827) M & M 108.

[27] See e.g. *R v Owen and Mitchell*, *The Times*, 9 July 1801; *R v Jacobs*, *The Times*, 23 January 1819; *R v Webster*, *The Times*, 20 December 1823, and *R v Maurice*, *The Times*, 16 April 1824.

[28] *R v Watson* (1817) 2 Stark 116.

[29] Frost v Holloway (1818) (unreported cited in Phillipps, 922n).

[30] *R v Pitcher* (1823) 1 C & P 85 and Alderson B in *Boyle v Wiseman* (1855) 10 Ex 647; contra Holroyd J in *R v Watson* above.

[31] PD 1853 CXXIV, 1368–69; W. M. Best, *Evidence* (1st edn, 1849), para 117.

sought to put the matter beyond doubt by abolishing the privilege, but the clause did not pass. In 1865 any lingering doubt as to the right to question witnesses as to previous convictions was removed by section 6 of the Criminal Procedure Act of that year, which provided that, if a witness declined to answer such questions, the conviction might be proved against him, thereby extending to criminal cases a rule laid down for civil cases by the Common Law Procedure Act (1854).

Although the 1865 edition of *Russell on Crime* had treated it as arguable that the privilege still survived, eight years later it was laid down by Cockburn LCJ in the clearest terms that there was no such privilege.[32] After this it was treated by text writers as defunct.[33] The only vestige which remained was in relation to jury challenge, albeit that the privilege had displayed a considerable capacity for survival in relation to rape prosecutions.[34]

By 1892 the want of such a privilege was being keenly felt. Two of the leading advocates of the day, who had the previous year in two notorious cases pushed cross-examination as to character to its limits, found themselves roundly condemned both in the leader and the correspondence columns of *The Times*.[35] Several letters suggested that English law adopt the plan of the Indian Evidence Act (1872) (already adopted in English courts martial) and give the judge power to disallow any question as to credit, unless of the opinion that the imputation conveyed by it would, if true, seriously affect the credibility of the witness.[36] Judges probably already had such power at common law.[37] In any event, as *The Times* leader pointed out, leaving the matter to the discretion of the judge did not always solve the problem. Judges were always reluctant to intervene because they could never feel sure they had a complete knowledge of the facts of the case. Also to disallow the question was to shut the stable door after the horse had bolted, as by the time the question had been asked the damage had been done. In the end one had to trust to the discretion of the advocate not to ask such questions. In the event the storm passed and nothing was done.[38]

---

[32] *R v Castro*, 1873 (Kenealey edn) 32nd day, i, 396 cited Halsbury's *Laws* (3rd edn), xv, 424n.

[33] See Stephen's *Digest*, art. 120, and Roscoe's *Criminal Evidence* (12th edn, London, 1898), 132. Contra Powell on *Evidence* (8th edn, London, 1904), 100, which speaks of the privilege as still possibly existing.

[34] See *R v Hodgson* (1812) Russ & Ry 211; *R v Barker* (1829) 3 C & P 589; *R v Mercier* (1842) 6 Jur 243; *R v Swann* (1851) 15 JP 420; *R v Cockroft* (1870) 11 Cox 410; and *R v Holmes* (1871) 12 Cox 137.

[35] Sir Charles Russell in *Osborne v Hargreave and Wife* (slander) and Sir Edward Clarke in *Russell v Russell* (divorce); see *The Times*, 2 January 1892 (leader) and letters 1, 2, 7 and 12 January 1892.

[36] Indian Evidence Act, 1872, ss 148–52; a similar rule applied in civil actions (see RSC, O 34, r 38).

[37] *Cooper v Curry* (1846) 11 JP 22 and 8 LT 238.

[38] In its *Annual Statement* for 1917 the Bar Council did, however, lay down rules as to the conduct of cross-examination modelled upon the Indian Evidence Act.

4. The Rule in The Queen's Case

Another fetter on cross-examination as to credit was that imposed by the judges in 1820 by their ruling in *The Queen's Case*.[39] There they had advised the House of Lords that a party seeking to cross-examine a witness about a previous statement in writing by him had to show the writing to him and, if he acknowledged it as his, read it as part of his (the party's) evidence. In criminal cases, the document upon which defence counsel would most frequently seek to cross-examine would be the witness's deposition, although prior to 1836 the refusal of the law to allow a prisoner either to inspect or have a copy of the depositions represented an obstacle (albeit not an insurmountable one) to such cross-examination. When prisoners were, by the Prisoners' Counsel Act (1836), given the right to a copy of the depositions, the judges took steps to ensure that cross-examination upon depositions should henceforth be in accordance with the rules laid down in *The Queen's Case*. In 1837, before going out on circuit, they issued a Practice Direction.[40] A Crown witness was not to be asked about what he did or did not say in his deposition, unless it had first been read out; and, if it was so read out, it was to be treated as evidence for the prisoner. Such a rule was extremely disadvantageous to the defence. It deprived the cross-examiner of the advantage of surprise. It also meant that exposure of the discrepancy between the witness's evidence and his deposition was bought at the price of having the whole deposition go in. Since the deposition, when read, became part of the defence case, such cross-examination automatically gave the Crown the right to the last word with the jury.

Before 1837 was out a determined attempt had been made to test the resolution of the judges to enforce the Practice Direction. In *Edwards*, a murder case tried before Littledale and Coleridge JJ (neither of whom had been present when the Practice Direction had been agreed to by the judges), defence counsel claimed that not all the judges were applying the new rules.[41] Tindal CJ, it was said, had treated it as an open question whether the new rules were binding. Further, it was argued that, under the new rules, a prisoner was in a worse position than he had been before the Act, which could scarcely have been Parliament's intention. Before the Act, it was claimed, defence counsel had commonly been allowed to cross-examine upon depositions without putting them in (Adolphus for the Crown conceded the existence of such a practice but claimed it was irregular), and that moreover the judges had frequently themselves undertaken such cross-examination. In the end the judges in *Edwards* cut short the debate by doing just that.

Edwards thus affirmed a possible avenue of escape from the rigours of the Practice Direction. However, few judges were it seems prepared to allow it

---

[39] *The Queen's Case* (1820) 2 Brod & Bing 286.
[40] 7 C & P 676.
[41] *R v Edwards* (1837) 8 C & P 26.

to be used. The report of *Edwards* refers to the Practice Direction being enforced by most judges and gives a long list of judges who had enforced it. Occasionally, one finds over the next twenty years examples of judges being prepared to follow *Edwards*, themselves cross-examining on the depositions, or allowing counsel to be their mouthpiece, without putting them in.[42] The general attitude appears, however, to have been that ascribed by the Common Law Commissioners to Patteson J: 'I will not break the law and you must not'.[43]

Another device resorted to was that of placing the deposition in the witness's hand, asking him to read it to himself, then asking him when he had done so whether he stood by his answer.[44] The justification offered for not putting in the deposition in such a case was that the witness was not being cross-examined on it, simply being invited to refresh his memory. However, in 1843 the Fifteen Judges, in a reserved case, declared the ploy illegal.[45] Their decision (probably because it was never reported) appears to have gone unnoticed, and certainly it did not put a stop to the practice. In *Matthews* (1849), Pollock LCB described it as on the extreme verge of established rules of practice.[46] In *Ford* (1851) the matter was considered by the Court for Crown Cases Reserved and the 1843 ruling affirmed.[47] Even after this, one finds occasional, albeit unsuccessful, attempts to revive the practice.[48]

Yet another way of evading the Practice Direction was simply to ask the witness whether he had ever said what he was now saying before.[49] Strictly, the question was improper. As Patteson J stressed in *Shellard* (1840), all that could lawfully be asked was 'Have you always said so except before the magistrates?'[50] But it was not unknown for judges to turn a blind eye and allow irregular questioning, despite prosecution objections. The judges never applied the Practice Direction to depositions irregularly obtained.[51] Whether it applied to coroner's depositions was uncertain.[52]

That the rule in *The Queen's Case* operated as a powerful disincentive to cross-examining upon depositions is beyond doubt. Counsel, upon being told that he must put the deposition in, would commonly abandon this line

---

[42] *R v Tooker* (1849) 4 Cox 93 n; *R v Peel* (1860) 2 F & F 21.

[43] 2nd Report of the Common Law Commissioners PP 1830 (123) XI, 547 (at p. 20).

[44] See e.g. *R v Barnet* (1850) 4 Cox 269; for a variant on the same theme see *R v Newton* (1850) 4 Cox 262.

[45] Referred to in *R v Ford* (1851) 5 Cox 184.

[46] *R v Matthews* (1849) 4 Cox 93.

[47] *R v Ford* (1851) 5 Cox 184.

[48] *R v Palmer* (1851) 5 Cox 236; *R v Brewer* (1863) 9 Cox 409.

[49] *R v Moir* (1850) 4 Cox 279; *R v Price* (1857) 7 Cox 405.

[50] *R v Shellard* (1840) 9 C & P 277.

[51] *R v Griffiths* (1841) 9 C & P 746; *R v Christopher* (1850) 4 Cox 76.

[52] In *R v Barnet* (1850) 4 Cox 269 it was held that the rule applied to coroner's depositions but contra *R v Maloney* (1861) 8 Cox 6.

of cross-examination.[53] In 1854 the rule was abolished as regards civil cases by the Common Law Procedure Act.[54] Henceforth a witness in a civil case could be cross-examined about previous written statements without the statement being put in, although, if it was sought to contradict him from the statement, then it had to go in. In 1856 Greaves, in a Report on Criminal Procedure, recommended that criminal law be brought into line with civil law on this point.[55] This was done by the Criminal Procedure Act (1865).[56]

5. The Submission of No Case to Answer

If at the close of the Crown's case there was no evidence upon which the jury could properly convict, it was open to the accused to submit that there was no case to answer.[57] Such submission if upheld would normally lead to a directed acquittal. However, if there was a co-accused who intended to call evidence, the judge could properly wait to see if this supplied the missing proof before ruling.[58] It was by a submission of 'no case' that objections based upon indictment variance were taken.[59]

---

[53] *R v Taylor* (1839) 8 C & P 726; *R v Brewer* above.

[54] S 24.

[55] Greaves, Report on Criminal Procedure, PP 1856 (456) L 79.

[56] S 5.

[57] *R v Burdett* (1820) 1 St Tr NS 1 at 140.

[58] *Carpenter v Jones* (1824) 1 Moo & M 197 n; *R v Martin* (1889) 17 Cox 36.

[59] A submission founded on variance was sometimes made immediately after the prosecution opening, see e.g. *R v Aslett* (first case) (1803) 2 Leach 954; *R v Aslett* (second case) (1803) 2 Leach 958.

15

The Prisoner's Incompetence to Testify

'Now where a man who is interested in the matter in question, would also prove it, 'tis rather a cause for distrust than any just cause for belief ... and the law removes them from testimony to stop them sliding into perjury.'

Gilbert, *Evidence*, p. 122.

1. The Incompetency Rule

The Crown having closed its case, the judge would call on the accused to make his defence. In seeking to get his version of events before the jury, the accused faced a severe handicap. The law denied him the right either to give evidence in his own defence or to call his wife to do so.

Lawyers explained the disability in terms of a larger rule: the doctrine of incompetency through interest. This barred from the witness-box, in civil and criminal suits alike, any person regarded as having an interest in the outcome of the proceedings. However, for all that text writers spoke of the incompetence of the accused and of parties to a civil suit as being of a piece, and offered the same justification for the rule in both cases, namely that the evidence of an interested person would inevitably be biased and therefore worthless,[1] the two cases were not in fact the same. In the first place, an accused was permitted to do something which the parties to a civil suit could not do, namely to make an unsworn statement. Secondly there was, so it was claimed, a far more compelling reason for refusing to allow an accused to give evidence on his own behalf. This was the need to protect prisoners against self-incrimination. To abolish the incompetency rule would, so the argument went, lead to the establishment in England of something akin to the disliked French form of procedure, with prisoners compelled by rigorous cross-examination (conducted, where there was no prosecuting counsel, by the judge) to convict themselves out of their own mouths.[2] The country had had experience of such a system in the days of Scroggs and Jeffreys.[3] After the Glorious Revolution of 1688 it had set its face against prisoners being subjected to such 'moral torture'. Faced with the law's refusal to allow him to testify, an accused had to resort to other means to get his story across.

---

[1] Sir G. Gilbert, *Evidence* (London, 1756), 122; he also argued that such evidence was incredible by reason of bias.

[2] See e.g. the Attorney-General: PD 1865 CLXXVII, 942.

[3] See e.g. Stephen (1857) 29 LT 146 and Ashley, PD 1876 CCXXIX, 1182.

2. Cross-Examination

One such means was cross-examination. By putting his case to the prosecution witnesses in cross-examination, an accused not only could make clear, at an early stage, what his answer was, but occasionally might even succeed in getting those witnesses to agree that the facts were indeed as he asserted. But cross-examination is a lawyer's tool and, although in reports of nineteenth-century trials one occasionally comes across undefended prisoners capable of cross-examining with real skill, effective cross-examination was beyond most of them. The common error of the undefended prisoner, when called upon to cross-examine, was to make assertions instead of putting questions; this would frequently produce a rebuke from the bench after which the accused would lapse into silence. Nor was this an area in which the judge could do much to aid the prisoner. He could probe weaknesses and inconsistencies in the prosecution evidence but he could not, save where the prisoner had given his account on arrest or at committal (or where during his attempts at cross-examination he disclosed his defence), put the prisoner's version to witnesses because he had no means of knowing what it was.

3. The Pre-Trial Statement

Another device was the pre-trial statement: a statement made by the accused either on arrest to the arresting officer or before the examining magistrate. The Crown, although not obliged to lay such statements before the jury, would generally do so.[4] Indeed many judges openly favoured this course.[5] One of the grounds on which Patteson J in 1844 exhorted police officers not to stop prisoners volunteering statements was that such statements were often a means of demonstrating the innocence of the accused.[6] But many prisoners made no such statements. At committal hearings, prisoners who were legally represented would, even in the 1800s, commonly reserve their defence, despite the adverse judicial comment this attracted.[7]

4. The Unsworn Statement

The method of getting the prisoner's story before the jury, which approximated most closely to the giving of evidence, was the making of an unsworn statement. Yet the privilege of making such a statement was not accorded

---

[4] (1882) 73 LT 229 and (1884) 18 Ir LT 316.

[5] See e.g. *R v Moore, The Times*, 7 March 1844 (Alderson B).

[6] *R v Dickinson* (1844) 1 Cox 27.

[7] See e.g. *R v Nutts and Riley, The Times*, 9 December 1800; *R v Locke, The Times*, 20 August 1808 and *R v Broughton, The Times*, 13 March 1819; see also Beattie, 276.

to all prisoners. Undefended prisoners and defended prisoners charged with treason and (until 1836) felony enjoyed the right, but a defended prisoner charged with misdemeanour did not. In *White* (1811) Lord Ellenborough sought to justify the rule in misdemeanour on the grounds of 'the confusion which would necessarily follow if a case were to be conducted at the same time both by counsel and by the party himself'.[8]

Reports of misdemeanour trials in *The Times*,[9] and in the *State Trials Reports*,[10] suggest that *White* was confirming an existing practice rather than laying down any new rule. However, the practice was certainly not one of any great antiquity. As recently as 1795 Rooke J, at the trial of Redhead Yorke for misdemeanour, had allowed the defendant and his counsel to share the task of examining and cross-examining witnesses, and at the end of the evidence had given the defendant the option of addressing the jury in person or by his counsel.[11] The rule laid down in *White* was reaffirmed by Abbott CJ in 1824 in *Parkins*: 'If', said the Chief Justice, the party addresses the jury in person, he must cross-examine the witnesses, for if counsel cross-examined and the party spoke great inconvenience would ensue.'[12] Abbott was, however, prepared to admit one qualification to the rule: that a defendant who employed counsel merely to argue points of law and suggest questions to him for cross-examination would not thereby lose his right to address the jury. Ellenborough's argument about confusion was less than convincing. In felony trials it was, and had been for many years, regular practice for counsel to cross-examine and the accused to address the jury. No one appears to have found the practice productive of confusion there.

An undefended prisoner was called on to make his unsworn statement (or defence as it was commonly called) at the close of the prosecution case, as was the defended prisoner in felony. In treason, however, the prisoner if defended (and prisoners in treason invariably had counsel) was called on for his defence after his counsel had addressed the jury and his witnesses had given evidence.[13]

The law was remarkably indulgent to prisoners as to the content of unsworn statements. All manner of hearsay could be and was introduced.[14] Passages from newspapers and books could be read.[15] However, there were limits to judicial tolerance. In the early part of the century blasphemy cases

---

[8] *R v White* (1811) 3 Camp 98.

[9] E.g. *R v Roper*, *The Times*, 28 December 1816 (perjury); *R v Macklin and Others*, *The Times*, 25 July 1818 (riot).

[10] E.g. *R v Peltier* (libel) and *R v Hedges and Hedges* (conspiracy) (1802) 28 St Tr 529 and 1315 respectively.

[11] *R v Redhead Yorke* (1795) 25 St Tr 1003.

[12] *R v Parkins* (1824) 1 C & P 548.

[13] 7 St Tr NS 276 n.

[14] *R v Bellingham*, *The Times*, 15–16 May 1812 (letters).

[15] *R v Stephens* (1839) 3 St Tr NS 1189 (newspapers); also *The Trial of Thurtell and Hunt*, Notable British Trials series.

were a recurrent problem in this respect. The accused would frequently seek to defend himself by quotations from religious texts. This would lead to an admonition from the bench that he should not try and justify one blasphemy by another, which would be followed by a protest from the accused that the judge was preventing him from defending himself.[16]

Another indulgence was that the prisoner, instead of delivering his defence *ex tempore*, could, if he wished, put in a written defence and either read it himself or have it read for him by an officer of the court.[17] A written defence offered in many ways the best method of getting across the prisoner's answer. Often such defences were the handiwork of friends or lawyers.[18] Indeed, in Newgate in the 1820s, there seems to have been a flourishing trade in written defences, a prisoner who could not afford to brief counsel using what money he had to pay for a defence to be written.[19]

The written defence had disadvantages, of which the gravest was that, being of necessity prepared in advance of trial, by the time the prisoner was called on to deliver it it might well have been rendered wholly inapposite by the turn the evidence had taken. This difficulty could, of course, be avoided if the defence was actually prepared as the case was going on, which was sometimes done.[20] Bought defences were a particular source of danger to prisoners. They rarely assisted and could often do the prisoner dreadful harm. It was not unknown for a prisoner to hand in a paper to be used in his defence, only to discover, when it was read, that it was an admission of guilt coupled with a plea in mitigation.[21] Some judges sought to protect prisoners handing in bought defences by insisting on reading the defence themselves, or having it read and explained to the prisoner, before it was put in.[22]

Prisoners who had no written defence to hand in generally made a poor show of explaining their case. Young children would often merely sob and say nothing.[23] Many adults fared no better. Illiterate, inarticulate, terrified for their lives, without friends or advice, not knowing what to say, they said

[16] *R v Carlile, The Times*, 13 October 1819; *R v Carlile* (1821) 1 St Tr NS 1033; *R v Davidson, The Times*, 24 October 1820; *R v Waddington, The Times*, 24 October 1822; *R v Tunbridge, The Times*, 21 January 1823.

[17] See e.g. *The Trial of Thurtell and Hunt* above; also *R v Perrot, The Times*, 1 April 1800 (read by counsel).

[18] Drafted by a friend: *R v Booth, The Times*, 18 July 1823; by a lawyer: *R v Harry, The Times*, 19 August 1817; *R v Ripley and Others, The Times*, 7 April 1815; *R v Taylor and Taylor, The Times*, 17 January 1816; and *R v Woodyear, The Times*, 2 March 1859 (where the lawyer's handiwork is very obvious).

[19] Reply of the Inspectors of Prisons to the Report of the Court of Aldermen, PP 1836 (486) XLII, 283; also *The Times*, 7 July 1836 (Court of Aldermen).

[20] *R v Brunt* (1820) 33 St Tr 1177.

[21] *R v Mayo, The Times*, 4 and 5 September 1818 and *R v Burgess, The Times*, 28 May 1819.

[22] *R v Meetham, The Times*, 23 August 1825; see also *R v Cain, The Times*, 14 and 16 January 1826.

[23] See e.g. *R v Hunt, The Times*, 25 October 1823 and *R v Mumford, The Times*, 8 March 1854.

nothing. In a case before the Reading special commission in 1831, of ten prisoners jointly indicted for riot only one, when called upon, offered a defence.[24] Newspaper reports of trials show that this was by no means an uncommon phenomenon, even where the charge was capital.[25] Those prisoners who did manage to get a few words out rarely went beyond a bare denial ('I am as innocent as the child unborn';[26] or 'I know nothing of it');[27] a few words of explanation ('I was intoxicated');[28] or the offering of a stock defence (such as the pickpocket's claim: 'I found the handkerchief under my feet, I picked it up got on the footpath and the policeman collared me').[29] Yet others, making no attempt at defence, simply begged for mercy ('I hope you will be merciful, I have a wife and two children').[30] Where the evidence was circumstantial or complicated, it was an exceptional prisoner who was able to deal with the points against him in an orderly and reasoned fashion. Most, if they attempted to speak at length, descended into rambling irrelevance.[31] At a trial in 1843 the jury were so irritated by having to sit through the prisoners' speeches that they asked the judge whether it was necessary for them to give attention to matters as entirely irrelevant as the last two speeches.[32] Even a man of education might find the task of making an effective address beyond him.[33]

For all that most undefended prisoners, when addressing the jury, cut poor figures and did their cases little good, a few were able to use the right effectively.[34] One way of making the statement of an undefended prisoner a more effective vehicle for getting across his defence would have been for the trial judge, at the close of the prosecution case, to call his attention to the principal points against him, and to invite him to deal with them one by one. This was in fact the solution adopted in the Indian Code of Criminal Procedure Act (1861);[35] there is evidence that by the 1880s and 1890s it was also being adopted unofficially at some Quarter Sessions.[36] In the 1800s one occasionally finds the technique used by examining magistrates, but in jury trials it was apparently unknown.

---

[24] *R v Hicks and Others*, *The Times*, 4 January 1831.

[25] See e.g. *R v Gibbs*, *The Times*, 27 March 1819: 'I don't know that I can say anything'.

[26] A stock phrase: see *The Times* trial reports and the CCC Sess. Papers for the first quarter of the century.

[27] See e.g. *R v Jones* (1844–45) 21 CCC Sess Pap 137, *R v Williams* ibid., 887.

[28] See e.g. *R v Pratt* (1845) 21 CCC Sess Pap 921 and *R v Kirby* ibid., 954

[29] *R v Edwards* (1845) 22 CCC Sess Pap 179.

[30] *R v Mitchell*, *The Times*, 12 January 1805; *R v Richardson and Others*, *The Times*, 7 June 1813; *R v Oughton and Lee*, *The Times*, 22 August 1811; *R v Johnson*, *The Times*, 16 January 1817 and *R v Clark*, *The Times*, 12 September 1823.

[31] *R v Tibbs*, *The Times*, 13 September 1809; *R v Andrews*, *The Times*, 19 August 1816.

[32] *R v O'Connor and Others* (1843) 4 St Tr NS 935.

[33] *R v Barstow*, *The Times*, 15 April 1813 (ex-clergyman).

[34] *R v Pilkington*, *The Times*, 22 August 1808.

[35] India Act No. XXV of 1861; and see also Code of Criminal Procedure Act, 1882, s 342.

[36] Letter to *The Times*, 27 October 1897.

Where a prisoner was defended by counsel, it was often a nice question whether he should make an unsworn statement.[37] Where the charge was treason, there was much to be said against his doing so (most prisoners in practice did not), for if he made a statement he would make it after his counsel had addressed the jury. The danger was that he would merely end up doing, for a second time and less well, what his counsel had already done, thereby risking trying the jury's patience. In felony the position was different. If the prisoner did not make a statement, the jury would hear no address either from him or his counsel (except in so far as his counsel had been able to address argument to them under the guise of submission to the judge on law) and this was clearly a factor to be weighed in the balance. In some cases the decision was easy to make. Where the defence was insanity, the best way of convincing the jury that the prisoner was mad would in some cases be to allow him to address them. If the prisoner had an explanation or facts to offer, which could not be otherwise got before the jury, it was clearly essential that he offer a defence; in such a case, it was obviously prudent for the defence to be written and approved, if not drafted, by counsel.

Where there was nothing to be gained by a defended prisoner making an unsworn statement, the sensible course was for him, when called upon, to 'leave it to his counsel'. But not all prisoners were prepared to do what was sensible. Some, when called upon, proceeded to offer an *ex tempore* defence which left their counsel in despair. Nor was it unknown for a prisoner to hand in, to be read, a written defence which his counsel had not even seen, still less approved.[38] In some of these cases, poor communication between counsel and client was no doubt to blame (a far from uncommon problem in an age in which it was unusual for counsel to have conferences in criminal cases, and in which many counsel were instructed so late in the day as to render a conference impractical). In others, the explanation was pigheadedness, dissatisfaction at counsel's failure to bring out a point which the prisoner mistakenly believed vital to his defence, or fear that, if he said nothing, it would go badly for him with the jury. In capital cases, it was not unknown for defended prisoners to seek to make a second statement to the jury at the end of the judge's summing up. Such requests were usually indulged *in favorem vitae*.[39]

The prisoner who succeeded in making an effective defence to the jury was still not out of the wood. In the first place, he might find prosecution witnesses being recalled so that matters raised by him in his defence could be put to them. In *Carey* (1803) the prisoner, charged with the murder of

---

[37] See the comment of Alderson B in *R v Malings* (1838) 8 C & P 242.

[38] *R v Skene, The Times,* 16 February 1812; *R v Bennett, The Times,* 29 May, 1819.

[39] *R v Codling* (1802) 28 St Tr 177; *R v Ashcroft and Holden, The Times,* 9 September 1817; *R v Kerr, The Times,* 31 October 1815; *The Trial of Thurtell and Hunt* above.

his wife, handed in a written defence in which he alleged that the deceased had been afflicted with asthma and consumption for some years before her death.[40] The judge had the deceased's father called to deal with the point. In the early years of the nineteenth century the course was one commonly adopted at the Old Bailey,[41] and it was still being followed by some judges as late as 1884.[42] That such a course should be adopted where the prisoner had not put his case to the witnesses was understandable but, on occasion, one finds witnesses being recalled even where he had done so.

Secondly, the prisoner's statement would be subject to comment from the judge. In the eighteenth century, it was the practice to tell juries that a statement by a prisoner, uncorroborated by evidence, was worthless.[43] This mode of direction was still being employed at the start of the nineteenth century. Not all judges took such a strict line.[44] Thus, in *Power* (1805), one finds the recorder of London commending the explanation given by the prisoner in her defence as 'probably true'.[45] By 1840 judges, whilst warning juries that the prisoner's statement was made without the sanction of an oath and had not been tested by cross-examination, were generally prepared to concede to such statements some evidential weight. In *Beard* (1837), Coleridge J said that a prisoner's statement would carry such weight with the jury as, all the circumstances considered, it was entitled to.[46] In *Dyer* (1844), Alderson B said that if it fitted in with the rest of the evidence it would be very material.[47] By the 1880s the doctrine laid down in *Dyer* seems to have gained general acceptance.[48] How far juries in fact heeded such directions is hard to say. The point that the prisoner had failed to call witnesses to support what he said, where if he was speaking the truth such witnesses did exist, was obviously a powerful (if often unfair) one. Where the prisoner was the only person who could prove the truth of what he was saying, it can hardly have struck an intelligent jury as fair to criticise him for failing to do what the law did not permit him to do.

Thirdly, if the account which the prisoner gave in his unsworn statement was one which he had not mentioned on his arrest or before the examining

---

[40] *R v Carey*, The Times, 17 September 1803.

[41] *R v Cullen and Others*, The Times, 12 August 1800; *R v Jackson*, The Times, 5 July 1804; *R v Heath*, The Times, 7 November 1811; *R v Peru*, The Times, 13 July 1816; *R v Abbott*, The Times, 25 February 1822.

[42] Letter to *The Times*, 8 January 1884 (Littler).

[43] See Scroggs CJ's retort to the prisoner in *Coleman's Trial* (1688) 7 St Tr 1 at p. 65.

[44] *R v Mansfield*, The Times, 15 August 1803; *R v Maddocks*, The Times, 31 October 1815; *R v Vamplere*, The Times, 2 March 1822; *R v Jackson*, The Times, 12 July 1826; *R v Donovan*, The Times, 4 January 1839.

[45] *R v Power*, The Times, 25 September 1805; *R v Duncan*, The Times, 21 March 1807; *R v Anon.*, The Times, 24 October 1808 (Clerkenwell Sessions).

[46] *R v Beard* (1837) 8 C & P 142.

[47] *R v Dyer* (1844) 1 Cox 113.

[48] See e.g. *R v O'Donnell*, The Times, 3 December 1883 per defence counsel Sir Charles Russell.

magistrate, he courted the risk of adverse judicial comment on this score.[49] This risk was at its height in the closing years of the century.

5. The Calling of Witnesses

The fourth and final means of getting the prisoner's version before the jury was by the calling of witnesses to fact: persons who had witnessed the events giving rise to the charge, or who could otherwise (e.g. by the giving of evidence of alibi) demonstrate the prisoner's innocence. In the matter of the calling of witnesses, the position of prisoners had during the seventeenth and eighteenth centuries been much improved. The common law rules, which denied a prisoner in a capital case process to compel the attendance of his witnesses and the right to have them sworn, had been swept away.[50] By 1835 it was also settled law that, in a criminal case, there was no obligation to tender conduct money to a witnesses subpoenaed on behalf of a defendant.[51]

For all these improvements in the law, poor prisoners often had the greatest difficulty in getting material defence witnesses to court. A prisoner who was in custody and who could not afford an attorney, even if he knew of his right to issue subpoenas (and many did not), would rarely be able to serve them. Even if he could get a message to his witnesses, and they were anxious to help, their poverty would frequently prevent their doing so. Attending as a witness at Assizes or county Quarter Sessions would usually involve travel. If the accused came from a part of the county remote from the county town, attendance would for his witnesses involve a costly journey or, if they could not afford to pay for transport, a walk of days.[52] Having made the journey to the court of trial, the witnesses would then have to wait until the case was called on. The wait could extend over many days, during which they would have to provide themselves with food and accommodation. At the Old Bailey in 1819 it was by no means unusual for witnesses in Middlesex cases to have to hang about the court for ten to twelve days and upwards.[53]

Sometimes prisoners' attorneys would try and reduce the expense by warning witnesses for the day or time at which they believed the case was likely to come on. But this was a risky game. All cases in the calendar were

---

[49] *R v Herbert*, *The Times*, 4 December 1807; *R v Rush*, *The Times*, 2–5 April 1849; *R v Thompson*, *The Times*, 25 March 1854.

[50] 7 & 8 Will III, c. 3, s 7 (treason, prisoner to have process to compel appearance of defence witnesses); 1 Anne st 2, c. 9 (witnesses for prisoner to testify on oath in all cases of treason or felony); after the latter statute the power to subpoena witnesses was granted to prisoners charged with felony (Hawk 2 P C, c. 46, s 30).

[51] *R v Cooke* (1824) 1 C & P 321 and *Pell v Daubney* (1850) Ex Rep 955 per Alderson B (arguendo).

[52] *R v Simmons*, *The Times*, 29 March 1830; and Report of the Judges concerning Circuits, PP 1878 (311) LXIII, 1.

[53] Report of Select Committee on Gaols, PP 1819 (579) VII, 1.

liable to be called on at any time and if, when a prisoner's case was called on, his witnesses had not arrived, judges would rarely put the case back to wait for them to arrive.[54] The publishing of a daily list would have done much to alleviate the problem. This modest reform had been canvassed before a royal commission in 1816, but it was to be many years before it was implemented.[55]

Where a prisoner had witness difficulties, it was in theory open to him to apply to the court to postpone his trial. However, such applications were sparingly granted. The application had to be supported by an affidavit, a requirement which would not be dispensed with simply because the prisoner was poor.[56] In the affidavit the prisoner would have to give the name of the witness, indicate the nature of the evidence he would give and detail the efforts he had made to procure his attendance.[57] Even where the prisoner had good grounds for postponement, he might still be refused if he made his application too late.[58] It was by no means unknown for a prisoner not to raise the matter of his absent witnesses until asked by the judge, at the close of the Crown case, whether he had any witnesses to call. There were some judges who held that an application made after the jury had been sworn came too late.

How reluctant judges were to grant postponements in the early years of the century is well demonstrated by the case of Nesbitt, tried for murder at Maidstone Assizes in July 1820.[59] When the case was called on Nesbitt's counsel applied to have it stood over to the next Assize, on the ground that the prisoner on his arrest had had his money taken off him, in consequence of which he had been unable to secure the attendance of his witnesses. Counsel added that an affidavit in support of the application was being prepared and would be ready in a few hours. Wood B rejected the application out of hand, declaring that plenty of time had been allowed. As well as granting postponements, judges would on occasion give cases a fixed day. Predictably, the majority of such applications appear, in practice, to have been made and granted for the convenience of counsel rather than for the assistance of their clients and their witnesses.[60]

---

[54] See PD 1824 XI, 219; *R v Jones* (1803) 8 East 31; *R v Lowther, The Times,* 8 March 1833; *R v Lyons, The Times,* 29 October 1835.

[55] Report of Committee on State of Police of Metropolis PP 1816 (510) V, 1 (evidence p 65); see also the complaints of Old Bailey counsel that it was impossible to know when cases would come on (*The Times,* 18 December 1834 and 7 February 1835). At the end of 1835 it was announced that henceforth homicide cases would be taken at the Old Bailey on Friday and other capital cases on Wednesday (*The Times,* 18 November 1835); as to daily lists, see *The Times,* 18 December 1835 and 5 January 1837 (list to be published day before).

[56] *R v Palmer, The Times,* 13 December 1843; *R v Langhurst* (1866) 10 Cox 353.

[57] Lefroy B in *R v Mitchel* (1848) 3 Cox 1.

[58] *R v Wardle* (1842) C & Mar 647 (not followed in *R v Fitzgerald* (1843) 1 Car & K 201.

[59] *R v Nesbitt, The Times,* 24 and 29 July, 1820; *R v Luie and Brown, The Times,* 9 April 1874.

[60] *R v Lyons* above.

Witnesses had to be competent at law, and the doctrine of incompetency through interest debarred the accused from calling two important categories of potential witnesses: his wife; and co-prisoners standing trial with him. It was not unknown for unscrupulous prosecutors to silence potential witnesses for an accused by indicting them with him.[61] Also barred from the witness-box were children, Quakers and atheists.

To these fetters upon the calling of defence evidence, Jeremy Bentham was for adding another. He urged that the prisoner's right to call alibi evidence be made conditional upon his having served before trial an alibi notice, giving details of the alibi and the witnesses to be called in support of it.[62] Alternatively, the court might, he suggested, be empowered to adjourn the trial to enable the prosecution to investigate a late disclosed alibi. In 1835 his idea was taken up briefly by a House of Lords' Select Committee, but in the end it was dropped.[63] It was not until 1967 that the alibi notice became part of English criminal procedure. In fact in the nineteenth century such a reform was hardly needed. Alibi evidence had a bad name,[64] and was universally distrusted,[65] nowhere more so than in Ireland where the word 'aliboy' was in everyday speech a synonym for a false witness,[66] and where a false alibi was classified as a Kerry or Tipperary alibi, according to whether it bore upon the whereabouts of the accused or a Crown witness at the material time.[67] Foster, writing in 1762, had warned that the only alibi deserving of credit was that disclosed at the first opportunity: an alibi raised only at trial, which the prosecution had had no opportunity to investigate, ought to be 'heard with uncommon caution',[68] a point regularly hammered home to nineteenth-century juries.[69]

6. The Right to Make an Unsworn Statement

When the Prisoners' Counsel Act (1836) gave prisoners charged with felony the right to have counsel address the jury on their behalf, the question immediately arose as to whether the prisoner's right himself to address the

[61] Gilbert, 131–32, East, 1 P C, 313n.; Archbold (1st edn, 1822), 97; *R v Wright, The Times,* 12 December 1809 is a case which has this appearance and led to strong criticism of the prosecutor from Lord Ellenborough.

[62] Jeremy Bentham, *Rationale of Judicial Evidence* (London, 1827), bk 5, ch 16.

[63] HL Select Committee on the Prisoners' Counsel Bill, PP 1835 (HL 130) XLVI, 317.

[64] Bentham, *Rationale of Judicial Evidence,* bk 5, ch 16; see also the evidence of the recorder of London to the HL Select Committee on the Prisoners' Evidence Bill, 1835 above at p 22.

[65] As to the prevalence of false alibis in the nineteenth century see R. N. Gooderson, *Alibi* (London, 1977), 1 et seq.; Wills, *Circumstantial Evidence* (6th edn), 285n and G. Howson, *Thief-Taker General* (New York, 1971), 141.

[66] A. M. Sullivan, *The Last Serjeant* (London, 1952), 109.

[67] M. Healy, *The Old Munster Circuit* (London, 1939), 168–70.

[68] Foster, 368.

[69] See e.g. an article in (1870) 48 LT, 367 referring to observations made by Hannen J in a recent assize case.

jury had survived. There was nothing in the Act to suggest that it had not. Its wording in fact followed that of the treason statutes (the prisoner was to have the right to make 'full defence' by counsel), and under the Treason Acts a prisoner represented by counsel was always permitted to make a statement.

The judges, however, chose to construe the Act restrictively. In *Boucher*, at Gloucester Assizes (1837), Coleridge J, at the conclusion of counsel's speech in a felony case, refused an application by the prisoner to make a statement saying: 'Prisoner, your counsel has spoken for you, I cannot hear both.'[70] This ruling was followed by Bosanquet J the next year in *Burrows*.[71] He gave as his reason that

> the recent statute only meant to put prisoners in the same situation as they were before when defended by counsel in cases of misdemeanour, and in those cases certainly a defendant could not be allowed the privilege of two statements, one by himself and another by counsel.

He rejected the analogy of treason, saying that treason had always been considered an exception, the reason for the greater privilege being that the statute giving the right to counsel in treason said that the accused was to be permitted a full defence. This reasoning, of course, ignored the fact that a prisoner's unsworn statement was not simply an exercise in advocacy, a second speech, but a vital opportunity to give his explanation. If denied the right to make a statement when represented, this meant that he was in a worse position in this respect than if undefended. Further, so far as the treason point is concerned, Bosanquet seems to have overlooked the fact that the wording of the 1836 Act was, if anything, wider than that of the treason statutes (it empowered accused to make 'full answer and defence by counsel'). In *Rider* (1838), Patteson J offered another reason for the rule, namely if a prisoner stated to a jury what he could not prove the jury ought to dismiss it from their minds and, in so far as what he said was a comment upon the evidence, his counsel could do this much better than he could.[72] This analysis ignored the fact that unrepresented prisoners had always traditionally been allowed to say whatever they wished in answer to the charge and, in particular, had always been permitted to give explanations of the evidence against them. Not all judges denied such explanations evidential weight. In *Taylor* (1859), Byles J offered a third objection: that to allow unsworn statements would 'lead to prisoners being examined on their own behalf without the sanction of an oath and then a speech commenting on their statement'.[73]

If a prisoner defended by counsel could not make a statement, could he get round the difficulty by giving his explanation through his counsel? In

---

[70] *R v Boucher* (1837) 8 C & P 141.
[71] *R v Burrows* (1838) 2 M & Rob 124.
[72] *R v Rider* (1838) 8 C & P 539.
[73] *R v Taylor* (1859) 1 F & F 535.

Beard, decided at the same Gloucester Assize as *Boucher*, Coleridge answered this question with an emphatic 'No'.[74] 'I cannot permit counsel', he said, 'to tell the jury anything which he is not in a position to prove.' The following year he repeated this ruling in *Butcher*.[75] It was, in fact, in line with that which had been given in a clutch of civil cases in the early 1830s.[76]

Not all judges, however, were willing to construe the new Act as excluding the prisoner's right to make an unsworn statement. In March 1838, at Oxford Assizes in *Malings*,[77] defence counsel was in his speech to the jury, bemoaning the fact that his client could not make his own defence, when the judge, Alderson B, interrupted him saying:

> I see no objection in this case to his doing so. I think it is right that a person should have an opportunity of stating such facts as he may think material ... besides it is often the genuine defence of the party and not an imaginary case invented by the ingenuity of counsel.

Later that same day, Gurney B, sitting in the adjoining court, was persuaded to follow the same course in the case of *Walkling*,[78] but it is clear that he was influenced principally by considerations of judicial comity. He was at pains to stress that *Malings* was a very peculiar case and that he did not wish his (Gurney's) ruling to be drawn into a precedent. In 1884 Serjeant Ballantine in a letter to *The Times* claimed that Alderson B later 'recalled' the decision in *Malings*.[79] Whether this is right or not, there seems no justification for Gurney's comment that it was a very peculiar case. It was a charge of wounding with intent where the prisoner had made a statement to the magistrates in the same terms as his unsworn statement to the jury. If counsel in *Burrows* was correct, Alderson had, prior to *Malings* given a similar ruling on the Northern Circuit. Six years after *Malings* we find him declaring, in *Dyer* (1844), 'I would never prevent a prisoner from making a statement though he has counsel ... If it were otherwise the most monstrous injustice might result to prisoners.' Another judge who was for allowing a defended prisoner to make an unsworn statement was Denman LCJ, who is cited by counsel in *Burrows* as having recently ruled to that effect in a case on the Western Circuit. In *Williams* in 1846, Rolfe B, after having *Malings* cited to him, said there was good sense in the decision and elected to follow it.[80]

Cases like *Malings*, *Dyer* and *Williams* were, however, against the trend. By 1850 the practice, followed it seems by almost all judges of the superior courts, was to allow a prisoner to make a statement in a felony case only if

---

[74] *R v Beard* (1837) 8 C & P 142.
[75] *R v Butcher* (1839) 2 M & Rob 228.
[76] *Smart v Rayner* (1834) 6 C & P 721; *Stevens v Webb* (1835) 7 C & P 60; *Duncombe v Daniell* (1837) 8 C & P 222.
[77] *R v Malings* (1838) 8 C & P 242.
[78] *R v Walkling* (1838) 8 C. & P. 243.
[79] (1883–84) 76 LT 187.
[80] *R v Williams* (1846) 1 Cox 363.

unrepresented. This was what was claimed in 1884 in the course of the correspondence in *The Times* generated by the *O'Donnell Case*. Confirmation of the claim is to be found in case reports. The *Old Bailey Sessions Papers* for 1846 show that in only one out of the hundreds of felony trials held there that year did a defended prisoner make an unsworn statement. The reaction of Rolfe B in *Williams*, when first confronted by counsel's application that his client be allowed to address the jury, is equally revealing: 'I never heard of such a thing. It is contrary to all the rules of practice.' There is also the comment of Crown counsel in *Manzano* (1860) that the application that the prisoner be permitted to make a statement was unusual.[81] In fact, it was the post-1836 refusal of judges to allow defended prisoners to make unsworn statements that gave rise to a defence tactic of complaining to the jury that the prisoner's mouth was closed: what a *Times* leader was to refer to as 'the stock argument about the marvels the prisoner could prove if his mouth were not shut'.[82]

It may be that at Quarter Sessions a laxer rule prevailed than at Assizes and the Old Bailey. Certainly, this was the claim made in one legal journal in 1879.[83] Even at the Old Bailey and before Assize judges there were occasional deviations from normal practice. In *Taylor* (1859), Byles J allowed a prisoner the option of having his counsel make a speech to the jury or making a statement himself. In *Manzano* (1860), a murder case, Martin B allowed the prisoner to make a statement explaining how he came into possession of certain clothes belonging to the deceased. The judge said he did so because of the importance of the case but added that it was a bad practice, requiring, as it did, the judge to make comments on the prisoner's statement (perhaps adverse to him), inasmuch as counsel for the Crown had no right of reply. In 1871 at Hampshire Assizes Pigott B, in the case of *Stephens*, allowed accused represented by counsel to make statements, saying: 'I think no harm or injustice is ever done by permitting prisoners to tell their own story. It is often a truthful statement'.[84] In the early 1860s two unsuccessful applications that prisoners be allowed to make unsworn statements made at the Old Bailey were thought worth reporting in extenso by the editors of the *Old Bailey Sessions Papers*.[85]

Where the judge refused to allow a statement by the prisoner and there was no pre-trial statement, defence counsel, if he could not get the prisoner's version out by cross-examination or by the calling of witnesses, had only one course open to him: to put his client's account to the jury as a hypothesis.[86]

---

[81] *R v Manzano* (1860) 2 F & F 64.

[82] 13 December 1883.

[83] (1879) 13 Ir LT 566 (reproducing an article from the *Law Journal*).

[84] *R v Stephens* (1871) 11 Cox 669.

[85] *R v Crane and Debock* (1861) 54 CCC Sess Pap 154; *R v Brown* (1863) 61 CCC Sess Pap 240.

[86] (1882) 26 Sol J 191; (1879) 13 Ir LT, 566; *The Times*, 9 April 1898 (letter from Mead).

16

The Incompetency Rule: The First Reforms

'If they threw on the accused the onus of proving that he had used all means of making a ship seaworthy, they must in justice allow him to be called as a witness.' The Attorney-General (1876) PD XXVIII, 900.

1. First Attacks upon the Incompetency Rule

If 1836 saw the prisoner's right to make an unsworn statement curtailed, the 1820s and 1830s witnessed a major assault on the doctrine of incompetence through interest. In 1827 it was violently attacked by Bentham,[1] and six years later ridiculed by Dickens in *The Pickwick Papers*.[2] In Parliament the cudgels were taken up by two convinced Benthamites, Thomas Denman, the Lord Chief Justice, and Henry Brougham, the former Lord Chancellor. Gradually the rule began to buckle.

In 1828 it was enacted that in prosecutions for forgery the person whose name had been forged should be competent to prove the forgery.[3] In 1843 Lord Denman's Act abolished the rule, except in the cases of the parties individually named on the record and their spouses.[4] Next to fall was the rule rendering the parties to a civil suit incompetent. This was abolished as regards county courts by the Act of 1846 which created them,[5] and as regards the superior courts by Brougham's Law of Evidence Amendment Act of 1851. The reform was bitterly opposed by the Lord Chancellor and viewed with great mistrust by the profession.[6] The incompetence of the spouses of the parties, which the 1851 Act had left untouched, survived only two years longer, being abolished by Brougham's Evidence Further Amendment Act (1853).

Following the reform of the rule in civil cases, it was perhaps inevitable that there would be an attempt to end the incompetence of the accused in criminal cases. This came in 1858 with Brougham's Law of Evidence Further Amendment Bill, which proposed that the accused and his spouse should

---

[1] Bentham, *Rationale of Judicial Evidence*.
[2] *Pickwick Papers*, chapter 34, and see W. B. Odgers, *A Century of Law Reform*, 217.
[3] 9 Geo IV, c. 32, s 2.
[4] 6 & 7 Vict, c. 85.
[5] 9 & 10 Vict, c. 95, s 83.
[6] PD 1851 CXVI, 16; (1851) 17 LT 99 and E. Bowen Rowlands, *Seventy-Two Years at the Bar*, 26.

be competent but not compellable in all trials on indictment.[7] The Bill got no further than a first reading. It was reintroduced the following year.[8] On the motion for leave, it was strenuously opposed by the Lord Chancellor and other Law Lords. It would, they argued, entirely alter the administration of justice. Like the 1858 Bill it never got beyond a first reading.[9]

In 1860 Brougham tried again with a Bill of more modest scope: it was only to apply to trials in misdemeanour. It was greeted with a marked lack of enthusiasm, although Lord Campbell was prepared to concede that a relaxation limited to cases of assault and libel might have value. Like its predecessors, it was dropped after its first reading.[10] During the rest of the decade, no serious attempt at legislative reform of the criminal rule was made.

In 1863, a private Member, George Whalley, introduced a Petty Offences Bill which sought to make the accused competent in his own defence in all summary proceedings.[11] His object, he declared, was to counter police perjury in magistrates' courts. The Bill received no support and was withdrawn at the second reading stage. The following year it was reintroduced by Whalley and Patrick M'Mahon, an Irish barrister. The Solicitor-General spoke strongly against it, arguing that it would expose accused persons to cross-examination and to the risk of a failure to testify being taken as evidence of guilt. At this it was withdrawn.[12]

In 1865 Bills to make the accused a competent witness in all criminal proceedings were introduced by M'Mahon and Vincent Scully, and by Fitzroy Kelly, a future Chief Baron.[13] On the second reading debate on Kelly's Bill the Attorney-General, whilst speaking out strongly against reform, gave an assurance that the government would try to give an opportunity for full discussion of the question. Upon that assurance M'Mahon agreed to the second reading of his own Bill being deferred. Such opportunity was, however, never afforded and both Bills were lost.

If legislative reform was still many years off, during the 1860s several writers on criminal law and evidence did add their voices to the demand for change. In 1860 John Pitt Taylor, the author of the leading textbook on evidence (and the draftsman of the 1851 Act), pointed to the recent sensational case of the Reverend Henry Hatch (who, having been convicted

7 (1858) 22 JP 200.

8 Law of Evidence Further Amendment Bill; for the text see (1859) 23 JP 185 and 193–94.

9 PD 1859 CLII, 760–66.

10 Law of Evidence Further Amendment Bill, 1860, see (1860) 24 JP 426; debate, PD 1860 CLIX, 1084.

11 Petty Offences Bill, PP 1863 (240) III, 253; debate PD 1863 CLXXII, 1203.

12 Petty Offences Law Amendment Bill, PP 1864 (121) III, 237; debate, PD 1864 CLXXVI, 1433.

13 Criminal Cases Evidence Bill, PP 1865 (8) I, 471, Scully and M'Mahon; Law of Evidence etc. Bill, 1865 (not printed), Fitzroy Kelly; for the debate on latter Bill, see PD 1865 CLXXVII, 939–45.

of indecent assault, retaliated by prosecuting his accuser to conviction for perjury) as clear proof of the need for reform.[14] Two years later, J. F. Stephen published his *General View of the Criminal Law,* in which he restated and developed, before a wider public, arguments he had first put forward in a lecture in 1857.[15] Although calls for change excited no general enthusiasm, it was difficult to deny that the existing rule was open to severe criticism.

First, there was the charge of inconsistency. If the law excluded the accused from the witness-box on the ground of interest, why it might be asked was the prosecutor, who was frequently, by the payment of the expenses of the prosecution and otherwise, as much interested as the party accused, not similarly incompetent? The answer that the prosecutor was the Crown not the complainant hardly convinced. Also, if interest was a ground of incompetency, how came it that the law admitted accomplices as witnesses? Again, if the accused was incompetent he ought logically to be incompetent for all purposes and yet he was not. On a motion for a criminal information the court would receive affidavit evidence from him; and there were many interlocutory applications in proceedings on indictment where the law would act upon the affidavit of the accused.

Then there were the practical difficulties and anomalies to which the rule gave rise. In felony and misdemeanour, the effect of the rule, when combined with the prohibition upon an accused who had counsel making an unsworn statement, was literally to close the mouth of the accused and leave him to rely upon indirect expedients (such as pre-trial statements) in order to get his version across. There was the ridiculous state of affairs which could arise in cases of affray or factional violence, nowhere better described than by the Irish QC, O'Hagan:

> A fight took place between two factions ... coming home from a fair. Informations and cross-informations were sworn with the very object of including among the accused such individuals as could give evidence for the defence. The 'Ryans' ... were first put upon their trial. Their opponents, the 'Carrolls' came to the table one after another and told one side of the story. Where their evidence closed, the case closed. The jury retired to consider their verdict and then what occurred? The Carrolls all walked into the dock to take their trials before a new jury, and the Ryans walked out of it for a time in order to be examined as witnesses. The new jury heard a new case. Each jury was forced to decide upon one-sided evidence.[16]

A similar turning of the tables occurred where a person, convicted on the evidence of a single witness, prosecuted that witness for perjury. On such a prosecution, it would be the alleged perjurer whose mouth was closed. In the event that the prosecution was successful (and the device was, as in

---

[14] *The Times,* 18 May 1860.
[15] Lecture to the Juridical Society reported at (1857) 29 LT 146.
[16] (1874–75) 19 Sol J 575.

Hatch's Case, sometimes used as an indirect means of appealing a jury's verdict), one would have conflicting verdicts, brought in by different juries, in relation to the same subject matter, neither of which would have heard the principal witness in the case tried by the other.

The exclusion of the prisoner's spouse from the witness-box produced its share of absurdities. Of these none was more striking or notorious than the rule in bigamy prosecutions that the first wife was incompetent and the second wife competent.[17] Added to this was the problem that it was uncertain whether a reputed wife was caught by the bar.[18]

While Parliament showed no enthusiasm for reform of the rule, inroads were being made on it in the courts. In the first place, the problem posed by cross-indictments for assault was occasionally dealt with by trying them together.[19] Secondly, by the 1850s, it had come to be settled law that a prisoner who had pleaded guilty, or against whom the Crown had offered no evidence or entered a *nolle prosequi*, was competent to give evidence for an accused jointly indicted with him.[20] There were some judges who were prepared to push this principle even further. In 1845, at Maidstone Assizes, Alderson B allowed a prisoner to call his co-accused notwithstanding that the latter was herself contesting guilt.[21] In 1870 Mellor J, without giving reasons, took the same course in a trial at Worcester Assizes.[22] So too did a number of other Assize judges, including Pigott B, Lush J and the Irish judge Ball J. It was inevitable that sooner or later the point would be tested. The occasion came in *Payne*, in 1872, when Keating J reserved the question.[23] The Court for Crown Cases Reserved was emphatic that the practice was wrong. If a prisoner was allowed to be called for a fellow prisoner he would be subject to cross-examination, whereby lay great dangers; he might, for example, be cross-examined as to his past life; alternatively, he might be asked questions which he would find himself obliged to decline to answer on the grounds of self-incrimination. In either case the result would be seriously to injure his case.

Another stratagem one finds being used to render prisoners, both con-testing guilt, competent for each other was application for separate trials. Around mid century, such applications seem to have been rarely granted. In *Barber* (1844), an application supported by an affidavit from Barber's attorney to the effect that it was intended at such separate trial to call the other prisoners for the defence, and that it was believed that their evidence would lead to his acquittal, was rejected out of hand by Gurney B.[24] Separate

---

17 *R v Grigg* (1660) T Ray 1.
18 See Phillipps (8th edn, 1838), 172–73 and the cases there cited.
19 PD 1892 I, 667 (Lord Halsbury LC referring to Lord Campbell).
20 *R v Arundel* (1849) 4 Cox 260; *R v Fanny Archer* (1848) 3 Cox 228.
21 *R v Stewart and Stewart* (1845) 1 Cox 174.
22 *R v Deeley* (1870) 11 Cox 607.
23 *R v Payne* (1872) 12 Cox 118.
24 *R v Barber The Times*, 11–20, 23 and 29 April 1844.

trials, he said were often desired by prisoners, but the application was never granted save where, as in the recent case of *Sealey*,[25] the Crown consented to severance. It may be that later in the century judicial practice on the point grew more lenient. In the 1880s, it was being claimed in several quarters that applications for separate trials were seldom refused.[26] If that is right, the change appears to have been a very recent one. Trial reports from the 1870s and 1880s indicate a continuing judicial reluctance to grant separate trials.[27] The only class of case in which judges would always grant a separate trial was where conspiracy had been charged upon evidence disclosing substantive offences in respect of which the accused would have had to be tried separately.[28]

Yet another device which appears sometimes to have been employed, to enable prisoners jointly indicted to testify for each other, was that of severing their challenges. The prisoners would exercise their rights of challenge separately and to such extent as to create the risk of exhausting the panel of jurors present at court. Where prisoners took this course, the court (in order to prevent the panel being exhausted) could direct that one or more of them be separately tried; indeed, the Crown could apply to the court for such a direction.[29] The threat of severing challenges was, where the number of accused was large, a very powerful one, for exhaustion of the panel would involve delay whilst the sheriff summoned a fresh one.[30] One finds the device being employed successfully in Chartist trials in the 1840s.[31] In *Sealey* in 1844, severance of challenges was the means by which defence counsel proposed to try and achieve separate trials, until the consent of the Crown to severance of the indictment rendered such a proceeding unnecessary. In *Fisher* in 1848 Platt B, referring expressly to *Sealey*, said it was an ill practice for a judge to allow severance of challenges.[32] Ill practice or not, it was still sufficiently prevalent for Greaves to devote several paragraphs to it in his 1856 Report on Criminal Procedure.[33]

The practice of admitting a prisoner (who had been acquitted, had pleaded guilty, had had his trial severed, or was otherwise permitted to give evidence) to testify for a co-prisoner gave rise to some novel problems. Could such a

---

[25] *R v Sealey* (1844) 8 JP 328.

[26] *The Times*, 23 September 1882, report of the proceedings of the Social Science Congress (Hastings MP).

[27] *R v Littlechild* (1871) LR 6 QB 293; see also *R v Foote and Ramsay*, *The Times*, 6 March 1883.

[28] *R v Wright and Others*, *The Times*, 12 December 1809, *R v Rowlands* (1851) 5 Cox 436 and *R v Boulton* (1871) 12 Cox 87.

[29] Archbold (20th edn 1886), 171.

[30] A fresh panel was summoned because of doubt as to the power to award a tales, Archbold, 176.

[31] *R v Frost and Others*, *The Times*, 1 January 1840; *R v Turner Kelsall and Others*, *The Times*, 12 October 1842.

[32] *R v Fisher* (1848) 3 Cox 68.

[33] PP 1856 (456) L 79.

prisoner, called at the trial of his co-prisoners A and B, who gave evidence for A which incriminated B, be cross-examined by B? In *Woods and May* (1853), one of the City judges had held that he could.[34] The Court for Crown Cases Reserved gave the same ruling when the point was tested before them in *Burdett* (1855).[35] Jervis LCJ, however, left open the question whether there was a right to cross-examine where a prisoner called a witness who did not criminate his fellow prisoner. In that situation, he said, the latter would only have the right to examine the witness as his own witness. Attempts to outflank the prohibition upon the wife of a prisoner giving evidence for his co-accused at their joint trial went back further in time. The point had come before the Twelve Judges as early as 1826 in *Smith*, when they had upheld the trial judge's ruling that a prisoner could not call in proof of an alibi the wife of a co-prisoner.[36] However, *Smith* was a case where the wife's evidence was arguably capable of benefiting her husband as well as the prisoner seeking to call her. What if calling the wife on behalf of a co-prisoner would not in any way benefit her husband? Did the principle in *Smith's Case* apply then? Phillipps, writing in 1838, thought that it might well not,[37] and that was in fact the view taken (albeit with considerable hesitation) by Wightman J in *Bartlett and Anderson* (1844).[38] This aberrant authority was eventually overruled in 1872 by the Court for Crown Cases Reserved, which held that the wife of a prisoner jointly indicted stood in the same position, as regards the admissibility of her evidence, as her husband.[39]

2. United States and Colonial Reform

Outside England matters were, in the 1860s, moving at an altogether faster pace. In 1864 the state of Maine passed a statute making the accused and his spouse competent but not compellable witnesses.[40] Similar legislation followed in other states, and by 1878 no fewer than twenty-eight American states had passed statutes permitting prisoners and their spouses to testify.[41]

---

[34] *R v Woods and May* (1853) 6 Cox 224.

[35] *R v Burdett* (1855) 6 Cox 458.

[36] *R v Smith* (1826) 1 Moo 289.

[37] Phillipps, 160.

[38] *R v Bartlett and Anderson* (1844) 1 Cox 105; other cases where the wife of an accused was admitted for a co- prisoner include *R v Moore and Turner* (1843) 1 Cox 59 and *R v Denslow and Newbury* (1847) 8 LT 559.

[39] *R v Thompson* (1872) 12 Cox 202.

[40] Wigmore, *A Treatise on the Anglo-American System of Evidence* (3rd edn, Boston, 1940), art 579 n 2.

[41] Ibid.; see also (1878) 12 Ir LT 554; amongst the first states to follow the example of Maine were Massachusetts (1867), New Hampshire and New York (1869) and New Jersey (1871). But note that until 1962 defendants in criminal cases in Georgia were not permitted to testify on oath, Wigmore, *Treatise*.

Nor was it only in the United States that the reform was being brought in. Three years before the Maine statute, an Act had been passed giving judges in British India power to examine the accused, and to put to him such questions as they thought necessary (the provision did not, however, apply in the Presidency Towns of Calcutta, Madras and Bombay, where English law continued to apply).[42] In 1872 the Indian Evidence Act (drafted by Stephen) was passed, section 120 of which made the spouse of accused competent as a witness for the defence.

3. Piecemeal Reform in England

Although the Bill of 1865 seeking to effect major reform was lost, some modest inroads were made in England in the 1860s on the bar on prisoners' evidence. The first comprised a clutch of statutes designed to remove all doubt that the Acts of 1851 and 1853 applied to proceedings on the Revenue side of the Exchequer, which arguably were criminal.[43]

Next, in 1867, came the Master and Servant Act, which provided, as part of its framework for the enforcement of contracts of employment, certain penal provisions, breach of which was punishable summarily by fine and imprisonment. It gave those charged with such breaches, and their spouses, the right to give evidence in their own defence. This was no more than a small breach in the general rule, the offences being summary only and essentially civil in character. Nevertheless, it marked the beginning of a trend of creating ad hoc exceptions to the general rule which, by the 1890s, had succeeded in reducing the law to a state which cried out for reform.

Another such statute followed four years later: the Merchant Shipping Act (1871), a temporary Act but one which could scarcely be dismissed as an unimportant breach. Its provisions:

1. Made it an indictable misdemeanour punishable by two years' imprisonment to send an unseaworthy ship to sea.

2. Cast upon a person charged with such offence the burden of showing that he had used all reasonable means to ensure the ship being sent to sea in a seaworthy state, or that her going to sea under such circumstances was reasonable and justifiable.

3. Made such a person a competent witness in his own defence.

The exception was later to be justified, in parliamentary debates, on the ground that where the law cast a burden of proof upon an accused, common justice required that he be allowed to give evidence in order to discharge

---

[42] (1876) 1 Law Mag (4th series) 631; Code of Criminal Procedure Act, 1861 (India Act XXV of 1861).

[43] 17 & 18 Vict, c. 122, s 15; 18 & 19 Vict, c. 96, s 36; 20 & 21 Vict, c. 62, s 14; 28 & 29 Vict, c. 104, s 34; and Customs Consolidation Act, 1876, s 259.

such burden.[44] However, the argument was less convincing than it sounded. It was not difficult to instance cases, both at common law and under statute, where the accused bore a burden of proof but with no right to give evidence.

The 1871 Act marked the opening of the floodgates. In the next seven years no less than ten more Acts were passed giving persons charged with offences created thereby the right to give evidence in their own defence. In the case of six of these Acts the justification could be, and was, offered that the Act cast a burden of proof on the accused: the Coal Mines Regulation Act (1872); the Metalliferous Mines Regulation Act (1872); the Sale of Food & Drugs Act (1875); the Merchant Shipping Acts (1875 and 1876) (which placed on a permanent footing the provisions as to unseaworthy ships contained in the 1871 Act); and the Threshing Machines Act (1878). Another, the Conspiracy and Protection of Property Act (1875), can be regarded as merely extending the exception created by the Master and Servant Act (1867); and yet another, the Evidence Act (1877), can be claimed to deal with proceedings which, though criminal in form, were essentially civil in character. For the exception created by the remaining two Acts, the Licensing Act (1872) and the Contagious Diseases (Animals) Act (1878), no such apology could be offered.

These ten Acts were conspicuous for their failure to adopt any common form of wording. Seven of them were silent as to cross-examination of the accused as to credit, and none faced up to the issue of whether failure by an accused to give evidence might be used against him and made the subject of adverse comment.

4. Russell Gurney's Act

In the same year as Parliament passed the Master and Servant Act, it also tried to tackle the problem of the prisoner prevented by poverty from calling witnesses. The Criminal Law Act of 1867 required examining magistrates to ask the prisoner whether he wished to call witnesses. If he elected to do so, depositions were to be taken from them and, if they gave evidence material to establish his innocence (and not going simply to character), they were to be bound over to attend the court of trial, where the judge would have power to order their expenses paid out of public funds. The principle of the Act was not in fact new. A similar scheme was being operated by magistrates in the West Riding as early as 1851.[45]

Despite the hopes of its promoter, Russell Gurney, the Act proved of only limited value to prisoners. Ten years after it came into force getting witnesses

---

[44] This was the justification for the exception urged in the Commons debates on the 1876 Act, see PD 1876 CCVIII, 900; cf. the criticisms of the Habitual Offenders and Bankruptcy Bills of 1869 in (1869) 4 LJ 151.

[45] *The Times*, 17 March 1851.

to court was still a real problem for most poor prisoners.[46] One of the Act's shortcomings was that it was only witnesses who attended the committal hearing who could be bound over to attend, and for a prisoner in custody getting such witnesses to attend the committal hearing could be just as much of a problem as getting them to attend the trial. Also, since payment of witnesses' expenses was only made after trial, a prisoner whose witnesses were too poor to afford to make the journey to court and provide for their subsistence there, while waiting for the case to be called on, was in no better position after the Act than before it.[47] Thirdly, the Act, like the Poor Prisoners' Defence Act (1903), made assistance conditional on the prisoner showing his hand.

In the 1890s, to assist prisoners to get their witnesses to court, it was the practice in some gaols for the staff to go round the week before trial and ask remand prisoners if there were any witnesses they wished to have called at trial and, if there were, to request the police to contact them.[48] In 1892 the Home Secretary gave an undertaking to take steps to see that this practice was adopted at all gaols.[49]

5. Quakers and Atheists

A small reform passed in 1869 benefiting prisoner and prosecutor alike was the abolition of the incompetency of atheists to give evidence in criminal proceedings. By the Evidence Further Amendment Act such witnesses were to be permitted to affirm, thereby extending to them a privilege which Quakers had enjoyed, in criminal cases, since 1833.[50]

---

[46] Report of the Committee of Judges respecting Circuits, PP 1878 (311) LXIII, 1, para 4.

[47] An Order in Council made under the Winter Assizes Acts, 1876–77, enabled a judge or two JPs to order upto £20 to be advanced out of public funds to cover the travelling expenses, but not the subsistence, of defence witnesses.

[48] See *R v Woolf, The Times*, 10 January 1884; PD 1890/91 CCCLVI, 770; and *R v Watts and Hall, The Times*, 8 June 1896.

[49] PD (1890/91) ibid.; SO 213 (Local Prisons) gave effect to the undertaking.

[50] Quakers and Moravians Act, 1833.

17

The Campaign for a Prisoners' Evidence Act

'the rule of law which incapacitated the accused ... from giving evidence
on his own behalf had the effect of excluding the evidence of the person
who knew most about the transaction.

Sir Charles Russell PD, 1888, CCCXXIV, 70.

1. The Attack on the Incompetency Rule

Not only did the 1870s see the creation of ad hoc exceptions to the incompetency rule, they also saw the rule itself come under sustained attack. The subject was debated by the Social Science Congress in 1874.[1] A survey of the practice in the United States, published by the Society for the Amendment of the Law, showed a majority of American states had abolished the incompetency rule, and that the general view in those states in which the reform had been tried was that it had worked well.[2] The survey merely served to confirm this message, which had been put abroad by Russell Gurney upon his return from serving as one of the *Alabama* arbitrators. He had, he said, been assured by both the Chief Justice and the Attorney-General of New York that the system had been the means of preventing wrongful convictions, and that judges and lawyers, who had originally been hostile to the reform, were now fully convinced of its advantages and utility. In 1876, 1877 and 1878 Bills for abolition were introduced in the Commons.[3]

The scheme of the 1876 Bill was unoriginal. The accused and his spouse were to be competent but not compellable, with no fetter placed upon cross-examination as to credit. Introduced too late in the session to have any hope of becoming law, the 1876 Bill provided Evelyn Ashley, its promoter, with an opportunity to test the parliamentary water. The reception it received on its second reading debate was not encouraging. Of the eight Members who spoke in the debate, six came out strongly against the Bill, variously condemning it as a retrograde measure, a return to barbarism and a Bill for torture. The two members who spoke in its favour were George

---

[1] *The Times*, 6 October 1874.
[2] (1878) 12 Ir LT , 554, 563, 575 and 593.
[3] Criminal Law Evidence Amendment Bill, PP 1876 (61) I, 511; debate, PD 1876 CCXXX, 1925–39; Criminal Law Evidence Amendment Bill, PP 1877 (76) I, 481; Criminal Law Evidence Amendment Bill, PP 1878 (23) II, 243; debate, PD 1878 CCLVII, 657–88.

Whalley (the co-promoter of the Petty Offences Bills of 1863 and 1864) and Russell Gurney, the recorder of London. Whalley's support was more an embarrassment than a help, for, predictably, the reason he gave for favouring the Bill was that it would be an antidote to police perjury. Russell Gurney could not, however, be so easily dismissed. He had huge experience and a high reputation as a City judge, and he had recently discussed the working of the reform with a number of American judges and lawyers, and observed trials in which the accused had given evidence. At the end of the debate, Ashley withdrew the Bill, but indicated that he regarded Russell Gurney's support as important for changing public opinion. His words might have carried more conviction had not Russell Gurney's fellow Old Bailey judge, Sir Thomas Chambers, the common serjeant, spoken out strongly against the Bill in the debate, or had the Attorney-General (who only troubled to enter the Chamber towards the end of the debate) not been equally dismissive.

The 1877 Bill did not get beyond a first reading. The 1878 Bill, however, made much more satisfactory progress. On the second reading debate, the majority of those who spoke were in favour of the reform, while the language used by its opponents was more temperate than it had been in the 1876 debate (Serjeant Simon, for example, no longer saw fit to dub it a Bill for torture). At the end of the debate it was given its second reading by the substantial majority of 185 to 76.

The stance of the government had also changed. The Attorney-General, while pointing to drawbacks and confessing to a great difficulty in making his mind up on the reform, was not overtly hostile. On the contrary, he offered encouragement to the reform lobby. The government he told them, was, in the course of preparing a Criminal Code, which would contain a provision dealing with the matter of prisoners' evidence. He suggested to Ashley that the Bill ought to go to a Select Committee, so that the government should have the benefit of that committee's report when it brought in its own measure. This offer Ashley willingly accepted.

Why did the 1878 Bill fare so much better than that of 1876? A number of possible answers suggest themselves. First, the 1876 Bill had attracted a good deal of attention in the legal press and elsewhere, and some powerful voices had been raised in its support.[4] Furthermore, an extraordinary rape case, tried at Liverpool in 1877, had seemed to vindicate reformist claims that the right to give evidence would be a boon to the innocent.[5] Another factor must have been the decision of Ashley and Russell Gurney, the Bill's promoters, to include in it clauses protecting the accused against cross-examination as to previous convictions and against any adverse inference

[4] J. F. Stephen, 'The Reform of the Criminal Law' (1877) 2 *Nineteenth Century* 737 ; cf. A. Wills, 'Should Prisoners be Examined?' (1878) 3 *Nineteenth Century* 169.

[5] The case was *R v Greenwood Jackson and Wild*, referred to *R v Sutcliffe and Others, The Times*, 12 November 1877).

being drawn from failure on his part to give evidence,[6] thus meeting two of the major criticisms which had been made of the 1876 Bill. Perhaps, also, the speeches in the 1876 debate did not, even then, accurately mirror the state of opinion in the House.

In the Commons debates on the two Bills, the arguments marshalled for and against the reform were ones that were to be heard, again and again, over the next twenty years. On the one side, it was urged that the existing rule made it difficult for juries to get at the truth. They were denied the explanation of the one person who knew most about the facts. To allow the accused to give evidence would lead to the acquittal of the innocent and the surer conviction of the guilty. This, it was claimed, had been the experience of the American courts, and there was no reason to think that the reform would work any less satisfactorily in England.

The arguments against the reform were various. First, while it was not denied that the reform would lead to more convictions, it was disputed that it would benefit innocent prisoners. On the contrary, it would operate to their disadvantage. It would undermine the principle that it was for the prosecution to prove the guilt of the accused. The accused would, in practice, be compelled to go into the witness-box or risk the jury drawing a damning inference from his failure to do so. An innocent prisoner who had a criminal record, or was of bad character, would be placed in an impossible dilemma: if he gave evidence, he risked his record or character being brought out in cross-examination; if he did not give evidence, he risked the jury taking against him on that score. For the innocent but uneducated prisoner (undefended as most were) there was the real risk that his nervousness and confusion might create an impression of guilt and that, under cross-examination at the hands of skilled experienced counsel, he might easily be made to appear guilty (particularly if he yielded to the temptation to lie to make his case better), with no counsel of his own to undo the damage by re-examination. (Serjeant Simon suggested that no more than one prisoner in twenty would be capable of standing up to cross-examination.) In short, the reform, if carried, would set at nought the principle of English law that an accused could not be compelled to criminate himself, in favour of the continental system of moral torture of prisoners. It would result in prisoners, who under the existing system would be acquitted through the weakness of the prosecution case, convicting themselves under cross-examination out of their own mouths.[7]

Secondly, in the case of undefended prisoners, there were very real

---

[6] Cl 6 of the Bill prohibited cross-examination of the accused as to previous convictions or charges, or as to other offences (but not as to other matters of discredit) whilst cl 10 provided that the failure of an accused to give evidence should not give rise to any presumption against him nor be referred to or commented upon.

[7] This argument, although touched on during the debates on the 1876 and 1878 Bills, was first fully developed in the debates on the later Prisoners' Evidence Bills.

practical problems. With no counsel to examine and re-examine, how was the prisoner's story to be brought out, if he could not tell it? What guidance would he receive and from whom as to whether he should testify? Thirdly, the reputation of the bench would be compromised. Where there was no prosecuting counsel, or where prosecuting counsel was inexperienced or inept, the judge would be obliged to undertake the task of cross-examining the accused. This would destroy the appearance of judicial impartiality and lead to unseemly wrangles between bench and prisoner, particularly where (as at some county Quarter Sessions) the judge was biased and unscrupulous. Fourthly, the reform if carried would lead to the most shocking perjury, which would injure public morals and the administration of justice. Fifthly, it was untrue that under the existing system a prisoner could not give his explanation. On the contrary, he could do so on arrest or before the examining magistrate; or, where undefended, by an unsworn statement at trial.

2. The Criminal Code Bills

For the period 1878 to 1882 the focus for the reformers was a succession of Criminal Code Bills, each of which contained a prisoners' evidence clause. The scheme of a Criminal Code had originated with J. F. Stephen.[8] By late July 1877 the government was converted, with Stephen instructed to start work drawing up a Bill.[9] Using his own *Digest of Criminal Law* as his starting point, Stephen did the work with remarkable rapidity. When the Bill was introduced into the Commons in May 1878 it contained, as the Attorney-General had promised, a prisoners' evidence clause.[10] However, this clause was very different to Ashley's scheme. Modelled on the provisions of the Indian Code of Criminal Procedure,[11] it provided that a prisoner should at the close of the prosecution case have the option, if defended, of being examined by his counsel; if undefended, of making a statement. The examination or statement would not be on oath, but the prosecution would have the right to cross-examine him on it, although they would not be allowed to put questions going to either credit or character. After being cross-examined he might, if defended, be re-examined or, if undefended, give

---

[8] He wrote to the Lord Chancellor on the subject on 20 January 1877 (PRO, LCO 1/42); on 6 February he gave a lecture on the subject of 'A Penal Code' to the parliamentary committee of the TUC (*The Times*, 8 February 1877). Later in the year he published an article with the same title in the *Fortnightly Review* (1877) 27 OS 362.

[9] L. Stephen, *The Life of Sir James F. Stephen* (London, 1895) 380; for his efforts Stephen received 3000 guineas (PRO, LCO 1/42) and the promise of a knighthood, which was honoured on 3 January 1879 when he was appointed a QBD judge.

[10] Criminal Code (Indictable Offences) Bill, PP 1878 (178) II, 5, cl 368.

[11] Code of Criminal Procedure Act, 1861 (India Act No. XXV of 1861) s 342 and Indian Evidence Act, 1872, s 120.

such explanation as he pleased. His statement not being on oath, he would not be liable to prosecution for perjury.

In an article written in 1877, Stephen sought to justify dispensing with the oath in the case of prisoners on two grounds.[12] First, it would not be practical to prosecute prisoners who gave false evidence on oath for perjury, yet not to prosecute them would undermine respect for the administration of justice. Secondly, the temptation for an accused to lie was so great that it would overbear the ordinary sanction of truthfulness which the oath provided. The *Solicitors' Journal*, commenting on the 1878 Code Bill, offered another reason: 'dispensing with the oath solved the problem of cross-examination as to credit: 'if the prisoner's evidence is put forward as prima facie credible because the prisoner is examined on oath, the logical consequence is that he ought to be cross-examined as to credit; but, where his evidence is not on oath this reasoning does not apply'.[13]

One problem, which Stephen's clause did not attempt to deal with, was that of protecting the accused who chose not to give evidence against the risk of an adverse inference being drawn from his silence. By early June 1878 it was clear that the Bill had little hope of passing that session. It was too bulky and there was too little time left. On 15 August it was withdrawn and referred to a Royal Commission, consisting of Stephen, Lord Blackburn, Lush LJ and the Irish judge Barry, for report and revision.[14]

The commission worked at great speed, and by Spring it had produced a revised Code Bill.[15] As its later published report made clear, it was divided on the question of whether prisoners and their spouses should be allowed to give evidence.[16] Although its Bill contained such a provision, the clause was very different to that in Stephen's 1878 Bill. A prisoner, or his spouse, would become a competent witness for the defence. If they gave evidence, it would be on oath and, like any other witnesses, they would be subject to cross-examination, although the court would have a power to limit cross-examination of the accused as to credit to such extent as it thought fit.[17] Once again, the problem of the accused who chose not to give evidence was not addressed.

On 3 April 1879 the Bill was given its first reading in the Commons.[18] In introducing it, the Attorney-General was diffident in his approach to the prisoners' evidence clause, telling the House that on the subject his mind

---

[12] (1877) 2 *Nineteenth Century* 737 at 754; the idea was not new see PD 1876 CCXXX, 1926 and 1878 CCXXXVII, 668.

[13] (1877–78) 22 Sol J 277–78.

[14] PD 1878 CCXLII, 2040.

[15] PP 1878–79 (Cmnd 2345) XX, 169.

[16] Report of Criminal Code Commissioners PP 1878–79 (Cmnd 2345) XX 169 (p 37).

[17] Criminal Code (Indictable Offences) Bill, 1879 (PP 1878–79 (117) II, 175) cl 523).

[18] For the parliamentary debates and history of the Bill, see PD 1878–79, CCXLV, 310 and 1750; CCXLVI, 1915; and CCXLVII, 953 and 1281.

was evenly balanced. He acknowledged that there could be no means of arriving at the truth so surely as that of the examination of the accused. On the other hand, the change might operate harshly in the case of a man unjustly accused of crime whose antecedents were of a character which would unfairly prejudice him if they were exhibited to the jury. He should, he said, be glad of full and ample disussion of this point of the measure and, if the House should exhibit a feeling adverse to the introduction of such a principle, he would at once consent to its withdrawal. The debate which followed showed that the reform was far from popular in all quarters. By the summer of 1879 it was becoming obvious that the Bill, like that of 1878, would be lost through lack of parliamentary time. On 12 June the coup de grace was administered when Lord Chief Justice Cockburn wrote a long letter to the Attorney-General criticising the first part of the Bill (mainly on drafting grounds), promising further letters commenting on the other parts of the Code. A month later the Bill was withdrawn.

3. Weston and the Extension of the Right to Make an Unsworn Statement

At this juncture, Cockburn, who was reputed to be an opponent of the proposal that prisoners be permitted to give evidence,[19] saw fit unilaterally to introduce a major modification of the law as to unsworn statements. In 1879, in a murder case (Weston) at Maidstone Winter Assizes, he ruled that defence counsel might in his speech to the jury give the accused's account of how the fatal shot came to be fired, adding that counsel was in place of the prisoner and entitled to say anything which he might say.[20] This ruling represented a repudiation of Beard, which had, for nearly forty years, been regarded as settling the point. Being a decision of the Lord Chief Justice it was followed by several puisne judges, although at least one declined to do so.[21] In 1881, by coincidence, the very same point arose before Cockburn's successor in office, Lord Chief Justice Coleridge. Again the case was a murder case (Le Froy); again, the venue was Maidstone.[22] With some reluctance, Coleridge acceded to Montagu Williams' application that he be allowed to tell the jury his client's account of events. Once the case was over, he lost little time in calling a meeting of the Council of Judges to discuss the propriety of the practice adopted in Weston's Case.

At the meeting held in the Queen's Bench rooms on 26 November 1881 (three weeks after the Le Froy trial), the judges passed, by a majority of nineteen to two, a resolution that:

19 (1883–84) 76 LT 187; (1879) 13 Ir LT 566.
20 R v Weston (1879) 14 Cox 346.
21 (1883–84) 76 LT 187.
22 R v Le Froy, The Times, 5 and 7–9 November 1881; (1883) 17 Ir LT 643.

It is contrary to the administration and practice of the criminal law, as hitherto allowed, that counsel for the prisoner should state to the jury, as alleged existing facts, matters which they have been told in their instructions, on the authority of the prisoner, but which they do not propose to prove in evidence.

The two dissentients were Hawkins and Stephen JJ. (Stephen had at the meeting moved an amendment that it was undesirable to express any opinion upon the matter, but this had been lost, again nineteen to two, with himself and Hawkins its only supporters.)[23] In January 1882 North J announced the decision of the judges in a case at Reading Assizes, an announcement that was given publicity in legal journals.[24] This ought to have settled the point but, astonishingly, it did not.

In December 1883 at the Old Bailey, at the trial of O'Donnell for murder,[25] Sir Charles Russell, in the teeth of objection from the Attorney-General, prevailed upon Denman J to allow him to state the prisoner's account to the jury, arguing that he was only claiming the right to do that which the prisoner could do himself, if undefended. Denman offered to reserve the point, which led to the Attorney-General abandoning his objection. On the same day as the jury's verdict was received in *O'Donnell's Case*, the Attorney-General wrote to Coleridge LCJ, asking that the uncertainty as to the law upon the point be removed, suggesting that next time the question arose in a case of no great importance permission to make the statement should be refused and the point reserved. He added that if the practice was henceforth to be as laid down in *O'Donnell*, it was in his view essential that the Crown be allowed a right of reply. He mentioned that he had raised with Denman J the question of the judges having already had a meeting upon the point, but was assured by him that this was not so. (Denman, who had not been present at the meeting, was later to explain that he had forgotten about it.) Coleridge replied to the Attorney's letter by return, telling him of the November 1881 resolution and expressing the view that, because of possible difficulties about reserving the point, the best way forward might be to make the resolution generally known. This was done. The correspondence was published both in *The Times* and in a number of legal journals. A lively correspondence followed in *The Times*.[26] Several of those who wrote supporting the resolution did so on the ground that there was a danger that counsel, in placing his client's version before the jury, would embellish it or omit parts which he considered damaging to the

---

[23] (1883–84) 76 LT 100; (1883) 17 Ir LT 644.

[24] (1881–82) 26 Sol J 175 (so too did Lopes J in a case at Worcester Assizes (1881–82) 26 Sol J 191); the ruling was severely criticised in *The Times* on 23 January.

[25] *R v O'Donnell*, *The Times*, 3 December 1883, and (1883–84) 99 CCC Sess Pap 138.

[26] The correspondents were Williams J (29 December 1883 and 5 and 12 January 1884); Lord Bramwell under the pseudonym 'B' (2 and 5 January); Littler QC (2 and 8 January), Ballantine (5 January) and Dering (4 January).

prisoner.[27] Within months of Cockburn's ruling in the *Weston* case, another development took place which was to prove of lasting importance: judges began to allow prisoners represented by counsel to make unsworn statements to the jury.

Amongst those most prominent in fostering this change was Hawkins J, one of the dissentients at the November 1881 meeting. Hawkins was, in fact, either the first or one of the first judges to allow in an unsworn statement. The case was *Hull and Smith*, a robbery tried Leeds Assizes on 3 February 1880.[28] As defence counsel began to complain to the jury that his clients' mouths were closed, Hawkins observed that it was not so:

> Prisoners were at liberty to make any statement they chose; the jury were not bound to believe it, but it ought to be taken into consideration ... if the prisoner had made a statement in writing, he saw no objection to it being read, but if it were an oral statement, it might be better to have it from the prisoner himself.

Before finally committing himself to allowing the two prisoners before him to make written statements, Hawkins left court to consult with Lush LJ, who was sitting in the adjoining court. On his return, he said that Lush LJ entirely agreed with him and had himself so acted in more than one case. There was no decision of the Court for Crown Cases Reserved to the contrary and, in so far as the books contained dicta to the contrary, they were only the expressions of opinion of individual judges made probably under circumstances not fully set out in the reports. It would be a barbarous state of the law if a prisoner were not permitted to give his own explanation. In 1884 Lush LJ's marshal, in a letter to *The Times*, revealed that the former's reason for agreeing to the course proposed by Hawkins was that, under Jervis's Act, a prisoner had a right to make a statement before the examining magistrates. Any such statement might go before the jury. If he had the right before the magistrates, why should he not have the same right when actually before the jury?[29]

The course taken by Hawkins J in *Hull and Smith* represented a substantial change of view and stance on his part. In the *Penge Murder Case* three years before, he had listened to Sir Edward Clarke's lament that his clients could not give their explanation, and had certainly not proferred to them the opportunity to make a statement to the jury.[30] Hawkins' example was followed by Bowen J in August 1880;[31] and by Coleridge LCJ in January 1881.[32]

---

[27] The point was made by Williams J in his letter of 29 December; see also Stephen J in *R v Ross*, *The Times*, 24 April 1884.

[28] *R v Hull and Smith* (1880) 68 LT 264; *The Times*, 5 and 7 February 1880.

[29] *The Times*, 22 January 1884 (letter signed ML).

[30] *The Trial of the Stauntons* (Notable British Trial Series), 200 (the trial was held in September 1877).

[31] *R v Blades* (Leeds Assizes), *The Times*, 5 August 1880.

[32] *R v Gerrish*, *The Times*, 14 January 1882.

At the November 1881 meeting of the judges, the propriety of allowing prisoners, represented by counsel, to make unsworn statements was raised but the matter adjourned sine die.

Opinion was, however, clearly moving in favour of the new practice. On 4 May 1882 at Liverpool, in the case of *Shimmin*, Cave J declared that for the future he intended to allow prisoners, whether defended by counsel or not, to make a statement at the conclusion of counsel's speech, subject to the prosecution having a right of reply.[33] He added that the rule was one in which the other judges of the High Court concurred. In a later case at the same Assize, he reiterated what he had said in *Shimmin*, adding that it was important that the profession generally should be acquainted with the practice intended to be followed in future.[34] Some assumed that Cave J was declaring a new rule of practice, decided upon by the Council of Judges,[35] but subsequent events make this doubtful.[36] In *Everett* in January 1883, Hawkins J laid down the same rule as had Cave J at Liverpool.[37] That year also saw Day J, Lush LJ and North J adopt the new practice.[38] It was also spreading to Quarter Sessions.[39]

However, there were dissentient voices. In *Taylor and Boynes*, tried in May 1883, Coleridge LCJ, upon the application of counsel, and after consulting with the Master of the Rolls, 'against his better judgment' allowed the defendants to make an unsworn statement.[40] Before the case was over he had repented of his decision, declaring that he would not do so again until the opinion of all the judges had been obtained. In December 1883 Williams J, in a letter to *The Times*, had come out strongly in favour of the practice, stating that nothing but an Act of Parliament would induce him to depart from it. His letter produced a spirited rejoinder from Lord Bramwell condemning the new practice root and branch. In *Houltby*, an arson case tried at York Assizes in late January 1884, Field J refused an application by defence counsel for leave for the prisoner to make an unsworn statement, saying that he could not change the law because he thought the law unjust.[41] By March 1884 Day J had had a change of heart. In *Velasquez*, tried at the Old Bailey in that month, he refused to allow a defended prisoner to make a statement, observing that the last time he had done it had been in a capital case and that the result had been disastrous for the prisoner.[42] In *Attwood and Tatham*,[43]

---

[33] *R v Shimmin* (1882) 15 Cox 122.
[34] *R v Pembroke*, *The Times*, 10 June 1882.
[35] See letter (1883–84) 76 LT 150.
[36] Letter from Paget to *The Times* quoted at (1883–84) 76 LT 187.
[37] *R v Everett* (1883) 97 CCC Sess Pap 329 at 355.
[38] (1883) 47 JP 343 and 355.
[39] (1883) 47 JP 343 (Essex); (1881–82) 26 Sol J 39 (Sheffield).
[40] *R v Taylor and Boynes* (1883) 15 Cox 265.
[41] *R v Houltby* (1883–84) 28 Sol J 256.
[42] *R v Velasquez*, *The Times*, 21 March 1884.
[43] *R v Attwood and Tatham*, *The Times*, 4 November 1884.

tried in November 1884, A. L. Smith J reverted to the practice, adopted by Byles J in *Taylor* (1859),[44] of putting the prisoner to his election whether he would make the statement himself or have counsel address the jury on his behalf, ruling that he could not do both.

Understandably, there was uncertainty at the bar as to what the position was. In *Ross*, tried at the Old Bailey in April 1884, Gerald Geoghegan, a very experienced counsel, expressed regret that a recent rule of the judges prevented the prisoner from giving his own version of the matter.[45] The trial judge, Stephen J, had to interpose to make clear that the November 1881 resolution merely prohibited counsel relating his client's instructions to the jury and did not prevent the prisoner himself making a statement. *Watters* in 1883 appears to be the first case in which Stephen J (the other dissentient at the 1881 meeting) is recorded as permitting an unsworn statement by a defended prisoner.[46] From this time on, he was in the forefront of those supporting the change in the law, particularly after 1885.

By early 1885 it appears that the matter had recently been before the Council of Judges again and a resolution in favour of the new practice adopted. In *Millhouse*, in January 1885, Coleridge LCJ declared himself bound by a resolution of the judges (with which he did not agree) to allow a prisoner represented by counsel to make an unsworn statement, but claimed that the resolution did not extend to a case where the prisoner proposed to call witnesses and declined to allow him to do both.[47] Certainly, from 1885 onwards, there are numerous instances of successful applications by counsel for their clients to be allowed to make unsworn statements.[48] But it is clear that there was still dissension and reluctance on the part of some judges to accept the new practice. In 1888 complaint was made, in a Commons' debate, that there were judges who still refused to allow a prisoner defended by counsel to make an unsworn statement.[49] Divergent judicial practice was offered as the principal justification for amending the Criminal Evidence Bill (1898) so as to include a clause preserving the right of prisoners to make unsworn statements.[50]

If the rule allowing defended prisoners to make unsworn statements was the subject of dissension, so was the manner in which the right was to be exercised. First, there was the question of the stage in the case at which such statements should be made. Stephen J always insisted that the statement be made before counsel's address on the grounds that it would otherwise

[44] *R v Taylor* (1859) 1 F & F 535.
[45] *R v Ross, The Times*, 24 April 1884.
[46] *R v Watters* (1883) 47 JP 756; *The Times*, 28 November 1883.
[47] *R v Millhouse* (1885) 15 Cox 622.
[48] *R v Hay, The Times*, 6 November 1885; *R v Masters, The Times*, 14 January 1886; *R v Rowe, The Times*, 3 November 1886; *R v Doherty, The Times*, 20 December 1888; *R v Jones* (1891) 114 CCC Sess Pap 1058.
[49] PD 1888 CCCXXIV, 120–21.
[50] PD 1898 LXII, 750.

be merely a corroboration of what counsel had said – this had been the course taken in *Malings* and *Dyer* in the 1840s.[51] Other judges took the view that the statement ought to be made after counsel had addressed the jury.[52] Then there was doubt about whether written statements were to be permitted. In *Riegelmuth* (1886), Stephen J refused to allow a statement, which the prisoner had not himself composed, to be read.[53] In the *Maybrick* trial (1889) he similarly declined to permit Sir Charles Russell to put in a written statement.[54] This represented a departure from the practice in treason cases, in pre-1836 cases and in undefended cases, and it was certainly not the practice followed by all judges.[55] Less controversial was the rule that the making of a statement gave the prosecution a right of reply. In 1883, in his letter to the Lord Chief Justice, the Attorney-General had asked for such a right. This was in fact quickly established by cases such as *Shimmin*. It represented a tacit acknowledgement that what was said in such statements was evidence, for (the Attorney-General's prerogative right apart) only the calling of evidence gave the Crown a right of reply. It also represented a reversal of the rule laid down in *Taylor* in 1859 and *Manzano* in 1860.

What prompted the judges to overturn, in the space of six years, a rule which had stood since the 1840s? Cockburn's decision in *Weston*, which started the ball rolling, came at a time when the Criminal Code Commissioners, in a Bill which he had recently publicly criticised, were proposing (albeit with some diffidence) that prisoners and their spouses be rendered competent witnesses. He was a reputed opponent of that reform. Was *Weston* an attempt by him to head off the reform by introducing an alternative solution to the problem of the defended prisoner's inability to place his explanation before the jury? Or was it simply a 'hard case'? (Certainly it would be difficult to find a case which demonstrated more forcibly the injustice of denying a defended prisoner an opportunity of placing his explanation before the jury.) Perhaps both. The practice which evolved out of the controversy engendered by the *Weston* and *Le Froy* cases, of allowing defended prisoners to make unsworn statements, was hailed by opponents of reform as having solved the problem of the prisoner's mouth being shut.[56] It enabled the defended prisoner to give his explanation (as Stephen had proposed in his 1878 Bill) while at the same time safeguarding him from cross-examination. It was, as one correspondent to *The Times* put it in November 1881, 'a wholesome ... compromise between the old idea of the

---

[51] *R v Ross* above; *R v Millhouse* above.
[52] E.g. Coleridge LCJ in Millhouse above.
[53] *R v Riegelmuth, The Times*, 11 March 1886.
[54] *R v Maybrick, The Times*, 27 and 29 July and 1–8 August 1889.
[55] See e.g. *R v Edgar, The Times*, 18 September 1886, and *R v Valli* (1890) 112 CCC Sess Pap 1058.
[56] PD 1882 XXLXVII, 433.

prisoner's mouth being closed ... and the new idea – a very dangerous one – of administering an oath to and cross-examining him'.[57]

There is no reason whatever to believe that this was the object of Hawkins and Stephen JJ, the two principal architects of the new practice. Stephen had for over twenty years been an advocate of allowing prisoners to give evidence, while Hawkins was, in the 1880s, no less enthusiastic for the reform. They may have seen it as a temporary solution to the problem of the defended prisoner until a Prisoners' Evidence Act could be passed, but certainly not as a substitute for such an Act.

For all the controversy which the subject of unsworn statements by defended prisoners generated in the 1880s, the right, once established, was one of which the bar seems to have availed itself very sparingly. In the majority of trials on indictment in the 1880s and 1890s, where the prisoner had counsel, the right seems not to have been taken up, counsel taking the view 'that they could put the case for the defence much better than the accused' and fearing 'the possible effect of an unwise statement from their client'.[58] However, it remained a valuable right in cases like *Weston* where the true facts were known only to the prisoner and the complainant or deceased, and where a statement was the only way of getting the prisoner's account before the jury.

4. The Later Criminal Code Bills

Whilst the judges were busy hammering out the new rules on unsworn statements, in Parliament attempts were still being made to get the Code, with its prisoners' evidence clause, passed into law. On 6 February 1880 the Conservative government introduced its third Criminal Code Bill. On the same day three private Members introduced a Criminal Code (No. 2) Bill containing a batch of wordy clauses dealing with prisoners' evidence.[59] The government Bill passed its second reading but the calling of a general election put an end to its further progress, the private Members' Bill having in the meanwhile been dropped. When Parliament reassembled after the election, the Attorney-General in the new Liberal government announced that the government did not intend to introduce a Criminal Code Bill in the present session.[60]

In 1882 came another attempt to pass the Code into law – this time in

---

[57] *The Times*, 19 November (quoted (1881–82) 26 Sol J 39) and see PD 1898 LXII, 751 ('an expedient of judges').

[58] T. Humphreys, *Criminal Days*, 45; see also PD 1898 LXII, 751.

[59] Criminal Code Bill, PP 1880 (2) II, 1 (the prisoners' evidence clause (cl 471) was identical to that in the 1879 Bill; the Private Members Bill (the Criminal Code (No. 2) Bill, PP 1880 (47) II, 223 contained a batch of wordy clauses dealing with prisoners' evidence; it was given a first reading but later dropped.

[60] 31 May 1880 (PD CCLII, 770).

the form of a Criminal Law Amendment Bill, which contained a large portion of the code.[61] The Bill passed its second reading but was dropped at the committee stage. 1883 saw what was to be the final government attempt to pass the Code into law. Honouring a promise made during the second reading debate on the 1882 Bill, the government introduced a Bill containing only the procedural part of the Code: the Criminal Code (Indictable Offences Procedure) Bill.[62] The prisoners' evidence clause was in the same terms as that in the 1879 Bill.[63] During the second reading debate, a number of Members touched upon the subject of prisoners' evidence. Most who did were in favour of reform but not all – Morgan Lloyd, for example, moved an amendment to the effect that no Bill would be satisfactory which directly or indirectly compelled an accused, or his spouse, to submit to cross-examination. When the Irish Nationalist MPs came into the Chamber (they arrived to the Attorney-General's evident annoyance at a late hour), the atmosphere changed markedly. They launched into a fierce criticism of the Bill, attacking a number of its clauses as calculated to lead, in Ireland, to oppression and abuse. (Interestingly the prisoners' evidence clause, although criticised by one of their number, was not a particular target of their anger; indeed one of them actually conceded that there might be something to be said for it.) When to the opposition of the Irish Members were added complaints from English Members that the House was not being afforded a proper opportunity to debate the measure, the fate of the Bill was virtually sealed. Predictably it ended up being withdrawn. One thing of value which the debate did throw up, which was ultimately to find its way into the 1898 Act, was the suggestion that prisoners should give evidence from the witness-box and not the dock.

5. The Bills of 1884

With the dropping of the 1883 Bill, the Criminal Code passed into history. The attempts to abolish the bar on prisoners' giving evidence, however, continued unabated. By now there were clear signs that public opinion was moving in the reformers' favour. In 1882 the subject had been debated at the Social Science Congress and in the correspondence columns of *The Times*, and most of those who had spoken and written called for reform, a call echoed in 1883 in a *Times* leader and by the Law Society.[64] The response was the introduction in 1884 of Bills in both Lords and Commons.

---

[61] Criminal Law Amendment Bill, PP 1882 (15) II, 1 (the prisoners' evidence clause followed the 1879 model); debate PD 1882 CCLXVII, 402–40.

[62] Criminal Code (Indictable Offences Procedure) Bill, PP 1883 (8) II, 249; debate PD 1883 CCLXXVIII, 90–166 and 332–49.

[63] Cl 100.

[64] Letters to *The Times* had been favourable (PD 1884 CCLXXXV, 1301); the Law Society had also come out in favour (ibid., 1880).

The Commons Bill was a government Bill.[65] The Lords Bill was sponsored by Lord Bramwell, who was fast emerging as one of the principal advocates of the reform.[66] He told the House that he had long been in favour of it and that recent correspondence in the press had convinced him that it was now within the range of practical politics. He explained that if the Bill currently going through the Commons passed there, he would withdraw his own Bill.

Both Bills were extremely short. They declared that a prisoner and his spouse should be competent at every stage of the proceedings. In the matter of cross-examination as to credit, however, they diverged. The government Bill provided that the accused should not be asked any question tending to show that he had committed or been convicted of any offence other than that charged, save where such evidence was admissible to prove his guilt of the offence charged or where he had given evidence of good character. Bramwell's Bill contained no such restriction (like Hawkins he believed that an accused who gave evidence should enjoy no special privileges). Both were silent as to the matter of comment upon an accused's failure to testify.

Bramwell's Bill passed through the Lords quickly and easily, completing all its stages in just over three weeks. At the second reading debate, of the six peers who spoke five were enthusiastically in favour, whilst the sixth, Lord Brabourne, while expressing some misgivings, declared that he would not oppose the Bill. The Commons Bill had a much more difficult passage. After it had passed its second reading, the government succeeded in getting it referred to the Grand Committee rather than to a Committee of the Whole House. This led to loud complaints that it was stifling debate. In the committee itself so many amendments were moved that in the end the government was obliged to withdraw the Bill. At this the Lords' Bill was also dropped.

In the 1884–85 session the government tried again. In November Lord Bramwell reintroduced his Bill of the previous session.[67] Like the 1884 Bill it passed through its stages in the Lords quickly and without difficulty. In December it was given its first reading in the Commons. In February 1885 the government introduced its own Bill (couched in identical terms to that of 1884).[68] This never got beyond the first reading stage and in July it was withdrawn and Lord Bramwell's Bill dropped.

---

[65] Law of Evidence in Criminal Cases Bill, PP 1884 (4) III, 525; debate, PD 1884 CCLXXXV 466–68.

[66] Law of Evidence Amendment Bill, PP 1884 (130) III, 521; debate, PD 1884 CCLXXXIV 1301–4.

[67] Law of Evidence Amendment Bill, 1885, PP 1884–85 (45) II, 359.

[68] Law of Evidence in Criminal Cases Bill, 1885, PP 1884–85 (65) II, 363.

6. More Ad Hoc Reform

Whilst attempts to secure general reform were proving unavailing, the trend established in the 1870s of individual statutes creating ad hoc exceptions to the rule continued. In the space of three years five statutes, the Married Womens' Property Acts (1882–84), the Corrupt and Illegal Practices Prevention Act (1883), the Explosive Substances Act (1883) and the Criminal Law Amendment Act (1885), were passed, containing provisions rendering accused persons charged on indictment with certain specified offences competent in their own defence and their spouses similarly competent. Also in 1881 the statutory exceptions to the incompetency rule were imported into the law as to courts martial.

Of these statutes by far the most important were the Explosive Substances Act (1883) (passed in a single night following a wave of dynamite outrages) and the Criminal Law Amendment Act (1885). Section 3 of the 1883 Act made manufacture or possession of explosives in suspicious circumstances an offence, save where the accused proved that the manufacture or possession was for a lawful purpose; and made an accused charged with such offence and his spouse competent in his own defence (a provision justified on the familiar ground that the section cast a burden of proof on the accused).

That the 1885 Act contained a prisoners' evidence clause was due to the efforts of private Members. During the passage of the Bill through the Commons a handful of backbenchers persuaded the government to include such a clause as a safeguard against blackmailing prosecutions.[69] The clause (section 20) was particularly far-reaching, conferring upon the prisoner and his spouse the right to give evidence not only in relation to offences charged under the Act (i.e. unlawful sexual intercourse, procuring prostitution, permitting premises to be used for unlawful sexual intercourse, abduction, gross indecency and brothel keeping), but also in respect of charges of rape, indecent assault on a female, and abduction contrary to sections 53–55 of the Offences against the Person Act (1861). The section was silent as to cross-examination as to credit. Section 4 of the 1883 Act, however, was explicit: the prisoner was to be subject to cross-examination to the same extent as an ordinary witness. Neither Act sought to safeguard from adverse comment or inference the prisoner who elected not to give evidence. In this they followed a pattern set by earlier Acts.

After the 1885 Act nothing was ever to be quite the same again. The Act meant that, at almost every Assize and Old Bailey session, there would now be in the calendar for trial a number of serious indictable offences in respect of which the accused had the right to give evidence in his own defence. The experience of the practical working of section 20 would henceforth regularly be prayed in aid in Parliament and elsewhere both for and against the

---

[69] PD 1885 CCC, 904–11.

proposal for general reform. The Act also exposed the law to the charge that it was fragmentary and inconsistent. If a prisoner accused of rape could give evidence in his own defence, what logic denied the privilege to a man on trial for his life?

Within a year of the coming into force of the Act different opinions were being expressed as to how well it was working. Stephen J, in an article in *The Nineteenth Century*, claimed that it was working well.[70] Cross-examination of prisoners was not being used as an instrument of torture. Very little use was in fact made of the power to cross-examine; and cross-examination as to credit was rare. The *Law Journal* was less satisfied.[71] It pointed to the inconsistent way in which the provisions of the Act were applied by different judges. Where a prisoner did not tender himself as a witness, it was, said the journal, the habit of Denman J to discourage comment on the fact, while Lopes J had declared in terms that it was unfair to suggest that it was fear of admitting facts showing his guilt which had caused the prisoner to stay out of the witness-box. Stephen J, on the other hand, adopted the opposite practice, not only allowing the prosecution to comment upon the prisoner's failure to testify, but commenting upon the fact himself in his summing up. He also subjected the prisoner, if called, to a form of *interrogatoire*. The *Times* reports of criminal trials for 1886 confirm the justice of the criticism. At Exeter in February, in a case of indecent assault, Hawkins J expressly warned the jury against drawing any adverse inference from the accused's failure to testify.[72] Three months later, in a trial under the Corrupt and Illegal Practices Prevention Act (1883), Pollock J stood by and allowed Avory, who was prosecuting, to comment strongly on such failure.[73]

[70] 'Prisoners as Witnesses' (1886) 20 *Nineteenth Century*, 453.

[71] (1886) 20 LJ 323.

[72] *R v Labbett*, *The Times*, 2 February 1886 (indecent assault) where Hawkins J directed the jury that no adverse inference ought to be drawn from the prisoner's failure to give evidence.

[73] *R v Wigger*, *The Times*, 10–11 May 1886.

18

Reform

'the prisoner [now] was entitled to go into the witness-box, much to his disgust in many cases, and tell the truth or what he called the truth.'

Bigham J (grand jury charge, 1904).

1. Irish Obstruction

Between 1886 and 1895 no less than nine Bills were introduced in Parliament seeking to make the accused and his spouse competent in all cases. Such of the Bills as started life in the Lords (as seven did) encountered, in general, little opposition there. Where the Bills ran into trouble was in the Commons, where the Irish Nationalist MPs were determined that the reform should not pass. They were prepared to adopt any and every obstructionist tactic to defeat any Bill introduced on the subject. They conceded readily enough that in England the reform might be advantageous, but were adamant that: 'Ireland was not in a suitable condition for the application of such a reform ... owing to agrarian and political conditions there the administration of public justice inspired little confidence'.[1] An accused had to cope with biased magistrates and judges, packed juries and Crown counsel overzealous to secure convictions, whilst in summary cases his rights of appeal were far more limited than those of his English counterpart. However desirable it was in principle, in Ireland the reform would simply lead to oppression.

By the time the Irish MPs turned their attention to the Prisoners' Evidence Bills, the Commons had already experience of their ability to block legislation. The most notorious incident was in 1881 when, on the first reading of the Protection and Property Bill, they had responded with forty-one hours of obstruction. To try and limit their obstruction the Commons had in 1882 amended their standing orders.[2]

The 1886 Bill ended up being counted out on its Commons second reading,[3] but William O'Brien, the MP for Tyrone North, left the House in no doubt that, had it not been, it would have been blocked.[4] During the

---

[1] C. Jackson, 'Opposition to the Passage of the Criminal Evidence Reform', in McEldowney and O' Higgins, *The Common Law Tradition*, 186.

[2] Ibid. 190–91.

[3] Law of Evidence Amendment Bill, PP 1886 (286 Sess. 1) III, 85.

[4] PD 1886 CCCVI, 1874.

Commons second reading of the 1887 Bill,[5] the government attempted to buy off the Irish Members by offering to exclude Ireland from its provisions, but the offer was spurned. A Bill excluding Ireland would be the thin end of the wedge: 'once the principle was established in England, the temptation to extend it to Ireland would be irresistible'. The debate ended up being adjourned in the early hours of the morning, to complaints by the Attorney-General of Irish obstruction, in order that MPs might 'get away for some little though much needed rest' after the Irish Members had prolonged it by moving a succession of adjournment motions.

The offer to exclude Ireland having been rejected, the government, in reintroducing the Bill in 1888, offered no such concession.[6] At the second reading stage, a number of MPs urged on the government the wisdom of excluding Ireland, but it stood firm, arguing that if the Bill conferred, as it believed, a benefit upon accused persons, it would be both illogical and wrong to deny Irish prisoners that same benefit. The Nationalists' response was a promise to use all their efforts to defeat the Bill. Predictably, it became bogged down in committee and eventually, in November, the government was obliged to withdraw it. The spectre of Irish opposition, coupled with pressure of parliamentary business, almost certainly lay behind the dropping of the 1889 and 1891 Bills (the former was withdrawn at the second reading stage; the latter was dropped, after having passed all its stages in the Lords, without ever reaching the Commons).[7]

On the Lords' second reading of the 1892 Bill, the government was once more urged to exclude Ireland.[8] It would not. In the Commons several Members tendered the same advice. By the end of the second reading debate the government indicated that it was ready to give way on the point but this did not save the Bill, which ultimately foundered in committee. In introducing the 1893 Bill, the Lord Chancellor accepted that for the last six years the measure had been blocked by Irish opposition.[9] Like its predecessors, this Bill also ended up being withdrawn, not this time due to Irish obstruction, but to the delay that had been caused by the government seeking the opinion of the judges upon a proposal, by the Society of Chairmen and Deputy Chairmen of Quarter Sessions in England and Wales, that there should be included in the Bill a clause empowering the court to assign counsel (to be paid out of public funds) to prisoners who desired to be defended by counsel.[10] In 1895 the government introduced two identical Bills in the

---

[5] Law of Evidence Amendment Bill, PP 1887 (316) III, 137; debate, PD 1887 CCCXVII, 454–75.

[6] Criminal Evidence Bill, PP 1888 (132) II, 407; debates, PD 1888 CCCXXIV 68–148; CCCXXV, 1564–91, and 1929–33.

[7] Criminal Evidence Bill, PP 1889 (96) I, 491; Evidence in Criminal Cases Bill, 1891 (the only references to the Bill is at PD 1891 CCCLIII, 1057–71 and 1170).

[8] Evidence in Criminal Cases Bill, PP 1892 (228) III, 135; debates, PD 1892 I, 665–69 (HL); 1892 IV, 284–311.

[9] Evidence in Criminal Cases Bill, PP 1893–94 (315) III, 93; debate PD 1893 X, 187–93.

[10] PRO, HO 45/9784/B2907E.

Lords.[11] Both excluded Ireland. The first never reached the Commons and the second got no further than a second reading. Although attempts to carry the reform during this decade were defeated, the parliamentary debates at least had the merit of throwing up new points for discussion. In the Lords debate on the 1887 Bill, Lord Salisbury argued for unrepresented prisoners to be given assistance from the bench in order to get across their defence,[12] while in the Commons Bradlaugh pressed for the inclusion of a clause requiring magistrates to caution prisoners that they were not obliged to give evidence.[13] In the 1888 debate, Wharton asked whether a prisoner's giving evidence without calling other witnesses would give the prosecution a right of reply, observing that, if it would, the Bill was a trap.[14]

The opposition of Irish Members was in stark contrast to the state of English opinion, which after 1885 was very much in favour of reform. The speeches of English MPs and Lords during the debates on the Bills were overwhelmingly favourable.[15] *The Times*, in a leader in 1891, treated the matter as too clear for argument.[16] Four senior criminal judges publicly expressed dismay that what they regarded as an essential reform still had not been enacted,[17] adding their voices to that of Stephen J, who had written extensively on the subject,[18] and to those of the Law Lords who had spoken in Parliament. Moreover, events both at home and abroad were making it increasingly difficult to deny the need for reform.

During the period 1882 to 1893 no less than six colonial legislatures passed statutes rendering the accused and his spouse competent witnesses in criminal proceedings: India (1882), South Australia (1882), New Zealand (1889), New South Wales (1891), Queensland (1892) and Canada (1893).[19] According to Windeyer, the Chief Justice of New South Wales, in a letter to *The Times* in 1896, in that jurisdiction the reform had been found to work well.[20]

---

[11] Evidence in Criminal Cases Bill and Evidence in Criminal Cases (No. 2) Bill, PP 1895 (236 Sess. 1) III, 87; debate, PD 1895 XXXII, 2–8.

[12] PD 1887 CCCXI, 433.

[13] PD 1887 CCCXVII, 456–57.

[14] PD 1888 CCCXXIV, 73. The 1876 and 1878 Bills both gave the Crown the right; later Bills were silent on the point.

[15] PD 1886 CCCVI, 1822 (Attorney-General); 1887 CCCXVII, 455 and 474.

[16] *The Times*, 11 November 1891.

[17] Huddleston B (*R v Massey and Others*, *The Times*, 15 January 1885); Wills J 1888; Matthew J (charge to grand jury, Bodmin, *The Times*, 21 July 1890); and Hawkins J (charge to Norwich grand jury, *The Times*, 24 November 1890).

[18] Most recently in 'Prisoners as Witnesses' (1886) 20 *Nineteenth Century*, 453.

[19] Code of Criminal Procedure Act, 1882 (India, Act No. X of 1882); Evidence Amendment Act, 1882 (South Australia, 45 & 46 Vict, No. 245); Justices of the Peace Act, 1882 (New Zealand, No. 15 of 1882) applying only to summary trials but extended to all criminal trials by the Criminal Code Act, 1893 (New Zealand, 57 Vict, No. 56); Criminal Law Amendment Act, 1883 (New South Wales, 46 Vict, No. 17); Criminal Law Amendment Act, 1892 (Queensland, 56 Vict, No. 3) and Canada Evidence Act, 1893 (Canada, 56 Vict, c. 31).

[20] *The Times*, 6 June 1896.

At the same time, back in England, Parliament was continuing to add to the list of statutory exceptions to the incompetency rule. No less than nine Acts creating such exceptions were passed between 1885 and 1895. Some of the new exceptions could be justified on the old ground that the Act threw a burden onto the accused: the Betting and Loans (Infants) Act (1892) and the Corrupt and Illegal Practices Act (1895). For the exceptions created by such statutes as the Public Health (London) Act (1891), the False Alarms of Fire Act (1895) and the Law of Distress (Amendment) Act (1895), it is difficult to find any explanation other than fashion. Of the new exceptions, the one of the most practical importance was that created by the Prevention of Cruelty to Children Act (1894), which like the Criminal Law Amendment Act (1885) permitted child complainants to give unsworn evidence subject to a corroboration requirement. Two of the statutes, the Diseases of Animals Act (1894) and the Merchant Shipping Act (1894), merely re-enacted exceptions created by earlier Acts.

These developments, in their turn, led to a change in the way the reformers argued their case. First, they increasingly began to pray in aid the way in which existing statutes, which permitted prisoners to testify, had been found to work in practice. In the debate on the 1888 Bill, the Attorney-General (drawing no doubt on Stephen J's article of 1886) claimed that the unanimous testimony of bar and bench was that the Criminal Law Amendment Act was working well.[21] In the debate on the 1895 Bill, Lord Halsbury cited the case of Barber, tried and convicted at the Old Bailey for fraud, and subsequently sued for damages for the same fraud. At the trial of the civil action, Barber had given evidence in his own defence so convincingly that the jury stopped the case, leading the trial judge, Lord Chief Justice Coleridge, to observe that, if the defendant had been able to give evidence at his criminal trial, he could not possibly have been convicted and punished.[22]

Secondly, it was urged that the law was now in a thoroughly anomalous and unsatisfactory state, and could not be allowed to remain in such condition. This was a multi-faceted point. There were first of all the anomalies and problems created by the poor drafting of the Criminal Law Amendment Act (1885). Of these the most glaring was the fact that a prisoner was competent in his own defence in cases of rape but not in cases of attempted rape. Then there was the difficulty which arose when the accused was charged in the same indictment with offences under the 1885 Act, in respect of which he was competent, and common law offences such as conspiracy and common assault, in respect of which he was not.[23] What was the status of evidence given by the prisoner, in the course of such trial, which bore upon the question of his guilt or innocence of the common law offence? Was it

[21] PD 1888 CCCXXIV, 69.

[22] PD 1895 XXXII, 3–4 and see *Coombs v Barber*, *The Times*, 27 June 1891 (case report and leader).

[23] The problem arose on the trial of Oscar Wilde, see *The Times*, 27 April 1895.

inadmissible and was it the duty of the judge to direct the jury to disregard it? To this problem, at least, an answer was not long in coming, the Court for Crown Cases Reserved ruling in *Owen* (1888) that if a prisoner, in the course of giving evidence upon a charge in respect of which he was competent to give evidence, made a statement in the nature of an admission of another charge, that statement stood in the same position as any other admission against interest.[24] But how satisfactory an answer was it? There was also the point, stressed by Lord Halsbury in the debate on the 1895 Act, that the prosecutor by the way he framed his charges (e.g. indicting for conspiracy rather than the substantive offence) could effectively determine whether the accused would be capable of giving evidence at his trial or not.

The 1885 Act was only part of the difficulty. Wherever one turned, one could find anomalies. A prisoner could be examined when charged with personation of a voter, but not where the charge was personation for the purpose of fraud. He could be examined where the charge was sending an unseaworthy ship to sea, but not where the charge was manslaughter by so acting. He was competent to give evidence where charged with unlawful possession of explosives, but not where charged with manslaughter arising from such possession. On a charge of forging a trade mark he was competent, but not when charged with another other species of forgery. Where the charge depended upon the sending of a letter he could give evidence if the case was one of libel, but not where the allegation was of sending a threatening letter.[25] Then there was the bizarre nature of some of the statutory exceptions. What public policy required that a man charged with giving a false alarm of fire, or levying distress when not the holder of a bailiff's certificate (both offences punishable by fine), should be competent to give evidence in his own defence, but denied the right to a person charged under the Chimney Sweepers Act (1894) with soliciting business in a manner calculated to cause annoyance (an offence likewise punishable by fine)? Again, the number of statutory exceptions was now so numerous that, as Lord Herschell claimed in the debate on the 1895 Bill (with some exaggeration), it now required a special education, on the part of those who presided at criminal trials, to know whether or not the persons accused before them were capable of giving evidence or not. Certainly the public was bemused to the extent that judges at the Old Bailey were, according to Poland, adopting the practice, in cases where the accused was incompetent to give evidence, of pointing this out to the jury lest they fall into error drawing an inference against the accused by reason of his failure to do what the law prohibited him from doing.

Added to the above were the problems caused by careless drafting, and lack of uniformity, in the wording of statutes creating exceptions to the

[24] *R v Owen* (1880) 16 Cox 397.
[25] Stephen J (1886) 20 *Nineteenth Century*, 453–54 and letter from Sir Harry Poland QC quoted by Lord Halsbury at PD 1898 LIV, 1172.

incompetency rule. The point was devastatingly made by Frederick Mead, a London stipendiary magistrate, in *The Nineteenth Century* in 1892.[26] 'Different words' he wrote,

> introducing varying incidents have been continuously used. For example in four cases a defendant but not the wife or husband, may be called [Merchant Shipping Act, 1894; Contagious Diseases of Animals Act,1878; Metalliferous Mines (Regulation) Act, 1872; and Threshing Machines Act, 1878]. In two cases a defendant may call his wife but a woman, when charged, is deprived of the reciprocal advantage [Sale of Food & Drugs Act, 1875]. Sometimes it is left to the discretion of the defendant whether the husband or wife shall be called, sometimes to that of the proposed witness, whether husband or wife.

The only way, so it was argued, of bringing the law to a satisfactory condition was either to abolish the incompetency rule or the exceptions to it, and of these two courses the latter was not a practical possibility. As Lord Chief Justice Coleridge put it, it was too late for any going back.[27]

2. Sir Herbert Stephen

1896 saw the government introduce yet another Prisoners' Evidence Bill.[28] Like so many of its predecessors, it passed through the Lords easily and quickly enough. In the Commons, however, it got no further than a first reading, being eventually withdrawn to ironic cheers in July. A private Member's Bill, introduced in February, seeking to make prisoners competent in all summary cases, fared no better.[29]

The same year also saw the beginning of a sustained English campaign against the reform. In the van of the campaign was Sir Herbert Stephen, the clerk of assize of the Northern Circuit, and the son of the late Stephen J. In 1895 he had written to *The Times* complaining that, in cases where prisoners gave evidence, the bar was departing from its traditional standards of fairness.[30] In April 1896 he published an article in *The Nineteenth Century* attacking the current government Bill.[31] It was provocatively entitled 'A Bill to Promote the Conviction of Innocent Prisoners'. The thrust of his argument was this. The only persons who could comment upon the merit of the proposed reform were those who had seen it working in practice. The chief class of cases in which prisoners gave evidence were those under the Criminal Law Amendment Act (1885) which were invariably tried either at the Central

---

26 F. Mead, 'The Accused as a Witness' (1892) 31 *Nineteenth Century*, 188.
27 PD 1890–91 CCCLIII, 1068.
28 Evidence in Criminal Cases Bill, PP 1896 (134), III, 37.
29 Prisoners Evidence Bill (limited in scope to summary proceedings), PP 1896 (56) VI, 221.
30 *The Times*, 11 June 1895.
31 (1896) 39 *Nineteenth Century*, 566.

Criminal Court or at Assizes. It followed that it was from amongst persons regularly present at or engaged in these cases that opinions as to its workings should be canvassed, not from judges like Lord Esher, Lord Halsbury and Lord Herschell who had spoken in favour of the Bill in the Lords, but who had probably never seen a trial in which a prisoner had given evidence, and had certainly not been engaged in such cases on any regular basis. He himself had considerable experience of such cases, first as a practising barrister on the South-Eastern Circuit and, since 1889, as clerk of assize of the Northern Circuit. His estimate was that there were 100–200 cases a year on that circuit in which prisoners were competent to give evidence, either under the Criminal Law Amendment Act or under one of the other statutes permitting prisoners to testify. His experience led him to the conclusion that, whereas in cases where prisoners were not competent to give evidence not one in a thousand was wrongfully convicted, in cases where prisoners did give evidence at least one a year was wrongfully convicted.

A number of factors, he thought, contributed to such wrongful convictions. First, where prisoners gave evidence, the jury decided the case on a balance of probabilities. Secondly, innocent prisoners were convicted because of the way they gave their evidence. If they gave it badly or dishonestly it went against them, and yet there were many prisoners who could not answer a series of questions, concerning a matter in which they had a strong interest, without looking as though they were lying. Not a few people were absolutely incapable of answering questions straightforwardly and to the point. Thirdly, where prisoners gave evidence, prosecuting counsel examined them and addressed the jury, not as ministers of justice but as if striving for a verdict at Nisi Prius. He conceded, however, that there might possibly be something to be said for allowing a prisoner to give evidence where statute cast upon him a burden of proof, or where the proceedings though criminal in form were litigious in substance.

Stephen had chosen his ground cleverly. Until then opponents of reform had never been able to dispute the claim that it had been tried in the United States and in the Colonies, and in England in civil cases and prosecutions under the 1885 Act, and had been found to work well. Now here was someone, with considerable experience of the 1885 Act, claiming that it worked not in favour of but to the prejudice of innocent prisoners. The article started a controversy which only stopped when the 1898 Act became law.

In May 1896 there was published a report upon the current Bill by a committee of the Bar Council. This reached quite the opposite conclusion to Stephen. It unanimously recommended that the principle of the Bill was, on the whole, a sound one, and should, in the interests of public justice, be made of general application. The committee's only misgiving was about 'the difficulty ... frequently experienced by prosecuting counsel under existing Acts in judging as to the propriety of commenting or not upon the prisoner's absence from the witness-box'. It suggested that if the Bill became law the judges should be invited to give guidance on the propriety of such comment.

George Pitt-Lewis, who was on that committee, published a reply to Stephen's article, in the May issue of *The Nineteenth Century*, under the title 'A Bill for the Protection of Innocent Prisoners'.[32] Despite its title, the article appeared to confirm several of Stephen's claims. In the first place, Pitt-Lewis conceded that it was difficult, if not impossible, to answer arguments based on personal experience, particularly when they came from a person 'as to whose opportunities of judging and whose sincere desire to judge rightly there can be no manner of doubt'. He further conceded that there were three classes of prisoner who suffered by giving evidence:

1. Those against whom the prosecution case was weak, but whose guilt was exposed in the course of their evidence.

2. Those who, though innocent, brought about their own conviction by lying on collateral matters.

3. Those who told the truth at their trial but told it so badly, and in such a bungling way, that the jury did not believe them.

The first class he claimed were deserving of sympathy only if one regarded a criminal trial not as a search for truth but as a game of skill in which the party on the defensive was entitled to be declared the winner of the same, and acquitted, unless the attacking party had strictly and conclusively proved their case, without any aid whatsoever from the party on the defensive.

The second class were equally undeserving of sympathy. The third class of sufferers was, he admitted, deserving of sympathy but it was extremely small, for the conviction of such persons required not merely a stupid accused but an equally stupid jury. Against the hardship suffered by them should be balanced the advantage, which other innocent prisoners reaped, through being able to prove their innocence in the witness-box. He concluded that there was no risk of the impartiality of the bench being compromised by the reform, lamenting the bar which the current Bill sought to place on the cross-examination of prisoners.

In June came Windeyer's letter to *The Times*, asserting that five years' experience of the working of the New South Wales Criminal Evidence Act had left him wholly in favour of the reform. Within days there appeared in *The Times* a letter from Stephen, claiming that the English experience was contrary.[33]

3. The 1897 Bill

1897 saw a yet further addition to the list of statutes which permitted accused persons charged thereunder to give evidence: the Chaff Cutting Machines

---

[32] (1896) 39 *Nineteenth Century*, 812.
[33] *The Times*, 16 June 1896.

Act. The Act was passed without opposition, the ground of the exception being the casting by the Act of a burden of proof on the accused. It also saw the government introduce yet another Criminal Evidence Bill.[34]

It would seem that the government's original intention was that the Bill should extend to Ireland, yet, on the motion for leave, when the Attorney-General was pressed upon the point by Maurice Healy, he equivocated and said that he would consult with the Attorney-General for Ireland and the Chief Secretary. Healy's warning shot worked, for when the Bill was introduced it had a clause excluding Ireland. In the second reading debate, the Attorney-General admitted that this had been done for purely 'parliamentary reasons'.

This was not its only omission. Unlike the Bill of the previous year (and the majority of the Bills introduced between 1884 and 1896), it failed to give any protection to the accused in the matter of cross-examination. In moving the second reading, the Attorney-General sought to explain this volte-face. It had been urged, he said, by many lawyers, including Lord Selborne and Lord Bramwell, that it was not right to throw any immunity around the accused. He had asked many judges whether they found that the power of cross-examination worked hardly to the prisoner who had given evidence. One and all they said that it had not. It seemed better to have one uniform and single code of law. He was confident that the judges would never allow the position of the prisoner to be prejudiced, or the licence of counsel to go too far in the matter of examination or cross- examination of prisoners.

During the second reading debate, little emerged that was new. The Attorney-General predictably prayed in aid the unsatisfactory state of the existing law, with all its anomalies. There were, he said, two systems under which accused were now tried and one or other ought to be abandoned. He argued that the reform had worked well in the United States and the Colonies. It had been supported by such great judges as Stephen J, Lord Bramwell, Lord Coleridge, Lord Selborne and many others; coming to living judges, almost every judge on the bench was in favour. The Bill was also supported by a number of important bodies including the Law Society.

Several lawyer MPs (Edward Carson, Llewellyn Atherley-Jones and Lloyd Morgan) spoke against the Bill, as did the radical liberal Edward Pickersgill. They were particularly severe in their criticism of the failure of the Bill to protect against cross-examination as to credit; it was pointed out that in the Colonies, where the reform was said to be working well, such protection was given. Nor was the Attorney's claim that the 1885 Act had worked well allowed to pass unchallenged. That was not, said Lloyd Morgan, the view of the rank and file of the bar who had actual experience of its working. Irish Nationalist Members intervened to make clear that they had not been

---

[34] Law of Evidence (Criminal Cases) Bill, PP 1897 (101) IV, 199; debates, PD 1897 XLV 266–68, XLVIII, 780–826.

appeased one whit by the exclusion of Ireland and remained as fiercely opposed to the measure as ever. The bulk of the House, however, was pro-reform and the Bill passed its second reading by a substantial majority (210 to 41). Despite this encouraging vote it became a victim of the pressure of parliamentary business and ended up being withdrawn.

4. The Bar Council Report

In the meanwhile, a committee of the Bar Council had, in March 1897, produced a report on the Bill. This time Stephen was on the committee. The majority of the committee came out in favour of the principle of the Bill but, with the exception of Pitt-Lewis, were strongly in favour of there being included a clause, along the lines of clause 1(d) of the 1896 Bill, restricting cross-examination as to credit. They also repeated what the 1896 committee had said about the matter of prosecution comment upon the prisoner's failure to give evidence.

Stephen produced a minority report. This repeated the arguments of his 1896 article, but with additional criticisms: the Bill would offer a strong temptation to the prosecution to be careless in preparing their cases, because they would trust to the prisoner's evidence, or his refusal to give any, to make out their case. It would produce perjury which, in practice, it would be hopeless to punish. And given that the current conviction rate stood at over 80 per cent, the slight increase in convictions which the Bill would procure seemed to him an advantage of little importance. He acknowledged that the question of cross-examination was one of difficulty. To protect prisoners against cross-examination as to previous convictions or character would place them in a position to which, as witnesses, they were not entitled. On the other hand, if they were not given protection, a man of suspicious character would always be convicted. He thought that, on the whole, the second was the greater evil of the two. In an attempt to draw the sting of the report, he expressed regret that the committee had not attempted to ascertain the opinion of the relatively small number of barristers who had been engaged in defending prisoners since the passing of the Criminal Law Amendment Act. Such men had an experience of the results of prisoners being allowed to give evidence, which made their opinion of unusual weight when compared with that of the leaders of the profession and other eminent persons.

The following month, in a letter to *The Times*,[35] Stephen took the matter a stage further. After claiming that, of the judges, Collins, Day, Lawrence, Vaughan and Williams were all of the opinion that the Bill was a mistake, he stated that on the Northern Circuit between five and ten innocent persons were convicted each year as a result of giving evidence. He also launched an attack on the absence of a provision in the Bill protecting the prisoner

---

[35] *The Times*, 16 April 1897.

against cross-examination. It was forgotten, he said, that you may not ask any other witness whether the prisoner was convicted of so and so. The true purpose of cross-examining a prisoner as to previous convictions was not to damage his credit, but to make the jury think that, because he had done it or something like it before, he had done it again. This operated very harshly on habitual criminals, who were often arrested and charged simply because a crime had been committed and they were in the neighbourhood at the time.

Nor was Stephen without support. In April the North London and Middlesex Sessions Bar Mess sent to the Lord Chancellor a copy of a resolution they had passed, protesting strongly against the Bill. The letter which accompanied it invited the Lord Chancellor to read Stephen's article in *The Nineteenth Century*, if he had not already done so.[36]

The correspondence columns of *The Times* for 1897 also contained a number of letters supporting Stephen.[37] Frederick Mead confirmed that, in his experience, defence counsel was considerably hampered in those cases where the prisoner could now give evidence. If counsel failed to call his client, the failure would be the subject of a damning comment on the part of the prosecution. If he did call him, he thereby lost the right of reply. If the prisoner had a tainted character, he would be cross-examined about it. All this was a hard price to pay for the privilege of taking an oath. The absence of a restriction in the 1897 Bill on cross-examination as to credit was also criticised in articles in both *The Times* and the *Scots Law Times*.[38] Another correspondent pointed out that the problem was particularly acute in magistrates courts, where the average borough justice of the peace believed that the past of the prisoner was as much or more to do with the case as the evidence for the prosecution. The plight of the innocent prisoner without counsel was also referred to in letter after letter. A chairman of Quarter Sessions argued that such a prisoner was far better served by making an unsworn statement than by going into the witness-box and running the risk of being reduced to confusion and self-contradiction under cross-examination. Alfred Lyttelton, the recorder of Oxford, suggested that the type of reform needed was something along the lines of the Indian Code of Criminal Procedure Act (1882), under which the judge was required to call the prisoner's attention to the heads of evidence against him one by one, and invite him to offer his explanation if he wished.[39] Stephen took up the suggestion with enthusiasm, whilst at the same time ridiculing a claim by Evelyn Ashley that what Lyttelton was advocating was the exact replica of existing procedure at Quarter Sessions.[40]

[36] PRO, HO 45/9784/B2907L.
[37] *The Times* for 16, 19 and 24 April and 25 and 29 October 1897.
[38] (1895–96) 3 Scots LT, 275.
[39] *The Times*, 25 October 1897.
[40] *The Times*, 29 October 1897.

The start of the New Year saw the debate still continuing in the columns of *The Times*. A correspondent, with experience of the Indian Code, pointed out that that also had its shortcomings, since judges, in drawing the attention of prisoners to the points against them, often cross-examined and put questions which assumed the guilt of the prisoner; while a failure to answer would lead to an adverse inference being drawn by the jury. Another correspondent predicted that the need for impecunious prisoners to be legally defended would be rendered all the greater by the Act.

In March 1898 Stephen published a sixty-four page pamphlet, obviously written with an eye on the forthcoming Bill, entitled *Prisoners on Oath: Past, Present and Future*. The pamphlet, in addition to restating his case on the matter, contained a detailed analysis of and reply to every argument advanced by the reformers in both the 1897 Commons debate and in *The Times* correspondence. On 2 March Grantham J wrote to *The Times* urging that there should be no restriction on cross-examination of prisoners, citing a case which he had tried in which the cross-examination of a prisoner as to his past had prevented a guilty man escaping and a complainant's reputation being blasted.

5. The Passing of the Criminal Evidence Act (1898)

In the meanwhile, the legislative round had begun again, with the government introducing into the Lords its latest Criminal Evidence Bill.[41] In the debates on the Bill, one senses that it was realised on all sides that this time the reform would finally be carried. The 1897 Bill had passed its Commons second reading by a large majority and the government now made a determined attempt to buy off all remaining opposition. The new Bill 'for purely parliamentary reasons' excluded Ireland and, in order to head off the critics of unrestricted cross-examination, included a clause limiting cross-examination as to credit.

As was to be expected, the Bill passed quickly through the Lords. On the Lords' second reading debate in March, the Lord Chancellor and Lord Herschell both went out of their way to try and discredit Stephen's claim that the 1885 Act was yielding an annual crop of five to ten wrongful convictions on the Northern Circuit. They stressed that no particulars, no facts, no proof had been offered in support of the claim and asked how, if specific cases had been cited, Stephen could hope to prove either that the prisoner in question was innocent or that it was his giving evidence which convicted him. They also cited Home Office statistics to show that his figure of 100 to 200 for the number of cases, tried annually on the circuit, in which prisoners gave evidence, was hopelessly overstated (it was in fact less than

---

[41] Evidence in Criminal Cases Bill, PP 1898 (132)(277)(324) IV, 345, 351 and 357; debates, PD 1898 LIV, 1170–84; LV 977–1082; LX 303–38, 516–34 and 650–750; and LXII 662–758.

one hundred per year). Further, said the Lord Chancellor, if Stephen were right, one would expect to find complaints about the working of the Act in petitions to the Home Office, but extensive research by the Home Office had failed to reveal a single such complaint. (When, in the Commons debate, this bad point was repeated by the Attorney-General, it was speedily demolished by Maurice Healy, who pointed out that a prisoner was hardly likely to petition on the ground that his own evidence had got him convicted.) Lord Herschell rounded off the attack on Stephen by refuting the latter's claim that he (Lord Herschell) had no experience of prisoners giving evidence. He had, he said, in fact appeared for the Crown in one of the first prosecutions brought under the 1883 Act.

It is clear from Home Office files that, prior to the debate, a good deal of work had been done by the department's officials to try and unearth material which could be used to discredit Stephen's arguments. Embarrassingly, the research, as well as yielding the statistics deployed in the debate, also resulted in an internal memorandum stating that there could be no doubt that the proportion of 'shaky' convictions was larger in cases under the Criminal Law Amendment Act than in others. Considering how few such cases were in proportion to the total number of convictions, the number of petitions on the ground of innocence was striking. One of the reasons for this, it was suggested, was the law of evidence. In rape cases, for example, if he did not give evidence, the accused suffered. If he did, almost inevitably the jury would frame the question to be decided by them 'Which is telling the truth: he or she?' If they did, no doubt they would convict many guilty men who under the general law of evidence would escape, but the result would be a number of shaky convictions. Home Office experience showed this was the case, and one could not help thinking that, among the shaky convictions, there might be an unusual proportion of miscarriages of justice. The memorandum concluded:

> the experience of the Department ... does seem to ... suggest that the assimilation of the general law of evidence to the law applicable to rape and other similar cases was likely, among other effects, to increase the number of shaky convictions founded rather on a strong probability than a probability which excludes reasonable doubt [which] would, of course, tend to increase the number of wrongful convictions.[42]

If the Lord Chancellor was aware of this memorandum, he made no reference to it, but concluded the debate by presenting a petition from the Law Society in favour of the Bill.

Between the Lords' second reading in March and the Commons' second reading in April there was a flurry of correspondence in *The Times*.[43] An Indian judge had pointed out that under the Indian system the problem of

---

[42] PRO, HO 45/9784/B2907M.
[43] *The Times*, 15 March and April 9 1898.

innocent prisoners telling obvious lies, in a foolish attempt to better their case, was well known. Frederick Mead wrote that with undefended prisoners, who were often too ignorant even to understand what was meant when they were called upon to ask questions, there was, in his experience, rarely difficulty if they were allowed or encouraged to make any statement they pleased as the evidence proceeded. But a rigid adherence to procedure, which required them to reserve all their explanations until the end of the prosecution case, put them at the same disadvantage whether they were in the dock or the witness-box.

Hawkins J, during the same period, also pronounced against the Bill on the ground that, under the law as it then stood, the prisoner had every opportunity of telling his story under the best possible circumstances, namely when first before the magistrates. If his story was truthful, it might lead to his being discharged there and then, while if he went to trial the fact that he had disclosed his story at the first opportunity and thereby given the prosecution the chance to investigate it would be in his favour.[44]

At the second reading debate in the Commons twelve Members spoke against the Bill. The majority were lawyers. Two were Irish Nationalists. The Attorney-General's speech opening the debate was, in the main, a repetition of the arguments he had used the previous year. There were, however, some differences. In the first place, he had to explain why the government had changed its mind, yet again, on cross-examination. He gave as the reason fairness to the prisoner. He repeated the Lord Chancellor's attack on Stephen's claims, and rejected calls for the adoption of the Indian practice of the judge calling the prisoner's attention to the points against him. Interestingly, throughout the progress of the Bill, he declined to be drawn on the question of judicial opinion on the subject (a change of stance from the previous year which did not pass unremarked).

A theme picked up by several of those who spoke against the Bill was that opposition to it had increased over recent years and was still growing.[45] Atherley-Jones claimed that the rank and file of the bar were against it, as were the judges. The real object of the Bill was not to protect the innocent, but to increase the number of convictions. Of those who were tried and convicted, 60 per cent had been previously convicted and 90 per cent were of depraved character. Persons of this sort, guilty or innocent, would make a poor showing in the witness-box. It was their habit, innocent or guilty, to tell lies to get out of scrapes and, if liable to cross-examination as to their way of life, they would have little hope of escaping conviction, innocent or not. Several Members commented upon the government's about-turn upon the subject of cross-examination, Gibson Bowles observing that the Bill

---

[44] In the Lords second reading debate, on 10 March, Hawkins had been claimed as a supporter of the Bill but by July he was inveighing strongly against it in his charge to a grand jury at Chelmsford (*The Times*, 2 July 1898).

[45] This had been commented on in (1896) 31 LJ 250.

changed every year. A remark of Cotton LJ about the adverse change the Bill would work in the relationship between judge and prisoners was cited. One of the arguments which had been used against the Prisoners' Counsel Bill in 1836 was disinterred, namely that the Bill would also lead to an increase in the length of trials. The Bill nevertheless passed its second reading by a large majority.[46]

In June there was a long debate upon a motion that the Bill should be referred to a Select Committee. The motion, if passed, would have destroyed all hope of the Bill passing that session, and the government would have none of it. The principle of the Bill had been clearly established by the large majority with which it had passed its second reading. In the end it was referred to a Committee of the Whole House.

The discussion of the Bill in committee was extensive and wide-ranging. Some Members, recognising that it was going to pass, embarked on a damage limitation exercise. Amendments were moved proposing that the Bill should be for a trial period of three, five or seven years; that it should not apply to magistrates' courts; that it should not apply to prisoners under sixteen years of age; and even that it should not apply to Wales. All were blocked.

A matter which it was predictable would loom large in the committee's deliberations was the absence of a clause in the Bill prohibiting comment upon the failure of the prisoner to give evidence. And so it proved. Lloyd Morgan moved that the Bill be amended to include a clause to the effect that such failure should not raise any presumption against the prisoner, and that no reference to or comment thereon should be made during the trial. To omit such a provision, he argued, was to compel prisoners to give evidence. The Solicitor-General was dismissive. Although in many cases it was a hard thing that comment should be made upon a prisoner's failure to give evidence, there was a residue of cases in which comment was necessary. As to the rest, the judges could be relied upon to see that the right of comment was not abused. Also, there were practical problems about prohibiting comment. How was such a prohibition to be enforced? Was a counsel who commented to be guilty of contempt? Were proceedings to be instituted against a judge who made comment? (In fact a very effectual remedy had been proposed by Lloyd Morgan as long ago as 1892: the quashing of any resulting conviction.)[47] Then again prohibiting comment would prevent a judge telling the jury not to allow themselves to be prejudiced by the accused's failure to give evidence. He could have added that none of the existing statutes which allowed prisoners to give evidence contained such a clause, nor had any Prisoners' Evidence Bill since 1878. But Lloyd Morgan was not alone in his misgivings. Other Members pressed the Solicitor to give way. His response was to offer a partial concession. He would agreed to a prohibition upon comment by counsel for the prosecution.

---

[46] 218 votes to 91.
[47] PRO, HO 45/9784/B2907E.

On the question of comment by the judge, however, he declined to yield. It would, he argued, be wrong to place such a fetter upon the judge. Where an accused's defence reflected gravely on the character of prosecution witnesses, to the extent that an acquittal would mean their ruin, it was only just that the judge would be allowed to comment upon the failure of the accused to back up his attack with evidence. In the end, this was where the committee agreed to draw the line. A suggestion by Abel-Thomas that the judge should, in a case where the accused failed to give evidence, be required to charge the jury that no adverse inference should be drawn therefrom was lost.

The clause restricting cross-examination of a prisoner as to his character and previous convictions unsurprisingly generated much discussion. Gibson Bowles urged the government to drop the clause, while Healy from the Irish benches called for a complete prohibition upon all cross-examination of the prisoner as to his character. Others urged the government to strike out the provision permitting a prisoner, who had attacked the character of the prosecutor or his witnesses, to be cross-examined as to his own bad character. Such a provision, they argued, would inhibit him in his defence. Further, it represented a substantial change in the law and one wholly to his disadvantage. Under the existing law a prisoner was unrestricted in his right of cross-examination. He could attack the character of prosecution witnesses without any fear of having his own record put in. But the Attorney-General stood his ground and the sub-clause to the proviso remained. One important drafting concession was, however, won from him. He agreed that in clause 1 the words 'person charged' should be substituted for 'person called'. This small amendment had the effect of preventing the Crown cross-examining a prisoner's spouse as to his character in cases where he attacked the character of a prosecution witness but did not himself give evidence.

The government also agreed to the inclusion in the Bill of clauses providing that the giving of evidence by the accused should not give the Crown a right of reply (a particularly vital safeguard); and that an accused who gave evidence should do so from the witness-box. It also accepted an amendment which made it clear that the Act would leave unaffected the right of a prisoner to make an unsworn statement, both at committal hearings and at trial.

A proposal that the Bill include a clause putting it beyond doubt that the right to testify was not to extend to hearings before the grand jury was however lost, as were proposals that prisoners should have the right to refuse to answer questions criminating them of the offence charged; that there be included a clause declaring that nothing in the Bill should affect the burden of proof; that prisoners under sixteen should not be subject to cross-examination; that prisoners and their spouses giving evidence should not be subject to prosecution for perjury; and that the trial judge should be under a duty to caution an undefended prisoner that he was not obliged to give evidence, but that if he did he would be subject to cross-examination. An amendment proposing that undefended prisoners be assigned counsel was rejected by the chairman of the committee as outside the scope of the Bill.

The committee stage was concluded in late July. The Bill received its Commons third reading the following day and on the 12 August 1898 it received the royal assent.

6. The First Year of the New Act

The new Act got off to an inauspicious start, with uncertainty as to its commencement date,[48] and controversy as to whether it gave prisoners the right to testify before the grand jury.[49] No sooner had the Court for Crown Cases Reserved ruled against such a right[50] than Hawkins J began openly to question whether prisoners were entitled thereunder to give evidence before examining magistrates.[51] Nor were prisoners showing any great enthusiasm to avail themselves of their new right. At the July 1899 session less than half of the prisoners tried at the Old Bailey gave evidence in their own defence, while of sixty-one prisoners charged with murder, whose cases were reported in *The Times* for 1899, only nine went into the witness-box.[52]

Part of the reluctance of prisoners to testify may have been due to fear of prosecution for perjury, for during 1898–99 there was much debate as to whether a perjury prosecution should follow as of course where a prisoner was convicted after giving evidence in his own defence.[53] Wright J even talked of raising the question before the Council of Judges.[54] The policy ultimately adopted was to reserve prosecution only for aggravated cases. Really there was no alternative. To have indicted everyone who gave perjured evidence for himself would, as Grantham J pointed out, have meant the judges being on circuit almost continuously.[55]

At the same time as the issue of prosecution for perjury was being debated, the judges were also adopting the practice (aped by prosecuting counsel) of criticising, as open to suspicion, any explanation offered by a prisoner in

---

[48] S 7 provided that the Act should come into operation at the expiration of two months from the passing thereof. The doubt was whether the two months included the day on which it received the royal assent.

[49] *The Times*, letters 10, 12, 14 and 18 October; see also charge of Hawkins to the Cambridge grand jury,*The Times*, 29 October 1898.

[50] *R v Rhodes* (1899) 19 Cox 182.

[51] See *The Times* letters 22 November and 27 December 1898 and 9 and 18 January 1899

[52] See CCC Sessions Papers and *The Times* reports of criminal trials.

[53] Wills J at the Mold Summer Assizes, 1898, had advised a grand jury against finding a bill for perjury against a prisoner who had given evidence on his own behalf, saying that otherwise there would be no finality (referred to in a letter to *The Times* from a chairman of Quarter Sessions published on 10 October 1898). Ridley J however strongly favoured prosecution, see reports in *The Times* for 17 November and 10 December 1898.

[54] *The Times*, 11 February 1899.

[55] *The Times*, 23 January 1899.

the witness-box which had not been given before the examining magistrates. This marked the beginning of an attack upon the 'reserved defence' which was to find its clearest expression in the Poor Prisoners' Defence Act (1903).[56] Some prosecuting counsel were also beginning to adopt practices disloyal to the spirit, if not the letter of the Act, such as telling the jury in opening that the only satisfactory answer to the charge could be the answer of the prisoner; or, where the prisoner did give evidence, making the sneering comment that his evidence was only that of a prisoner.[57]

7. The Significance of the Act

The most important effects of the 1898 Act were, first, to strip the accused of his old immunity from cross-examination (henceforth if he wished to offer an explanation of the evidence against him he would have to give it from the witness-box, or run the risk of the jury drawing an inference to his discredit); and, secondly, to expose an accused who attacked the character of Crown witnesses to a new peril: retaliation in kind should he venture into the witness-box. With the Act the shape of the criminal trial was decisively and drastically altered, and with it both the trial system and the law of criminal evidence entered the modern age. Its coming into the force made a scheme of criminal legal aid daily more urgent and quickly put an end to the practice of judges prosecuting. The opponents of the Act, although they could not prevent it passing into law, did succeed in ensuring that it incorporated safeguards for the accused. But there was always a danger that once it was in force these would sooner or later be stripped away or whittled down. So it has proved. In 1994 Parliament repealed section 1(b) of the Act (which prohibited comment by the prosecution upon the accused's failure to give evidence) and enacted that henceforth such failure would be a matter from which an inference might be drawn. There have also been calls for abolition of the shield against cross-examination as to credit provided by section 1(f). The object of such changes is to prevent the guilty escaping justice. But then that was always one, if not the principal, objective of the 1898 Act.

---

[56] See for example *R v Larder*, *The Times*, 26 January 1899.
[57] Letter to *The Times*, 7 November 1898.

19

The Rules of Criminal Evidence

'the testimonies and proofs of the offence ought to be so clear and manifest as there can be no defence of it.'

Coke, *Institutes*, iii, 29, 137.

Throughout the nineteenth century the protection conferred upon the accused by the law of evidence was substantial. Not only did the law cast the burden of proof on the prosecution, it rigorously excluded hearsay, involuntary confession and evidence of the accused's bad character. It also insisted that juries be cautioned about the danger of convicting without corroboration where the charge was perjury, or where the evidence came from an accomplice or a rape complainant.

1. The Burden and Standard of Proof

That it was for the prosecution to prove guilt beyond reasonable doubt was, in 1800, a rule well known to lawyer and layman alike. One has to look no further than the Commons debates on the early Prisoners' Counsel Bills to see this.[1] This is not to say, however, that juries always received a direction on the matter.[2] Where a direction was given it might take one of a number of forms, ranging from one framed in terms of proof beyond reasonable doubt, to a direction to convict if guilt was proved (or clearly proved), or proved to their (complete) satisfaction, or if they believed the prosecution witnesses (this was the direction contained in the precedent of a summing up given in Chitty's *Criminal Law* published in 1816).[3]

---

[1] See e.g. PD 1826 XV 611–12 and 617.

[2] See Chapter 24, below.

[3] There are countless cases, reported and unreported, in which judges can be found directing juries that guilt must be proved beyond reasonable doubt, e.g. *R v Rowe*, *The Times*, 21 September 1805 and *R v White* (1865) 4 F & F 383. For other forms of direction, see e.g. *R v Higgins* (1829) 3 C & P 603 ('satisfied'); *R v Hazy and Collins* (1826) 2 C & P 458 ('perfectly satisfied'); *R v Howlett* (1836) 7 C & P 273 ('satisfactorily shown'); *R v Beeson* (1835) 7 C & P 142 and Chitty, *Criminal Law*, iv, 331–32 ('believe'); *R v Small* (1837) 8 C & P 46 ('if you think'). Such text writers as discussed the topic at all (and most did not) talked of proof beyond reasonable doubt, see e.g. Starkie, *Law of Evidence* (4th edn, London, 1853), 817 and 865, Best (1st edn, 1849), 100–102, Taylor (7th edn, 1878), 113.

In the heyday of capital punishment, a judge who intended to leave a prisoner for execution if convicted would sometimes warn the jury of this when directing them on the standard of proof.[4] Even in the second half of the century it was not unknown for summings up in capital cases to buttress the direction as to the standard of proof with a warning that the life of a fellow creature was at stake.[5] Such warnings proved, if anything, too effective. In the 1850s and 1860s Pollock LCB reacted to the acquittal rate in capital cases by trying to water down the standard of proof.[6] His much criticised initiative, which consisted of directing the jury that the degree of certainty for a conviction was merely that upon which they were accustomed to act in their own 'grave and weighty concerns', did not survive his retirement from the bench in 1866.[7]

That the burden upon the prosecution included a duty to disprove defences raised by the accused was less than clear. Text writers and judges often wrote and talked as if the burden of proving defences was on the accused.[8] Whether the burden referred to was persuasive or merely evidential was rarely made plain, but this is hardly surprising given that the distinction between the two burdens was at the time imperfectly understood.[9] One defence upon which the accused undoubtedly did bear the persuasive burden was insanity. The law presumed a man to be sane; if a prisoner relied upon insanity as a defence it was for him to prove it. This had been clear law since *Arnold's Case* in 1724, if not before.[10] But insanity seems not to have been regarded as a case alone. In 1816 one can find Abbott J directing a jury that it was for a prisoner who relied on the defence of duress 'to make

---

[4] See e.g. *R v Brittle, The Times*, 15 March 1822: 'if they should feel compelled to return a verdict of guilty no judge could, in the discharge of his lawful duty, give the prisoners the least hope of mercy this side of the grave' (Garrow B); *R v Weston and Eastwood, The Times*, 28 December 1822: 'This was a case in which, if the prisoners were convicted, their lives would undoubtedly be forfeit' (Bayley J); contrast *R v Gould* (1840) 9 C & P 364, where the jury were told that the trial did not affect the prisoner's life.

[5] See *R v Belaney* (1844) 20 CCC Sess Pap 441: 'if you convict while there is any rational doubt ... you may commit that foulest of all enormities – murder under colour of the law ...' ; and Campbell LCJ in *R v Palmer* 1856 (Notable British Trials Series, 268): 'the life of the prisoner is at stake and if you find him guilty he must expiate his crime by an ignominious death'. See also *R v Kain, The Times*, 3 March 1824.

[6] On this episode, see the footnotes to the report of *R v White* above.

[7] For examples of cases in which Pollock CB directed juries in these terms, see *R v Manning and Manning* (1849) 30 CCC Sess Pap 654; *R v Exall* (1865) 4 F & F 922 and *R v Kohl* (1865) 4 F & F 935 n.

[8] See e.g. Archbold (1st edn, 1822), 243 in relation to the defences of accident and self defence in assault.

[9] J. B. Thayer, *A Preliminary Treatise on Evidence at the Common Law* (1st edn, Boston, 1898) 355 and 359–64.

[10] *Arnold's Case* (1724) 16 St Tr 695 at 764: 'it must be very plain and clear before a man is allowed such an exception'; see also *R v Offord* (1831) 5 C & P 168 and *R v Oxford* (1840) 9 C & P 525.

it out most satisfactorily'.[11] Again take murder. It had been laid down, by both Gilbert and Foster,[12] that in murder, once the fact of killing was proved against a prisoner, the burden was then on him to prove that the case was not one of murder, either by proving matters (such as provocation or lack of intent) which reduced the offence to manslaughter, or which showed that the killing was justifiable or excusable (i.e. self-defence, accident), the law presuming malice from the fact of the killing, and throughout the century it was normal practice so to direct juries.[13] In *Woolmington* in 1935, the House of Lords held that the burden on the accused was only evidential,[14] but in the nineteenth century it was spoken of and seemingly regarded as persuasive.[15] It may well be that the rule laid down by Foster spread over into non-fatal assault as well. Certainly, in two cases this century, *Davies* (1913) and *Lobell* (1957),[16] the Court of Criminal Appeal has had to overturn rulings by High Court judges that in assault the burden of proof on the issues of accident and self-defence was on the accused (rulings which the prosecution in each case sought to uphold by reference to dicta from nineteenth-century homicide cases). Also, it must not be forgotten that during the century in an increasing number of statutory offences the burden of proof was cast by statute on the defendant.[17]

A question never answered at any time during the century was to what standard the accused was required to prove an issue upon which he bore the burden of proof. When in 1843 the judges in *M'Naghten's Case* delivered what still remains the definitive exposition of the law of insanity in criminal cases, they wholly ignored the question.[18] Indeed it seems not to have been asked or answered (in England at least) until the 1930s, either in relation to insanity or to issues upon which the accused by statute bore the burden

---

[11] *R v Dennis and Others*, The Times, 20 June 1816.

[12] Gilbert, *Evidence*, 273, and Foster 255 (cited verbatim on this point by most nineteenth-century text writers). In India the rule was given statutory force: Indian Evidence Act, 1872, s 105.

[13] See e.g. *R v O'Callaghan and Others*, The Times, 17 January 1818; *R v Greenacre* (1837) 8 C & P 35 and *R v Little*, The Times, 6 May 1886.

[14] *Woolmington v DPP* (1936) 25 Cr App R 72 (the trial judge's direction here was in identical terms to that commonly given in the nineteenth century).

[15] See R. Cross, *Evidence* (6th edn, London, 1979), 109: 'The speech (of Lord Sankey in *Woolmington*) can be regarded either as making a change in the law or as an insistence on a distinction ignored by the old authorities between the legal and evidential burden.'

[16] *R v Davies* (1913) 8 Cr App R 211 (accident); *R v Lobell* [1957] 1 QB 547 (self-defence); Archbold (1st edn), 243.

[17] For a list of statutes which cast a burden of proof on the accused see Taylor (7th edn), 339–44; see also the line of cases which cast on an accused, who relied on an exemption, proviso, exception or qualification contained in the statute creating the offence charged, the burden of proving the same, especially where the subject matter of the exception was peculiarly within his own knowledge – e.g. *R v Stone* (1801) 1 East 639; *R v Turner* (1816) 5 M & S 206, and *Apothecaries Company v Bentley* (1824) 1 C & P 538.

[18] *M'Naghten's Case* (1840) 10 Cl & Fin 200.

of proof.[19] The usual jury direction in such cases was that it was for the accused to make out, to prove (clearly) the defence or issue; that it was for him to satisfy them upon it; or that they must believe the defence made out.[20] It may be that many, if asked, would have said that the standard of proof required of the accused was proof beyond reasonable doubt.[21] The use of expressions such as 'believe', 'satisfy' and 'clearly prove' certainly suggests this.

2. Procedural Aspects

The area in which the nineteenth-century law of criminal evidence most clearly lacked maturity was its procedural aspects. In 1800 some elementary questions as to admissibility still awaited resolution. For example, by whom was a factual issue upon which admissibility depended to be determined, the judge or the jury? Upon whom did the burden of proof in relation to such issue rest? Was it open to the accused to call evidence on the issue and, if so, at what stage? In *Woodcock* in 1789,[22] Eyre LCB had held that it was for the jury to determine the admissibility of a dying declaration and, although this aberrant ruling was within a matter of years overturned by the Twelve Judges,[23] as late as 1853 one could find doubt being expressed as to whether it was for the judge or the jury to decide if a prosecution witness was married to one of the accused, and therefore incompetent.[24] As for the burden of proof, in a case in the Court for Crown Cases Reserved in 1848 Patteson J observed *arguendo* that it was for the prisoner to prove that a confession had been procured by an inducement.[25] Although in *Warringham*,[26] three years later, Parke B laid down precisely the opposite rule, there is no certainty that this settled the point; forty years on counsel can be found arguing before the Court for Crown Cases Reserved that the burden was on the prisoner.[27] *Warringham* had, however, been followed in

---

[19] The first English case in which the standard of proof in insanity is discussed appears to be *R v Sodeman* [1936] 2 All ER 1138. In Canada the question had been discussed as early as 1918: see *R v Kierstead* (1918) 42 DLR 193 (also *R v Clark* (1921) 61 SCR 608) and in the United States earlier still, see Wigmore, *Treatise*, 2497.

[20] 'Make out', *R v Leigh* (1866) 4 F & F 915; 'prove', *R v Stokes* (1848) 3 Car & Kir 185; 'clearly prove', *R v Kopsch* (1925) 19 Cr App R 50; 'satisfy', *R v Offord* above; sometimes the question was framed in terms of whether the jury 'believed' the defence evidence, *R v Davies* 1858 1 F.& F 69.

[21] Cf *R v Nobin Chunder Banerjee* (1873) 13 BLR 20 ('clearly and distinctly proved').

[22] *R v Woodcock* (1789) 1 Leach 500.

[23] The fact of its being overturned is referred to by Lord Ellenborough in *R v Hucks* (1816) 1 Stark 521.

[24] By Huddleston in *R v Blackburn* (1853) 6 Cox 333.

[25] *R v Garner* (1848) 3 Cox 175.

[26] *R v Warringham* (1851) 2 Den 447 n.

[27] *R v Thompson* (1893) 17 Cox 641.

Jenkins in 1869,[28] where Kelly LCB had held that, where a question arose as to the admissibility of a statement as a dying declaration, the burden of proof of the state of mind of the declarant was on the Crown and the standard of proof was proof beyond reasonable doubt. In a case heard at the Old Bailey in 1828, Gaselee J refused to allow defence counsel to call evidence bearing upon the voluntariness of a confession, save as part of the defence case, despite counsel's protests that by that time the confession might well have been allowed in and the damage done.[29] There was, said his lordship, no precedent for such a proceeding.

3. Trying Admissibility in Front of the Jury

From an accused's point of view no feature of the law of evidence was more unsatisfactory than the way issues of admissibility were tried. Eighteenth-century practice had been for legal argument as to the admissibility of confessions to take place in front of the jury.[30] The advent of the nineteenth century brought no change. Reported cases indicate that, where the Crown sought to put in confession evidence, the procedure followed was for the witness who was to prove the confession to be questioned minutely as to what passed between him and the prisoner prior to the making of the confession and, if anything emerged to cast doubt on its admissibility, the judge would hear argument on the point and rule.[31] Reports make no mention of the jury being invited to withdraw at any stage and the clear impression one gains is that the jury was present throughout. That would be consistent with all we know about eighteenth-century trials. It would also explain cases such as *Yarham* (1846), where defence counsel, in his closing speech, is to be found making reference to a statement earlier ruled inadmissible by the judge.[32]

Nor do confessions appear to have been a case apart. On the contrary, there are grounds for believing that throughout the century the normal practice was for all legal argument, whether as to admissibility or otherwise, to take place in the presence of the jury. In the debate on the 1824 Prisoners' Counsel Bill, Denman claimed that counsel in felony cases used legal objection and argument as an indirect means of making a jury speech. Other evidence is afforded by reports of trials. In 1840 one finds a judge explaining in his summing up a ruling he had earlier given on admissibility, which suggests that the jury had been present when the point was argued.[33] In an

---

[28] In *R v Jenkins* (1869) 11 Cox 250 at 256.

[29] *R v Fenn, The Times*, 12 September 1828.

[30] See Beattie, 365.

[31] See e.g. *R v Day* (1847) 2 Cox 209 (boy of eight; Cresswell J conducted the investigation); *R v Griffin* (1853) 6 Cox 219; *R v Frewin* (1855) 6 Cox 530 (prisoner unrepresented).

[32] *R v Yarham, The Times*, 30 March 1846.

[33] *R v Megson Battye and Ellis* (1840) 9 C & P 420.

1843 case legal argument as to the right of reply took place before the jury.[34] In *Forster* in 1855 a jury, in convicting the accused of uttering counterfeit coin, added that they found this verdict without considering in the least the evidence of a subsequent uttering which had been adduced by the Crown, which strongly suggests that they had been present when the admissibility of the evidence was argued.[35] The case of *Ingrey*, tried before the Lord Chief Justice in 1900, is even clearer.[36] Then there is the frequency with which one finds objections to admissibility being taken during the prosecution's opening speech – a state of affairs difficult to explain except on the basis that there was no duty on the Crown to refrain from opening potentially inadmissible evidence, and consistent with a practice of arguing admissibility in front of the jury.[37] There are twentieth-century cases which appear to look back to such a practice. In the judgement of the Lord Chief Justice in *Thompson* (1917), there are dicta which seem to imply that argument in front of the jury was the normal rule, sending them to their room the exception.[38] Lastly, there is the difficulty, which the Court of Appeal was still having as late as 1973, of stamping out the practice of arguing submissions of no case in front of the jury.[39]

Gradually attempts were made to protect the accused against the prejudice to which the practice gave rise. A variety of expedients was resorted to. In a handful of 1820s cases there is evidence of something resembling the American practice of counsel discussing points of law with the judge at his bench in voices too low to be heard by the jury.[40] It does not, however, seem to have taken root and no more is heard of it after this. In *Taylor* in 1851, the judge, on the application of both counsel, gave a ruling, before the trial began and out of the hearing of the waiting jury, upon a question of similar fact evidence.[41] In *Winslow* in 1860, again before the trial began, and with the express object of avoiding prejudice to the prisoner, Martin B received written submissions from counsel upon the admissibility of similar fact evidence and gave a ruling thereon in private.[42] During the remainder of the century this practice was occasionally adopted in other cases.[43] In 1917,

[34] *R v Brooks* (1843) 1 Cox 6.

[35] *R v Forster* (1855) 6 Cox 521 at 522.

[36] *R v Ingrey* (1900) 64 JP 106.

[37] See e.g. *R v Overfield, The Times*, 22 March 1824; *R v Peel* (1860) 2 F & F 21; *R v Bedingfield, The Times*, 14 November 1879 (where the trial judge intervened of his own motion) and *R v Honour, The Times*, 30 July 1898.

[38] *R v Thompson* (1917) 12 Cr App R 261 at 269; see also *R v Anderson* (1929) 21 Cr App R 178 at 182.

[39] *R v Falconer Atlee* (1973) 58 Cr App R 348 per Roskill J at 354; this case prompted the editor of the 1976 edition of Phipson to observe that formerly it had been the practice for the jury to be present during such submissions.

[40] *R v Turpin, The Times*, 9 August 1824; *R v Dewesbury, The Times*, 7 September 1824; *R v Fauntleroy, The Times*, 1 November 1824; and *R v Scott, The Times*, 10 September 1827.

[41] *R v Taylor* (1851) 5 Cox 138.

[42] *R v Winslow* (1860) 8 Cox 397.

however, it was severely condemned by the Court of Criminal Appeal on the ground that it gave rise to no shorthand note.[44] An expedient occasionally resorted to at the Old Bailey in the 1860s was that of requiring a witness, before he answered a question, the answer to which it was thought might well be inadmissible, to write down the answer so that the judge might consider it.[45] Yet another was to couch the objection or argument in terms which the jury were unlikely to be able to follow.[46]

The first case in which an English court is reported as sending a jury away whilst a question of admissibility was argued would appear to be *Ivimy*, tried at the Old Bailey in 1880.[47] The practice was slow to take hold. By 1910 it was becoming more common.[48] Seven years later, in *Thompson*, the Lord Chief Justice, in expressing his disapproval of *Winslow*, observed that, where the judge considered that it would unfairly prejudice the accused to hear legal argument in front of the jury, he should direct them to retire to their room. However, he made clear that the accused had no right to require that the jury be sent out. The matter was one for the discretion of the judge. This was the same rule as had been laid down by the American courts in the 1880s and 1890s.[49] The first practitioners' book to make mention of it appears to have been the 1921 edition of Roscoe, which noted that the jury was sometimes asked to retire while questions of law were argued.[50]

When inadmissible evidence got in front of the jury, the judge would normally strike it from his notes and tell the jury to disregard it.[51] By the start of the twentieth century, however, there were signs that the courts were beginning to recognise that there were some cases where justice demanded that the trial be stopped and the jury discharged.[52]

---

[43] *R v Beesley, The Times*, 18 March 1889; *R v Davis and Others, The Times*, 28 July 1893; *R v Scott, The Times*, 1 December 1896.

[44] *R v Thompson* above.

[45] *R v Ward* (1860) 54 CCC Sess Pap 576 and *R v Carlos* (1864) 59 CCC Sess Pap 292 (where the witness instead of being asked to write down his answer was asked to whisper it to the clerk of the prosecuting solicitor).

[46] See e.g. *R v Bartlett and Dyson, The Times*, 13 April 1886, and the observation in the judgement in Thompson supra that it was not necessary to send the jury out where the question was capable of being argued in the abstract, as it frequently was when the evidence objected to appeared in the depositions.

[47] *R v Ivimy* (1880) 107 CCC Sess Pap 570.

[48] One finds references to the jury being sent out whilst admissibility was argued in two appeal cases from around this time, namely *R v Booth* (1910) 5 Cr App R 177 and *R v Ballard* (1914) 12 Cr App R 1.

[49] See the note on *The State v Kelly* in 42 *Central Law Journal*, 158 and the authorities there cited.

[50] Roscoe's *Criminal Evidence* (15th edn), 287.

[51] See e.g. Bosanquet J in *R v Crockett* (1831) 4 C & P 544, 'I must strike the whole of the evidence out of my notes'; see also *R v Blackburn* (1853) 6 Cox 333, and *R v Drage* (1878) 14 Cox 85.

[52] *R v Rose* (1898) 18 Cox 717 at 718.

4. The Judge's Exclusionary Discretion

Of an exclusionary discretion one finds no trace. If evidence was admissible the judge was bound to admit it, however slight its probative value.[53] As late as the 1870s and 1880s, even in capital cases, arguments that similar fact evidence tendered by the Crown had little weight, or would cause damning prejudice, were simply brushed aside.[54] Such matters had no bearing upon admissibility. However, although a judge had no power to exclude prejudical evidence, a suggestion to prosecuting counsel not to press the evidence (coupled where there was doubt as to admissibility with a threat to reserve the point) would often suffice to prevent its being laid before the jury. As early as 1862 one finds Williams J, when faced with an argument that prior utterings of forged documents relied upon by the Crown were too remote in time to have any probative value, declaring: 'the judge reposes confidence in counsel that they will not give in evidence what has no tendency to prove guilty knowledge but only prejudice the prisoner'.[55] By the early twentieth century, the practice of urging counsel not to press evidence was sufficiently firmly established to be described by Lord Moulton, in *Christie*, as 'very salutary' and 'usually sufficient' to prevent evidence being put in.[56] Prior to 1898 it was by this means that judges were able to prevent prisoners who availed themselves of a statutory right of giving evidence being cross-examined as to character.

---

[53] See Grose J in *R v Eriswell (Inhabitants)* (1790) 3 T R 707 at 711 and Lord Halsbury in *R v Christie* (1914) 10 Cr App R 141 at 149.

[54] See e.g. Lush J in *R v Roden* (1874) 12 Cox 630, and Butt J in *R v Flannagan and Higgins* (1882) 15 Cox 403 at 410 ('The question of its prejudicing the prisoners was not what he had to try').

[55] *R v Salt* (1862) 3 F & F 834.

[56] *R v Christie* above (n. 53) at 160.

20

Hearsay

'You must not tell us what the soldier or any other man said', interrupted the judge, 'it's not evidence'.

Charles Dickens, *The Pickwick Papers* (1837), chapter 34.

The rule against hearsay had roots going back to the seventeenth century. It was throughout the nineteenth century strictly enforced in criminal cases. In the early years of the century this strictness led to severe curbs being placed upon the leading of complaint evidence in rape and sexual assault. That such evidence was admissible was too clear for argument. The practice of admitting it went back to Hale's day and far beyond.[1] Indeed, without evidence of fresh complaint, a rape prosecution stood little change of success.[2] A complaint was in law not evidence of the truth of the facts stated, merely of consistency on the part of the complainant.[3] Because of this, judges were by the 1830s refusing to allow the prosecution to lead more than the fact of a complaint having been made.[4] (It was left to the prisoner to elicit the terms of the complaint if he wished, as he might do where the story the complainant had told initially differed from that which she was now telling.) The rule, which had been criticised by Parke B in 1839,[5] was seen at its most bizarre in *Wink* (1834), where Patteson J held that a police constable, who had received a complaint of robbery from the prosecutor, could not be asked whom the prosecutor named as his attacker.[6] He could only be asked whether, in consequence of the name given, he went in search of any person and who that person was (a distinction which proved too subtle for

[1] Hale 1 P C, 632–33.

[2] Phillipps (8th edn) 204 n 2.

[3] See *R v Brasier* (1779) 1 Leach 199, *R v Tucker* (1808) in D. R. Bentley, *Select Cases from the Twelve Judges' Notebooks*, 102; Archbold (1st edn) 260; *R v Megson Battye and Ellis* (1840) 9 C & P 418 and *R v Guttridge* (1840) 9 C & P 471.

[4] See *R v Wink* (1834) 6 C & P 397; *R v Walker* (1839) 2 M & Rob 212; *R v Osborne* (1842) Car & M 622 and the Irish cases *R v Maclean* (1840) 2 Craw & D 350, *R v Alexander* (1841) 2 Craw & D 126 and *Quigley's Case* (1842) Ir Circ Rep 677.

[5] *R v Walker* (1839) 2 M & Rob 212.

[6] *R v Wink* above; for instances of judges admitting evidence of complaint in cases other than rape, see *R v Ridsdale* (1837) Starkie, *Evidence* (4th edn) 469 n; *R v Lunny* (1854) 6 Cox 477; and *R v Folley* (1896) 60 JP 569.

some of Patteson's brethren).[7] In the second half of the century some judges were openly refusing to follow the rule, allowing the prosecution to adduce both the fact and the terms of the complaint.[8] Eventually in 1896 the question came for decision before the Court for Crown Cases Reserved in *Lillyman*, which held that the terms as well as the fact of a complaint could be led.[9] One of the justifications the court gave for the ruling was that it prevented the jury speculating as to what the terms of the complaint were.

Confession aside, the most important exceptions to the rule in criminal cases were those relating to dying declarations and the reading of depositions.[10] The law as to the first became ever more strict, while the scope for the latter was progressively enlarged. At the end of the eighteenth century it had commonly been thought that dying declarations were admissible in all cases civil and criminal. Indeed one finds the law so stated by text writers as late as 1810.[11] Such a view of the law seemed in accordance both with principle and authority. With principle, because the reason given for admitting such declarations in evidence – the unlikelihood of a man dying with a lie on his lips – applied as well to civil suits as to criminal.[12] In accordance with authority, because there existed a handful of pre-1820 cases which appeared to show that admissibility was not confined simply to homicide cases. Of these the most important was *Wright v Littler*,[13] in which Lord Mansfield had held the deathbed confession of an attesting witness to a deed that he had forged it admissible to impeach the validity of the deed (a decision later followed by Heath J in an unreported case, cited with approval by Lord Ellenborough in judgements given in 1805 and 1808).[14] The others were the *Douglas Peerage Case* (1769), where the dying declarations of Lady Douglas as to the paternity of the claimant had been held admissible;[15] and *Drummond* (1784), in which, on an indictment for robbery, the dying confession of a man who had recently been executed (that he was the true robber) had been rejected solely because, as a convict, the deceased would have been incompetent to give evidence.[16]

In 1836 Parke B was able to describe the theory of the general admissibility

---

[7] Cresswell J in *R v Osbourne* above.

[8] *R v Eyre* (1860) 2 F & F 579 (Byles J); *R v Wood* (1877) 14 Cox 46 (Bramwell LJ), and Stephen's *Digest* (12th edn) N 1.

[9] *R v Lillyman* (1896) 18 Cox 346 (the court added that such evidence was also admitted to show want of consent).

[10] The other exception most commonly encountered in criminal cases was that relating to statements made by persons as to their bodily health and feelings.

[11] Z. Swift, *American Law of Evidence* (Hartford, 1810), 125; see also L. McNally, *The Rules of Evidence on Pleas of the Crown* (Dublin, 1802), 381 and 386.

[12] As to which see Wigmore, *Treatise*, art 1430 n 1 and 2 and the cases there cited.

[13] *Wright v Littler* (1761) 3 Burr 1244.

[14] *Aveson v Kinnaird* (1805) 6 East 188 at 195, and *Bishop of Durham v Beaumont* (1808) 1 Camp. 206.

[15] *Douglas Peerage Case* (1769) 2 Harg Collect Jurid 387,389 and 397.

[16] *R v Drummond* (1784) 1 Leach 337.

of declarations in extremis as 'long exploded', the only class of case in which such evidence was by then admissible being homicide prosecutions.[17] The first English case in which this new strict rule was applied was *Doe d Sutton v Ridgway* in 1820.[18] (There was a New York case to like effect in 1818).[19] There the King's Bench refused to admit a dying declaration to prove pedigree in an ejectment action, *Wright v Littler* being explained away on the basis that the declaration was admitted so that the party impeaching the deed should not, by the death of the attesting witness, lose the benefit of a matter which he could have put to him in cross-examination had he lived. Four years later came the important ruling of the same court, in *Mead* (a perjury prosecution),[20] that dying declarations were only admissible where the death of the deceased was the subject of the charge. Although the court did not condescend to give reasons for its ruling, it again apparently felt obliged to distinguish *Wright v Littler*, this time on a somewhat different ground to that offered in 1820, namely that the declaration was self-accusatory and not accusatory of others. After these two decisions all that was need to get rid of the old doctrine altogether was to administer the coup de grace to *Wright v Littler*. This was done in 1836 by a strong Court of Exchequer in *Stobart v Dryden*.

This dramatic change of direction in the law probably stemmed from increasing judicial unease about the anomalous nature of this exception to the hearsay rule and the scope which it offered for fraud. But why was the exception allowed to survive in homicide cases? The explanation offered by contemporary text writers was necessity. If dying declarations were not received, murderers would escape justice.[21] The reality, however, is probably that their admissibility in homicide cases was too well established to be questioned, there being numerous decisions (including several by the Twelve Judges) in favour of their reception,[22] some dating back to the seventeenth century.[23]

Mead did not quite mark the end of the old doctrine so far as criminal cases were concerned. In *Lindfield* (1848),[24] and in *Hind* (1860),[25] both of which were abortion prosecutions, the dying declaration of the woman was admitted by the trial judge (Hind's conviction was in consequence quashed by the Court for Crown Cases Reserved; in *Lindfield* the jury's acquittal of

---

[17] *Stobart v Dryden* (1836) 1 M & W 615 at 626.

[18] *Doe d Sutton v Ridgway* (1820) 4 B & Ald 53.

[19] *Wilson v Boeram* (1818) 15 Johnson's Rep 286 (Supreme Court of New York).

[20] *R v Mead* (1824) 2 B & C 605 (perjury) and *R v Hutchinson* (1822) cited 2 B & C 608 n.

[21] East, 1 P C (1803) 353.

[22] See e.g. *R v Tinkler* (1781) East 1 P C 354; *R v Radburne* (1787) East 1 P C 356 and *R v John* (1790) East, 1 P C 357.

[23] *R v Earl of Pembroke* (1678) 6 St Tr 1309; *Lord Mohun's Trial* (1691) 12 St Tr 950 at 967 and see Wigmore, *Treatise*, art 1431.

[24] *R v Lindfield* (1848) 12 JP 745.

[25] *R v Hind* (1860) 8 Cox 300.

the accused prevented the point being reserved). Unsuccessful attempts were made in 1830, 1841 and 1859 to get dying declarations admitted in prosecutions for robbery, shooting with intent to murder (in this case, the deathbed confession of a man, alleged by the defence to be the perpetrator of the offence, was sought to be put in to exculpate the accused) and rape.[26]

The rules applied after *Mead* to determine the admissibility of statements tendered as dying declarations in homicide cases were essentially the same as had been laid down in the eighteenth century. The declarant must have been a person competent in law to give sworn evidence;[27] the declaration must relate to the cause of his death;[28] and at the time he made it he must have been under a settled and hopeless expectation of almost immediate death.[29] What was new, however, was the strictness with which judges now demanded that the declarant's state of mind be proved. This resulted in rulings against which, in Wigmore's words, 'common sense revolts', rulings such as that in *Mooney* (1851), where a declaration made by a woman, after she had been warned by a clergyman to prepare for death and had been heard commending her soul to God, was rejected on the grounds that the proof that she was aware that she was in a dying state was insufficient.[30] A celebrated instance of this excessive judicial scrupulosity occurred in the 1870s. It had been held in several eighteenth-century cases that the fact that a deceased knew he was in a dying state could properly be inferred from the nature of his wounds or illness alone.[31] One finds the same proposition laid down both by text writers and in reported cases in the first half of the nineteenth century.[32] In *Morgan* (1875), however, Denman J, after consulting Cockburn LCJ, refused to draw the inference, declaring that there was no case in which a judge had admitted the statement entirely upon an inference drawn from the nature of the wound itself and from giving the deceased credit for ordinary intelligence as to its natural results.[33] Four years

[26] *R v Lloyd* (1830) 4 C & P 233; *R v Gray* (1841) Ir Cir 76; *R v Newton and Carpenter* (1859) 1 F & F 641.

[27] *R v Pike* (1829) 3 C & P 598 (four-year-old child).

[28] *R v Mead* above; *R v Murton* (1862) 3 F & F 492; but contra *R v Baker* (1837) 2 M & Rob 53.

[29] *R v Mooney* (1851) 5 Cox 318; *R v Peel* (1860) 2 F & F 21; *R v Jenkins* (1869) 17 WR 621: 'an unqualified belief in the nearness of death'; Eyre CB in *R v Woodcock* (1789) 1 Leach 500: 'soon to answer to his maker'; *R v Van Butchell* (1829) 3 C & P 629: 'almost immediate dissolution'; *R v Jenkins* above: 'expectation of impending and almost immediate death'; *R v Osman* (1861) 15 Cox 1: 'if he thinks he will die tomorrow it is not enough'; but contra *R v Bonner* (1834) 6 C & P 386.

[30] *R v Mooney* above; see also *R v Spilsbury* (1835) 7 C & P 187 (deceased stated he should not recover; declaration rejected because his failure to take his leave of his relatives and settle his affairs suggested he entertained hope); and *R v Nicholas* (1852) 6 Cox 120 (declaration rejected although, immediately after making it the deceased said 'Oh God I am going fast. I am too far gone to say any more.')

[31] *R v Woodcock* above; *R v John* above.

[32] Phillipps, 297; *R v Bonner* above.

later, in *Bedingfield*, Cockburn LCJ rejected out of hand, as a dying declaration, a statement made by a woman minutes before dying of a throat wound inflicted inside a house from which she had just fled.[34] There was, he ruled, no evidence that she was aware she was dying. The two cases were severely criticised by commentators as based on a mistaken view of the law, and were thereafter generally so regarded.[35] Had they stood, however, the result would have been that the dying words of a victim who expired within minutes of the fatal injury being inflicted would in many cases not have been receivable.

The judges justified their scrupulosity on the ground that dying declarations, not being subject to cross-examination, were a dangerous species of evidence.[36] Their admission was an anomaly to be confined within as narrow bounds as possible. In the main the judges' stance was supported by text writers such as Phillipps and Taylor, who were at pains to point out the dangers inherent in such evidence (misreporting, animosity or resentment on the part of the deceased at his condition, or mistake or confusion caused by his injuries).[37] Phillipps' assiduity had even thrown up a case of a man wrongly convicted and executed in 1749 for rape on evidence of a dying declaration.[38] A factor which must have played a part in shaping judicial attitudes was the frequency with which such evidence was tendered in homicide cases. Nowadays medical science has rendered the dying declaration well nigh obsolete. Victims of violence who remain conscious or recover consciousness now usually live to tell their tale in the witness-box. In the nineteenth century any serious injury carried with it a high risk of a fatal outcome.[39] For this reason, it was commonplace for a victim of serious assault to be pressed (particularly if his condition took a turn for the worse) to give his version, with a view to its being adduced in evidence in the event of his succumbing.

From the accused's point of view, the progressive narrowing of the scope for the admission of dying declarations in evidence was obviously welcome, as indeed were two principles laid down early in the century: that he could pray in aid a declaration which exculpated him;[40] and that in cases where

---

[33] *R v Morgan* (1875) 14 Cox 337, based on a misunderstanding of *R v Cleary* (1862) 2 F & F 850.

[34] *R v Bedingfield* (1879) 14 Cox 341.

[35] See especially 14 Cox 339–40 and 343–45.

[36] See *Ashton's Case* (1837) 2 Lew 147; *R v Jenkins* above; *R v Hind* above; *R v Gloster* (1888) 16 Cox 471.

[37] Phillipps, 305; Taylor (7th edn) 612.

[38] Phillipps, 306 n 1; the case was that of Richard Coleman executed in 1749.

[39] The prospects of recovery improved somewhat in the second half of the century with the introduction of new surgical techniques, in particular the use of anaesthetics (ether was first used in 1845) and antiseptics (first used in the 1860s), see L. Woodward, *The Age of Reform* (2nd edn), 620.

[40] *R v Scaife* (1836) 2 Lew 150.

a dying declaration was used against him he could lead evidence to show the deceased's bad character or unreliability as a witness.[41]

One result of the judges' strictness was the enactment in 1867 of a provision designed to make it easier to get in evidence statements made by dangerously ill patients who subsequently died. Russell Gurney's Act (1867) empowered magistrates to take out of court the deposition in relation to an indictable offence of any person dangerously ill and unlikely to recover.[42] It made the same admissible in evidence at trial, provided that the accused was given notice of the taking of the deposition and the opportunity to attend and cross-examine, and that the deponent was, by the date of trial, either dead or ill with no probability of his ever being well enough to attend trial.

In cases where the accused died within minutes of the fatal blow, his dying words could arguably be received in evidence as part of the *res gestae*. Indeed, in 1834, the dying words of a man run down by a coach were admitted on a prosecution of the coach driver for manslaughter.[43] However, the door was effectively slammed shut by the ruling of Cockburn LCJ in *Bedingfield* that, to be admissible on this ground, the words spoken had to be contemporaneous with the fatal attack. The decision in *Bedingfield*, although severely attacked in the legal press, was none the less accepted as authoritative on the point.[44] Even before this judges had shown a lack of enthusiasm for admitting dying statements on this ground in criminal cases.[45]

So far as depositions were concerned, in 1800 these could be put in only in felony,[46] and then only subject to two stringent conditions: first, that it be shown that the witness was dead,[47] so ill as not to be able to travel,[48] or was being kept out of the way by the accused;[49] and, secondly, that the deposition had been taken in the presence of the accused, and he had had full opportunity to cross-examine the deponent.[50] The condition that the accused must have been present and have had the opportunity to cross-examine was one which some eighteenth-century judges had been inclined

[41] *R v McCarthy* (1842) unreported cited in Russell (6th edn), 270.

[42] Criminal Law Act, 1867 (30 & 31 Vict., c. 35), s 6.

[43] *R v Foster* (1834) 6 C & P 325 followed in the Irish case of *R v Lunny* above.

[44] (1880) 15 LJ 5 and 18.

[45] See *R v Jackson* (1864) 61 CCC Sess Pap 128 (declaration made within thirty seconds of injury; trial judge prepared to admit in evidence but said he would reserve the question of its admissibility, at which the Crown abandoned the attempt to get the evidence in); *R v Williams* (1872) 77 CCC Sess Pap 27, statement made ten minutes after injury held inadmissible. In *R v Morgan* above, evidence that the deceased, whilst lying mortally injured, had pointed at the prisoner was let in without argument.

[46] Under 1 & 2 Ph & M, c. 13, and 2 & 3 Ph & M, c. 10.

[47] Hale, 1 P C, 305; Buller, N P 242; applies even where witness accomplice, *R v Westbeer* (1739) 1 Leach 12.

[48] Hale, 1 P C, 305

[49] *Lord Morley's Case* (1666) 6 St Tr 769.

[50] *R v Woodcock* above; *R v Dingler* (1791) 2 Leach 561; *R v Forbes* (1814) Holt 599 n.; *Errington's Case* (1838) 2 Lew 148.

to dispense with in the case of coroners' depositions.[51] But in the nineteenth century it was strictly insisted upon in all cases, not least because it formed the principal justification for letting in this species of hearsay. None the less, in practice, the supposed safeguard was in many respects a hollow one. It was, in fact, rare for witnesses who gave evidence at committal hearings to be rigorously cross-examined. Most prisoners were undefended and had little skill in cross-examination, and attorneys, when they were admitted (and many benches excluded them) would often for tactical reasons ask few questions.[52] Effective cross-examination was frequently also made difficult by the objectionable but common practice of taking statements from witnesses out of court, then merely having a witness's statement read out and confirmed by him in the prisoner's presence.[53] Again, because of the careless way in which depositions were taken, it was not uncommon for a deposition to omit important answers given in cross-examination.[54]

The scope for putting depositions in evidence was increased by statute. In 1826 depositions taken by examining magistrates in misdemeanour became admissible to the same extent as in felony.[55] More thoroughgoing reform came with Jervis's Act of 1848. This empowered examining magistrates to conduct preliminary examinations into all indictable offences, treason included.[56] It laid down strict rules as to how magistrates should take depositions and declared in what circumstances they could be given in evidence at trial, namely in any case where the deponent was dead or too ill to travel.[57] This poorly drafted section gave rise to a host of problems. What of witnesses kept out of the way by the accused: could their depositions still be read? In *Scaife* (1851), the Court for Crown Cases Reserved held that they could, also ruling that a deposition put in on this ground was, on a trial of co-accused, admissible only against the prisoner responsible for the witness's absence (thereby obliging the jury to undertake a feat of mental gymnastics of the type already common in confession cases).[58] The Act was also silent as to the case of the witness who had become insane since committal (pre-1848 the deposition of such a witness had been held admissible upon the basis that he was to be regarded as to all intents and purposes

---

[51] *Lord Morley's Case* above; *Bromwich's Case* (1667) 1 Lev 180; dicta of Lord Kenyon and Buller J in *R v Eriswell (Inhabitants)* (1790) 3 T R 721 citing *Radburne* above, which is not in fact in point, and a ruling of Coleridge J in *Sills v Brown* repudiated by Starkie, Phillipps and Russell and by M Smith J in *R v Rigg* (1866) 4 F & F 1085.

[52] For the practice of excluding attorneys, see *R v Borron* (1820) 3 B & A 432; *Cox v Coleridge* (1822) 1 B & C 37; *R v Staffordshire JJ* (1819) 1 Chit KB 217; *Collier v Hicks* (1831) 2 B & A 663. As to tactics see Phillipps, 565.

[53] See e.g. *R v Hake* (1845) 1 Cox 226.

[54] Phillipps, 567.

[55] 7 Geo IV, c. 64, s 3.

[56] 11 & 12 Vict, c. 42, s 1.

[57] Ibid. ss 17 and 18.

[58] *R v Scaife* (1851) 5 Cox 243.

dead).[59] Then what of the words 'too ill to travel': how they were to be construed? Before 1848 it had been held that illness would only justify the reading of a deposition where it could be shown that the witness was so ill that he was unlikely ever to be fit to come to court.[60] Where the illness was not of this seriousness, the appropriate course was postponement of the trial. The courts, however, felt obliged to construe the words of the Act literally, with the result that even temporary illness was now enough to allow a witness's evidence to be read.[61] In 1856 Greaves, in his Report to the Lord Chancellor on Criminal Procedure,[62] recommended that the section be redrawn to cover the cases omitted, including that of pregnancy (a constant source of difficulty in this connection).[63] Nothing was done. The only reform made came in 1867 when Russell Gurney's Act, by requiring examining magistrates to take depositions from witnesses tendered by the defence, made it possible for the first time for the evidence of defence witnesses who had died or were ill to be read at trial.

[59] *R v Eriswell (Inhabitants)* above.

[60] *R v Hogg* (1833) 6 C & P 176; *R v Wilshaw* (1841) Car & M 145; and *R v Savage* (1831) 5 C & P 143.

[61] *R v Wilson* (1861) 8 Cox 453 (witness too ill to give evidence but not too ill to travel; held deposition could be read) *R v Croucher* (1862) 3 F & F 285 (pregnancy) and *R v Stephenson* (1862) 9 Cox 156 (pregnancy and illness).

[62] PP 1856 (456) L, 79.

[63] See e.g. *R v Walker* (1857) 1 F & F 534; *R v Stephenson* (1862) 9 Cox 156; *R v Heesom* (1878) 14 Cox 40; *R v Goodfellow* (1879) 14 Cox 326; and *R v Harney* (1850) 4 Cox 441.

21

Confessions and Police Interrogation

'For a constable to press an accused person to say anything with reference to the crime of which he is accused is very wrong.'

Preface, *Vincent's Police Code* (1882).

1. Confessions

One of the main exclusionary rules inherited by nineteenth-century judges was that rendering involuntary confessions inadmissible. In *Warickshall* in 1783, the judges had defined an involuntary confession as one 'got by promises or threats', a definition which left unanswered two important questions.[1] First, did the identity of the person offering the inducement matter? Secondly, what of the inducement itself? Would any promise or threat exclude, however trivial and whatever its subject matter?

Upon the first question judicial opinion was divided as late as the mid 1830s, but by 1840 the rule was settled: only an inducement held out by, or with the sanction of, a person in authority (that is a person in a position to influence the conduct of the prosecution) would exclude.[2] Taylor was later to suggest that the adoption of this rule was due principally to fear of opening 'a wide door to collusive practices [with] perjured witnesses ... called to affirm that they had urged the prisoner [that it would be best] to confess'.[3]

As to the second question, if the reason for the exclusionary rule was (as *Warickshall* and later cases suggested) the likely unreliability of confessions obtained by inducements, it followed that the only inducements which ought to exclude were those of a kind calculated to lead the prisoner to make an

---

[1] *R v Warickshall* (1783) 1 Leach 263.

[2] Early cases in which inducements held out by persons not in authority were held not to exclude are *R v Row* (1809) Russ & Ry 153, *R v Hardwick* (1811) 1 C & P 98 n and *R v Gibbons* (1823) 1 C & P 97. One of the doughtiest advocates of the exclusion of confessions obtained by inducements held out by those not in authority was Bosanquet J, see *R v Dunn* (1831) 4 C & P 543 and *R v Slaughter* (1831) 4 C & P 544 n. In *R v Spencer* (1837) 7 C & P 776 Parke B observed that there was a difference of opinion among the judges upon the question, but two years later, in *R v Taylor* (1839) 8 C & P 733, Patteson J claimed that they favoured admissibility. As to inducements held out with the sanction of a person in authority see *R v Pountney* (1836) 7 C & P 302, *R v Moody* (1841) 2 Craw & D 347 and *R v Laugher* (1846) 2 C & K 225.

[3] Taylor (7th edn), 735; Taylor favoured exclusion, ibid., 734.

untrue confession.[4] This approach in fact received a measure of judicial support. Indeed, the ruling of the Twelve Judges in *Gilham* in 1828 (a decision never thereafter questioned) that a purely spiritual inducement would not exclude seems to have been based on just this reasoning.[5] Likewise the refusal of the judges to treat exhortations to tell the truth as inducements. How could it be said that telling a man to be sure to tell the truth was advising him to confess what he was not really guilty of?[6] Or yet again the 1840 ruling that property discovered in consequence of an inadmissible confession rendered the confession pro tanto admissible (the finding of the property, so the argument ran, demonstrated that in that respect at least 'the party was not accusing himself falsely').[7] In 1842, Joy, the former Irish Lord Chief Baron, published a treatise on confessions in which he sought to argue that reliability was the true test of admissibility. The 'threat or inducement held out must', he wrote 'have reference to the charge, and be such as would lead [the prisoner] to suppose that it would be better for him to admit himself guilty of an offence which he had never committed.'[8] He was able to cite in support a handful of English cases, in particular those of *Green* and *Lloyd* (both from 1834), where the removal of the prisoner's handcuffs (desired by him as the price of a confession), and a promise to allow him to see his wife, were respectively held not to render the confessions which followed inadmissible.[9]

When Joy wrote, the reliability test was in fact relatively little employed in cases of temporal (as opposed to spiritual or moral) inducement. Proof of any such inducement was commonly treated as sufficient to exclude, without the need for any inquiry as to whether the inducement was one which, in the particular circumstances, would have been likely to lead the particular accused to make a false confession. The judges justified this uncritical approach on two grounds. First, the difficulty of assessing the influence of an inducement on a prisoner's mind.[10] Secondly, the need for great caution before admitting confessions in evidence. Had not Hotham B said in *Thompson* (1783) that it was 'impossible to be too careful on the subject'?[11] Indeed, in one class of case, namely where the prisoner had been told it would be better to confess, the rule as early as the 1830s was rigid

---

[4] *R v Warickshall:* 'It comes in so questionable a shape ... that no credit can be given to it'; for other dicta suggesting that the reason for excluding involuntary confessions was their unreliability, see *R v Thomas* (1837) 7 C & P 345; *R v Court* (1836) 7 C & P 486; and *R v Moore* (1852) 5 Cox 555.

[5] *R v Gilham* (1828) 1 Moo 186; *R v Nute* (1800) 2 Russ C & M 832 is to the same effect.

[6] *R v Court* above.

[7] *R v Gould* (1840) 9 C & P 364; *R v Butcher* (1798) 1 Leach 265 n.

[8] H. H. Joy on *Confession in Criminal Cases* (Dublin, 1842), 13.

[9] *R v Green* (1834) 6 C & P 655; *R v Lloyd* (1834) 6 C & P 393.

[10] Starkie, *Evidence*, ii, 36.

[11] *R v Thompson* (1783) 1 Leach 291: 'It is almost impossible to be too careful ... on this subject' (Hotham B).

and fixed. The use of any such expression rendered any confession which followed automatically inadmissible (even where the phrase had been intended and understood by the prisoner to be no more than an exhortation to tell the truth).[12]

As well as failing to make reliability the touchstone of admissibility, the judges were by the 1830s also displaying an increasing astuteness in spelling inducements out of seemingly innocuous phrases. In *Enoch* (1833), for example, an admonition to a prisoner to confess 'otherwise the matter would lie on her and the guilty would go free' was held to be an inducement.[13] Yet, as Joy complained, it is difficult to see what threat or promise was held out. In *Mills* (1833), telling a prisoner 'it is of no use for you to deny it for there is the man and boy who will swear they saw you do it' was held by Gurney B to render his confession inadmissible, on the ground that it was 'an inducement to say something'.[14] In *Fleming* (1842), an admonition from a police inspector to a constable accused of stealing a watch, 'Be cautious in the answers you give to the questions I am going to put to you about the watch', was held to exclude.[15] In *Croydon* (1846), an attorney's telling a suspect 'I dare say you had a hand in it; you may as well tell me about it' was treated as equivalent to saying it would be better to tell, therefore rendering what followed inadmissible.[16]

Perhaps the most bizarre of all was the line of cases which fashioned an inducement out of the forms of caution in daily use by police officers and magistrates. The starting point of this line of authority was *Drew* (1838), where Coleridge J held that to caution a person that anything he said would be given in evidence for or against him constituted an inducement.[17] It might, he explained, lead the prisoner to put forward an untrue story which he believed would help him at his trial. He repeated the ruling in later cases.[18] It was followed in Ireland.[19] Police officers, in the light of *Drew*, altered the form of caution telling prisoners simply that what they said would be used in evidence against them, only to find that this would not do either. To tell a man what he says will be used against him was, said Maule J in *Jones* (1843), little different from telling him that it may be used for or against him.[20] It was just as likely to lead him to say something that

---

[12] See e.g. *R v Kingston* (1830) 4 C & P 387; *R v Dunn* above; and *R v Jarvis* [1867] LR 1 CCR 96.

[13] *R v Enoch* (1833) 5 C & P 539.

[14] *R v Mills* (1833) 6 C & P 146.

[15] *R v Fleming* (1842) Arm M & O 330.

[16] *R v Croydon* (1846) 2 Cox 67.

[17] *R v Drew* (1837) 8 C & P 140.

[18] *R v Morton* (1843) 2 M & Rob 514; explained by Coleridge J in *R v Hornbrook* (1843) 1 Cox 54.

[19] *R v Simpson* (1849) 1 Ir Jur 200.

[20] *R v Jones* (1843) cited in *R v Attwood* (1851) 5 Cox 322 and followed in *R v Holmes* (1843) 1 C & K 248; *R v Furley* (1844) 1 Cox 76 and *R v Harris* (1844) 1 Cox 106 and in Ireland in *R v Hallam* (1846) 1 Bl D & Osb 88.

he supposed might make for him at this trial, and so constituted an inducement.

To many, the judges' approach to the question of voluntariness was far too favourable to the prisoner. The law was also coming under criticism for its obscurity.[21] By the 1840s the case law on confessions had swollen to huge proportions, with some of the cases difficult, if not impossible, to reconcile. Inevitably, there were calls for reform. A scheme suggested by the *Law Magazine*,[22] and by a number of those who answered a questionnaire put put by the Criminal Law Commissioners in 1844,[23] was that all confession evidence should be admitted, leaving it for the jury to decide what weight it deserved, subject to the safeguard that no jury should be permitted to convict upon confession evidence alone. The first limb of the scheme, which had been canvassed by Bentham twenty years before, won a measure of judicial support. In *Baldry* (1852), Parke B and Campbell LCJ both declared themselves attracted by it.[24] As for the proposed corroboration requirement, this was already part of United States law where, taking as their starting-point dicta of Hale as to the danger of convicting a man of homicide where no body had been found, judges had developed the doctrine that a man could not be convicted upon his own confession without independent proof of the corpus delicti.[25] The justification offered for the rule was based on well-known cases of false confession such as those of Perry, Hubert, Wood and the Boons.[26] Where English law stood upon the point in the 1840s was uncertain. Apart from Hale's dicta there was a decision of Pollock LCB in 1847 to the effect that in bigamy some evidence of the legality of the prisoner's first marriage was required apart from his confession.[27] Against this was an imperfectly reported case in which Lord Kenyon had, seemingly, ruled that a man could be lawfully convicted on his own uncorroborated confession,[28] and two rulings at Nisi Prius. In addition there was a succession of cases from the first half of the century in which English courts had contrived to avoid ruling on the point at all.[29]

In the end, the *Law Magazine* proposal was not taken up. Reform, when it came, came at the hands of the judges themselves. In 1851 Campbell LCJ

---

[21] This criticism was made as early as 1809 in *R v Row* above; see also Joy on *Confession*, 3–4.

[22] (1842) 28 Law Mag (1st series) 17.

[23] Criminal Law Commissioners, 8th Report, app A, p 281 and p 307.

[24] *R v Baldry* (1852) 5 Cox 523.

[25] Taylor, 728; Hale, 2 P C 290.

[26] *Perry's Case* (1660) 14 St Tr 1312; *Hubert's Case* (1666) 6 St Tr 807; *Wood's Case* 1810, *Life of Sir Samuel Romilly* (by himself)(London, 2nd edn, 1840), ii, 188, and the case of the Boons (cited by Taylor, 723).

[27] *R v Flaherty* (1847) 2 C & K 782.

[28] *R v Wheeling* (1789) 1 Leach 310 n. The two other cases were *R v White* (1823) Russ & Ry 508 and the curious case of *R v Sutcliffe* (1850) 4 Cox 270.

[29] See *R v Eldridge* (1821) Russ & Ry 440; *R v Falkner* (1822) Russ & Ry 481; *R v Tuffs* (1831) 5 C & P 167.

(fresh from piloting through Parliament his Criminal Procedure Act, which had severely reduced the scope for the taking of technical points on indictments – at that time at least as great a cause of disquiet as the indulgent state of the law on inducements), turned his attention to confessions. In *Baldry*, a case which he had himself reserved, the Court for Crown Cases Reserved, at the same time as overruling the *Drew* and *Jones* line of cases, made it clear that in their view the pendulum had swung too far in favour of prisoners.[30] 'I cannot but concur', said Parke B, 'with the observations of Mr Pitt Taylor that justice and common sense seem to have been sacrificed on the altar of mercy', and with these words the other judges agreed. After *Baldry* one undoubtedly sees a stricter approach being adopted to the question of voluntariness. The old inclination 'to torture words and speculate as to what words may have been misunderstood to mean' was now a thing of the past. In 1872 a confession extracted from two young lads was actually let in, notwithstanding that it had been preceded with the exhortation 'you had better as good boys tell the truth' – an outcome which would have been unthinkable thirty years before.[31]

Baldry did not, however, put an end to the calls for reform. In 1856 a Bill was presented to Parliament by Fitzroy Kelly which proposed, inter alia, that no confession should be excluded on the ground that a promise or threat had been held out, unless the judge considered it of such a character as to cause an untrue admission to be made;[32] and that confessions made to spiritual advisers should be privileged (this latter being a rule which Alderson B had six years before vainly tried to establish).[33] It did not pass. The battle to import a corroboration requirement into the law of confessions was lost by default. The Irish courts (while leaving open the position in homicide) twice came out against such a rule.[34] By the end of the century (despite the lack of any recent English ruling on the point), it had come to be generally accepted that the rule was not part of English law.[35] Calls for such a requirement were during this period based not, as today, upon the risk of police fabrication, although dicta such as those of Cave J in *Thompson* (1893) show that not all judges were blind to this danger,[36] but rather upon the danger of false confession.

The criticism which has been heaped on the judges, most notably by Wigmore,[37] for their indulgent approach to voluntariness pre-*Baldry*, tends to

---

[30] *R v Baldry* above per Lord Campbell.

[31] *R v Reeve and Another* (1872) 12 Cox 179.

[32] PP 1856 (111) V, 523, cl 13 (Sir Fitzroy Kelly later became Lord Chief Baron).

[33] Ibid., cl 15 ; the decision of Alderson B referred to is *R v Griffin* (1853) 6 Cox 219.

[34] *R v Unkles* (1874) Ir 8 CLR 50 and *R v Sullivan* (1887) 16 Cox 347.

[35] See e.g. Best, *Evidence* (9th edn, 1902) 459, and the lack of reference to the point in Stephen's *Digest*.

[36] *R v Thompson* [1893] 2 QB 12.

[37] See Wigmore, *Treatise* (3rd edn), art 820a; for nineteenth-century criticism, see e.g. Phillipps (8th edn, 1838), 424 and the dictum of Taylor cited in Baldry.

obscure the fact that in the first half of the century (and indeed after *Baldry*) the law of confessions was, on some points, far from favourable to the prisoner.[38]

Take, for example, the practice of the Crown opening disputed confessions to the jury,[39] or again the practice of arguing their admissibility in front of the jury.[40] Then there was the way in which the voluntariness rule was disregarded in the case of accomplices, called as king's evidence, who in the witness-box failed to come up to proof. Any 'evidence' behaving in this way would be forthwith indicted, and would have adduced in evidence against him the admissions he had made before the examining magistrate. The fact that such admissions had been made under the clearest possible inducement was brushed aside. He had broken his compact with the Crown and that breach, so it was argued, justified the Crown in using his statements against him.[41] This rule was not finally reversed until 1861 when, in *Gillis*, the Irish Court for Crown Cases Reserved held that, though the Crown was fully entitled to put on trial an accomplice who broke his bargain, they were obliged to prove their case against him by legal evidence.[42] Confessions made under a promise of immunity were not lawful evidence nor did nor could his breach of bargain make them so.

Most significant of all there was the refusal of the courts to treat oppressive and unfair conduct towards a prisoner, falling short of improper inducement, as a ground for exclusion. Their stance was that improper inducement was the only ground of exclusion. If none was used, the prisoner's confession was admissible, no matter how unfair or reprehensible his treatment might have been in other respects.[43] Admissions and confessions obtained from a prisoner when drunk,[44] or when in a highly distressed state,[45] or when in severe pain and about to go into labour,[46] were thus admissible. Likewise confessions obtained by such means as the browbeating interrogation of a child,[47] holding a prisoner in custody illegally,[48] intercepting his mail,[49]

---

[38] In addition to the examples given in the text one can point to the emergence during the first half of the century of the 'person in authority' requirement and the refusal of the judges to have any truck with the argument that admissions made on oath in other proceedings were made under compulsion and so inadmissible. For the extensive case law on this point see Archbold (20th edn, 1886), 265–68.

[39] *R v Elsley* (1844) 3 LT 6 overruling *R v Swatkins* (1831) 4 C & P 548.

[40] See Chapter 19, above.

[41] See *R v Burley* 2 Starkie, *Evidence*, 13 n and 37 and Pollock CB in *R v Dingley* (1845) 1 C & K 637.

[42] *R v Gillis* (1886) Ir 17 CLR 512.

[43] *R v Derrington* (1826) 2 C & P 418 (Garrow B).

[44] *R v Spilsbury* (1835) 7 C & P 187; *R v Carter, The Times*, 23 March 1835.

[45] *R v Dewey, The Times*, 27 July 1825.

[46] *R v Mitchell, The Times*, 26 December 1823 (confession excluded on another ground).

[47] *R v Wild* (1835) 1 Moo 452, and *R v Risborough* (1847) 11 JP 280.

[48] *R v Thornton* (1824) 1 Moo 27 (fourteen year old illegally detained); contra *Ackroyd's Case* (1824) 1 Lew 49.

[49] *R v Derrington* (1826) 2 C & P 418.

deceiving him as to the strength of the case against him,[50] playing on his emotional vulnerability,[51] promising that any disclosure he made would go no further,[52] or sending a clergyman to his cell to persuade him that divine forgiveness depended upon full repentance, and that full repentance involved making full disclosure to the civil authorities,[53] also stood. This gap in the law, which was never plugged during the nineteenth century, gave rise to a much disliked but common police practice of sending into a prisoner's cell a fellow prisoner, or a policemen disguised as a prisoner, to win his confidence and worm admissions out of him, a practice still in use in Cumberland as late as 1883.[54]

Another aspect of the nineteenth-century law of confessions, which has generally been overlooked, was the attempt made by the judges in the first half of the century to find solutions to two problems which are still with us: the misreporting of confessions; and the plight of the prisoner who denied guilt but was incriminated by a confession made by a co-accused jointly tried with him. The danger of confessions being misreported had been stressed by Foster and others after him, and it was a matter about which many felt unease.[55] In the 1820s and 1830s an attempt was made to do something about the problem. In *Sexton* in 1822, Best J refused to allow a police officer to give evidence of a confession which he had not written down at the time it was made.[56] In *Mallett* in 1830, Littledale J took the same course, excluding a statement, returned by the examining magistrate and signed by the prisoner, written in language which the prisoner herself almost certainly had not used.[57] In the end the initiative came to nothing. In *Roche* (1841) Denman LCJ, despite having *Sexton* and *Mallett* cited to him, declined to exclude a statement of the prisoner taken down in the third person, although he offered to reserve the point (a course rendered unnecessary by the jury's acquittal of the prisoner).[58] That was the last that was heard of the doctrine. Thereafter judges, while stressing the dangers of misreporting, no longer treated paraphrasing as a ground of exclusion. In the last quarter of the century an attempt was made to deal with the problem by the Metropolitan Police General Orders.[59] These stressed the need for officers to record at the time and in the prisoner's own words any statement volunteered by him.

[50] *R v Burley* (1818) 2 Starkie, *Evidence* (3rd edn) 13 n.
[51] *R v Gibney* (1822) Jebb Cr & P Cas 15 and *R v Nolan* (1839) 1 Craw & D 74.
[52] *R v Shaw* (1834) 6 C & P 372 and *R v Thomas* (1837) 7 C & P 345.
[53] *R v Gilham* (1828) 1 Moo 186.
[54] (1844) 8 JP 514 referring in particular to *R v Smith*; see also Criminal Law Commissioners, 8th Report, app A (evidence of Cobbet p 294) and (1884) 18 Ir LT 617 (Carlisle Assizes, Day J).
[55] Foster, 243; see also *R v Simons* (1834) 6 C & P 540.
[56] *R v Sexton* (1822) 1 Burn's *Justice of the Peace* (29th edn, 1848–49) 1086.
[57] *R v Mallet* (1830) MSS Greaves, cited in Russell (4th edn, 1865), 867.
[58] *R v Roche* (1841) C & M 341.
[59] Metropolitan Police General Orders, 1873 (PRO, MEP 8/3); Metropolitan Police General Regulations and Orders, 1893 (PRO, MEP 8/4).

The confession of a prisoner was in 1800, as now, no evidence against others named in it (this rule had been settled for well over a century),[60] but the danger was that the jury, despite a warning from the judge not to do so, would use it as evidence against all named in it.[61] How could the judge prevent their doing this? In 1789 Buller J had hit upon an imaginative solution.[62] Faced with a case in which prisoner A was implicated in a confession made by prisoner B, he summed up the evidence as it affected A, requested the jury to come to a decision in his case but not to say what that decision was. Upon their announcing that they had done so, he summed up the evidence as it affected B. It is difficult to be sure how widespread this technique became but one can find it in use at Assizes as late as 1844.[63]

Another device resorted to in the 1830s (and much favoured by Parke J) was that of reading out the confession with the names of all the persons implicated omitted (juries were not, as today, furnished with a copy of a prisoner's statement; instead it was merely read out by the clerk of the court). For a short time, this practice enjoyed some currency on the Oxford Circuit, but the majority of judges were against it (in part due to the practical difficulties to which it could give rise).[64] Within a few years it had passed into limbo, not to resurface again until the *Broadwater Farm Case* in 1987.[65]

Oddly enough, there was an even more obvious answer: to have the prisoners separately tried. There was a method by which this could be achieved: namely the severing of challenges. (Each prisoner would exercise separately and to the full his right of jury challenge, thereby obliging the Crown to choose between agreeing to separate trials or seeing the jury panel exhausted and the trial delayed by the challenges.) In practice, however, it seems to have been little used. Where prisoners were unrepresented, it is easy enough to understand why (it was an exceptional prisoner who knew of the right, still less appreciated the tactical advantages to be reaped from its use). It is more difficult to explain why counsel appearing for prisoners jointly accused so rarely availed themselves of it. The answer may lie in judicial disapproval of the practice. Platt B had certainly been condemnatory of it in a case in 1848.[66] If that is not the explanation, the case of *Blackburn*

---

[60] Hale 1 P C, 585; Hawkins 2 P C, c. 46, s 3; and see *R v Boroski* (1682) 9 St Tr 1 and *R v Tong* (1662) Kel 17.

[61] See the remarks of the jury foreman in *R v Shakespeare and Clarkson*, *The Times*, 16 February 1899.

[62] *R v Young* (1789) 1 Leach 505 (where Buller J claimed that Yates J had followed the same practice).

[63] *R v Clothier and Tiler* (1844) 1 Cox 113; also *R v Holloway and Kennard*, *The Times*, 15 and 17 December 1831.

[64] *Maudsley's Case* (1830) 1 Lew 110; *Barstow's Case* (1831) 1 Lew 110; *R v Fletcher* (1829) 4 C & P 250; *R v Hearne* (1830) 4 C & P 215; *Hall and Ritson's Case* (1833) 1 Lew 110; *Foster's Case* (1833) 1 Lew 110; see also Russell (4th edn 1865), 867; *R v Harding, Bailey and Shumer* (1830) MSS Greaves, cited Russell, 867n.

[65] *R v Silcott* [1987] Crim LR 765.

[66] Platt B in *R v Fisher* (1848) 3 Cox 68 at 69.

in 1853 becomes very difficult to understand.[67] There counsel for one of three co-prisoners applied to the trial judge for an order that his client be tried separately, on the ground that he was named in the confession of one of his co-accused and would be prejudiced if tried together with that accused. He conceded that the application was novel, and in the event it was refused. But why did he not simply persuade the accused to sever their challenges? Was it that he tried to persuade them but they refused to agree (possible but unlikely); or was it out of deference to judicial pronouncements on the subject? The only other possibility (again unlikely) is that the jury panel was so large that even the severing of challenges would not have won the prisoners a separate trial. Although one hears no more of severance of challenges in this connection, later in the century the practice of applying for and granting separate trials in confession cases did gain limited currency.[68]

2. *Questioning of Suspects by the Police*

The transfer of the function of detecting crime from the magistracy to the reformed police inevitably raised the question of how far police officers were to be permitted to question those they arrested. Even in the 1820s there was occasional judicial criticism of police officers who took it upon themselves to question prisoners. In 1823, in the course of a summing up, Bayley J expressed the view that officers should refrain from attempting to pump prisoners,[69] whilst two years later Gaselee expressed his disapproval of 'the habit of constables and gaolers getting into conversation with prisoners, who then made disclosures unfavourable to themselves, not supposing that those disclosures would afterwards be used against them'.[70] The law at this period was, however, a long way from placing any bar upon such questioning. As recently as 1820 the judges of Ireland had, on a reserved case, held admissible a confession extracted by police questioning;[71] four years later their English brethren reached a like decision in the case of *Thornton*.[72] In each case more eloquent than the decision is the fact that defence counsel did not seek to found any objection upon the fact that the confession had been elicited by interrogation. In so far as any limitation did exist at this period upon the power of the police to question, it appears to have lain in the customary practice of cautioning – adopted, it seems, in imitation of magisterial

---

[67] *R v Blackburn* (1853) 6 Cox 333.

[68] See *R v Anon.*, *The Times*, 1 November 1862 (Old Bailey); PP 1856 (456) L, 79; and Russell, 868.

[69] *R v Young and Aynsley*, *The Times*, 5 August 1823.

[70] *R v Baker*, *The Times*, 2 August 1825; also Park J in *R v Read*, *The Times*, 2 January 1844.

[71] *R v Gibney* (1820) Jeb Res Cas 15.

[72] *R v Thornton* (1824) 1 Moo 27.

procedure and, as there, having the advantage of rendering less likely the exclusion of any admission thus obtained.

By the late 1830s the climate had changed. Judges were now setting their faces against police questioning. In 1838 Patteson J threatened with dismissal from the force an officer in the habit of interrogating prisoners,[73] while in 1839 both the Lord Chief Justice of England and one of the Irish Chief Justices expressed their strong disapproval of the practice.[74] Not all judges were happy about this new fetter on the police. The evidence published as an appendix to the Eighth Report of the Criminal Law Commissioners spoke of a divergence of opinion and practice amongst the judges upon the point.[75] Even amongst those who disapproved of police questioning, there was disagreement as to where the real evil lay. To some all police interrogation of prisoners was improper,[76] while to others it was objectionable only when not under caution.[77] By the 1850s, however, the new doctrine had carried the day. All questioning, whether under caution or not, was improper. One of the strongest affirmations of the rule came from Lord Chief Justice Campbell in *Baldry*, where, while overruling the absurd rule in *Drew* (1837) that to caution a prisoner was an inducement rendering his reply inadmissible, he stated emphatically that in England prisoners were not to be interrogated.[78] This case, together with decisions in the 1860s, such as *Mick* (1863), settled the rule for the rest of the century.

Prior to Jervis's Act, a justification commonly offered by the judges for the rule was that police questioning was a usurpation of the function of the examining magistrate, without any of the safeguards which attended a magisterial examination.[79] When Jervis's Act deprived magistrates of their power to examine prisoners, there was a change of judicial tack. Stress was now laid upon the fact that judges and magistrates were prohibited by law from questioning prisoners. If they could not question a prisoner, it was unthinkable that inferior officers of justice, such as policemen, should be allowed to do so. Indeed this became the standard justification of the rule for the rest of the century and into the twentieth century.[80] These magisterial analogies were not, however, the only reasons offered by the judges. The

---

[73] *Hill's Case* (1838) cited in Roscoe, *Criminal Evidence* (10th edn), 51.

[74] Denman LCJ in *R v Anon.*, *The Times*, 1 August 1839, and Dougherty CJ in *R v Hughes* (1839) 1 Craw & D 13.

[75] Criminal Law Commissioners, 8th Report, app A, 219, and 281; and see *R v Anon.* (1844) 2 LT 175.

[76] See Dougherty CJ in *R v Doyle* (1840) 1 Craw & D 396; *R v Toole* (1856) 7 Cox 244; and *R v Bodkin* (1862) 8 Ir Jur NS 340.

[77] Crampton J in *R v Martin* (1841) Arm M & O 197.

[78] *R v Baldry* (1852) 2 Den 430.

[79] *R v Glennon Toole and McGrath* (1840) 1 Craw & D 359.

[80] *R v Mick* (1863) 3 F & F 822; *R v Johnston* (1864) 15 Ir CLR 60, at 88 and 133; *R v Anon.* (1866) 11 Sol J 1168; *Yeovil Murder Case* (1877) 41 JP 187; *R v Davitt*, *The Times*, 16 July 1870; *R v Marshall*, *The Times*, 28 February 1874; *R v Gavin* (1885) 15 Cox 656; and *R v Male and Cooper* (1893) 17 Cox 689.

risk of unfairness to the prisoner was also stressed.[81] An officer might mistake or misunderstand an accused's reply,[82] or imperfect recollection might cause him to misrepresent it.[83] Even if he reported the prisoner's words with accuracy, the jury would have no idea of the tone of voice used or the manner in which the reply was given. Also, given a police officer's 'natural ambition to convict',[84] there was always the danger of his unconsciously twisting or distorting a prisoner's words.[85] Then again, as Alderson B pointed out, it was 'very easy to put captious and leading questions to a prisoner to induce him to give an answer which might be taken entirely contrary to its true sense'.[86] Another concern (although rarely openly expressed) was almost certainly the fear of invented confessions. The Metropolitan Police, in particular, had none too savoury a reputation in this respect in the 1840s.[87] To others the real objection lay in the relation in which the police questioner stood to his prisoner. It tended, they claimed, to make any statement obtained from the prisoner the very reverse of voluntary. The very act of questioning was an indication that the questioner might liberate the answerer if the answers were satisfactory, or detain him if they were not.[88]

Joy, writing in 1842, had suggested that the police should forbid the practice of officers questioning prisoners.[89] This is in fact what ultimately happened. The Metropolitan Police General Orders, published in 1873,[90] prohibited any attempt by officers or others to extract a statement in the nature of a confession from a person brought to a police station on a charge of felony, while the General Orders and Regulations issued by the Commissioner in 1893, as well as repeating the prohibition, contained specific reference to the impropriety of putting questions to accused persons.[91] Nor was this all. When in 1882 it was decided to publish a Police Code for the use of officers, included in it was a foreword from Hawkins J on the duties of police constables, which laid down in clear terms that it was wrong for an officer to question a person who was in custody or whom he was about to arrest. This foreword was still being included unaltered in revised editions of the Code in the mid 1920s.

Inevitably the new rule spawned its share of practical problems. One of the first was that some officers took the prohibition upon questioning to

---

[81] See Alderson B in *R v Stokes* (1853) 17 Jur 192: 'We are not always certain it is fairly done.'
[82] Denman LCJ in *R v Anon.,The Times*, 1 August 1839.
[83] *R v Toole* (1856) 7 Cox 244.
[84] *R v Anon., The Times*, 5 March 1845 per Alderson B.
[85] Cox at (1844) 2 LT 356; *R v Toole* (1856) 7 Cox 244; *R v Stokes* above.
[86] Cox at (1844) 2 LT 356; *R v Stokes* above per Alderson B.
[87] Criminal Law Commissioners, 8th Report, app A, at p 294 and 318.
[88] Per Piggott B in *R v Johnston* supra at 122–23; cf. Christian J in *R v Hassett* (1861) 8 Cox 511.
[89] Joy on *Confession*, 38.
[90] PRO, MEP 8/3 Prisoners, para 8.
[91] PRO, MEP 8/4, paras 203, 203 and 306.

mean that it was their duty to stop up the mouth of any prisoner who attempted to confess to them, by immediately cautioning him.[92] The matter was commented upon by the Lord Chief Justice in a letter to the Criminal Law Commissioners in 1844.[93] It was also the subject of judicial pronouncement in several reported cases from around the same period, with judges emphasising that, while it was no part of the duty of an officer to question a prisoner, neither was it his duty to caution and shut the mouth of a prisoner who was about voluntarily to confess.[94]

Another question was that of how far officers might legitimately question persons against whom there was suspicion, but who had not yet been arrested. To this the judges' answer was that, once an officer had taken the decision to take a suspect into custody, it was not proper for him to put questions to him.[95] Until that point was reached a suspect might be questioned after a proper caution, although even here the power should be exercised sparingly.[96]

The most intractable problem was what stance the law should take where a police officer obtained admissions by questions in breach of the rule – as continued to happen with rather depressing frequency.[97] Upon this question the Irish judges initially took a very firm line. Until 1864, almost every reported Irish case on the point favoured the exclusion of answers so obtained.[98] In 1864, however, the point came before eleven of the Irish judges on a reserved case (*Johnston*).[99] By a majority of eight to three they held that improper questioning did not, of itself, render inadmissible answers so obtained. The admissibility of such replies, like that of all confessions, depended upon their voluntariness. This decision was in accord with the views of the leading text writers[100] and with a number of English cases, not least *Wild* (1835), in which the Twelve Judges had held admissible a confession obtained by a civilian browbeating a fourteen-year-old boy who was in custody, and *Cheverton* (1862) and *Mick* (1863).[101] Amongst English judges the question had provoked its share of disagreement. Indeed, in *Mick*, Mellor

[92] See the anecdote recounted by W. Forsyth in a letter to the Criminal Law Commissioners, 8th Report, app A, 253 and in *Hortensius the Advocate* (3rd edn, London, 1879), 292.

[93] Criminal Law Commissioners, 8th Report, app A, p 211.

[94] *R v Dickinson* (1844) 1 Cox 27; *R v Watts* (1844) 1 Cox 75; and *R v Priest* (1847) 2 Cox 378.

[95] *R v Davitt, The Times*, 16, 18 and 19 July 1870 (Cockburn LCJ).

[96] *R v Berriman* (1854) 6 Cox 388 and *R v Reason* (1872) 12 Cox 228.

[97] See e.g. *R v Reason* above, *The Yeovil Murder Case* above, and (1882) 46 JP 665.

[98] Evidence excluded: *R v Doyle* (1840) 1 Craw & D 396; *R v Martin* (1841) Arm M & O 197; *R v Devlin* (1841) 2 Craw & D 151; *R v Toole* (1856) 7 Cox 244; *R v Warrell* (1861) 13 Ir Jur 357; *R v Bodkin* (1863) 15 Ir Jur NS 340; the only case in which answers obtained by questioning had been received was *R v Hughes*, cited in Joy on *Confession* at p 39.

[99] *R v Johnston* above.

[100] Taylor (1st edn, 1848), 421; Joy on *Confession*, 34 et seq ; Phillipps (8th edn, 1838), 427.

[101] *R v Wild* (1835) 1 Moo 452; *R v Cheverton* (1862) 2 F & F 833; *R v Mick* (1863) 3 F & F 822.

J, whilst ruling the evidence in, observed that many judges would not have received it. The year 1864, however, seems to have represented a turning point, and after this the rule laid down in *Johnston* (1864) was to prevail unchallenged both in Ireland and England for the next twenty years. In *Johnston*, O'Brien J had suggested a compromise rule:

> that the police should be at liberty, without risk of censure, to question a prisoner so far as might be requisite for the guidance of their own conduct, and for the discovery of other evidence, but the answers to such questions should not be given against the prisoner at his trial.[102]

Neither this suggestion, nor the scheme adopted by the Indian Evidence Act (1872) of making all confessions to police officers inadmissible, took root.[103]

In 1885 the controversy was resurrected when A. L. Smith J in *Gavin* refused to admit evidence of admissions obtained by police questioning.[104] His lead was followed by Cave J in *Male and Cooper* in 1893 and in *Morgan* in 1895 and by Hawkins J in *Histed* in 1898.[105] However, in *Rogerson* in 1886, the Chief Justice of New Zealand declined to follow *Gavin*, and it was expressly dissented from by Day J in *Brackenbury* in 1893.[106] The sharpest denunciation came in *Rogers v Hawken* (1898), where Lord Chief Justice Russell declared that if *Male and Cooper* laid down that 'a statement made by an accused person in answer to a policeman ... which statement has not been brought about any inducement ... or threat ... is inadmissible' it was both wrong in law and mischievous.[107] In *Gavin*, the police interrogation had taken the form of confronting the prisoner with one of his co-accused and reading over to him the latter's statement, whilst in *Male and Cooper* one of the accused had had a witness's statement read over to her. This technique of interrogation (which seems to have been particularly prevalent in the Metropolitan Police and was no doubt seen as a way of outflanking the prohibition on questioning) lingered on into the twentieth century.[108] It served to keep alive the controversy which *Gavin* had started, with several judges treating admissibility in such cases as a matter for the trial judge's discretion. In *Ibrahim* in 1914 Lord Sumner summarised the position:

> the ... law is still unsettled, strange as it may seem for the point is one that constantly occurs in criminal trials. Many judges in their discretion exclude

---

102 *R v Johnston* above, at 105.
103 Indian Evidence Act, 1872, s 25.
104 *R v Gavin* (1885) 15 Cox 656.
105 *R v Male & Cooper* (1893) 17 Cox 689; *R v Morgan* (1895) 59 JP 827; *R v Histed* (1898) 19 Cox 16 ; in *R v Miller* (1895) 18 Cox 54 Hawkins J said he did not dissent from *Gavin*; see also (1894) 58 JP 310 where it was claimed that judges constantly rejected and discredited such evidence.
106 *R v Rogerson* (1870) NSWCR 234; *R v Brackenbury* (1893) 17 Cox 628.
107 *Rogers v Hawken* (1898) 19 Cox 122.
108 *R v Pearson* (1908) 1 Cr App R 77; *R v Firth* (1913) 8 Cr App R 162; *R v Grayson* (1921) 16 Cr App R 7; *R v Adams* (1923) 17 Cr App R 77; see also (1900) 109 LT 389.

such evidence, for they fear that nothing less than exclusion of all such statements can prevent such improper questioning of prisoners by removing the inducement to resort to it ... Others less tender to the prisoner or more mindful of the balance of decided authority would admit such statements, nor would the Court of Criminal Appeal quash the convictions thereafter obtained if no substantial miscarriage of justice had occurred.[109]

Of the nineteenth-century prohibition upon the questioning of suspects nothing now remains.[110] Interrogation, conducted in accordance with the code of practice issued by the Home Secretary,[111] is recognised as a legitimate

[109] *Ibrahim v R* [1914] AC 599.

[110] The decisions of the Court of Criminal Appeal, in the capital cases of *Voisin* (1918) 13 Cr App R 89 and *Booker* (1924) 18 Cr App R 47, tipped the balance heavily in favour of admitting in evidence admissions obtained by the questioning of prisoners, thus clearing the way for the emergence of the modern system of police interrogation. The undermining of the bar upon police questioning had, however, begun before this. It started, in fact with the 1912 Judges' Rules for the guidance of police officers. Not only did these contained no prohibition upon the questioning of persons in custody, but rule 3 provided: 'Persons in custody should not be questioned without the usual caution first being administered', implying that such questioning was lawful if preceded by a caution. The part played by the rules in overturning the old practice is confirmed by the Report of the Royal Commission on Police Powers and Procedure (1929). The Commission found that whilst most police forces (headed by officers trained on the principles set out in Hawkins' foreword to the Police Code) were still adhering to the old practice of not questioning prisoners, some limited the application of the principle to the offence for which the prisoner was in custody, and approved questioning as to other offences. A few, taking their lead from rule 3, permitted a prisoner to be questioned even on the charge for which he was in custody (Report, paras 161–62). In 1930, in an attempt to ensure uniformity of police practice, the Home Office, after consultation with the judges, issued a circular stressing that: 'Rule 3 was never intended to encourage the questioning or cross-examination of a person in custody after he had been cautioned on the subject of the crime for which he is in custody' (Home Office Circular of 24 January 1930, 536053/29). This was a point which was periodically reinforced by judicial pronouncement, see e.g. in *R v Brown and Bruce* (1931) 23 Cr App R 56 and *R v Dwyer* (1932) 23 Cr App R 156. The interpretation given to rule 3 in the circular, was never embodied in the rules themselves, see R. N. Gooderson, 'The Interrogation of Suspects' (1970) 48 Can Bar R 272. Also it appeared by implication to legitimise questioning concerning charges other than that for which the accused was in custody, which meant, of course, that the rules could easily be outflanked by the use of holding charges (The DPP had described the practice as 'a first rate procedure' but the Royal Commission condemned it, para 159). It had been used in *Booker* above and upheld in *R v Whiteway*, *The Times*, 29 October 1953. By the 1950s the circular was a dead letter (see Glanville Williams, 1960 Crim LR 330) and all trace of the old rule disappeared when the judges' rules were revised in 1964 (see Rule 1 of the 1964 Rules). The growth in the practice of police interrogation created an obvious need for safeguards to protect suspects against the risk of their replies to questions being misreported or, worse still, fabricated. In their absence malpractice and false allegations of malpractice flourished. By 1974 the problem had become so serious that the Court of Appeal called for something to be done, as a matter of urgency, to make evidence of admissions to police offices difficult both to challenge and fabricate (*R v Turner*, 1975, 61 Cr App R 67 at p 77). Nothing was done, however, until the Police and Criminal Evidence Act, 1984, grasped the nettle.

[111] Code of Practice for the Detention, Treatment and Questioning of Persons by Police Officers (1995 revision) issued by the Home Secretary under s 66 of the Police and Criminal Evidence Act, 1984.

investigatory tool and, since 1995, an accused who fails to mention when questioned by the police a matter relied upon by him in his defence runs the risk of an adverse inference being drawn from such failure.[112]

---

[112] Criminal Justice and Public Order Act, 1994, s 34 (which came into force on 10 April 1995).

22

Character and Similar Fact Evidence

'Generally speaking it is not competent to a prosecutor to prove a man guilty of one felony by proving him guilty of another unconnected felony.'

Bayley J, in *R. v. Ellis* (1826)

1. Character Evidence

The calling by the prisoner of witnesses to speak to his character was a common incident of criminal trials at around the start of the nineteenth century. If an accused was of good character judge and jury would indeed expect to hear the fact confirmed by witnesses.[1] If not, the obvious inference was that he was of bad character. In capital cases character evidence was often of critical importance. Without it an accused would generally have little hope of mercy at the hands of either jury or judge.[2] There is no doubt that prisoners realised the importance of calling witnesses to character.[3] It was not unknown for as many as twenty or more such witnesses to be called by a single accused.[4] Even lads of fourteen or fifteen, too poor to fee counsel, would sometimes manage to have a witness or two in court to give them a character.[5] Prisoners who had no witnesses would try and explain their absence: they were too poor to travel or had not yet arrived.[6]

Although character evidence would weigh with judges in matters of sentence, and in particular when deciding whether to recommend a man capitally convicted to mercy, the law placed limits on the use which juries might make of it. Jurors were always told that it was only where the case was doubtful that they should pay any attention to evidence of good

---

[1] See e.g. *R v Landfriede*, The Times, 30 October 1805; *R v Budge*, The Times, 27 August 1811; *R v Howe*, The Times, 20 March 1813; *R v Fonswick*, The Times, 22 September 1819; Beattie, 448.

[2] See Beattie, 443 and T. A. Green, *Verdict According to Conscience* (Chicago, 1985), 177.

[3] Beattie, 447.

[4] See e.g. *R v Bryan*, The Times, 5 August 1814 (twenty-one character witnesses); *R v Blackburn*, The Times, 29 March 1815 (over twenty); *R v Stent*, The Times, 20 September 1819; *R v Fauntleroy*, The Times, 1 November 1824 (sixteen).

[5] See e.g. *R v Allen*, The Times, 31 October 1814.

[6] E.g. *R v Solomon*, The Times, 25 January 1817.

character.[7] Also character witnesses were debarred from deposing to particular acts reflecting credit on the prisoner. The only matter to which they might speak was the accused's general character.[8] In *Rowton* (1865), the Court for Crown Cases Reserved sought to refine the law still further, ruling that a character witness was not entitled to give his own opinion of the accused's character but must confine himself to the accused's general reputation.[9] This ruling, which ran counter to existing practice,[10] was strongly criticised and widely ignored.[11] Text writers added two further glosses: character evidence should bear reference to the nature of the offence charged; and relate to the same period as the offence.[12]

Where evidence of good character was elicited or called by the accused, it was open to the prosecution to contradict it. If he had previous convictions, his character witnesses might be cross-examined about them.[13] Indeed, according to a ruling of Parke B, they could also be cross-examined about matters of which he had in the past been suspected.[14] Rebuttal evidence could also be called. Where the charge against the accused was committing felony or misdemeanour after previous conviction, the prosecution was by statute entitled to rebut any claim of good character by proving the previous conviction.[15] There was also a right to call witnesses to prove the accused's bad character.[16] This latter right was seldom exercised in practice, with some judges denying that it existed.[17] When it was exercised the evidence given by the rebuttal witnesses would on occasions go far beyond matters of general character. For example, at an Old Bailey trial in 1844 the prosecution were allowed to call, in rebuttal of the prisoner's claim of good character, a police officer to say that the previous Saturday he had seen him at the haunts of the 'swell mob' at around 2 a.m.[18] In *Rowton* the Court for Crown Cases

---

[7] E.g. Lord Ellenborough in *R v Cock*, *The Times*, 3 May 1802; *R v Davison* (1809) 31 St Tr 99; *R v Haigh* (1813) 31 St Tr 1092. This form of direction had, semble, been in use since the late seventeenth century, see *R v Turner* (1664) 6 How St Tr 565. It was still being used as late as 1918, see *R v Broadhurst and Others* (1918) 13 Cr App R 125. It had been strongly criticised by Greaves, Russell (4th edn, 1865), 786.

[8] Archbold (1st edn, 1822), 70, Phillipps (8th edn, 1838), 491.

[9] *R v Rowton* (1865) 10 Cox 25.

[10] This was conceded by Cockburn LCJ at p 30. The ruling was at odds with earlier reported cases, in particular *R v Davison* above and *R v Hemp* (1833) 5 C & P 468.

[11] Some of the strongest criticism came in Stephen's *Digest* (1st edn, 1876), 167.

[12] These glosses seem to have originated with Phillipps and to have then been generally adopted.

[13] *R v Hodgkiss* (1836) 7 C & P 298.

[14] *R v Wood and Parker* (1841) 5 Jur 225; contra *R v Rogan and Elliott* (1846) 1 Cox 291.

[15] Previous Convictions Act, 1836 proviso; Prevention of Offences Act, 1851, s 9; Larceny Act, 1861, s 116; Coinage Offences Act, 1861, s 37; and Prevention of Crimes Act, 1871, s 9.

[16] *R v Hughes* (1843) 1 Cox 44; *R v Lovejoy* (1850) 14 JP 592.

[17] *R v Burt* (1851) 5 Cox 284.

[18] *R v Collins*, *The Times*, 17 April 1844. There was by the time of *Rowton* some authority for allowing in such evidence, viz. *R v Hains* (1695) Comb. 337.

Reserved upheld the Crown's right to call rebuttal evidence but, at the same time, insisted that such evidence must be limited to evidence of general reputation, which ruling had the consequence of preventing the Crown (statutory exceptions apart) proving in rebuttal the prisoner's previous convictions.[19]

In the early part of the century, the calling of perjured character evidence was apparently common, an evil with which the law was ill-equipped to cope.[20] Unless the case was prosecuted by counsel (and most were not), there would be no channel through which the matter could be taken up, save where the judge himself recognised the prisoner as an old offender and stepped in to expose him.[21] Even where there was prosecuting counsel, because it was the practice to warn the defence if the Crown had evidence of bad character, the prisoner who was represented would, by the time the trial began, know whether the case was one in which he could risk calling perjured character evidence.[22]

If the accused did not give evidence of good character, it was not normally open to the Crown to adduce evidence of his bad character. In 1810 in *Cole*,[23] the Twelve Judges overturned a capital conviction for buggery because the trial judge had allowed to be adduced in evidence an admission, made by the accused on arrest, that he had a 'natural inclination' to such practices. That case administered the coup de grace to any lingering remains of the eighteenth-century practice of allowing the Crown to bolster up its case with evidence of the prisoner's bad character and past convictions.[24]

To the prohibition on the prosecution adducing evidence of bad character there were then, as now, exceptions. Of these perhaps the most important was that relating to admissible similar fact evidence considered below. But there were others. An accused who had on a previous trial pleaded his clergy would have the letter F branded on this thumb for all the world to see.[25] An accused facing multiple indictments (a far more common situation in the nineteenth century than today, due to the bar on charging more than one felony in an indictment) had little hope of concealing this fact from his jury. He would be arraigned on all indictments, in the presence of the

---

[19] See Cockburn LCJ at p 31 and Willes J at p 39. This was certainly the view of the text writers, e.g. Taylor (7th edn), 322, and was the view taken by a Canadian Court in *R v Triganzie* (1888) 15 O R 294.

[20] *R v Roberts*, *The Times*, 23 September 1820: 'no man ever had a character until he came to the Old Bailey'.

[21] *R v Roberts* affords one example of a judge intervening in this way; for others, see *R v Norris*, *The Times*, 2 August 1804, and *R v Kelly*, *The Times*, 21 December 1838.

[22] See the judgment of Martin B in *Rowton* at p 36.

[23] *R v Cole* (1810) in D. R. Bentley, *Select Cases from the Twelve Judges' Notebooks*, 109, and noted in Phillipps (1st edn), 69–70.

[24] As to such practice see J. H. Langbein, 'The Criminal Trial before the Lawyers' (1975) U Chicago LR 1 at 303.

[25] Ibid. 304.

waiting jurors,[26] and would then be tried successively on the indictments he faced, usually by the same jury. (The Crown normally only called a halt when they had secured a conviction on one of them.)[27] If his case had attracted public interest (and sometimes even if it had not), he would often find that the whole of his past life had already been laid before the jury by the newspapers. Sometimes the very offence charged would reveal him as a criminal (e.g. returning from transportation). And there were still other possibilities. In a case in 1885 the prosecution were allowed to put in evidence a ticket of leave found on the accused at the time of his arrest (on the ground that anything found on the prisoner was evidence against him).[28] A prisoner's character might also be disclosed as a result of the inadvertent or malicious remark of a witness, or an improper or imprudent question by counsel.[29] By the early years of the twentieth century, judges were in such cases prepared to consider discharging the jury.[30] For much, if not all, of the nineteenth century, a direction to the jury to disregard what they had heard was the most that the accused could hope for.[31]

To all these perils, Parliament in 1827 added another. By section 11 of the Criminal Law Act, persons committing a non-capital felony, after a previous conviction for felony, were made liable to 'exemplary punishment'. The practical working of this provision was gravely disadvantageous to the accused, for the jury trying him knew throughout of the previous conviction. Not only was it read out when he was arraigned, but any verdict of guilty brought back by them had also to state whether they found the allegation of previous conviction proved. The Previous Convictions Act of 1836 attempted to correct this unfairness by directing that in such a case the subsequent offence should be tried first; and that only after they had brought in a verdict of guilty should the jury be charged to inquire into the previous conviction, or have the part of the indictment concerning the same read to them. This ought to have solved the problem. It did not. Before the accused could be put in charge he had to be arraigned. The courts held that the arraignment still had to be on the whole indictment, and such arraignment

---

[26] See e.g. *R v Fauntleroy* above, *The Times*, 8 March 1843, reports the waiting jurors complaining at being kept out of court during the trial of Daniel M'Naghten (public interest was such that their seats had been taken by others). See also the exchange between counsel and the judges in *R v Shrimpton* (1851) 2 Den 319.

[27] For examples of cases of prisoners being tried successively on a number of indictments, see *R v Oliver*, *The Times*, 31 July 1800; *R v O'Donnell*, *The Times*, 24 September 1806; *R v King*, *The Times*, 15 July 1811; *R v Napier*, *The Times*, 18 September 1839 and *R v Carn*, *The Times*, 10 January 1885.

[28] 101 CCC Sess Pap 5. The common serjeant appealed in vain to prosecuting counsel not to press the evidence.

[29] See *R v Anon.* (Guildford Assizes), *The Times*, 2 August 1862; *R v Tuberfield* (1864) 10 Cox 1.

[30] *R v Smith* (1916) 80 JP Rep 199.

[31] In the first case noted at 29 above Bramwell B, although remonstrating with the officer, did not discharge the jury.

invariably took place in the presence of the jury in waiting.[32] When in *Shrimpton* (1851), a case concerning a similarly worded section in the Prevention of Crime Act (1851), defence counsel protested about the unfairness of arraignment in the presence of the waiting jury, the judges would have none of it. 'You are crediting the jury', said Alderson B, 'with attending to matters not before them', while from the Lord Chief Justice he drew the pedantic riposte 'the jurors then present are not a jury in the case'.[33] To modern eyes an obvious solution would have been to have had the waiting jurors out of court during arraignment, but in the 1860s sending the jury out of court at any stage would have struck lawyers as a very novel idea. In 1861 the law was recast: the 1827 Act was repealed but the principle of punishing more severely those convicted after previous conviction was continued by the Larceny and Coinage Offences Acts. There was, however, an improvement made: the accused was not to be arraigned upon the previous conviction until the jury had brought in a verdict of guilty of the subsequent offence. This happily solved the problem.[34]

In the last third of the century practitioners had a fresh and worrying problem to cope with: statutes containing prisoners' evidence clauses, which gave the prisoner who chose to give evidence no protection against cross-examination as to credit. Not until 1898 was anything done to remedy this desperately unfair situation.[35]

2. Similar Fact Evidence

In eighteenth-century criminal trials one finds instances of evidence admitted as relevant which would today be dubbed similar fact evidence.[36] These cases were almost wholly ignored by contemporary text writers, no doubt because they were not regarded as involving any point of principle. In the nineteenth century, however, all this changed. In the first decade alone, the Twelve Judges heard two cases, both destined to become landmarks in this area of law, *Tattersal* (1801)[37] and *Cole* (1810).[38]

In *Tattersal's Case* the question for the judges was whether, upon a charge of uttering a forged bank note, it was open to the prosecutor to prove other similar utterings to show guilty knowledge. The question was important. Bank note forgery was in 1801 a growing problem, and was to remain so for the

---

[32] *R v Anon.* (1851) 5 Cox 268, and *R v Shuttleworth* (1851) 3 C & K 375.

[33] *R v Shrimpton* (1851) 2 Den 319.

[34] See *R v Maria Fox* (1866) 10 Cox 502, and *R v Martin* (1869) 11 Cox 343.

[35] By s 1(f) proviso of the Criminal Evidence Act, 1898.

[36] See e.g. *R v Rickman* (1789) East 2 P C 1035; *R v Pearce* (1791) Peake Add Cas 106; and *R v Neville* (1791) Peake 91.

[37] *R v Tattersal and Others* (1801) in Bentley, *Select Cases from the Twelve Judges' Notebooks*, 89. It is referred to by Ellenborough LCJ in *R v Whiley and Haines* (1804) 2 Leach 983.

[38] *R v Cole* above.

duration of the Napoleonic Wars and indeed for some years after, yet it was far from easy to bring offenders to book.[39] The actual forgers were rarely caught,[40] and prosecutions for uttering often failed because of the inability of the prosecution to prove guilty knowledge. Not more than one uttering could be charged in the same indictment, and an accused facing but a single charge could always plausibly claim that he had come by the note innocently, not realising when he passed it on that it was forged. In *Tattersal* the judges gave the bankers the answer they wanted: evidence of other utterings was admissible. The ruling did not command universal support in the profession. Precedent was against it (in prosecutions for passing bad coin the evidence was always limited to the uttering charged in the indictment).[41] The admission of such evidence also appeared to undermine the rule prohibiting the Crown from charging more than one felony in an indictment,[42] as well as compelling the prisoner to defend himself against charges of which he had no notice. Three years later the King's Bench judges emphatically reaffirmed it in *Whiley*.[43] The case, declared Lord Ellenborough, was one of necessity. Since the mere fact of uttering did not of itself show guilty knowledge, proof of such knowledge had 'necessarily to be collected from other facts and circumstances'. The only significant limitation placed on the rule was a requirement that the notes, the subject of the other utterings, be actually produced and proved forgeries by clear evidence.[44]

In *Cole* the point reserved was whether similar fact evidence, which went to show only that the accused was a man with a propensity to commit crimes of the type with which he stood charged, was admissible. The judges held that it was not. The decision, having been brought to the attention of the profession by Phillipps in the first edition of his work on evidence, quickly became the leading authority on the point. It has never since been questioned – perhaps not surprisingly given that to admit such evidence would be to drive a coach and horses through the prohibition upon the Crown leading evidence of bad character. For most of the first half of the century the rule in *Cole* was commonly rendered by lawyers and text writers in terms which looked back to the old pleading rule in felony, that it was not competent for a prosecutor to prove a man guilty of one felony by proving him guilty of another unconnected felony.[45] It was left to Lord Chief Justice Campbell,

---

[39] See PD 1816 XXXIII, 1178–79; XXXIV, 309–10; PD 1818, XXXVII, 1223–24; XXXVIII, 272–84 and xxxv–xl.

[40] See e.g. the charge of Hullock B to the grand jury at the York Summer Assizes 1828, *Sheffield Courant*, 25 July 1828.

[41] Per counsel in *R v Whiley and Haines* above.

[42] Chitty, *Criminal Law* (1st edn, 1816), i, 252–55.

[43] *R v Whiley and Haines* above.

[44] *R v Millard* (1813) Russ & Ry 245; *Phillips' Case* (1829) 1 Lew 105 and *R v Moore* (1858) 1 F & F 73. The rule was departed from by Coleridge J in *R v Forbes* (1835) 7 C & P 224.

[45] See e.g. counsel in *R v Smith* (1827) 2 C & P 633 and *R v Dossett* (1846) 2 C & K 306; *R v Ellis* (1826) 6 B & C 145; and Russell (4th edn, 1865).

in *Oddy* (1851) to give it a more modern sound, when he declared that it was not open to the Crown to seek to prove its case by evidence showing that the accused was a 'very bad man and likely to commit such an offence'.[46] With the rulings in *Tattersal* and *Cole* the law began to assume something of its modern shape. This is not to say, however, that the eighteenth-century case law was discarded. In 1789 Buller J had held that the finding in the accused's possession of items stolen from a house at the time it was set on fire was admissible to prove that the accused was the arsonist.[47] This ruling was followed in several cases in the first half of the nineteenth century. These included *Westwood* (1813) where, on a charge of night poaching, evidence that a coat, lost by a gamekeeper during a struggle with poachers, had been found in the prisoner's home was held admissible to show that he was one of the gang;[48] and *Fursey* (1833) where, upon a charge of wounding a constable, the shape of the stab wound, which the accused had inflicted upon another officer in the same incident, was held admissible to show that the wound charged in the indictment was caused by the same weapon and the same assailant.[49] These cases, although commonly cited as authority for the proposition that similar fact evidence was admissible to prove identity, could equally well be regarded as an application of another eighteenth-century evidence rule: that, where several offences were so intermixed to form a single transaction,[50] or amounted to a continuous offence, evidence of all was admissible upon the trial of an indictment for any of them.[51] This rule (and the linked pleading rule which permitted offences forming a single transaction to be charged in a single felony count) was one which was constantly invoked and applied throughout the nineteenth century in cases ranging from group rape to the theft of coal from twenty different landowners by means of a continuous mining operation, but with the courts drawing the line at multiple poisoning and systematic embezzlement.[52] It was often in practice prayed in aid by advocates with no better argument to offer.

As well as drawing upon precedents from the previous century, the judges were at the same time also steadily adding to the categories of admissible

---

[46] *R v Oddy* (1851) 2 Den 264.
[47] *R v Rickman* above.
[48] *R v Westwood* (1813) 4 C & P 547.
[49] *R v Fursey* (1833) 6 C & P 81.
[50] E.g. *R v Young* (1789) 3 T R 98, *R v Thomas* (1800) East, 2 P C, 934.
[51] Per Lord Ellenborough in *R v Whiley and Haines* above.
[52] *R v Folkes* (1832) 1 Moo 354; see also *R v Giddins* (1842) 2 Car & M 634; *R v Birdseye* (1839) 4 C & P 386; *R v Trueman* (1839) 8 C & P 727; *R v Bleasdale* (1848) 2 C & K 765 (mining); *R v Firth* (1867) 11 Cox 234 (theft of gas); *R v Winslow* (1860) 8 Cox 397, and *R v Hall* (1887) 5 NZLR 93 (poisoning); *R v Williams* (1834) 6 C & P 626 (embezzlement); the Larceny Act, 1861, s 71, created an exception to the prohibition on charging more than one felony in an indictment, permitting in cases of theft and embezzlement up to three charges, separated in time by no more than six months, to be included in the same indictment.

similar fact evidence. In *Donnall* (1817), to show that the deceased had been poisoned by the accused, evidence was admitted that on a previous occasion, after taking tea with him, she had developed identical (albeit less severe) symptoms to those she exhibited immediately prior to her death.[53] In *Egerton* (1819), evidence of an attempt by the defendant to rob the prosecutor on the day following the robbery charged in the indictment was admitted by Holroyd J, on the ground that the latter incident corroborated the prosecutor's evidence as to the first.[54] In *Clewes* (1830), evidence of one murder was held admissible to show the motive (silencing a witness) for committing another.[55]

From 1823 came *Voke*, the first reported case in which similar fact evidence was admitted to rebut a defence of accident.[56] The accused was charged with maliciously shooting at A. His counsel had cross-examined prosecution witnesses with a view to showing that the shooting might have been accidental, only to be confronted with evidence that the accused had shot at A on a second occasion that day. After *Voke* one also begins to get an increasing number of cases in which similar fact evidence was admitted as going to prove intent. In *Winkworth* (1830), for example, upon an indictment for robbery founded upon the defendant's actions in advising the prosecutor to give money to a mob, evidence was admitted of his presence on other occasions that day when the mob made demands for money at other houses.[57] In *Boynes* (1843), upon a charge of making a false declaration before a magistrate, Erskine J held evidence, that documents which the accused had sent together with a declaration to a benefit society in support of a claim, were forged, was admissible to prove that the declaration was wilfully false.[58] In *Mahoney* (1848), upon a charge of using an instrument to procure an abortion, in order to show with what intent the instrument had been used, the prosecution were allowed to adduce evidence that the accused had procured miscarriages of other women.[59] In *Cooper* (1849), upon an indictment for accusing a person of an unnatural offence with intent to extort money, evidence that the defendant had in the past obtained money in this way was admitted to prove with what intent the accusation was made.[60]

Shortly after *Voke*, the guilty knowledge principle laid down in *Tattersal*, which had by this time already been applied to utterings of bad coin,[61] and forged bills of exchange,[62] was applied to a wholly new category of offence,

[53] *R v Donnall* (1817) 2 C & K 308 n.
[54] *R v Egerton* (1819) Russ & Ry 375.
[55] *R v Clewes* (1830) 4 C & P 228.
[56] *R v Voke* (1823) Russ & Ry 531 followed in *R v Dossett* above.
[57] *R v Winkworth* (1830) 4 C & P 444.
[58] *R v Boynes* (1843) 1 C & K 65.
[59] *R v Mahoney* (1848) 12 JP 377.
[60] *R v Cooper* (1849) 3 Cox 547.
[61] *R v Whiley and Haines* above.
[62] *R v Hough* (1806) Russ & Ry 120.

receiving stolen goods. The Twelve Judges held in *Dunn and Smith* (1826) that, upon such a charge, the fact that there had been found in the accused's possession goods stolen from the prosecutor on other occasions was admissible to show guilty knowledge.[63] Despite *Dunn and Smith*, there were still those in the profession who doubted the soundness of the decision in *Tattersal*.[64] Further, in relation to uttering offences, there was uncertainty as to the true bounds of the rule. It was, for example, unclear whether the Crown was entitled to rely upon utterings subsequent to,[65] or remote in time from, that charged in the indictment.[66] There was also doubt as to whether utterings could be led which were the subject of other indictments,[67] or which were of notes of a different bank or different denomination to that charged, in the indictment.[68] By the 1850s most of these questions had been resolved and resolved against the accused,[69] although upon some points the controversy was a long time dying.[70]

The unhappiness of some at least of the judges with the principle of the uttering cases surfaced in a very public fashion in *Oddy* (1851), where the Court for Crown Cases Reserved refused to extend *Dunn and Smith*, holding that it was not open to the Crown in a receiving case, in order to prove guilty knowledge, to adduce evidence of the possession by the prisoner at the date of the receiving of other goods stolen at other times from other persons.[71] In delivering the judgement of the court, Lord Chief Justice Campbell declared that the uttering cases went a great way, and that he was 'by no means inclined to apply them to the criminal law generally'. His words inspired one defence counsel to make an unsuccessful attempt, in the following year, to keep out similar fact evidence in an uttering case.[72]

So far as receiving cases were concerned, the ruling in *Oddy* stood until 1871, when it was in effect overturned by section 19 of the Prevention of Crimes Act,[73] a provision strictly construed by the courts,[74] and in practice

---

[63] *R v Dunn and Smith* (1826) 1 Moo 146.

[64] See Vaughan B in *Sunderland's Case* (1828) 1 Lew 102.

[65] *R v Taverner* (1809) 4 C & P 413n; *R v Smith* (1831) 4 C & P 411.

[66] *R v Whiley and Haines* above; *R v Ball* (1808) 1 Camp 324; *R v Millard* (1813) Russ & Ry 245.

[67] *R v Smith* (1827) 2 C & P 633; *Hodgson's Case* (1828) 1 Lew 103; *Kirkwood's Case* (1830) 1 Lew 103.

[68] *Hodgson's Case* above; *Sunderland's Case* (1828) 1 Lew 102.

[69] *R v Harrison* (1834) 2 Lew 118 and *R v Forster* (1855) 6 Cox 521 (later uttering); *R v Jackson* (1848) 3 Cox 89 n (remote utterings); *R v Jones & Hayes* (1877) 14 Cox 3 (subject of another indictment); *R v Harris* (1836) 7 C & P 416 (notes of different denomination or description).

[70] *R v Forster* (1855) 6 Cox 521; *R v Salt* (1862) 3 F & F 834.

[71] *R v Oddy* (1851) 2 Den 264.

[72] *R v Green* (1852) 3 C & K 209.

[73] This made evidence of the finding of other stolen property in the possession of the accused within the period of twelve months preceding the alleged receiving admissible to prove guilty knowledge.

[74] See *R v Drage* (1878) 14 Cox 85 and *R v Carter* (1884) 15 Cox 448.

little used. In relation to offences other than receiving, the courts, despite
Oddy, showed no particular reluctance to extend the principle of the guilty
knowledge cases. In *Roebuck* (1855), for example, such evidence was admitted
to fix guilty knowledge on a confidence trickster, who had tried to pass off
as silver a chain of base metal.[75] In *Parker v Green* (1862), upon a charge of
permitting persons of bad character to assemble on licensed premises,
evidence of the same prostitutes having gathered on the premises on previous occasions was admitted to prove that the licensee knew of their
character.[76]

By the second half of the century the principle in *Voke* had also been
extended, the Crown now being permitted to adduce evidence of anonymous
incidents (incidents which could not positively be linked with the accused)
to rebut any possible suggestion that the death or other event charged in
the indictment was accidental. One of the earliest such cases was *Bailey*
(1847) where, upon the trial of a maid for arson of a stable, evidence of
two other recent fires at the prosecutor's premises was admitted to show
that the stable fire was not accidental.[77] The trial judge, Pollock LCB, cited
in support of this ruling a murder case (*Donnallan*), in which the Crown, in
order to show that the poisoning of the deceased was not accidental, had
been permitted to call evidence to the effect that shortly before his death
the branch of a tree, which overhung a dangerous and deep pool where he
had been accustomed to fish, had been found sawn nearly through. One
finds the principle regularly applied after 1850 in cases of poisoning, in
murder cases such as *Roden* (1874) (evidence that a number of the deceased's
children had died at an early age admitted to show that the death of a child
who had been found suffocated was not accidental),[78] *Waters and Ellis* (1870),
a pre-*Makin* baby-farming case,[79] and in arson.[80]

Multiple poisoning cases were, in fact, the class of case where the admission
of similar fact evidence was perhaps most calculated to cause dismay to the
defence. Under the rules of criminal pleading, a prisoner accused of multiple
murder could only be tried for one murder at a time, but this rule was
substantially eroded by the ease with which the Crown, after *Geering* in 1849,
was able to get in evidence of other poisonings.[81] In *Geering*, Pollock LCB
held such evidence was admissible on two grounds. First, it was admissible
along with the domestic history to show that the administration of poison
to the deceased was felonious and not accidental (for authority he cited his
own ruling in *Bailey*). Secondly, evidence that others connected with the

---

[75] *R v Roebuck* (1856) 7 Cox 126 followed in *R v Francis* (1874) 12 Cox 612.
[76] *Parker v Green* (1862) 9 Cox 169.
[77] *R v Bailey* (1847) 2 Cox 311.
[78] *R v Roden* (1874) 12 Cox 630.
[79] *R v Waters and Ellis* (1870) 72 CCC Sess Pap 544 and *The Times*, 22–24 September 1870.
[80] *R v Gray* (1866) 4 F & F 1102.
[81] *R v Geering* (1849) 8 Cox 450n. and (1849) 18 LJ MC 215.

accused had died, after exhibiting the same symptoms displayed by the deceased whose death was the subject of the indictment, and that poison had been found in their bodies, was admissible as evidence that death had been caused by poison. (This was a rule less unfair than it looks today, given the difficulty which the Crown, with the science of forensic pathology still in its infancy, often experienced at this date in establishing poison as the cause of death.)[82] *Geering* was to remain the leading authority on the question for the rest of the century. It was repeatedly followed in murder cases such as *Garner* (1864), *Cotton* (1873), *Heeson* (1878) and *Flanaggan and Higgins* (1884), and was treated as rightly decided by the Judicial Committee in 1894 in *Makin*.[83]

Not all judges were happy to follow it. In *Winslow* (1860), where there was evidence that the prisoner's employers and three members of his family had died of antimony poisoning at a time when they and the prisoner were residing under the same roof, Martin B refused to allow the Crown to call evidence of the other deaths or their cause, despite prosecuting counsel's submission that it went to show that the death of the deceased from antimony was not accidental, that the prisoner had had antimony in her possession and (more desperately) that the deaths were all one transaction.[84] In 1887 the New Zealand Supreme Court took the same course in *Hall*.[85] There, upon a charge of murder by antimony poisoning, the Crown, despite defence objections, had been permitted to adduce evidence of an attempt by the accused, at a date after the murder, to poison his wife with antimony. On appeal, the Crown sought to uphold the trial judge's ruling on three grounds. The evidence of the attempted poisoning was, they argued, admissible to show that the administration of antimony to the deceased was not accidental; secondly, the poisoning and the attempt were all one transaction; and, thirdly, the evidence went to prove what the symptoms of antimony poisoning were. The Supreme Court rejected all three submissions and allowed the appeal. For its rejection of the Crown's third submission the court gave no reasons, but it may well be that Sir Herbert Stephen was right in his comment that the court probably considered that there was abundant other evidence to show that the death was due to antimony.[86] For its rejection of the first submission it did, however, give a reason: for evidence to be admissible on this ground there must first be proof *aliunde* that it was the prisoner who administered the poison to the deceased. It may be that this same reasoning

---

[82] See e.g. *The Trial of William Palmer* (1856), *The Trial of Dr Smethurst* (1859) and *The Trial of Mrs Maybrick* (1889) (Notable British Trials series).

[83] *R v Garner* (1864) 3 F & F 681 and 4 F & F 346; *R v Cotton* (1873) 12 Cox 400; *R v Heeson* (1878) 14 Cox 40; *R v Flannagan and Higgins* (1884) 15 Cox 403; *Makin v AG for New South Wales* [1894] AC 57.

[84] *R v Winslow* (1860) 8 Cox 397

[85] *R v Hall* (1887) 5 NZLR 93.

[86] H. Stephen, 'Evidence in Criminal Cases of Similar but Unconnected Acts' (1888) 13 LQR 71.

lay behind Martin B's ruling in *Winslow*. Surprisingly late in the century (1861) one gets the first reported instance of similar fact evidence being admitted to rebut a defence of mistaken accounting in embezzlement.[87]

By about 1870 one also finds lawyers and judges beginning to speak of 'system' as a ground of admissibility of similar fact evidence.[88] In 1876 this unhelpful proposition found its way into the first edition of Stephen's *Digest*,[89] and thereafter continued to enjoy currency for the rest of the century (although it received no mention when, in *Makin's Case*, the Judicial Committee took the opportunity of stating the principles considered to govern the admissibility of similar fact evidence).[90]

Makin's Case served to stress a point, which was in danger of being overlooked as the number of reported cases on similar fact evidence burgeoned, that the underlying principle governing the admissibility of such evidence in criminal cases was relevance.[91] By 1894 it was possible to list over eleven categories of admissible similar fact evidence. It was in terms of such categories (conceived of as exceptions to a general exclusionary rule) that the subject now tended to be discussed both by lawyers and text writers.[92]

For the accused, the steady expansion of the categories of admissible similar fact evidence meant a corresponding erosion of the prohibition on the Crown's leading evidence of his bad character. Given that the justification for admitting such evidence was always that it had probative value going beyond mere proof of propensity, prisoners never had any realistic hope of being able to stop, let alone reverse, the trend. What prisoners and their counsel could legitimately protest about (and they had to wait until the present century for the complaint to be heeded) was the absence of any exclusionary discretion on the part of the trial judge. If similar fact evidence was legally admissible, judges considered themselves bound to admit it, no matter how slight its weight nor how great the prejudice it would generate. In uttering cases, for example, the oft-posed question as to whether utterings remote in time from that charged in the indictment could be proved was invariably answered affirmatively. In *Jackson* (1848), Rolfe B expressed the view that evidence of utterings twenty years before was in law receivable, although he added that he would in such a case 'direct the jury to pay no attention to it'.[93] For the same reason, prosecuting counsel was commonly

---

[87] *R v Richardson* (1861) 8 Cox 448 followed in *R v Murphy* (1864) 59 CCC Sess Pap 77; *R v Proud* (1861) 9 Cox 22; *R v Stephens* (1888) 16 Cox 387.

[88] See e.g. *R v Waters and Ellis* above.

[89] Stephen's *Digest* , 139.

[90] *Blake v Albion Life Insurance* (1878) 4 CPD 94, at 166; *R v Rhodes* (1898) 19 Cox 182, Halsbury's *Laws* (1st edn), ix, para 742.

[91] See letter from Hawkins J to Windeyer J printed at 1893 14 LR (NSW) 1 and see generally J. Stone, 'The Rule of Exclusion of Similar Fact Evidence: England' (1933) 46 Harv LR 954.

[92] See e.g. counsel in *R v Winslow* above, Stephen's *Digest* and Archbold (20th edn, 1886), 245–50.

[93] *R v Jackson* (1848) 3 Cox 89 n.

allowed to adduce similar fact evidence to rebut a defence, which it was theoretically open to the defence to raise, even though defence counsel had expressly disclaimed the intention of either raising or relying upon it. In *Dale* (1889), evidence of previous abortions was held admissible to show the intent with which the accused had inserted a quill pen into a woman's vagina, despite the fact that his counsel had already made it clear that the issue was not intent but whether the instrument had been used at all.[94] In *Phillips* (1848), Rolfe B held similar fact evidence admissible in an uttering case, despite defence counsel's protests that on the facts guilty knowledge was not an issue, giving as his reason that it was just possible it might become an issue.[95] Occasionally, a judge would hint to prosecuting counsel not to press evidence of dubious cogency,[96] but the more usual judicial stance was that taken by Lush J in *Roden* (1874): that 'the value of evidence cannot affect its admissibility'.

---

[94] *R v Dale* (1889) 16 Cox 703.

[95] *R v Phillips* (1848) 3 Cox 88; and see *R v Oriel* (1845) 9 JP 170–71.

[96] For an example of counsel being invited not to press evidence see *Martin and Collins' Case* (1830) 1 Lew 104; for a threat to reserve the point see *R v Smith* (1831) 4 C & P 411 and *R v Phillips* (1848) 3 Cox 88.

23

Corroboration and Identification

'An accomplice of the name of Durant ... admitted that he came forward in the expectation of saving his life by convicting the prisoner.'

R. v. Lynell, The Times, 5 March 1831

At the start of the nineteenth century the law required corroboration in three classes of criminal case: prosecutions for treason; for perjury; and in cases involving the use of accomplice evidence. By 1900 further categories had been added to the list. Identification evidence was never subject to such a requirement, nor indeed to any special rules for all that the dangers of mistaken identification were well known.

1. Treason

In high treason, by the statute 7 & 8 William III, c. 3, the overt acts alleged by the Crown had to be proved by two credible witnesses.[1] Treasons relating to coining fell outside this protection, however, as did those where the overt act alleged was assassination, wounding or maiming of the sovereign or an attempt thereat. Treason felony was also outside the rule. Petty treason, until its abolition in 1828, was, like high treason, subject to a two witness requirement.[2]

2. Perjury

The corroboration requirement in perjury too. a different form: a rule forbidding the conviction of the accused on the evidence of a single witness. This rule had been laid down as early as 1713,[3] and its roots go back even further, but it was not until the first half of the nineteenth century that the law was set out with clarity. After hesitation as to whether there had to be direct evidence from two witnesses as to the fact alleged as falsely sworn,[4]

---

[1] 7 & 8 Will III, c. 3, s 2.

[2] 1 Ed VI, c. 12, s 22.

[3] R v Muscot (1713) 10 Mod Rep 192.

[4] Champney's Case (1836) 2 Lew 258; Jordan v Money (1854) 5 HL Cas 185; and R v Braithwaite (1859) 8 Cox 254.

the courts had by 1850 settled for a less rigorous rule, holding that it was sufficient for the prosecution to prove the falsity by the evidence of a single witness supported by some independent corroborating circumstance (such as a letter written by the accused admitting the falsehood), or even by circumstantial evidence coming from more than a single source.[5] Evidence of contradictory statements made by the accused (whether or not on oath) was however held insufficient per se,[6] whilst in *Parker* in 1842 Tindal LCJ, in an important ruling, held that where the indictment contained a number of assignments of perjury, each such assignment was subject to a separate corroboration requirement.[7]

3. Accomplices

For the detection and conviction of criminals the law in the early nineteenth century depended heavily upon the services of accomplices – a state of affairs which began to change only after the reform of the police.[8] The means by which accomplices were induced to come forward were various. To criminals at liberty the law offered substantial incentives to betray others. More than a dozen statutes (all repealed in the late 1820s) offered a pardon to an accomplice, not being in custody, who secured the conviction of two others for specified offences.[9] (The accomplice could also claim a reward of up to £40 a head.)[10] In addition, private reward advertisements (with Home Office permission) regularly offered pardons to accomplices, a practice which lingered on until well into the second half of the century.[11]

It was from amongst those in custody that accomplices were most frequently recruited. Attempts were commonly made to persuade arrested gang members to become 'evidence', that is to buy immunity for themselves by making full disclosure of, and giving evidence against, their associates.[12] It was not unknown for them to be exhorted to do so by examining magistrates in open court.[13] In many cases, however, it was from the arrested man that the initiative came.[14]

---

[5] *R v Mayhew* (1834) 6 C & P 315.

[6] *R v Wheatland* (1838) 8 C & P 238.

[7] *R v Parker* (1842) Car & M 639.

[8] See Radzinowicz, ii , chapter 2.

[9] The most important of these statutes were 4 Will III, c. 8; 10 & 11 Will & Mary, c. 23; and 5 Anne c. 31.

[10] 58 Geo III, c. 70 (1818) made the payment of rewards a matter for the court's discretion.

[11] For an example of a reward advertisement see *R v Blackburn* (1853) 6 Cox 333; the practice of the Home Office offering rewards was discontinued by Harcourt in the 1880s, see PRO, HO 45/9961/X6851.

[12] See J. H. Langbein, 'Shaping the Eighteenth-Century Criminal Trial' (1983) 50 Chicago LR, 1 at 84–89 and Beattie, 367–69.

[13] See e.g. *R v Sharpe, The Times*, 17 May 1833.

[14] For an example of an approach by a prisoner to be admitted approver, see *R v Read* (1844) 1 Cox 65.

If the evidence against him was strong, his only way of saving his neck would often be to get himself admitted king's evidence. Where several members of a gang were caught red-handed there might be a race to be admitted 'evidence'. The decision as to whether a man was to be so admitted rested with the examining magistrate.[15] Magistrates were urged to be cautious in whom they admitted,[16] and to select the least infamous.[17]

Before the examining magistrate, the accomplice would be examined on behalf of the Crown, with a warning from the bench to be frank in his evidence. He would also be told that no hope or promise was held out.[18] If, upon his evidence, a case was made out against those accused, he and they would be committed for trial in custody.[19] At the court of trial, counsel for the prosecution would, on the first day of the session, apply to the judge for leave to admit the accomplice as evidence.[20] If leave was given (as it normally, but not invariably, was),[21] he would be taken to give evidence before the grand jury; if they found a bill he would be called at the trial. His fate would depend upon how he gave his evidence. If he was frank and truthful, he would earn immunity (whether or not a conviction followed).[22] Although the law books speak of his being entitled to a pardon, the reality appears to be that accomplices who came up to proof were not pardoned but simply not prosecuted.[23] If, however, he sought to resile from his deposition, either before the grand jury or on the trial, the judge would forthwith direct the prosecution to get a bill against him from the grand

---

[15] In strict law magistrates had no power to admit accomplices king's evidence; see *R v Rudd* (1775) 1 Leach 115; but as Langbein puts it ('Shaping the Eighteenth-Century Criminal Trial', 96) they had total command of that power in practice.

[16] See Radzinowicz, ii, 44 n 42; see also *The Times* police reports for 18 July 1819.

[17] *R v Dunne* (1852) 5 Cox 507.

[18] *R v Strange Chandler and Kansley*, *The Times*, 14 January 1823, and Stone's *Justices' Manual* (17th edn, 1874), 44.

[19] As to the desirability of remanding the accomplice in custody to ensure he did not abscond, see Chitty, *Criminal Law* (2nd edn), i , 83, and *R v Beardmore* (1837) 7 C & P 497. To avoid the risk of collusion the accomplice would normally be committed to the Bridewell and the other prisoner to the County Gaol (Chitty, *Criminal Law* (2nd edn), i, 83.

[20] *R v Barnard* (1823) 1 C & P 87 and nn thereto; also *Walter Scott's Case* (1858) 2 Lew 36.

[21] See Phillipps (10th edn, 1852) 91; following the cases of *R v Lee* (1818) Russ & R 361 and *R v Brunton* (1821) Russ & Ry 454 judges ceased to admit prisoners against whom other indictments were pending, see *R v Anon.* (1826) 2 C & P 411. Also not more than one accomplice would normally be admitted per case: *The Barnsley Rioters' Case* (1830) 1 Lew 5 (but contrast *Walter Scott's Case* above where three were admitted).

[22] The immunity of an approver (like the right to a pardon under the reward statutes) depended upon his securing a conviction but the court had declined to extend this rule to accomplices: *R v Rudd* above.

[23] See Langbein, 'Shaping the Eighteenth-Century Criminal Trial' 94 and Beattie, 367; see also *R v England* (1796) 2 Leach 767 and the figures for prisoners committed for trial but not prosecuted given in the *Judicial Statistics* for 1856–1900.

jury. He would then be put on trial himself.[24] Hence the popular saying that accomplices: were 'fished for prey, like tame cormorants, with ropes around their necks'.[25]

Occasionally, accomplices were recruited at trial. A prisoner jointly indicted who pleaded guilty, might (as now) receive an approach from the Crown to give evidence against his co-accused. Until 1843 it was essential in felony cases that he be called before sentence, for, once sentenced, he became incompetent until he had served the sentence.[26] This was not, however, normally a source of difficulty, given the practice of putting off the sentence of felons until the last day of the Session or Assize. After Denman's Act (1843) had removed the bar on incompetency, some judges began to adopt the practice of sentencing prisoners who were to be called against co-accused before they gave evidence, on the ground that there was then no sentencing advantage to be gained by false testimony.[27] If the Crown's case was weak, it was not unknown in a multi-handed case for the Crown to offer to enter a nolle prosequi,[28] or even take an acquittal, against the prisoner considered least culpable if he would undertake to give evidence against his fellows.[29] As late as 1839 one can find an example of prosecuting counsel making such an offer to an accused in front of the jury, with the trial already well under way.[30] *Winsor's Case* in 1866 established a yet further option.[31] A jury, having failed to agree in the case of two women jointly accused of child murder, the Crown on the retrial, elected to try only one of them, calling the other as a witness without either entering a nolle prosequi or taking an acquittal against her. This procedure, for which some slight precedent could be found,[32] was to the surprise of some held unexceptionable by the Court for Crown Cases Reserved.

Judges were only too well aware of the dangers of accomplice evidence, but justified its use on grounds of expediency. Against all arguments that accomplices were incompetent from infamy of character,[33] or from

---

[24] *R v Burley* (1818) Starkie, *Evidence* (3rd edn), ii, 13, and *Moore's Case* (1837) 2 Lew 37; for an example of a judicial warning to a temporising accomplice see *R v Baker*, *The Times*, 5 March 1828 and *R v Hinks* (1845) 2 C & K 462.

[25] Cited by Taylor (7th edn, 1878), 811 n 8.

[26] Chitty, *Criminal Law*, i , 601; *R v Lyons* (1840) 9 C & P 555. The only alternative was for the judge to impose a nominal sentence such as a fine of 1s., *R v Noble*, *The Times*, 17 July 1819.

[27] See *R v Jackson* (1855) 6 Cox 525 (refusal to allow prisoner who had pleaded guilty to testify for his co-accused until he had been sentenced) and Cockburn LCJ in *R v Winsor* (1865) 10 Cox 276.

[28] See *R v Storer*, *The Times*, 8 September 1813 (after the nolle prosequi but before he embarked upon his evidence the accomplice asked the judge if he was safe).

[29] See e.g. *R v Rowland* (1826) Ry & Moo 401; *R v Peacock* (1849) 13 JP 254.

[30] *R v Owen Ellis and Thomas* (1839) 9 C & P 83.

[31] *R v Winsor* (1865) 10 Cox 276.

[32] See *R v Gerber* (1852) T & M 647.

[33] H. H. Joy on *The Evidence of Accomplices* (Dublin, 1836), 2; *R v Durham and Crowder* (1787) 1 Leach 478.

interest,[34] they resolutely set their faces. Such matters, they ruled, went merely to credit; a conviction based upon the evidence of an accomplice alone was none the less a legal conviction.[35] This strict legal rule was, however, tempered by a practice of advising juries to acquit where the only evidence against the accused was the uncorroborated evidence of an accomplice. Joy, writing in about 1824, claimed that the practice was less than half a century old.[36] In this he was almost certainly wrong. Langbein found evidence that as early as the 1750s judges at the Old Bailey were directing juries to acquit where accomplice testimony was not corroborated by independent evidence.[37]

The protection afforded by this practice was much reduced by the way the judges chose to define corroboration. The stance they took was that any evidence which confirmed an accomplice's story to any material extent, whether or not it implicated the accused, amounted to corroboration of it.[38] Evidence from the victim confirming that the facts of the offence were as the accomplice stated (e.g. that four men took part; that they had blacked faces and wore shirts over their clothes;[39] that one had a brazen-mounted pistol;[40] that one fired a warning shot) was deemed ample corroboration. Again, where there were co-accused, confirmatory evidence implicating one was treated as corroboration as against all.[41] In *Despard* (1802), Lord Ellenborough even went so far as to suggest that confirmation need not always come from an independent source, but might be found in the clearness and consistency of the accomplice's testimony in the witness-box.[42] With corroboration defined in such wide terms, a practice of warning juries not to convict upon unconfirmed accomplice evidence was hardly to be wondered at. If an accomplice could not even be confirmed as to the circumstances of the offence, there was cause for suspicion indeed.

It was from Ireland that calls for a stricter definition first came. In 1824 an anonymous Irish barrister published a pamphlet arguing that evidence, to be corroborative of an accomplice, must implicate the accused.[43] The

---

[34] *R v Tonge and Others* (1662) 6 St Tr 225.

[35] *R v Rudd* above; *R v Atwood and Robins* (1788) 1 Leach 464; *Jordaine v Lashbrooke* (1798) 7 T R 601; *R v Jones* (1809) 2 Camp 131; *R v Thistlewood* (1820) 33 St Tr 681; *R v Hastings and Graves* (1835) 7 C & P 152.

[36] Joy, *Accomplices*, 3.

[37] Langbein, 'Shaping the Eighteenth-Century Criminal Trial' 99–100, and Sir John Fielding, *Enquiry into the Recent Increase of Crime in London* (London, 1751), 111.

[38] Archbold (1st edn, 1822), 96; *The York Trials* (1813) 31 How St Tr 967 and 981; and *R v Birkett* (1813) Russ & Ry 251.

[39] *R v Swallow* (1813) 31 How St Tr 971.

[40] *R v Mellor* (1813) 31 How St Tr 998; see also *R v Charnock King and Keys* (1698) 12 St Tr 1377; *R v Despard* (1803) 28 How St Tr 489; and *R v Carroll, The Times*, 2 January 1823.

[41] *R v Jones* above; see also *R v Swallow* above; *R v Haigh* (1813) 31 How St Tr 1092 and *R v Dawber* (1821) 3 Stark 34.

[42] *R v Despard* above, an observation taken up by Park prosecuting counsel in *R v Swallow* above.

[43] Referred to by Joy, *Accomplices*, 19.

following year Jebb J applied this test when trying a case of murder.[44] In *Sheehan* (1826) the point was considered by eleven judges on a reserved case.[45] By a majority of six to five, they held that juries should be told in most cases to disregard accomplice testimony, unless there was some corroboration of it; and that corroboration as to the circumstances of the case merely, and not of the person charged, was deserving of very slight consideration. Joy, writing in rebuttal of the 1824 pamphlet, sought to demolish this new-fangled doctrine. In Ireland the subject was being treated as though it were *res integra* but it was not. No English judge, he argued, had ever held that corroboration need go to confirm the guilt of the accused – nor was there any reason why it should. The office of corroborative evidence was not to prove the guilt of the accused but to restore the credit of the accomplice, by showing the truthfulness of his evidence; any evidence which confirmed the truth of his story on any material point served to do that.[46] Joy, however, was fighting a losing battle. By the time his book was published in England in 1836, the English courts were already beginning to embrace the Irish rule. In the space of three years no less than five English judges held that evidence, to amount to corroboration, must not merely confirm the accomplice but must also implicate the accused.[47] At the same time, the old rule that what was corroboration against one was corroboration against all was abandoned.[48] Henceforth, it became increasingly common for judges to advise juries to acquit those against whom the accomplice was not corroborated. Indeed, it was almost inevitable that they should do so. Given the new stricter definition of corroboration, adherence to the old rule would not only have been illogical, it would have made the prospects of acquittal dependent upon the accident of whether the accused were tried alone, or with others against whom there was corroboration.[49]

A further refinement introduced at this time was the rule that an accomplice could not be corroborated by another accomplice,[50] or by his spouse.[51] But not all judges were subscribers to the new thinking. As late as 1838 an Irish Chief Justice openly declared his disagreement with the new definition

---

[44] *R v Green* (1825) 1 Craw & D 158.

[45] *R v Sheehan* (1826) Jebb Cr & P Cas 54.

[46] Joy, *Accomplices*, 2, 10–11, and 97.

[47] *R v Webb* (1834) 6 C & P 595; *R v Addis* (1834) 6 C & P 388; *R v Wilkes and Edwards* (1836) 7 C & P 272; *R v Farler* (1837) 8 C & P 106; *R v Dyke* (1838) 8 C & P 261 and *R v Birkett* (1839) 8 C & P 732.

[48] *R v Moores and Spindlo* (1836) 7 C & P 270; *R v Jordan* (1836) 7 C & P 432; *R v Fletcher* (1838) 2 Lew 45 n; *R v King and Hancock, The Times*, 18 July 1834; *R v Jenkins* (1845) 1 Cox 177.

[49] Joy, *Accomplices*, 17–18, used this point as an argument in favour of the old rule.

[50] *R v Noakes* (1832) 5 C & P 326 followed in *R v Buncher, The Times*, 7–12 January 1863. The view of the Irish judges was different; they considered that one accomplice could corroborate another where, since their apprehension they had been kept separate so as to avoid all possibility of collusion, *R v Aylmer and Behan* (1839) 1 Craw & D 116; the same view was expressed by Hawkins J in *R v Levy and Others* (1882) 74 LT 121.

[51] *R v Jones* (1835) 7 C & P 167; *R v Neal and Taylor* (1835) 7 C & P 168.

of corroboration,[52] while in 1845 Coleridge J was still directing juries that confirmation as to one accused was confirmation as to all.[53] The new rule was, however, placed beyond doubt when, in *Stubbs* (1855), the Court for Crown Cases Reserved held that a jury should always be told to acquit a prisoner accused by an accomplice unless there was corroboration as to that prisoner.[54] The reason for this change of judicial stance was a recognition that evidence which confirmed an accomplice's participation in a crime offered no sort of guarantee that his accusations against others were true. As Jervis CJ put it in *Stubbs*, nothing was easier than 'for the accomplice speaking truly as to all the other facts of the case to put the third man in his own place'.

Of the twentieth-century practice of telling juries that it was open to them to convict upon the uncorroborated evidence of an accomplice, if they were sure he was telling the truth, one finds but little trace in the nineteenth.[55] Where there was no corroboration of an accomplice, the usual practice was for the judge to advise the jury to acquit.[56] Some indeed went further and actually directed an acquittal.

This latter practice had a long history. Joy thought it went back to about the 1780s. According to him, shortly after *Rudd's Case* (1775) 'a practice began to prevail of even not sending to the jury to be considered the uncorroborated testimony of an accomplice'.[57] He cites *Durham and Crowder* (1787), where Perryn B described the practice as 'a matter of discretion of the court'.[58] He might also have referred to the case of *Smith and Davis*, decided three years earlier, where the court declared that, notwithstanding that an uncorroborated accomplice was legal evidence, it considered it too dangerous to suffer a conviction to take place on such evidence, and *semble* directed an acquittal.[59] In *Atwood and Robins* (1788), the Twelve Judges affirmed unequivocally the propriety of founding a conviction on uncorroborated accomplice evidence (so much so that the case came to be regarded as the *locus classicus* on the point); however, they apparently felt some unease about the matter for the judges' notebook records that they recommended the prisoners to pardon, thinking that they 'ought not to be executed merely on his [the accomplice's] testimony unconfirmed in any circumstance'.[60]

---

[52] *R v Curtis* (1838) 1 Craw & D Abr Cas 274.

[53] *R v Andrews and Payne* (1845) 1 Cox 183.

[54] *R v Stubbs* (1855) Dears 555.

[55] For examples of judges reminding juries of their right to convict, see *R v Jarvis* (1837) 2 M & Rob 40, and *The Trial of the Stauntons* (Notable British Trials), 251.

[56] *R v Wells Hudd and College* (1829) Moo & M 325; *R v Noakes* above; *Kelsey's Case* (1838) 2 Lew 45; *R v Stubbs* above; *R v Boyes* (1861) 1 B & S 311; *R v Myles* (1889) 8 NZLR 324 and In *Re Meunier* [1894] 2 QB 415.

[57] Joy, *Accomplices*, 3 and Langbein, 'Shaping the Eighteenth-Century Criminal Trial', 98.

[58] *R v Durham and Crowder* (1787) 1 Leach 478.

[59] *R v Smith and Davis* (1784) 1 Leach 479.

[60] 1 JN 43.

The practice was still in evidence by the early nineteenth century, and was indeed to persist for the rest of the century. In *Jones* in 1809, Lord Ellenborough, in rejecting a defence objection that on some counts the only evidence was unconfirmed accomplice evidence, restated in emphatic terms the rule laid down in *Atwood and Robins*, complaining that 'strange notions on the subject have lately got abroad'.[61] In *Jordan and Sullivan* in 1836, Gurney B declared that he knew that persons had been convicted in the past on the evidence of an accomplice alone, but that he hoped that it would never be so again, and that, as far as he could, he would take steps to see that it should not.[62] In a burglary case in 1843, Coleridge J directed an acquittal on the ground of want of corroboration, being criticised by a law reporter for doing so.[63] In 1845 counsel, in making a submission of no case before Erle J, on the ground that the only evidence against his client was uncorroborated accomplice evidence, asserted that it was the constant habit of judges in such cases to direct an acquittal. From this proposition Erle did not dissent, but claimed that the position had been altered by Denman's Act, which had made even a felon who had been convicted and sentenced a competent witness.[64] Between 1830 and 1860 there was a line of cases in which judges refused to allow the Crown even to call an accomplice until they had demonstrated, by evidence called, that there was satisfactory corroboration of what he had to say. This was a practice justified by Hill J in *Sparkes* (1858), on the ground that it avoided the court's time being wasted.[65] In 1861 no less a judge than Blackburn J is reported as having directed the acquittal of accused in a fraud trial for want of corroboration of accomplice evidence,[66] for which he was roundly criticised in the *Solicitors' Journal*.[67] In 1895 on the trial of Taylor,[68] the man accused with Oscar Wilde, Wills J threw out some of the counts against the accused for the same reason – for which he was criticised by the future Lord Darling in a self-important letter to *The Times*.[69] Nor was the Taylor case an isolated example. In the 1898 edition of Roscoe the practice is referred to and its legality questioned.[70] Even as late as 1909 one finds the *Justice of the Peace* declaring it not unusual

[61] *R v Jones* above.

[62] *R v Jordan and Sullivan* (1836) 7 C & P 432.

[63] *R v Keats* (1843) 7 JP 484.

[64] *R v Skiller* (1845) 9 JP 314.

[65] *R v Sparks* (1858) 1 F & F 388; cf. *R v Mellor* (1833); *R v Saunders* (1842); *R v Salt* (1843) (all cited in Russell (5th edn), iii, 602.

[66] *R v Cunnings* (1861) 56 CCC Sess Pap 378.

[67] (1862) 7 Sol J 197.

[68] *R v Taylor, The Times*, 22 May 1895.

[69] *The Times*, 30 May 1895.

[70] P. 118; for other examples of directed acquittals see *R v Owen and Mitchell, The Times*, 9 July 1801; *R v Fox and Others, The Times*, 20 March 1824; *R v Huggins and Another, The Times*, 5 March 1847; *R v Druce, The Times*, 7 July 1847; *R v Desmond and Others, The Times*, 28 April 1868 and *R v Winkel* (1911) 76 JP 191.

for judges to direct an acquittal, at the close of the prosecution case, where there was no corroboration of the accomplice.[71]

Joy argued that these directed acquittals represented nothing more than an illustration of something that happened daily in criminal courts – namely a judge treating a particular witness, whether an accomplice or not, as one who ought not to be listened to.[72] This suggestion may not in fact have been far wide of the mark. Judicial distrust of accomplices was not always shared by juries. It was not unknown for a jury in an accomplice case to bring back a guilty verdict in the teeth of advice from the bench to acquit. (In a case in 1864 Pollock LCB, faced with the flat refusal of a jury to follow his advice to acquit, ended up seizing upon a supposed defect in the indictment and directing them to acquit on that ground, which very reluctantly they did.)[73] Where that happened, the courts of review (even where they had jurisdiction, for example, because the point had been reserved or because the case was one of misdemeanour tried in the King's Bench), would not interfere.[74] This being the state of the law, the only way in which a judge could make sure that an accused was not convicted upon the uncorroborated evidence of an accomplice he personally disbelieved or distrusted was by a directed acquittal.

4. The Criminal Law Amendment Act (1885)

The Criminal Law Amendment Act (1885) made significant additions to the categories of case in which the law required corroboration. The new pro-curation offences it created were all made subject to such a requirement. It was this Act which introduced into English law the principle of allowing an accused to be convicted on the corroborated but unsworn evidence of a child witness. Section 4 permitted a child, who in the opinion of the trial judge possessed sufficient intelligence to justify receiving her evidence, and who understood the duty to tell the truth, to give such evidence where the offence charged was defilement of a girl under thirteen or an attempt thereat. In 1894 the principle of section 4 was applied by the Prevention of Cruelty to Children Act to offences of child cruelty and neglect. More far-reaching reform had to wait until the present century.

5. Rape

Of the twentieth-century rule of practice requiring juries to be warned of the danger of convicting on the uncorroborated evidence of victims of sexual offences there was, at the start of the nineteenth century, no trace.[75] Hale,

---

71 (1909) 73 JP 251.
72 Joy, *Accomplices*, 47.
73 *R v Robinson* (1864) 4 F & F 43.
74 *R v Boyes* (1861) above; see also Cave J in *In Re Meunier* above at 418.
75 Cf. Wigmore, *Treatise* (3rd edn), para 2061.

writing in the seventeenth century, had warned of the danger of false accusation in rape cases, observing that the charge was 'easily to be made ... and harder to be defended by the party accused, tho' never so innocent'.[76] He had also urged that how far the complainant in such a case was to be believed depended upon her reputation and whether the attendant circumstances concurred with her testimony:

> if she be of good fame; if she presently discovered the offence and made search for the offender; if the party accused fled for it; these and the like are concurring circumstances which give greater probability to her evidence. But on the other hand if she be of evil fame and stand unsupported by the testimony of others; if she concealed the injury for any considerable time after she had opportunity to complain; if the place where the fact was alleged to have been committed were such that it was possible that she might have been heard and she made no outcry; these and the like circumstances carry a strong but not conclusive presumption that her testimony is false or feigned.[77]

Until the second decade of the twentieth century, Hale's words represented the only learning which law books offered upon the matter.[78] Inevitably they became part of the defence lawyer's stock in trade.[79] They also on occasions found their way into judges' summings up (especially where the judge was trying to secure an acquittal).[80] Unlike the twentieth-century corroboration direction, they never had the status of directions which a trial judge was required to give, and it would be wrong to imagine that all nineteenth-century judges gave rape juries a warning about the dangers of false charges. They did not.[81] The only topic on which there appears to have been something close to a uniformity of judicial approach was that of complaints: most judges treated failure by the complainant to make prompt complaint as fatal to the prosecution case.[82] Such indeed was the importance attached

---

[76] Hale 1 P C 635–36.

[77] Ibid. 633–34; and see Bayley J's summary of the rule in *R v Scallon, The Times*, 13 December 1825.

[78] They were repeated by Blackstone, Hawkins, East and Archbold and were still being quoted in Roscoe (13th edn, 1908) and *Halsbury's Laws* (1st edn), ix, 613k. In the early years of this century some textbooks on evidence (e.g. Starkie, Taylor and Stephen) made no mention of the topic at all.

[79] For examples of defence speeches praying in aid Hale see *R v Mariner, The Times*, 4 March 1837; *R v Osborn The Times*, 21 December, 1857; *R v Rudland, The Times*, 20 July 1865; *R v Hunter, The Times*, 22–25 November 1865.

[80] For examples of summings up containing borrowings from Hale see *R v Lippincott, The Times*, 21 April 1810; *R v Brown, The Times*, 21 March 1827; *R v Vessey, The Times*, 21 March 1843; *R v Osborn, The Times*, 14 July 1864; *R v Lord St Leonards, The Times*, May 24 1884.

[81] See e.g. *R v Chapman, The Times*, 9 September 1805; *R v Freeman, The Times*, 13 July 1867.

[82] Phillipps (8th edn, 1838), 204 n 2; see also *R v Connor, The Times*, 16 September 1802; *R v Scallon* above; *R v Webb, The Times*, 3 September 1818; *R v Osborne, The Times*, 22 March 1827; *R v Page, The Times*, 12 July 1853; *R v Hales, The Times*, December 3 1859; *R v Howard, The Times*, 16 April 1864; there are grounds for supposing that absence of fresh complaint was regarded as less critical in indecent assault than rape (see e.g. *R v Webb* above and R v West, *The Times, 20 July 1865*).

to fresh complaint that, in a case in 1817, defence counsel actually went so far as to tell a jury that, by a rule of evidence which had become a rule of law, failure to complain for a long time was a bar to a conviction for rape.[83]

By the 1920s Hale's learning had been supplanted by a new corroboration rule. Although the emergence of this rule is difficult to date, the seeds of change were probably sown by the Criminal Law Amendment Act (1885). This made several fundamental changes in the law of sexual offences, all of which had implications for the future development of this area of the law of evidence. In the first place, it made several of the new sexual offences it created subject to a corroboration requirement.[84] Secondly, upon a charge of unlawful carnal knowledge of a girl under thirteen, it permitted the complainant to give evidence unsworn, subject to a mandatory corroboration requirement (from which it was but a small step to giving a corroboration warning in a case where the child's evidence was sworn).[85] Thirdly, it raised the age of consent from twelve to sixteen. This meant that in future the number of sexual cases in which the complainant would have to be treated as an accomplice, whose evidence required corroboration, would be much greater than before.[86] Fourthly, it made the accused and his spouse competent witnesses in relation to a wide range of sexual offences including rape;[87] a reform which, in Nebraska and several other American states, had already led to the imposition of a corroboration requirement in sexual cases.[88]

The obvious starting-point in any attempt to date the corroboration rule is *Graham*, decided by the Court of Criminal Appeal in 1910.[89] It is the first reported case in which a criminal court is to be found stating that a jury should be given something akin to a corroboration warning in sexual cases. The actual words of the judgement were: 'the judge should explain ... it is dangerous to act on the evidence of one person'. Although the judgement is brief and cites no authority, it does not read as though the court considered that it was laying down any novel or revolutionary principle. But if the rule is older than *Graham*, how much older is it?

At the committee stage of the 1885 Bill, the Home Secretary and the Attorney-General both justified their opposition to the inclusion of a corroboration clause in the Bill on the grounds that it was already the practice of judges not to allow men to be convicted in sexual cases without corroboration.[90] This claim, although hotly disputed by a former Attorney-General

[83] *R v Woodward and Others*, The Times, 24 March 1817.
[84] Ss 2 and 3.
[85] S 4.
[86] S 5. The new offence of gross indecency created by s 12 was also one, the proof of which might involve the calling of accomplice evidence (see e.g. *R v Wilde*, The Times, 21 May 1895).
[87] S 20.
[88] 'The Rape Corroboration Requirement' (Note), 81 (1972) Yale LJ 1361.
[89] *R v Graham* (1910) 4 Cr App R 218.
[90] PD 1884–85, CCC, 914 and 915–16.

and another lawyer MP,[91] appears to find some confirmation in _The Times_ trial reports from the period. For instance, Field J is reported as telling a jury in a rape case in 1877 that the law required corroboration. 'Was there', he asked, 'corroboration and did the complainant afterwards make immediate complaint?'[92] Again, the report of a judge's charge to a grand jury in 1889 contains a passage in which he comments upon the lack of corroboration in a case of indecent assault in which they were being asked to return a bill.[93] All this appears to suggest that the rule goes back twenty years or so before _Graham_. But the matter becomes less certain when one remembers that at this period it was the habit of lawyers and judges to use the word corroboration very loosely as including any item of confirmatory evidence (whether or not it could properly be said to be independent of the complainant).[94] Perhaps the strongest evidence against a date as early as the 1880s is the complete absence of reference to such a rule or practice in textbooks, legal journals and reported cases from the period.[95]

The first reported case which affords any basis for suspecting the possible existence of such a rule is in fact _Moore v The Bishop of Oxford_ (1904),[96] in which the Privy Council overturned the conviction of a clergyman for the ecclesiastical offence of immoral intercourse with a woman on the ground that there was no corroboration of her testimony. The suspicion that such a rule was either in place or emerging at the date of the Criminal Appeal Act (1907) is increased when one discovers that, in the first two years of the new court's existence, want of corroboration was a ground of appeal in no fewer than three reported rape conviction appeals.[97]

Whatever its age, it took some twenty or so years after the passing of the 1907 Act for the rule to assume its twentieth-century shape, with the standard form of jury direction not emerging until 1924.[98] Two facts which appear to have played a part in helping it take root were the adoption of the practice of giving a corroboration warning in cases involving child complainants and the creation by the Punishment of Incest Act (1908) of yet

[91] Ibid. 916 and 919; see also a letter published in _The Times_ on 2 June 1882.

[92] _R v Watts, The Times_, 29 June 1877.

[93] _The Times_, 27 May 1889.

[94] See the jury direction given in _R v Osborn, The Times_, 14 July 1864 and _R v Lord St Leonards, The Times_, 24 May 1884. See also _R v Hedges_ (1909) 3 Cr App R 262 at 265; _R v George_ (1909) 2 Cr App R 262; _R v May_ (1912) 8 Cr App R 63 at 67; _R v Christie_ (1914) 10 Cr App R 141 at 147; and _R v Lovell_ (1923) 129 LT 638.

[95] The Report of the Departmental Committee on Sexual Offences against Young Persons 1925 (Cmnd 2561) was apparently unable to trace the rule back further than _R v Graham_ (see p 47).

[96] _Moore v Bishop of Oxford_ [1904] AC 283.

[97] _R v Goulding_ (1908) 1 Cr App R 121, _R v Baker_ (1909) 2 Cr App R 249 and _R v George_ (1909) 2 Cr App R 282.

[98] See e.g. _R v Salman_ (1924) 18 Cr App R 50; and _R v Jones_ (1925) 19 Cr App R 40. Earlier cases had tended to use the 'oath against oath' approach adopted by the court in _R v Graham_, see e.g. _R v Quinn_ (1911) 6 Cr App R 269.

another category of sexual crime in which an accomplice direction would commonly be necessary.[99]

What is perhaps most surprising about the corroboration rule is that it was so late to emerge. The absence of any requirement that the jury be given a Hale warning, coupled with the inability of the prisoner and his wife to testify, made the blackmailing prosecution a thing to be feared, and throughout the century blackmailing suits and prosecutions were far from uncommon. In Ireland in the 1820s it was by no means unknown for a woman, having been seduced, to launch a rape prosecution as a means of bringing her seducer to the altar.[100] In England a corroboration requirement had to be imposed in 1834,[101] to try and stem the flood of perjury and extortion in bastardy suits.[102] Nor does the position appear to have markedly improved as the century progressed. When in 1859 Parliament passed an Act to curb vexatious prosecutions, one of the six offences made subject to its provisions was indecent assault.[103] The following year saw the Reverend Hatch bring a successful prosecution against a young girl whose evidence had secured his conviction and imprisonment for sexual assault.[104] *The Times* considered the problem of false accusations against men sufficiently serious to devote a leader to it, concluding with an observation that, unless things changed, it would be necessary to form a Society for the Protection of Men.[105] In 1869, during the Lords debate on the Evidence Further Amendment Bill, a former Lord Chancellor argued that, if the bar upon parties giving evidence in breach of promise of marriage cases were to be removed, it would be essential to put in its place a corroboration requirement: otherwise 'every case of seduction would be turned into one of breach of promise'.[106] During the debates on the Criminal Law Amendment Bill (1885) and the Punishment of Incest Bill (1908), the Commons were warned that by adding

[99] For accomplice cases, see e.g. *R v Brown* (1910) 6 Cr App R 24; *R v Dimes* (1911) 7 Cr App R 43; *R v Bloodworth* (1913) 9 Cr App R 80. For child witness cases, see *R v Pitts* (1912) 8 Cr App R 126; *R v Cratchley* (1913) 9 Cr App R 232; *R v Dossi* (1918) 13 Cr App R 158 and *R v Warren* (1919) 14 Cr App R 4; as to the importance of these lines of cases in the development of the rule, see the citation of authority in *Hargan v R* (1924) 27 C L R 13.

[100] See *R v Clifford, The Times*, 2 August 1826; *R v Moloney, The Times*, 10 August 1824; *R v Callaghan, The Times*, 25 August 1825; *R v Baron, The Times*, 27 March 1828; and *R v Murphy, The Times*, 21 April 1829.

[101] Poor Law Amendment Act, 1834, s 72.

[102] Report of the Poor Law Commission PP 1834 (44) XXVII, 1 (at p 195 of the Report); PD 1834 XXIV, 522, 528–30, and 536–37; and PD 1834 XXV, 603.

[103] Vexatious Indictments Act, 1859.

[104] *R v Plummer, The Times*, 10, 11, 12, 14, 16 and 18 May 1860; cf. the cases of *Toomer* (the subject of a leader in *The Times*, 5 September 1866) and *Seth Adams* referred to in PD 1878/79 CCXLIV, 401.

[105] *The Times*, 11 October 1864; see also letters published in *The Times* for 12, 13, 14 and 18 October 1864.

[106] Lord Chelmsford, PD 1868–69 CXCVIII, 674.

to the calendar of sexual offences they would simply be creating fresh opportunities for extortion.[107]

In the second half of the century the move in other jurisdictions was towards a corroboration requirement. New York in 1886, following the example of several other states, adopted a corroboration requirement in rape cases,[108] while in England the newly-created Divorce Court was, as early as the 1860s, refusing to find allegations of sexual crime proved unless there was corroborative evidence to support them.[109]

6. Identification

Nineteenth-century lawyers were well aware of the fallibility of identification evidence. When in 1838 William Wills published his work on *Circumstantial Evidence*, he devoted several pages to the topic of mistaken identity.[110] Eight years later the *Law Times* called in a leader for the law to be changed. Juries should not, it argued, be allowed to convict on identification evidence alone.[111] In 1848 Patteson J wrote to the House of Lords Select Committee that the 'too ready credence' given by juries to identification evidence was a source of wrong convictions; he had, he said, had two such cases on his last Assize.[112]

Despite the known risks, judges did not in the main regard identification cases as calling for any special treatment. There was certainly no requirement that the judge give the jury any special direction or warning in such cases.[113] Dock identifications were regarded as acceptable.[114] Indeed in 1843 Lord Chief Justice Denman rejected out of hand a proposal by the recorder of Newcastle for the outlawing of such identifications at committal hearings.[115] There was no practice of withdrawing from a jury fleeting glance identifications, such as that based upon the view afforded by the flash from the discharge of an assailant's gun.[116] If defence counsel in his speech sought to impress upon the jury the fallibility of evidence of identification, he might

---

[107] Cavendish Bentinck, PD 1884–85 CCC, 912–14; Rawlinson, PD 1908 CXCI, 280 and Staveley Hill, ibid., 282.

[108] See Note (1972) 81 Yale LJ 1963 above.

[109] See *N v N* (1862) 3 Sw & Tr 234.

[110] Some of the more notorious of the late eighteenth- and nineteenth-century mistaken identity cases are described in Wills, *Circumstantial Evidence* (6th edn, London, 1912), 179–91.

[111] (1846) 6 LT 21 February.

[112] Report of the H. L. Select Committe on the Further Amendment of the Administration of the Criminal Law: PP 1847–48 (523) XVI, 423 (at p 51 of the report).

[113] This was an attitude which persisted until *R v Turnbull* (1976) 63 Cr App R 132; see in particular *Arthurs v AG for Northern Ireland* (1970) 55 Cr App R 161 especially the speech of Lord Morris at 170.

[114] See *R v Watson* (1817) 2 Stark 116 and *R v De Berenger* (cited Russell, 4th edn, 1865, 522).

[115] Criminal Law Commissioners, 8th Report, app A, No. 22.

[116] *R v Brook* (1813) 31 St Tr 1124 and the cases cited by Wills, *Circumstantial Evidence*, 182–83.

well find his arguments pooh-poohed in the judge's summing up. That was certainly the fate of a counsel who took this tack before Lord Denman at the Somerset Assizes in 1849.[117] But not all judges were of the Denman mould. Some, due no doubt to personal knowledge of miscarriages of justice, approached identification cases with especial care, buttressing counsel's arguments with warnings and examples of their own[118] and, on occasions, even went so far as to direct an acquittal where the quality of the identification was poor.[119]

In practice, one of the most substantial protections for prisoners was the identification parade (which, whatever its shortcomings, meant that there would be no dock identification). The precise origin of the identification parade is unclear. In a memorandum to the Home Office, written in January 1874, the Commissioner claimed that it had been a feature of Metropolitan Police procedure 'almost ever since the establishment of the … force'.[120] The earliest force order on the subject so far traced dates from March 1860.[121] As is clear from the order itself, the practice was older than this; one only has to look in the Middlesex Sessions reports from the previous month to find an example of a case in which the prisoner was picked out on an identification parade.[122] Outside London the practice appears to go back to at least the 1850s.[123]

In terms of fairness to the suspect, nineteenth-century identification parades fell well short of present-day standards. According to the Commissioner's memorandum of 1874, it was usual for parades to consist of between eight and ten persons. This receives some confirmation in reported cases (although it is possible to find a case in 1871 where over fifteen persons were used on each parade).[124] All this sounds satisfactory enough. However, because of the perennial difficulty of finding members of the public (particularly respectable persons) willing to stand on identification parades, a practice grew up of using police officers to make up the numbers.[125] Criticisms of the practice by defence counsel and judges (based upon the fact that police officers, even in plain clothes, were usually readily recognisable

---

117 (1849) 13 LT 55; see also *R v Howe and Others*, *The Times*, 4 February 1882.

118 *R v Martindale*, *The Times*, 26 September 1800; *R v Sweeper*, *The Times*, 1 March 1830 and *R v Sutcliffe, Crossley and Mallinson*, *The Times*, 12 November 1877.

119 See e.g. *R v Biscoe and Dane*, *The Times*, 23 July 1806.

120 PRO, HO 45/9386/30237; one finds no trace of the practice in the early eighteenth century, see the report of the arrest of Thomas Edwards in *Daily Courant* , 18 March 1781, and the court order from 1724 cited by G. Howson, *Thief-Taker General*, 230.

121 Order of 24 March 1860.

122 *R v Daley and Morgan*, *The Times*, 22 February 1860.

123 *R v Blackburn* (1853) 6 Cox 333; *R v Cain and Rayne*, *The Times*, 28 July 1856.

124 *R v Pook*, *The Times*, 8 June 1871; and see J. W. Shepherd, H. D. Ellis, & G. M. Davies, *Identification Evidence: A Psychological Evaluation* (Aberdeen, 1982), 9.

125 Referred to in a letter from the Commissioner dated 7 January 1874 and in a report from a police inspector included in the same Home Office file and dated 4 December 1873 (PRO, HO/9386/30237).

as such) led the Commissioner in 1873 to issue instructions that henceforth police officers were only to be used in cases of emergency, as a very last resort.[126] The use of police officers was in fact merely part of a wider problem. Under force orders there was no obligation upon the officer assembling the parade to ensure that those on it were of the same general appearance and dress as the suspect. All that he was required to do was to ensure that they were of the same sex and, if police officers, were in plain clothes.[127] This gap in force orders was capable of working great unfairness. It was plugged by the Commissioner in 1874,[128] but even after that, as the *Beck* and *Sheppard* cases were to demonstrate, cases of a suspect being placed on a line up containing men bearing not the slightest resemblance to him in dress or appearance continued to occur.[129]

Another source of unfairness was the practice of officers 'tipping off' identifying witnesses beforehand, by showing them a photograph or giving them a description of the suspect. Outlawed by Metropolitan Police General Orders in 1893,[130] the Court of Criminal Appeal was still trying to stamp it out twenty years later.[131] The shortcomings of identification procedures might have been more quickly remedied had text writers displayed the slightest interest in the subject, but none did, not even Wills.

Though nothing further was done in the nineteenth century to improve visual identification procedures, at the turn of the century there occurred a development which was to have major implications for the identification of criminals. In 1900 a Home Office Committee,[132] set up to advise on the identification of criminals, recommended that the existing methods used to identify criminals with previous convictions be replaced by the fingerprint classification technique invented by E. R. Henry.[133] The following year a

[126] Amendment to the Metropolitan Police General Orders, 1873, dated 20 January 1874 (PRO, MEP 8/3).

[127] See order of 24 March 1860 and the General Orders, 1873, para 65.

[128] See the amendment to the General Orders referred to at n 126 above.

[129] As to the Beck Case, see Shepherd Ellis & Davies, *Identification Evidence*, 11; for a full account of the Sheppard case see the Report of the Tribunal of Inquiry thereon: PP 1924–25 (Cmnd 2497) XV, 1049.

[130] Metropolitan Police General Orders and Regulations, 1893 (PRO, MEP 8/4), S XVII, para 304.

[131] Early Court of Criminal Appeal Cases dealing with the practice include *R v Bundy* (1910) 5 Cr App R 270; *R v Chadwick* (1917) 12 Cr App R 247; *R v Dwyer* (1925) 18 Cr App R 145; and *R v Chapman* (1911) 28 TLR 135.

[132] Report of Committee on Methods of Identification of Criminals, 1900 (PRO, HO 144/566/A62042/3).

[133] The identification of those with previous convictions was a matter of importance given the policy of the legislature (initiated by the Criminal Law Act, 1827) of visiting with heavier penalties offences committed by persons who had been previously convicted. Prior to the introduction of fingerprinting, the principal method of identification was having prison and police officers inspect remand prisoners to see if there were any familiar faces amongst them; other methods, such as photography (developed at Bristol Gaol in the 1850s) and the Habitual Criminals Register set up in 1869, had proved of very limited value.

Central Fingerprint Bureau was established at Scotland Yard. The implications of the new technique for criminal investigation were quickly realised. Its use and value as evidence was placed beyond doubt when, in 1910, the Court of Criminal Appeal upheld a conviction based solely on fingerprint evidence.[134]

[134] *R v Castleton* (1909) 3 Cr App R 74; the attitude of some judges to fingerprints had initially been one of distrust see e.g. *R v Chadwick* (1908) cited by Wills, *Circumstantial Evidence*, 204.

24

The Concluding Stages of the Trial

'The Chairman said he would not take up the time of the jury recapitulating the evidence and the jury immediately pronounced the defendant guilty.'

R v Robinson (Surrey Sessions), *The Times*, 14 October 1802

1. The Last Word

After the defence evidence, if any, the accused or his counsel would address the jury. To this speech prosecuting counsel had, if the accused had called evidence, the right of reply. Throughout the century, the fear of giving the prosecution the last word with the jury operated as a powerful deterrent to the calling of defence witnesses. Where the prosecution was conducted by the Attorney-General there was nothing the accused could do to prevent the Crown having the last word, the Attorney having a prerogative right of reply. In all other cases, however, whether the Crown had the reply depended upon the nature of the charge and the course the defence took.

In treason, if the defence called evidence, both prosecution and defence counsel made closing speeches, with the Crown having the last word. If no defence evidence was called, the defence had the last word. In misdemeanour, the accused's position was more disadvantageous still. If he called evidence, not only would this give the prosecution the last word, but his counsel had no right to a closing speech. (Only one speech by defence counsel was allowed which, irrespective of whether he had witnesses to call, had to be made immediately upon the close of the Crown case.)[1]

These rules meant that, in deciding whether to call witnesses, the defence would have to weigh the benefit it hoped to reap from their evidence against the harm it might suffer from a prosecution reply. In misdemeanour that harm could be particularly great if the defence witnesses failed to come up to proof or were badly mauled in cross-examination, for the defence, lacking a closing speech, would have no opportunity to try and repair the damage. That counsel frequently chose to hold back available evidence rather than risk a reply is beyond doubt.[2]

Nor was this the only impact which the reply had on trial tactics. After 1820

[1] Greaves, Report on Criminal Procedure, PP 1856 (456) L 79.

[2] See Greaves ibid.; also PD 1826 XV, 601; PD 1836 XXXI, 498; PD 1898 LIV, 1180; and (1859–60) 34 LT 201.

it was but rarely that defence counsel would risk cross-examining a Crown witness on discrepancies between his testimony and his deposition, for, in order to do so, he would have to put the deposition in, and the putting in of any document by the defence gave the prosecution the reply.[3] Again, defence counsel, when addressing the jury, had to take care not to state facts not in evidence for this too would give the Crown the reply.[4] Unless one knew one's opponent, even the calling of character witnesses involved an element of risk; it was exceptional for prosecution counsel to claim a reply in such a case but, if he decided to do so, there was no way of preventing it.[5] The only situation in which the defence could be conducted without worrying about the reply was where the prosecutor was in person, as an unrepresented prosecutor was not permitted to address the jury either by way of opening or reply.[6]

Before 1836 the rules in misdemeanour in theory applied also in felony. Since in felony the accused's counsel could not address the jury on his behalf, the practice was for Crown counsel not to avail themselves of the right of reply where defence evidence was given.[7] Indeed, on some circuits, indulgence went even further than this, it being the custom for prosecuting counsel not even to make an opening speech (except in complicated cases).[8] Thus, in felony trials, at the close of the prosecution case, what the jury would hear would be the accused's unsworn statement followed by any evidence he chose to call, with no prosecution reply to either.

The Prisoners' Counsel Bills had obvious implications as regards the reply, as the Attorney-General was not slow to point out in debate.[9] If felony prisoners were given the right to make full defence by counsel, the Crown would beyond doubt henceforth exercise the same right of reply in felony as in misdemeanour. The point appears to have been overlooked by the draftsmen of the early Bills, for they are completely silent on the matter. The first to deal with it was that of 1833, which proposed that the prisoner should have the last speech in both felony and misdemeanour. In 1835 the Criminal Law Commissioners came out strongly in favour of allowing the accused the last word,[10] and both the 1835 and the 1836 Bills contained a

---

[3] See Chapter 14.

[4] See *R v Horne* (1777) 20 How St Tr 651 at 664; *R v Bignold* (1823) Dow & Ry 59; *R v Carlile* (1834) 6 C & P 636; Taylor (7th edn), 354 thought that the judge had a discretion to permit a reply in a flagrant case.

[5] *R v Stannard* (1837) 7 C & P 673; *R v Hayes* (1840) 1 Cr & D 367; *R v Corfell* (1844) 1 Cox 123; *R v Briggs* (1858) 1 F & F 106. Occasionally one finds judges refusing to allowing the reply in such a case, see e.g. *R v Loughnan* (1842) Arm M & O 253; *R v Brooks* (1843) 1 Cox 6; and *R v Dowse* (1865) 4 F & F 492.

[6] *R v Brice* (1824) 2 B & Ald 606; *R v Gurney* (1869) 11 Cox 414.

[7] PD 1824 XI, 208; *R v Edwards* (1837) 8 C & P 26; *R v Codling and Others* (1802) 28 St Tr 177 and *R v Fursey* (1833) 3 St Tr NS 543.

[8] Common Law Commissioners, 2nd Report PP 1852–53 (1626) XL 701 at p 10. For an example of the survival of the practice post-1836 see *R v Jackson and Fisher* (1837) 7 C & P 773.

[9] PD 1824 XI, 207–08; PD 1826 XV, 600–1.

[10] Common Law Commissioners, 2nd Report, p 16.

clause to that effect. When the 1836 Bill reached the Lords, the clause was struck out at committee stage, the principal ground of objection to it being that it would create an inconsistency of practice between civil and criminal cases.[11] At the third reading an attempt to reinstate it failed by ten votes, and the Bill was sent back to the Commons with the clause struck out.[12] The Commons refused to accept the amendment but, with only a day of the session left, Ewart reluctantly gave in and the Bill was passed in the form in which it had come down from the Lords.[13]

The judges were not slow to spell out what the implications of the new Act would be as regards the reply. In early 1837 they issued a Practice Direction.[14] In felony cases, counsel for a prisoner was not to be permitted to cross-examine a prosecution witness upon his deposition without putting in the deposition, which would in turn give the Crown the right of reply; the calling of character witnesses would give the reply, although it would be a matter for discretion whether counsel would exercise it; the Law Officers would be entitled to reply although no evidence had been produced on behalf of the prisoner. As opponents of the Act had predicted, part of the price to be paid for the right to full defence by counsel in felony was that the prisoner who called evidence would be subject to the reply. A question which soon had to be faced was whether, in a case where there were several accused, the calling of evidence by one gave the prosecution a right of reply against all. It received from the judges no clear answer.[15]

Events took an important turn in 1853 with the publication of the Second Report of the Royal Commission on Common Law Procedure.[16] This stressed that, in civil cases, the one great object of counsel for a defendant was to avoid calling witnesses so as not to expose the case to the danger of a reply. The upshot of the report was section 34 of the Common Law Procedure Act (1854) which, while it did not abolish the reply in civil suits, did give counsel for a defendant who called evidence the right to make a second speech at the close of such evidence. This meant that henceforth the defendant's counsel would, at least, be able to deal with any ground that had been lost in the course of the defence case.

The passing of the 1854 Act obviously posed the question whether the reform should be extended to criminal cases. In 1856 the Lord Chancellor commissioned a report on criminal procedure from Charles Greaves. He

[11] PD 1836 XXXV, 183 and 1247–48. The argument that the clause would lead to four speeches in every case (see PD 1836 XXXV, 600) was one which Pollock easily demolished.

[12] PD 1836 XXXV, 228.

[13] PD 1836 XXXV, 599–602, 612–14, 1210–11, 1247–49 and 1323–25.

[14] Practice Direction 7 C & P 676.

[15] In *R v Hayes* (1838) 2 M & Rob 155 Parke B declined to allow the Crown a general reply but stressed that he was no laying down a general rule, whilst in *R v Jordan and Cowmeadow* (1839) 9 C & P 118 Williams J allowed a general reply but stressed that it was to be exercised with great forbearance.

[16] PP 1852–53 (1626) XL 701.

recommended that criminal and civil procedure be brought into line on this point.[17] He also argued forcibly against the Law Officers' prerogative right to the last word. On the question of whether the law should be altered to give the prisoner the last word in all cases, he pointed out that the Second Report of the Criminal Law Commissioners had favoured such a reform, and that the last word was given to the prisoner in civil law systems, in Scotland and under the New York Criminal Code. He also acknowledged that the existence of the Crown's right of reply led in many cases to evidence material to a prisoner's case not being called. However, in his view, the balance of convenience was against making such a change. There was no evidence that the right of reply had led to practical inconvenience. If defence counsel were allowed the last word, the judge would often be placed in the embarrassing position of having to expose in his summing up the unsoundness of the defence arguments. There would also be no incentive for prisoners not to bring forward all manner of irrelevant evidence.

The government took no steps to give effect to Greaves' recommendation, although in 1860 Denman and Ewart presented a Bill to bring the practice in felony and misdemeanour into line with that in civil suits.[18] It passed the Commons but the Lords sent it back with an amendment to the effect that it should be left to the discretion of the trial judge whether the defence should have a second speech (such discretion to be exercised in the light of the number of witnesses called and all other relevant factors). The amendment was strongly attacked in the Commons and in the end the Bill was lost.[19] In 1861 a similar Bill was introduced but did not get beyond a first reading.[20] Eventually, in 1865 the reform was carried in the form of section 2 of the Criminal Procedure Act. The Act, by permitting prosecution witnesses to be cross-examined on their depositions without the deposition being put in, also limited the scope for the reply.[21]

Although the 1865 Act did not, as Greaves had recommended, abolish the Law Officers' right of reply, that right was by now coming under attack from other quarters. In the Practice Direction of 1837 the judges had spoken of the right as being exercisable not only by the Attorney-General but by any counsel representing him, but by the 1860s not all judges were prepared to allow it so wide a scope. In 1858 Byles J declared the right limited to the Attorney-General personally,[22] and the following year he repeated this ruling in a Mint prosecution.[23] In 1865 Martin B denied the claim of the Attorney-General of Chester to exercise the right, declaring it exercisable

[17] At p 33 of his Report.
[18] PP 1860 (167) III, 243.
[19] PD 1860 CLX, 1319; as to the justification offered by the Lords for their stance, see ibid., 180–81.
[20] PD 1861 CLXIII, 221.
[21] S 5.
[22] *R v Beckwith* (1858) 7 Cox 505.
[23] *R v Taylor* (1859) 1 F & F 535.

only by the Attorney-General of England in person.[24] Also, hard on the heels of the 1865 Act, came arguments that the Act had abolished the prerogative right. This palpably unsound argument was rejected by a number of judges but it took a long time dying.[25] As late as 1872 the point was still being taken at the Old Bailey.[26] The judges gave equally short shrift to arguments that the right was limited to the Attorney-General and not claimable by the Solicitor-General. In 1878 Hawkins J attempted a reverter to the old rule, declaring that any counsel representing the Law Officers could claim the right,[27] but his decision was against the tide of opinion. In 1884 the matter was put beyond doubt by a resolution of the Council of Judges:[28] henceforth the right would be allowed only in cases where the Law Officers were personally involved.[29]

The problem of how the right of reply should be exercised in cases involving co-prisoners was one which still had not been fully solved even by the 1860s. In *Blackburn* in 1853, Talfourd J had held obiter that, where prisoners were jointly indicted for the same offence, the calling of evidence by one gave a right of reply against all.[30] There were other decisions, both earlier and later to like effect.[31] In *Marlow and Beesley* (1867), however, Smith J held that the Crown only had a right of reply against those prisoners who called evidence, a ruling which was followed in several subsequent cases, including *Burns* (1887), where it was further held that in such a case counsel for the prisoners on whose behalf no evidence was called could make their speeches after the reply for the Crown.[32] In *Trevelli* (1882) Hawkins J steered a middle course between these conflicting lines of authority, by holding that the calling of evidence by one prisoner would give the Crown a right of reply against all to whose cases the evidence was relevant.[33] This ruling too attracted its adherents.[34]

The Criminal Code Bills (1878–83) proposed no change in the law as to the reply. However, a clutch of cases in the 1880s, reversing the rule forbidding the making of unsworn statements by prisoners defended by counsel, brought a change in the law, with the rule laid down in *Manzano*

---

[24] *R v Christie* (1858) 1 F & F 75 (Attorney-General of Chester).

[25] *R v Currie* (1865) 62 CCC Sess Pap 479; *R v Toakley* (1866) 10 Cox 406; *R v Barrow* (1866) 10 Cox 407.

[26] *R v Dixblanc* (1872) 76 CCC Sess Pap 260.

[27] *R v Wood* (1878) 88 CCC Sess Pap 72.

[28] 5 St Tr NS 3 n.

[29] An attempt was made at the committee stage of the Criminal Evidence Bill 1898 to include a clause abolishing the prerogative right: PD 1898 LXVIII, 663–82.

[30] *R v Blackburn* (1853) 6 Cox 333.

[31] See *R v Jordan* above and *R v Serne* (1887) 107 CCC Sess Pap 122.

[32] *R v Marlow and Beesley* (1867–68), 12 Sol J 373 (followed in *R v Harrington*, 1869, English & Empire Digest 15(1) 15839 and *R v Kain* (1883) 15 Cox 388); *R v Burns* (1887) 83 LT 29, 16 Cox 195.

[33] *R v Trevelli* (1882) 15 Cox 289.

[34] It was followed in *R v Maslin* (1883) 98 CCC Sess Pap 183 and *R v Vass* ibid., 361.

(1860),[35] that the making of such a statement did not give the Crown the right of reply, being overturned.[36]

A point which was slow to be appreciated during the long debate about prisoners' giving evidence was that the reform, like that of 1836, had implications for the right of reply. One of the first MPs to raise the question was Wharton, who in the debate on the 1888 Bill asked whether the giving of evidence by a prisoner would give the Crown the reply, observing that if it did the Bill would be a trap.[37] By most it went unnoticed. Certainly, none of the Prisoners' Evidence Bills introduced in the 1880s and 1890s contained any provision on the point. It was only at the committee stage of the 1898 Bill that the government was prevailed upon to agree to the inclusion of a clause providing that the giving of evidence by the accused should not give the Crown the reply.[38]

For all that the reply had an impact upon trial tactics, its importance in this regard must not be overstressed. Many prisoners had no witnesses as to fact to call.[39] Also it was by no means in every prosecution that counsel was briefed; and where there was no prosecuting counsel there could be no reply. If the prisoner was undefended, he would usually not know what the rules as to the reply were and would thus not be influenced by them. The dilemma as to whether to call evidence and risk the reply assumed its most acute form in capital cases. This continued to be the case almost down to the abolition of the death penalty for murder in 1965.[40]

2. The Judge's Summing Up

After the closing speeches, the judge would sum the case up to the jury. In the first half of the nineteenth century the standard of summings up was generally low. In a simple case the summing up would be perfunctory, if not omitted altogether. One of the reasons why in the 1830s and 1840s the City judges were able to get through as many as trials as they did was that they habitually dispensed with summing up.[41] At many Quarter Sessions the same bad practice prevailed.[42] Charges to the jury by the common law judges in heavy cases were usually of a higher standard, dealing fully with both law and evidence, but even they would, on occasions, omit to sum up. As late

---

[35] *R v Manzano* (1860) 2 F & F 64; also *R v Taylor* (1859) 1 F & F 535.

[36] See e.g. *R v Shimmin* (1882) 15 Cox 122; *R v Doherty* (1887) 16 Cox 306.

[37] PD 1888 CCCXXIV, 73.

[38] PD 1898 LX, 747; see also PD 1898 LIV 1180.

[39] See e.g. PD 1836 XXXV, 613.

[40] See e.g. *R v Craig and Bentley*; D. Yallop, *To Encourage the Others* (London, 1990), 178–79.

[41] See e.g. *R v Barrett*, *The Times*, 17 September 1823; *R v Fawcett*, *The Times*, 11 December 1823; also R. Harris, *The Reminiscences of Sir Henry Hawkins*, 40–41.

[42] E.g. *R v Robinson*, *The Times*, 14 October 1802 (Surrey Sessions).

as 1836 one can find Patteson J acceding to a request from an Old Bailey jury not to trouble to sum the case up.[43]

After 1850 there was an improvement in standards. It was not universal. At the Old Bailey Mr Commissioner Kerr, who sat as third City judge between 1859 and 1901, would, until the day of his retirement, remain notorious for his one-line summings up and for his refusal to take a note of the evidence.[44] Indeed so deeply engrained were the old bad practices that some Quarter Sessions chairmen were still omitting to sum up as late as 1913, a state of affairs which the Court of Criminal Appeal astonishingly refused to condemn.[45] The vice of this was, of course, that the accused was denied the benefit of having the jury clearly directed upon such elementary but vital matters as the burden of proof, and the legal ingredients of the offence charged. Where he did sum up, the judge would often have no scruples about advising the jury to convict. Such conduct was viewed far less critically than it is today. It was the right of the judge, declared Brougham, to tell the jury what his opinion of the case was. This was not a minority view.[46]

3. Verdict and Judgement

The summing up completed, the jury would consider their verdict. Often juries reached a verdict without leaving the jury box.[47] If unable to agree on the spot, they would retire to the jury room to deliberate. Once enclosed, they would be kept without fire, food or drink until they reached a verdict.[48] If one of them became faint or ill (lack of food was the most usual cause) the judge would send for a surgeon. If, having examined the juror, the surgeon swore that further confinement would involve risk to life, the jury would be discharged. Nothing short of danger to life would, however, normally persuade a judge to discharge a jury.[49]

At Assizes, if a jury had not reached a verdict by the time the judge was ready to leave for the next Assize town, it was open to him to have them placed in a cart, carried along behind him and, if they had still not agreed

[43] *R v Elliott*, *The Times*, 18 June 1836.

[44] G. Pitt Lewis, *Mr Commissioner Kerr*, 251 and 259–64; F. W. Ashley, *My Sixty Years in the Law*, 97–99.

[45] *R v Newman* (1913) 9 Cr App R 134 (a decision still being cited as an authority in Archbold (28th edn, 1931), 219.

[46] *R v Hayden*, *The Times*, 13 December 1823; 'Jury Trial: Charging the Jury' (1882) 16 Ir LT 124 at 125; see also dicta of Cockburn LCJ in *R v Orton* cited in Wigmore, *Treatise* (3rd edn), art 2551a.

[47] PD 1859 CLIII, 1021 and see also *The Times* trial reports for the period.

[48] In the debate on the Juries in Civil Causes Bill (1859) it was said that juries were sometimes allowed a plentiful supply of lamps in order to provide them with some heat, and that one judge had permitted them water on the ground that it was neither meat nor drink (PD 1859 CLIII, 1014).

[49] (1844) 3 LT 113; (1857) 1 Sol J 128 (Old Bailey) and 298 (Middlesex Sessions).

by the time he reached the county border, shot into a ditch.[50] In a Lords debate in 1859,[51] and in *Winsor* (1865),[52] the judges were at pains to assert that carting had never been practised or sanctioned by the common law. This was, however, untrue. Carting may have been rare in the nineteenth century but it certainly took place. An Irish jury was carted at Tralee Assizes in 1825,[53] while as late as 1848 Platt B, when sitting at Oxford Assizes, gave orders for a cart to be got ready for a jury which could not agree.[54]

Until 1865 whether a judge had power (in the absence of danger to life) to discharge a jury which could not agree,[55] and whether there could be a second trial if he did,[56] were regarded as doubtful questions. The doubts were finally removed by the decision of the Court for Crown Cases Reserved in *Winsor v R*, but even after this judges remained slow to discharge deadlocked juries.

The law's tactic of starving juries into verdicts made jury trial a lottery in cases of disagreement. The feeling was that the loser in such lottery was usually the accused. As Alexander Pope had it: 'wretches hang that jurymen may dine'.[57] A solution to the problem of hung juries periodically canvassed was that of majority verdict. Majority verdicts in civil cases had been advocated by the Common Law Commissioners in 1831,[58] and investigated so far as criminal cases were concerned by the Criminal Law Commissioners in 1845.[59] During the second reading debate on the Juries Bill (1873), which proposed to reduce the size of the jury to seven in all save capital cases, the Attorney-General suggested abandoning the unanimity rule in non-capital cases, but by the committee stage, having ascertained that the judges were divided on the proposal, he dropped it.[60]

Where the jury could not agree, the prisoner would be remanded to be retried at the next session of the court. There was in theory no limit to the number of times a prisoner could be retried, and it was certainly not unknown for a prisoner to be retried more than once. In 1909 at Belfast a prisoner

---

[50] Bla Comm, iii , 376 citing Lib Ass fel 40, pl 11.

[51] PD 1859 CLIII, 1020–21.

[52] *R v Winsor* (1866) 10 Cox 276 per Cockburn LCJ at p 310 and Lush J at p 325.

[53] *R v M'Elroy, The Times,* 2 April 1825; for another instance, see (1832) 7 Law Mag (1st series) 46 n 1.

[54] *R v Anon., The Times,* 21 July 1848 (in the event the jury reached a verdict before the judge left town).

[55] Co Litt, 227b; Co 3 Inst, 110, Hawk 2 P C, c. 47, s 1; Foster, 29–39; also PD 1859 CLIII, 1038.

[56] The doubt was caused by the decision of the Irish Court of QB in *Conway and Lynch v R* (1845) 5 LT 458.

[57] A. Pope, *The Rape of the Lock,* III, 21.

[58] Third Report, PP 1831 (92) X, 375 (at p 70); the Juries in Civil Causes Bill, 1859 sought to carry the reform.

[59] It was one of the subjects covered by the questionnaire circulated by the Commissioners in 1844.

[60] PD 1873 CCXVI, 1511.

called Tease was retried three times.[61] A hung jury was not the only reason for discharge. If a juror died, became ill or absented himself during a trial, the judge was obliged to discharge the jury and start again. In such cases the practice was to call a new juror, swear the jury thus afforced again and then read over to them the evidence given in the aborted trial.[62] The eleven original jurors were thus subjected to the tedium of hearing evidence gone through twice, while the accused ended up being tried by a jury one of whom had not seen and heard all the witnesses.

In the second half of the century there was considerable pressure for the rules as to jury separation, retirement and discharge to be reformed. The first to be done away with was that denying a jury which was deliberating fire, food and refreshment.[63] By the 1860s the rule had been abolished in Ireland;[64] and, even in England, there had been occasional infractions in civil cases.[65] Between 1864 and 1869 no less than four Bills were presented to the Commons containing clauses for its abolition. It was finally done away with by the Juries Act (1870), which declared that henceforth the matter should be in the trial judge's discretion. The rule prohibiting jury separation in treason and felony trials proved much more enduring. Between 1864 and 1897 nineteen Bills on the subject were presented to Parliament,[66] but only in 1897 was the reform finally carried.[67] Even then treason, treason felony and murder were excepted (in these cases the prohibition upon separation continued right down to 1948).[68] The rule that illness, death or absence of a juror obliged the judge to dischage proved equally resistant. Bills for its reform introduced in 1868[69] and 1874 were lost;[70] not until 1925 was it finally altered.[71]

The jury were required to deliver their verdict in open court through their foreman. Usually it would be a general verdict (that is to say guilty or not guilty). But it was open to them, if they wished, to return a special verdict, stating the facts they found, and leaving it to the judge to say whether upon those facts the accused was guilty in law of the offence charged. Prior

---

[61] Kenny's *Outlines of Criminal Law* (Cambridge, 19th edn, 1966), 616.

[62] *R v Gould* (1763) 3 Burn's *Justice of the Peace* (30th edn, 1869) 98; *R v Edwards* (1812) Russ & Ry 224; as to reading over the evidence, see *R v Beere* (1842) 2 M & Rob 472.

[63] The practice had been repeatedly condemned by Royal Commissions, by judges and legal journals.

[64] (1866) 1 LJ 73–74.

[65] E.g. *Smith v GN Ry*, *The Times*, 20 December 1858 (juror allowed port and sandwiches on doctor's advice).

[66] Including the Juries in Criminal Cases Bills, 1864, 1865 and 1866, the Criminal Code Bills, 1878–83, and the Jurors' Detention Bills, 1886, 1887, 1888, 1889 and 1890.

[67] Jurors' Detention Act, 1897, s 1.

[68] Criminal Justice Act, 1948, s 35(4).

[69] Special and Common Juries Bill, 1868, cl 29.

[70] Juries Bill, 1874.

[71] Criminal Justice Act, 1925, s 15.

to the establishment of the Court for Crown Cases Reserved in 1848, judges would, in cases where the law was doubtful, sometimes invite the jury to return a special verdict so that it could be adjourned for argument before the Twelve Judges.[72] By 1900, however, special verdicts had gone almost entirely out of use.

If the verdict was not guilty, the judge would order the prisoner's discharge. If it was guilty of treason or felony, the court clerk would put the allocutus, that is ask the prisoner why the court should not give judgement against him. The object was to enable the accused to urge anything – such as a pardon, an indictment error, benefit of clergy or (in the case of a woman capitally convicted) pregnancy – which was a bar to judgement or a ground for respiting judgement. If no bar was shown, the court would proceed to sentence.

In 1800 the practice at Assizes and the Old Bailey was to sentence on the last sitting day. Those capitally convicted would receive the death sentence, lesser offenders would be sentenced to imprisonment, whipping or a fine. It all took very little time. Prisoners would be brought up in batches, told their fate and taken back down. Murderers and capital prisoners not reprieved by the Assize judge before he left town would usually be executed within a few days of sentence being pronounced.[73] Newgate prisoners, however, had a longer wait for death. Their cases would be referred to the King in Council for review, and it would be two to three weeks before the Council's decision was known.[74]

In 1823 judges were relieved of the obligation of passing the death sentence upon prisoners whom they intended to recommend to mercy. It was enacted that they might instead direct that sentence of death be recorded, which order would operate as a deemed reprieve.[75] No longer would a judge have to reassure a hysterical girl whom he had just sentenced to die that he did not mean to hang her. In 1837 the practice of referring Newgate cases to the Privy Council ceased.[76] The Act of 1752 which required murderers to be executed within two days of sentence was also repealed.[77] In future the period between sentence and execution in all capital cases would be not less than fourteen days, the power to reprieve resting in all cases with the Home Office.

By the 1840s the practice of sentencing prisoners in batches had been abandoned.[78] Sentence now followed immediately upon conviction. By the 1890s it had become customary for judges to hear police evidence as to

---

[72] E.g. *R v Hazel* (1785) 1 Leach 368.
[73] *Lord Eldon's Anecdote Book* (ed. Lincoln & McEwen)(London, 1960), anecdote 130.
[74] H. Twiss, *The Public and Private Life of Lord Chancellor Eldon* (London, 1844), i, 398–99.
[75] 4 Geo 4, c. 48.
[76] Central Criminal Court Act, 1837; Fenton Bresler, *Reprieve*, 52.
[77] By the Executions for Murder Act, 1836.
[78] W. Eden Hooper, *History of Newgate and the Old Bailey*, 129.

antecedents before sentencing.[79] The practice of 'taking offences into consideration' also dates from around this period.[80] Speeches in mitigation, whether from counsel or accused, were, however, rare.

---

[79] Referred to in *R v Gathercole* (1908) 1 Cr App R 43; see also Serjeant Robinson, *Bench and Bar*, 49.

[80] The practice appears to date back to the 1890s, see *R v Syres* (1909) 1 Cr App R 172, 173.

25

Appellate Remedies

'I am perfectly satisfied that many persons have suffered punishment where they have been positively innocent of the crime with which they were charged [where] if there had been any court of appeal ... there would have been a reversal of their conviction.' E. A. Wilde, former sheriff of London, giving evidence to the Criminal Law Commissioners (1836).

England in the nineteenth century had no system of criminal appeal, merely a handful of appellate procedures of limited scope: the motion for a new trial; the writ of error; and the practice of reserving cases.

1. The Motion for a New Trial

Of the three procedures, the most satisfactory from an accused's point of view was the motion for a new trial, since it afforded a remedy against both judicial and jury error and could be brought as of right.[1] Had it been generally available in criminal cases, the nineteenth century would have had a criminal appeal system falling little short of the present-day system. But it was not. It was available only in a tiny number of cases: the hundred or so cases of misdemeanour tried each year in the King's Bench. It was not available in treason or felony wherever tried,[2] nor in cases of misdemeanour tried elsewhere than in the King's Bench (although an accused desirous of ensuring that he had a right of appeal in the event of being convicted of misdemeanour could, before trial, move for certiorari to transfer the indictment into the King's Bench).[3]

2. The Writ of Error

The writ of error was available to any accused convicted before a court of record, but only in respect of legal errors apparent on the record. These

---

[1] Chitty, *Criminal Law* (1st edn), i , 654–58.

[2] A special verdict found in felony could however be removed to be argued in the King's Bench: *R v Hazel* (1785) 1 Leach 368.

[3] Criminal Law Commissioners, 8th Report, app C.

included indictment error and procedural irregularities such as want of jurisdiction, defective jury process, wrongful denial of a jury challenge, failure
to put the allocutus and the passing of a sentence contrary to law.[4] They did
not include errors made by the trial judge in his rulings upon questions of
admissibility of evidence, nor in his direction of the jury as to the law.[5] In civil
suits the scope of error was much wider, it being provided by the Statute of
Westminster II (1285) that, where a court gave a decision which would not
appear on the record, the judge could be asked to seal a bill of exceptions
recording the objection in a permanent form, which could then be used to
found a writ of error.[6] During the first half of the nineteenth century there was
much uncertainty as to whether there was a right to tender a bill of exceptions
in criminal cases.[7] Had the right been established, the effect would have
been to provide prisoners with a means of appealing all errors and irregularities occurring at trial. In the end, it was held that there was no such right,
with the result that, as in the eighteenth century, the principal use to which
the writ was put was challenging rulings on indictment objections.[8]

In the eighteenth century indictment error had been a happy hunting
ground for lawyers: many accused saw their convictions overturned because
of a trivial formal error in the indictment.[9] In the nineteenth century, as
has been seen, the scope for technical objections to indictments was progressively cut down by statute.[10] By 1851 their day was almost past, with the
result that the number of writs of error slowed to a trickle. By 1880 the writ
was being described by Stephen as obsolete.[11] Even in its heyday it had been
a cumbersome and expensive remedy. Before a writ could be brought, the
Attorney-General's fiat had to be obtained;[12] and when that had been done
there followed the time-consuming process of having the record drawn up
and checked for accuracy and completeness.[13]

---

[4] Chitty, *Criminal Law*, i , 741 and 747.

[5] See Holdsworth, HEL, i, 215–16.

[6] S 31.

[7] Pre-nineteenth century precedents suggested that a bill of exceptions would lie in
misdemeanour, *R v Higgins* (1683) 1 Vent 366, *R v Nutt* (1728) 1 Barn 307, but not in felony
or treason, *Sir Henry Vane's Case* (1661) Sid 85.

[8] Of the cases of error reported in Cox's *Criminal Law Cases* between 1851 and 1900 eleven
out of twenty concerned indictment points.

[9] See e.g. W. Eden, *Principles of Penal Law* (London, 1771), 181, repeating a complaint made
by Hale, 2 P C 193.

[10] See 7 Geo IV, c. 64, s 20 and 14 & 15 Vict, c. 100, ss 24 and 25.

[11] Stephen, HCL, i , 312.

[12] In treason and felony grant of the fiat was in the Attorney's discretion; in misdemeanour
it was grantable *ex debito justitiae* where the error was probable, and if the Attorney refused to
grant it the court would order him to do so, *Paty's Case* (1705) 1 Salk 504. As to the Attorney's
right to a fee, see *R v Costello* (1868) 11 Cox 81.

[13] As to the form of and materials from which the record was drawn up, see Report of Criminal
Code Commission, PP 1878–79 (Cmnd 2345) XX 169 (at p 37) and Stephen, HCL, i, 308.

3. Reserving Cases

Reserving was a review procedure of considerable antiquity.[14] A trial judge who entertained doubt as to the legal propriety of a conviction might reserve the case for consideration by the whole body of common law judges (the Twelve Judges), sentence being postponed or respited until their decision was known. The case would then be considered by the judges at a meeting held at Serjeants' Inn, with their decision (which was binding on the trial judge) announced in open court at the next sitting of the trial court. If it was in the prisoner's favour, he would be pardoned or judgement against him arrested. If it was against him, the law would take its course.

Whether a point of law was reserved was entirely in the discretion of the trial judge. The judges claimed that this was no hardship since they never refused to reserve points of substance. Many remained unconvinced. Judges varied enormously in their willingness to reserve cases. The risk that an obdurate judge would improperly refuse to reserve a point was all too real, as *Russell* (1832) and the *Case of the Brazilian Pirates* (1845) clearly demonstrated.[15] Faced with a refusal to reserve, an accused had only two courses open to him: first, where the point was capable of being so raised, to sue out a writ of error or move for a new trial; or, if it was not, to try and persuade the Lord Chancellor or other judges to bring pressure to bear on the trial judge.

Some courts had no power to reserve cases. It was only where the trial was held at the Old Bailey or at Assizes that a case could be reserved.[16] Courts of Quarter Sessions, for all that they were more likely to fall into legal error than the superior courts,[17] had no power to reserve.[18] Other aspects of the system which attracted cricitism were the informality and secrecy of the procedure (with cases argued in private and no judgement or reasons for decisions given),[19] and the fact that the judges had no power to order a new trial nor any power to quash convictions.[20]

---

[14] See generally D. R. Bentley, *Select Cases from the Twelve Judges' Notebooks*, 8–21 and 49–52.

[15] *R v Russell* (1832) 1 Moo 356; *R v Serva* (The Case of the Brazilian Pirates) (1845) 1 Cox 292.

[16] The Welsh judges reserved cases via petition to the king: *R v Harley* (1830) 4 C & P 369.

[17] The risk of error was at its greatest at county Quarter Sessions presided over by lay chairmen.

[18] Quarter Sessions could in theory reserve difficult points to the judge of Assize (see the Commission of the Peace under which they sat) or refer them to the Home Office (see Criminal Law Commissioners, 2nd Report, App 1, p 95 (Lord Wharncliffe).

[19] Stephen, HCL, i, 311.

[20] *R v Lea* (1837) 2 Moo 9.

4. The Narrow Scope of These Remedies

As a safeguard against miscarriage of justice, the three remedies were hopelessly inadequate. They offered no redress against jury error, save in King's Bench misdemeanor trials.[21] Where the judge misdirected the jury, or wrongly admitted or excluded evidence, his ruling could not be challenged without his consent. Against harsh sentencing there was no redress except where the sentence was illegal (in which case error would lie). In the main, the prisoners who benefited from the three procedures were those who had lawyers. Most reserved points were points taken by prisoners' counsel.[22] Without the money to fee a lawyer, the prospect of a prisoner being able to sue out a writ of error or move for a new trial (even if he was aware of the existence of the remedy) was negligible.[23] Even in the case of defended prisoners, the three procedures combined were in the 1820s giving rise to no more than forty or so cases a year.[24]

5. The Home Office

An inevitable consequence of the lack of adequate appeal remedies was reliance upon the royal prerogative of mercy as a means of putting right injustice. It was open to any prisoner to petition the Crown for a revision of his conviction or sentence and many did.[25] Upon receiving such a petition, the Home Secretary would call for a report from the trial judge and for his notes. If any 'new evidence' was exhibited to the petition the judge would be asked to consider and comment upon it.[26] The Home Secretary would also make such further inquiries of his own as the case appeared to warrant.[27] If the result of these inquiries was to cast doubt upon the rightness of the

[21] Explanations for the refusal to extend to felony the remedy of the motion for a new trial are offered by P. Devlin, *Trial by Jury* (London, 1966), 77; and in (1879) 150 *Edinburgh Review* 524 at 550.

[22] Occasionally a judge would reserve a point in which the prisoner had no counsel, see Bentley, *Select Caes from the Twelve Judges' Notebooks*, 12.

[23] In *Ryalls v R* (1846) 2 Cox 80 a prisoner sued out a writ of error *in forma pauperis* but this appears to have been an isolated case (cf. *R v Stokes* (1848) 3 C & K 185).

[24] In the years 1818–27 the average number of cases reserved annually was twenty-two, see Bentley, *Select Cases from the Twelve Judges' Notebooks*, 187–89; in the years 1820–22 writs of error averaged sixteen a year (this figure including civil as well as criminal cases), see PP 1823 (447) XV, 1; between 1824 and 1828 motions for new trial averaged four a year, see PP 1844 (408) XXXVIII, 681.

[25] In 1905 the committee of inquiry into the Beck Case was told that the Home Office received approximately 5000 petitions per year (PP 1905 (Cmnd 2315) LXII, 465, app 60).

[26] Report of Royal Commission on Capital Punishment, PP 1866 (3590) XXI, 1 and the Beck Report below.

[27] In the Smethurst Case he took the opinion of the Queen's Surgeon on the scientific evidence called at trial.

conviction or upon the justice of the prisoner's sentence, a pardon or reduction of sentence would follow.[28]

Successful petitions against conviction were rare.[29] A precondition to success was material casting doubt upon the correctness of the jury's verdict.[30] A prisoner in custody and labouring (as many were) under the twin handicaps of poverty and illiteracy was rarely in a position to marshal such evidence.[31] Prisoners capitally convicted had a further problem – lack of time: the interval between sentence and execution in such cases often being no more than a day or two.[32]

6. Attempts at Reform, 1844–48

It was not until the 1840s that a reform movement got under way. In the forefront were Fitzroy Kelly, a future Lord Chief Baron, William Ewart and Patrick M'Mahon, both of whom had played a prominent part in getting the Prisoners' Counsel Act (1836) on the statute book, and Isaac Butt, a leading member of the Irish bar. The case for reform was, they claimed, unanswerable.[33] The law as it stood was illogical and unjust. How could it be right that in civil suits the parties had an unfettered right of appeal, whilst in criminal cases, where men's lives and liberty were at stake, there was no appeal on fact, and an appeal on law only at the judge's discretion. What logic allowed a defendant convicted of misdemeanour in the King's Bench the right to move for a new trial, but denied the right to those convicted of treason or felony? Miscarriages of justice were not unknown in criminal cases. Yet against a mistaken verdict there was no appeal, merely a right to petition the Home Office, which was the worst possible tribunal of review with its secret and imperfect procedures. The cure for these ills

---

[28] The trial judge's view of the case always carried great weight with the Home Office (Report of Royal Commission on Capital Punishment above). Indeed it was always open to a judge who was dissatisfied himself to take the initiative and recommend the accused for a pardon without waiting for any petition, see Chitty, *Criminal Law*, i , 654. For examples of manoeuvres by counsel to secure a favourable report from the trial judge, see *R v Scott The Times*, 13 April 1824; and *R v Robinson, The Times*, 19–21 and 27 July 1824.

[29] See PD 1883 CCLXXVII, 1183 and the Beck Inquiry Report, PP 1905 (Cmnd 2315) LXII, 465, app 40.

[30] See the Beck Inquiry Report, app 60. New evidence usually took the form of affidavits from witnesses who had not given evidence at trial; as to such evidence, see generally PP 1856 (456) L 79.

[31] See the evidence of Edward Wilde to the Criminal Law Commissioners (2nd Report). Often a prisoner's best hope lay in having his case taken up by the press or an MP (see PD 1844 LXXV, 24).

[32] See 25 Geo II, c. 37, s 3; Criminal Law Commissioners, 2nd Report and PD 1836 XXXIII, 466–70.

[33] The reform arguments are set out at PD 1844 LXXV, 11–25 and in the evidence of Greaves, Fitzroy Kelly and Taylor to the 1848 Select Committee on Lord Campbell's Bill.

was to copy the system in civil cases and give to all persons convicted on indictment the right to move for a new trial on both fact and law.

The reform campaign got under way in 1844 with Kelly's introduction of a New Trials in Criminal Cases Bill.[34] Introduced too late in the session to have any real hope of becoming law, it was withdrawn upon an undertaking by the government to look at the whole matter.[35] Nothing came of this promise. The following year, however, the reformers' hand was greatly strengthened by the publication of the Eighth Report of the Criminal Law Commissioners, which came down strongly in favour of appeals on fact in criminal cases.[36] More than a year went by without any indication from the government that it intended to take action on the report. In December 1847 Ewart took up the matter in the Commons. Did the government intend to act on the report? The Home Secretary declined to say.[37]

The following year Ewart introduced his own Bill.[38] It was virtually identical with that of 1844. At the second reading he was prevailed upon by the government not to press the Bill, but instead to await a Bill which Lord Chief Justice Campbell was about to introduce in the Lords, which would in all probability cover the same ground.[39] When Campbell's Bill was introduced, it contained not a word about new trials but was merely concerned with making improvements to the system of reserving cases. However, there was to be a Lords' Select Committee on the Bill. Before that committee, the reformers would have the chance to make their case. The Select Committee sat for eight weeks taking evidence from ten witnesses: three judges, two ex-Lord Chancellors, two chairmen of Quarter Sessions and three pro-reform barristers (Fitzroy Kelly, Charles Greaves and John Pitt Taylor).[40] The questions on which it took evidence were reform of the law as to the reserving of cases and the desirability of allowing new trials in criminal cases.

On the first issue, Lord Campbell's proposal that the reserving of cases be placed on a statutory basis received general assent, but there were sharp divisions of opinion as to the advisability of allowing Quarter Sessions to reserve cases, and as to whether it should lie in the discretion of the judge to decide whether a case was reserved or not. On the question of extending the new trial system to all criminal cases, the judges were hostile. They put forward three arguments:

1. There was no call to change the law. Cases of wrongful conviction were extremely rare, and were dealt with as satisfactorily under the present system as they would be under a system of criminal appeal.

34 PP 1844 (367) I, 13.
35 PD 1844 LXXV, 1337–38.
36 It described the law as very defective and wrongful convictions not infrequent.
37 PD 1847 XCV, 527–30.
38 Appeal in Criminal Cases Bill PP 1847–48 (128) I, 193.
39 PD 1853 CXXVII, 969–70.
40 For the evidence given see PP 1847–48 (523) XVI, 423, Minutes of Evidence.

2. The argument that the same appeal remedies ought to be allowed in criminal cases as in civil was misconceived. The two cases were not the same. The criminal law incorporated safeguards for the accused which were wholly absent in civil suits. Civil suits frequently involved difficult questions of both law and fact, whereas in criminal cases the law and facts were usually straightforward. The delay incidental to appeal, whilst tolerable in civil suits, would in criminal cases be a great evil.

3. Granting a general right of appeal would give rise to a host of inconveniences which would far outweigh the supposed advantages.

No fewer than seven inconveniences were listed. First, it was said that if an unrestricted right of appeal were granted every prisoner would appeal, thereby generating a volume of work so great that the courts would be overwhelmed ('the Floodgates Argument'). Secondly, if appeal were not to be a rich man's remedy, it would be necessary for lawyers to be assigned to poor appellants at enormous expense to the public. Thirdly, unless the public met the cost of resisting motions for new trials, they would go unopposed due to the inability or unwillingness of prosecutors to bear the cost. Fourthly, juries knowing that their verdicts were subject to appeal would be more ready to convict in doubtful cases. Fifthly, the deterrent effect of the criminal law, which depended (especially in capital cases) on the speed with which execution of sentence followed verdict, would be watered down by the delays that an appeal system caused. Sixthly, to allow new trials in criminal cases would be to open the door to fraud and perjury on a massive scale. Seventhly, if a general right of appeal were granted to prisoners it would be difficult to deny a like right to the prosecutor, which would end the cherished principle that an acquittal was final.

When the Lords resumed their consideration of his Bill, Lord Campbell made it clear that, so far as he was concerned, there was to be no new trial clause and he carried the House with him.[41] The judges' arguments had won the day and would for the rest of the century remain the principal planks in the anti-reform case.

As a result the Bill, when it became law as the Criminal Law Administration Amendment Act (1848), made only minor and largely cosmetic changes in the law. Henceforth, reserved cases were to be heard by a court (to be known as the Court for Crown Cases Reserved) sitting in public with power to affirm or quash convictions, and consisting of at least five of the common law judges, including one of the Chiefs.[42] Quarter Sessions were given for the first time the power to reserve, but no other change in the law was made.

---

[41] PD 1848 C, 465–66; he was supported by Denman (466–67) and Brougham (467).
[42] Often called the Court of Criminal Appeal, see e.g. Cox's *Criminal Law Cases*.

7. Fluctuating Fortunes for the Reformers, 1848–60

After their defeat at the hands of the judges the reformers licked their wounds. In 1853, however, Butt decided to raise the subject again, introducing a Bill[43] modelled on those of 1844 and 1848, but containing provisions designed to meet 'the Floodgates Argument', and to ensure that appeals in capital cases were speedily heard.[44] It was met with a rehash of the arguments used before the Select Committee and failed to pass its second reading.

In 1856 there was published Greaves' Report on Criminal Procedure.[45] Before the Select Committee in 1848 Greaves had urged adoption of the principle of Ewart's Bill. In his report he again argued strongly for reform, this time not from the standpoint of the prisoner but from that of the public. He made two points. First, before the Court for Crown Cases Reserved a prisoner who succeeded in establishing that a legal error (for example the reception of inadmissible evidence) had been made during his trial, had his conviction quashed, even though the admissible evidence adduced at the trial was sufficient to justify his conviction. Secondly, the Home Office, in exercising its review function, had inadequate means of testing the truthfulness of 'new evidence' laid before it. In consequence there was the ever-present danger of its being imposed upon. It was also unsatisfactory that a verdict given after a trial in open court should be treated as a nullity, except after review proceedings of a kind which would satisfy all reasonable persons that it was erroneous. By way of solution he suggested that the Court for Crown Cases Reserved be given a discretionary power to order new trials, and that the Home Office be authorised to use district public prosecutors to investigate 'new evidence', with the further power to order a new trial where the result of their investigation was to cast doubt upon the conviction.

Whether Greaves' report was responsible for the shift of opinion is hard to judge, but when a New Trials in Criminal Cases Bill was introduced by M'Mahon in 1858, it received a much better reception than any of the earlier Bills had done.[46] The majority of those who spoke in the second reading debate were for reform. Although the stock anti-reform arguments were rehearsed, the most frequently voiced criticism of the Bill was that, as drafted, it would enable the prosecution to appeal an acquittal. The vote taken at the end of the debate produced a majority of fifty-four in favour of the Bill.

After the vote M'Mahon was urged by the Attorney-General not to attempt

[43] New Trials in Criminal Cases Bill PP 1852–53 (164) V, 215; for the debates thereon see PD 1852–53 CXXVII, 964–93; the Bill was to apply only to Ireland.
[44] Cl 6 and cl 21–23.
[45] PP 1856 (456) L 79.
[46] PP 1857–58 (137) III, 587; debate, PD 1857–58 CLI, 1051–64.

to carry the Bill further that session. While he was, he declared, in favour of the principle, in its present shape the Bill was open to substantial objections and required considerable revision. This suggestion did not go down well with all Members, particularly after the Home Secretary declined to give an undertaking to bring in a government Bill on the subject. By a reduced majority the House voted that it be sent to committee. In fact no further progress was made on it.

The following year M'Mahon introduced the Bill again.[47] It was cordially welcomed by the Attorney-General, who indicated that the government was in favour of making some alteration in the law and would introduce its own Bill.[48] A general election in June stopped any further progress on the Bill. When, following the election, M'Mahon reintroduced it,[49] the new Liberal government made it clear that it would oppose it. It got no further than an adjourned second reading.

M'Mahon, however, pressed on. In 1860 he and Butt introduced a modified version of the 1858 Bill.[50] The government, however, was as good as its word. When, on the second reading debate, the new Home Secretary, Sir Cornewall Lewis, was called on, he launched into a long speech rehearsing all the old anti-reform arguments. The most effective part of his speech was that which dealt with a provision in the Bill designed to meet 'the Floodgates Argument' (a clause empowering the Queen's Bench to make the grant of a new trial conditional upon the defendant submitting to terms as to costs). What this clause meant, he argued, was that the right of appeal which the Bill conferred would be a rich man's remedy. Poor prisoners would not be able to appeal, for they would not be able to comply with the terms as to costs. That was what currently happened in the case of appeals against summary conviction under statutes such as the Vagrancy Act (1824), which allowed appeals only on terms as to costs. Thousands had the right but, because of clauses as to costs, only a handful exercised it. Appeal to the Home Office might have its shortcomings but it was at least free and open to everyone. This was a very damaging point. M'Mahon's answer, that where there was merit in the appeal the question of costs might be waived, or if not, the money would be found by friends and family, did not convince. By the end of the debate it was becoming clear that the Bill was lost. It was refused a second reading without a division.

A Bill introduced the following session by Butt met the same fate, Sir Cornewall Lewis expressing surprise that it should have been thought necessary to introduce again a Bill which had been rejected without a division in the last session.[51] Three years later Sir Fitzroy Kelly brought in a Bill, offering

---

[47] Appeal in Criminal Cases Bill, 1859 (not printed).
[48] PD 1859 CLII, 1112–13.
[49] Appeal in Criminal Cases Bill, PP 1859 (15 Sess 2) I, 17.
[50] Appeal in Criminal Cases Bill, PP 1860 (I) I, 211; debate, PD 1860 CLVI, 407–24.
[51] New Trials in Criminal Cases Bill, PP 1861 (61) III, 613; debate, PD 1861 CLXXVI, 2070.

as his justification for doing so public dissatisfaction at the way in which the Home Office dealt with petitions for revision of conviction and sentence, but it came too late to have any hope of passing into law and was withdrawn.[52] It was fourteen years before another Bill for the granting of a general right of criminal appeal was introduced into the House.

8. Other Developments

Whilst the argument was continuing in Parliament, the power of Quarter Sessions to reserve cases was proving itself a useful reform. The Court for Crown Cases Reserved was not (as some had predicted) swamped with such cases, but the figures showed how necessary the reform had been. (During the first ten years of the operation of the 1848 Act, Quarter Sessions cases accounted for over half the work of the court: 126 out of 237 cases dealt with, a situation which was to change little during the remainder of the century.)[53]

The success of the reform may have been a factor in the enactment of the Summary Jurisdiction Act (1857), which gave persons summarily convicted a right to require the magistrates to state a case for the opinion of the Queen's Bench. The Act, which applied also to decisions of Quarter Sessions upon summary appeals, created the curious situation that a person whose appeal had been dismissed by Quarter Sessions could require them to state a case, while a person convicted before them could not. Indeed, during the period 1844 to 1864, it was a strange irony (oddly enough never referred to during debates) that whilst Parliament was setting its face against rights of appeal on fact for persons convicted on indictment, it was at the same time passing statutes giving such right to persons summarily convicted.[54]

Outside Parliament the legal profession were pushing forward the boundaries of existing appeal remedies.[55] In 1852 a defendant succeeded in obtaining from the Queen's Bench an order for a new trial in a felony case.[56] The case was one of theft removed before trial from Hull Quarter Sessions into the Queen's Bench by certiorari, then tried at Nisi Prius at York Assizes. Although the precedent it set does not seem to have been much followed,[57] fifteen years were to pass before it was finally overruled.[58]

---

[52] Appeal in Criminal Cases Amendment Bill, PP 1864 (14) I, 39; debate, PD 1864 CLXXVI, 1773–74.

[53] See Bentley, *Select Cases from the Twelve Judges' Notebooks*, 50 and 196.

[54] E.g. Hosiery Act, 1843, s 29; Factories Act, 1844, s 70; Larceny Act, 1861, s 110; Poaching Act, 1862, s 6.

[55] Occasionally one finds judges adopting very questionable procedures to reverse wrong verdicts, see e.g. *R v Holding, The Times*, 7 February 1857.

[56] *R v Scaife* (1851) 5 Cox 243.

[57] It was always regarded of doubtful authority (see the preamble to the Criminal Appeal Bills of 1853, 1858, 1859 and 1861).

[58] In *R v Bertrand* (1867) 10 Cox 618.

The previous year, in *Alleyne*, Lord Chief Justice Campbell had been prevailed upon to seal a bill of exceptions in a misdemeanour case.[59] He subsequently repented of his decision in *Esdale* in 1858,[60] but even as late as 1867 one finds an attempt being made by experienced counsel to get one of the City judges to seal a bill.[61]

In 1860 Hatch's lawyers demonstrated how a perjury prosecution could be made to serve as an appeal tool.[62] The case caused a considerable stir.[63] In 1866 the Home Office actually advised a prisoner, who was alleging that he had been wrongly convicted of rape, to proceed as Hatch had done.[64] In fact the remedy was beyond the means of most prisoners and during the rest of the century it was but little used.[65]

9. The Subject that Would Not Go Away

Despite the defeat of the 1864 Bill the question of criminal appeal would not go away. During the 1860s capital punishment was a subject of intense public debate, and in 1864 a Royal Commission was appointed which reported two years later.[66] It was inevitable that the commission should touch upon the question of the revision by the Home Office of capital convictions and sentences. Most of the witnesses from whom it took evidence favoured leaving things as they were, arguing that appeal to the Home Office was as favourable a procedure as could exist. Some, however, were more critical. The misgivings which Greaves had voiced in 1856 were echoed by Baron Bramwell, whilst to Lord Cranworth it was wrong for the Home Office to commute the death sentence where doubt was felt as to the correctness of the conviction; the proper course in such a case was to grant a pardon. In its report the commission diplomatically declined to make any recommendation as to whether there should be a right of appeal in capital cases, observing that the question of appeal did not concern just capital cases.

It was capital cases which formed the subject of the next Bill on criminal appeals introduced into the Commons: Sir George Jenkinson's Bill of 1870.[67] The scheme of this was that a person capitally convicted should have a right to appeal his conviction with the leave of the trial judge, such

[59] Unreported, cited Archbold (20th edn), 182.
[60] *R v Esdale* (1858) 1 F & F 213.
[61] *R v Jelly and Hall* (1867) 10 Cox 553.
[62] *R v Plummer, The Times*, 10–12, 14 and 16 May 1860.
[63] It provoked both a *Times* leader and a letter from Taylor (*The Times*, 16 and May 1860 respectively).
[64] *R v Toomer, The Times*, 5 September 1866 (leader).
[65] One finds occasional examples of its employment in *The Times* trial reports, e.g. *R v Kinnear*, 22–27 August 1872; as to the expense, see *The Times*, 3 September 1866 (letter).
[66] PP 1866 (3590) XXI, 1.
[67] Capital Sentences (Court of Appeal) Bill PP 1870 (85) I, 193; debate, PD 1870 CCII, 727–35.

leave to be granted where the trial judge was satisfied by affidavit that new evidence existed tending to support a defence of insanity or exculpatory of the prisoner. The appeal was be heard by a court consisting of three common law judges and three members of the Judicial Committee of the Privy Council. The time limits for appealing and the setting down of the appeal were to be very short. At the hearing of the appeal, the appeal court should have power to inquire into any matter of law or fact. It should have power to examine witnesses on oath, to receive affidavits and to send for the notes of the trial judge and for letters and papers. It should report to the queen as to the grant of a free pardon, the commutation of the death sentence or otherwise as should seem just. The Bill was given short shrift. It would, said the Attorney-General, lead to delay in the execution of capital sentences and so undermine the system of capital punishment; it would lead to evidence being kept back in order to ensure a right of appeal. Worst of all, it would lead to verdicts being set aside 'after an investigation of a bastard description unknown to law' in which the appeal court, never having seen the witnesses who had given evidence at trial, would proceed simply on written statements. Sir George pointed out that all of the objections raised applied equally to the revision of capital cases by the Home Secretary, but that was not enough to save the Bill which was refused a second reading without a division.

The topic was briefly alluded to again in 1874 by the Select Committee on the Homicide Law Amendment Bill, but here again the witnesses questioned showed no enthusiasm for a right of appeal in homicide cases.[68] In 1878 Serjeant Simon and Sir George Bowyer introduced a Bill proposing to give an unrestricted right of appeal on law and fact to those sentenced to death or penal servitude without previous convictions; and a right of appeal, with the leave of the judge, in other cases.[69] The most novel feature of this Bill was a clause giving an appellant the right to tender himself as a witness at the appeal hearing (with restrictions placed upon cross-examination as to credit, and the provision that failure to tender himself should not prejudice him). It was withdrawn at the second reading stage.

10. The Criminal Code Bills

May 1878 saw a far more promising development: the introduction of the government-sponsored Criminal Code Bill, providing, inter alia, for the establishment of a Court of Appeal in Criminal Cases and empowering trial judges to grant new trials.[70] The Bill, as already seen, was ultimately

---

[68] PP 1874 (315) IX 471.

[69] The Criminal Appeals Bill PP 1878 (92) II, 1.

[70] Criminal Code (Indictable Offences) Bill, PP 1878 (178) II, 5; debates, PD 1878 CCXL, 1671–73, and 1881; and CCXLII, 2038–40.

withdrawn. In 1879, after revision by the Royal Commission, it was reintroduced but again ended up being withdrawn.[71]

1879 was none the less an encouraging year for reformers. It saw the enactment of the Summary Jurisdiction Act conferring a general right of appeal in cases of summary conviction. Although the 1879 Code Bill did not pass, its appeal provisions met all the reformers' demands. The refusal of the trial judge to reserve a point of law would henceforth be subject to appeal. The powers of the court on hearing reserved cases were to include the power to order a new trial. Trial judges were to have the power to order a new trial on the grounds that the jury's verdict was against the weight of the evidence, with a right of appeal against refusal. So too was the Home Secretary in cases where a petition for mercy raised doubt as to the correctness of a conviction. To exercise criminal appellate jurisdiction a new court, the Court of Appeal in Criminal Cases, was to be constituted.

In 1880 the government introduced its third Criminal Code Bill (remodelled to take account of criticisms from the Lord Chief Justice but with the appeal clauses unchanged).[72] Three private Members also introduced a Criminal Code Bill of their own, the appeal clauses of which differed in significant respects from those of the government Bill.[73] A general election put an end to further progress on the government Bill, the private Members' Bill having in the meanwhile been dropped. After a lull in 1881, in 1882 no less than three Bills were introduced containing clauses dealing with criminal appeal: two Criminal Law Amendment Bills and a Death Sentences (Appeal) Bill.[74] In the end all three had to be dropped.

In 1883 the government made another major effort, with two Bills being introduced into the Commons in tandem.[75] The first was yet another Criminal Code Bill containing the same appeal clauses as the 1879 Bill; the other was a Criminal Appeal Bill providing for appeal on fact in capital cases. In the debate on the Criminal Code Bill, the government was criticised for bringing before the House two Bills containing different provisions on the same subject. The debate on the Court of Criminal Appeal Bill saw it attacked on a variety of grounds. To some it was unnecessary: because of the numerous safeguards for the accused, wrong convictions in capital cases simply did not occur. By providing an appeal remedy the government would cause delay in the execution of sentence, thus undermining the death penalty. To

---

[71] Criminal Code Bill PP 1878–79 (117) II, 175; debates, PD 1879 CCXLV, 310–47 and 1750–73; CCXLVI, 1238–89, 1719 and 1915; and CCXLVII, 953 and 1281.

[72] Criminal Code Bill PP 1880 (2) II, 1; debates, PD 1880 CCL, 244 and 1236–48; and CCLI, 1014–15.

[73] Criminal Code No. 2 Bill PP 1880 (47) II, 223.

[74] The Criminal Law Amendment Bill PP 1882 (15) II, 1, at p 60; Criminal Law Procedure Bill, PP 1882 (43) II, 81 at 119 and Death Sentences Appeal Bill PP 1882 (81) II, 155.

[75] Criminal Code (Indictable Offences Procedure) Bill PP 1883 (8) II, 249; Court of Criminal Appeal Bill PP 1883 (9) II, 211; for the debate on the latter see PD 1883 CCLXXVII, 1181–1248.

others the fault of the Bill was that it permitted appeals as of right in capital cases only. For all the criticism, the general reception to the Bill was favourable and, like the Criminal Code Bill, it passed its second reading by a comfortable majority. Yet, as before, it proved impossible to get the Criminal Code Bill through all its stages within the session, and both Bills in the end had to be dropped. This marked the end of government involvement in the subject of criminal appeal for the rest of the century. Within a few years the appeal clauses of the Code Bill were being publicly repudiated by Stephen, who announced that subsequent experience had led him to the view that: 'substantially the existing system cannot be improved'.

11. The Fight Continues

The efforts of the reformers, however, continued with Bills introduced in 1888, 1890 and 1892,[76] none of which got beyond the first reading stage. A novel feature of the 1888 Bill was that it proposed a right of appeal against sentence as well as conviction. In 1892 there occurred a wholly unexpected development . Out of the blue the Council of Judges, in its annual statutory report,[77] recommended to the Lord Chancellor the establishment of a Court of Appeal in Criminal Cases. Lack of uniformity in sentence was, argued the report, a serious problem, which could be solved if there was an appeal court with power to give authoritative guidance on sentencing. In order to discourage frivolous appeals the court should have power to increase as well as reduce sentence, and as a check on overlenient sentencing the Attorney-General should have a right of appeal, to be exercised only in cases of extreme or systematic inadequacy of sentence. It was conceded that, at first, the number of appeals would be large, but the possibility of an increased sentence and, after a short time, the increased uniformity of sentences throughout the country (and the consequent difficulty of obtaining an alteration of sentence) would combine to prevent hopeless appeals. As well as dealing with sentence appeals, the court should, the report recommended, also have the duty of reviewing convictions and sentences referred to it by the Home Secretary, with power in such cases to quash the conviction or diminish the sentence but not to order a new trial.

There was no government action on the report, but in 1895 a Private Member's Bill was introduced, which was the 1883 Bill rehashed with additions to give effect to the report's recommendations.[78] It was given an unopposed second reading and referred to a Select Committee. The committee reported on the Bill in July without amendment, stating it had not

---

[76] They were the Court of Criminal Appeal Bill, PP 1888 (377) II, 391; the Court of Criminal Appeal Bill, PP 1890 (83) I, 535; and the Criminal Cases Appeal Bill PP 1892 (163) II, 201.

[77] PP 1894 (127) LXXX 1, 173.

[78] Court of Criminal Appeal Bill, PP 1895 (53 – Sess. 1) I, 493); debates, PD 1895 XXX, 316; XXXI, 521 and 1517; XXXII, 875–76; XXXIII, 1347, 1497 and 1672; and XXXV, 54.

had sufficient time to conclude its investigations.[79] After this it made no further progress. A similar Bill the following year did not get beyond a first reading.[80]

In 1897 a revised Bill, limited in scope to the reforms recommended in the 1892 report, was introduced by the radical Edward Pickersgill.[81] On its second reading it was given a lukewarm welcome by the Home Secretary and the Attorney-General. The Home Secretary conceded that: 'there was a general consensus of opinion in favour of some alteration of the law giving some further appeal in criminal cases', but he thought that the scheme proposed by the Bill had serious shortcomings. He was unhappy about the Appeal Court being given power to increase sentences, and about the proposal that he, as Home Secretary, should have the power to refer cases to the court. This would put him in a difficult position. If he refused to refer a case he would be accused of denying access to the court, whilst if he sent all petitions to it the judges would complain that he was handing over his business to them. The Attorney-General, while acknowledging the problem of inequality of sentences, thought review by the Home Office an adequate remedy. There was also criticism from the backbenches. There was general dislike of the provision for the increase of sentence. The wisdom of giving a general right of appeal against sentence was also questioned: the court would be flooded out with cases. If the scheme were not to be a mockery, legal assistance would have to be provided for poor appellants at public expense. Disparities in sentencing were more apparent than real and, in so far as there was a problem, could it not be remedied by the judges issuing sentencing guidelines?[82] For some, the proposal that Appeal Court should have power to review convictions at the request of the Home Secretary went nothing like far enough. If sentence appeals were to lie as of right, why should conviction appeals require the Home Secretary's fiat? Why did the Bill give no right of appeal at all in capital cases? What was the logic in allowing a man convicted of stealing a pair of boots to appeal his sentence but denying the like right to a man sentenced to death? None the less, despite all the criticism, the Bill was given a second reading by a majority of 147 to 86. It made no further progress.

The following year Pickersgill introduced a revised Bill,[83] proposing that prisoners should have a right of appeal against conviction and sentence both on law and fact. The second reading debate, which was very thinly attended, saw a strong attack launched on it by both the Home Secretary

---

[79] PP 1895 (351) VII, 499.

[80] Court of Criminal Appeal Bill PP 1896 (60) I, 443.

[81] Court of Criminal Appeal Bill PP 1897 (17) I, 373; debates, PD 1897 XLV, 295, and XLVII, 1229–82.

[82] Hawkins J (1893), *New Review*, 617 and M. Crackanthorpe (1893) 34 *Nineteenth Century*, 614, had proposed a Royal Commission to report on the principles on which punishment should be based.

[83] Court of Criminal Appeal Bill PP 1898 (3) I, 413; debate, PD 1898 LV, 5–79.

anf the Attorney-General, with all the arguments used by Sir Cornewell Lewis in the debate on the 1860 Bill being deployed against it. When the matter was put to the vote the Bill was defeated by a majority of sixty-four. Still the reformers would not give up. In 1899 yet another Bill was introduced.[84] This failed to get beyond the first reading stage.

The 1899 Bill was the thirtieth Criminal Appeal Bill to be presented that century. Out of the thirty only one – Lord Campbell's Bill of 1848 – had got onto the statute book. In 1900 the prospects of reform looked no brighter than they had in 1848. There was still a general belief that wrongful convictions were rare, and that the procedures of reserving cases and petition to the Home Office provided an adequate remedy against error. However, a time bomb was ticking away. In 1896, in the course of an Old Bailey trial, the common serjeant had made a blunder which would, within less than ten years, lead to a Committee of Inquiry Report, which would pave the way for the Criminal Appeal Act (1907). His mistake was to refuse to admit evidence which, had it been received, would have proved beyond doubt that the case was one of mistaken identity; an error which he then compounded by refusing to reserve the point. As a result, the accused, Adolf Beck, was convicted. In 1904 the unfortunate Beck was wrongly convicted on mistaken identification evidence for a second time, but this time the error was discovered. The Committee of Inquiry into his case expressed the view that, had the common serjeant reserved the question of admissibility raised at the first trial, the first conviction would almost certainly have been set aside, and the second conviction would never have taken place. In short, Beck had been convicted as a result of an event (namely the refusal of a judge to reserve a point of substance) which judges had throughout the nineteenth century been claiming would never happen. The committee recommended a right of appeal on law in all cases, but another sensational wrongful conviction a year later – that of George Edalji – obliged the government to go the further step of allowing appeals on fact as well.[85]

The failure to reform appellate procedures had, as has already been seen, consequences which went beyond the misfortunes of individual prisoners wrongly convicted or overharshly sentenced who could get no redress therefrom. Lack of an appeal remedy meant that judicial misconduct went largely unchecked, with adverse press publicity the only sanction. It also meant that judges in the lower courts (of whom many were laymen) were almost wholly without authoritative guidance (of the kind now given by the Court of Appeal) as to how the duty of summing up was to be discharged. The result was that many prisoners were convicted after summings up which by twentieth-century standards were wholly deficient.

84 Court of Criminal Appeal Bill PP 1899 (58) I, 305.
85 See Beck Inquiry Report above and the Papers relating to the Edalji Case (PP 1907 (Cmnd 3503) LXVII, 403).

26

Conclusion

Nineteenth-century English criminal justice was swift and cheap, civil justice slow and expensive. The reason why criminal cases could be and were despatched so much more speedily than civil suits was that the vast majority of accused stood trial undefended. Where a prisoner through poverty was obliged to conduct his own defence the trial was usually quick and hopelessly one-sided. His efforts at defence were generally 'pitiable even if he [had] a good case'. Indeed many accused, knowing the task was beyond them, did not even attempt to defend themselves and were convicted with scarcely a question asked or a word spoken in their defence. For them the trial 'rushed by like a dream which [they could not] understand'. In 1800 calls for poor prisoners to be provided with legal representation would have been greeted with astonishment. What need had prisoners of counsel? Prosecutions, even on indictment, were rarely conducted by counsel and in any event what handicap was the lack of a lawyer to an innocent man? It required 'no manner of skill to make an honest defence'.

Lack of a scheme of criminal legal aid was and would remain throughout the century one of the most serious shortcomings of the trial system. But in 1800 there were others just as grave. The way summary trials was conducted was little short of scandalous. Bound by no code of procedure, fond of doing justice behind closed doors, their decisions in practice if not in theory unappealable, magistrates tried men as they saw fit and often with great unfairness. Although trials on indictment were better conducted, rights regarded today as lying at the heart of a fair trial were denied to the accused either as unnecessary or actually obstructive of justice. So that he could not use them to fabricate a defence, he was denied a copy of the depositions. To prevent him taking pleading points, he was denied a copy of the indictment. Where he had counsel, the help the latter was permitted to give him was in felony limited to the asking of questions and arguing law; he could not address the jury on his behalf. That the prisoner had to do for himself; any other rule would have robbed the jury of the opportunity of observing his demeanour as he made his defence and thus of an important means of getting at the truth. If poverty prevented him getting his witnesses to court, or if they arrived late, they would go unheard. If convicted he could not appeal either conviction or sentence. Most surprising of all, he could not give evidence in his own defence. This last disability was one which in practice worked to the advantage rather than the disadvantage of the illiterate undefended prisoner, for it meant that he could not be cross-examined.

There were other failings. The law tolerated laymen acting as judges at Quarter Sessions. In the London courts, for want of some one to guide them through the evidence, grand juries, year in year out, threw out indictments in clear cases which had already passed the scrutiny of an examining magistrate. In political prosecutions in the King's Bench jury-packing was an open scandal. For all its boasted tenderness to the accused, the law made him stand for the duration of his trial no matter how long it lasted. Prosecutions of child abusers regularly broke down because the victims were too young to be sworn. The rules of criminal pleading were so strict that each year trifling indictment defects and variances carried guilty men to an unmerited acquittal. In capital cases, rather than lock a jury up overnight, judges would sit on into the early hours of the morning, with the defence case taken at a time when jurors' powers of concentration were at their lowest ebb. Juries which could not agree would be starved into a verdict and, at Assizes, sometimes threatened with carting as well.

For all its shortcomings, jury trial at least enjoyed a high reputation and there was reluctance to tamper with it. Trials were held in public and in front of a watchful press. Against the risk of frivolous prosecutions, there were the safeguards of preliminary examination and grand jury. By denying the accused the right to testify but allowing him to make an unsworn statement, the law enabled him to tell his story but protected him against the 'moral torture' of cross-examination. Its evidential rules were highly favourable to him and, by casting on the Crown the burden of proving guilt beyond reasonable doubt and requiring unanimity of trial juries, the risk of wrongful conviction was reduced to a minimum. To many it was hard to see how such a system could be improved.

Yet change there was. Shamed perhaps by the spectacle of prisoners, sometimes as young as eight, standing trial for their lives undefended, the judges in the 1820s began to adopt the practice of assigning counsel to poor prisoners in capital cases. The abuse of jury packing in the King's Bench was stamped out. In 1836 felony prisoners were given the right to make full defence by counsel and the right to a copy of the depositions. With a clerk to assist them, London grand juries were no longer 'The Hope of the London Thief'. By mid century late sittings and the practice of judges prosecuting had been much curtailed. In 1848 Jervis's Act reformed the law of summary trial and placed it on its modern footing. This was as timely as it was necessary, for the second half of the century saw a huge growth in summary trials. After Campbell's Criminal Procedure Act (1851) trivial indictment flaws and variances no longer won an accused his freedom. The law of criminal evidence, already highly favourable to the accused, was from the 1830s onwards extensively reshaped by both judges and Parliament. Also by 1900 judges had begun to adopt the practice of hearing arguments about admissibility of evidence out of the earshot of the jury.

The majority of these reforms were accomplished before 1860. For the rest of century the burning issue was prisoners' evidence. Eventually in 1898 the government got the Criminal Evidence Act onto the statute book and with this the trial system moved much closer to the present-day model. Yet even in 1900 it had by modern standards grave deficiencies, of which the lack of an appeal remedy for those convicted on indictment (the nineteenth-century's 'standing lost cause') and the lack of a scheme of criminal legal aid were the most fundamental. In the evolution of the trial system since 1800 the great landmarks have been the Prisoners' Counsel Act (1836), the Criminal Evidence Act (1898), the Criminal Appeal Act (1907) and the Legal Aid Acts (1949–60). Between them they provide a useful measure of the progress made during the nineteenth century and of that which remained to be made at its end.

To the cause of reform the general public were largely apathetic. In 1884 the *Law Times* complained about the lack of public interest in the debate over prisoners' evidence.[1] Nor was the legal profession as a whole interested overmuch in such questions. Most lawyers made their livings away from the criminal courts and knew little of and cared less about their workings. Bentham's *Rationale of Judicial Evidence* might have been both an inspiration and agenda for the likes of Brougham and Denman, but for those concerned with earning a living in the law it held little interest. The trial system might be in need of reform but they were more than happy to leave the task to others who had an appetite for it. Yet for all the conservatism and lack of interest of many in the profession, reform and reform campaigns were in the main lawyer led. In the struggle to get the Prisoners' Counsel Bill on the statute book and to establish a criminal appeal court the leading figures were, with the exception of Martin and the admirable and indefatigable Ewart, all lawyers: Pollock, Lyndhurst, Fitzroy Kelly, Greaves, Pitt Taylor, Butt and M'Mahon. The long debate over prisoners' evidence was throughout lawyer-driven, with committed Benthamites such as Brougham, Denman and FitzJames Stephen to the fore in the the early years. The gospel the Benthamites were preaching took early root in the United States but in England they had less success. The turning point came in 1885 when a backbencher persuaded the government to amend its Criminal Law Amendment Bill by including in it a section giving those accused of serious sexual crime the right to give evidence in their own defence. Ironically the backbencher was not a lawyer at all but his intervention was decisive. Following such a major breach in the incompetency rule it could only be a matter of time before the rule was abolished.

What of the judges? It has long been fashionable to depict them as reactionary and anti-reform. Ellenborough's hostility to the relaxation of the capital laws and Park's threat to resign his judgeship if the Prisoners'

[1] (1884) 18 Ir LT 316.

Counsel Bill became law are examples usually cited. There are others. It was the opposition of the bench which put paid to Ewart's attempt to give convicted prisoners a right of appeal. In 1883 they were equally dismissive when their opinion was canvassed as to the desirability of a scheme of criminal legal aid. Yet not all judges set their faces against change. Brougham, Denman, Lyndhurst, Kelly and Stephen were all of a reformist bent and hugely influential. Also, and this needs to be stressed, the judges made a major contribution to the development of the law of criminal evidence.

Some of the weaknesses of the nineteenth-century trial system received early attention in the present century. In the wake of the Criminal Evidence Act (1898) there was enacted in 1903 the woefully inadequate Poor Prisoners' Defence Act, while in 1907 the Court of Criminal Appeal was finally set up. However, it was only in the 1960s that a scheme of criminal legal aid that was anything like satisfactory was established. From this same era date reforms such as the abolition of lay judges and the banning of the reporting of committal proceedings. The imposition upon the Crown of a duty to disclose material in their possession helpful to the defence had to wait until 1981.

The present century, as well as seeing the introduction of new rights for accused, has also seen the progressive stripping away of many old safe-guards. One of the first to go was the prohibition upon pre-trial interrogation of suspects. By the 1950s it had become standard police practice to interrogate those whom they had arrested. It was a practice which created an obvious need to protect the suspect against the risk of his replies to questions being misreported or worse still fabricated. Only in 1984, however, was this problem finally tackled. Of the old triple safeguard of preliminary examination, grand jury scrutiny and trial jury unanimity, only the first now remains and it is not expected to survive much longer. The accused's right of peremptory challenge of jurors, after being whittled down progressively to near vanishing-point, was finally abolished in 1988. Over the last twenty years many evidential safeguards have been either watered down or done away with altogether. In 1988 the mandatory corro-boration requirement for children's unsworn evidence was abolished. 1995 saw the abolition of the corroboration requirement in accomplice and sexual cases. There has also been a substantial relaxation of the hearsay rule. Child witnesses now enjoy the privilege of having videotape recordings of their answers to police questions stand as their evidence in chief. Since 1967 there have been imposed on accused obligations to make pre-trial disclosure of alibis, expert evidence and the general nature of his defence. Since April 1995 failure by an accused to answer police questions or to give evidence at his trial have been matters from which a jury can be invited to draw an adverse inference. The justification offered for this wholesale abolition of long-standing protections is the need to convict the guilty. Too many guilty people are slipping through the net. The acquittal rate in jury trials is currently running at 40 per cent and that is far too high.[2] Given the access which suspects and accused now have to free legal advice and representation, and given the safeguard of tape-recording at the interrogation stage, there can, so the argument goes, be no justification for allowing guilty men to shelter behind rules which look back to an age when accused regularly took their trials undefended. One might have expected that the spate of highly publicised miscarriages of justice which led to the setting up of the recent Royal Commission on Criminal Justice would have halted demands for the balance of the system to be tilted ever further against the accused. But in fact the erosion of evidential protections has simply continued. The nineteenth century was the springboard for many of the reforms which justify the description of our trial system as fair. If present trends continue we may yet come to look upon it, at least as far as its rules of criminal evidence are concerned, as a golden age.

---

[2] Crown Prosecution Service, Annual Report, 1996–97. Despite the low figure for convictions in jury trials, the overall conviction rate has gone up markedly over the last hundred years. In 1893 of those tried for indictable offences just under 18 per cent were acquitted; twenty years later the acquittal rate was 17 per cent for those tried on indictment and 10 per cent for those tried summarily, G. G. Alexander, *The Administration of Criminal Justice*, 202–3 and 224–25. In 1995–96 and 1996–97 the acquittal rate was 10 per cent for those tried in the Crown Court and 2 per cent for those tried summarily, Crown Prosecution Service, Annual Report 1996–97.

List of Cases

Index

Lightning Source UK Ltd.
Milton Keynes UK
UKOW030227251111

182662UK00002B/5/P